THE
ARNOLD SCHOENBERG
COMPANION

Arnold Schoenberg circa 1948. Photograph by Florence Homolka. Reproduced courtesy of the Arnold Schoenberg Institute, Los Angeles.

THE
ARNOLD
SCHOENBERG
COMPANION

Edited by
Walter B. Bailey

GREENWOOD PRESS
Westport, Connecticut • London

Library of Congress Cataloging-in-Publication Data

The Arnold Schoenberg companion / edited by Walter B. Bailey.
    p. cm.
    Discography: p.
    Includes bibliographical references (p.) and index.
    ISBN 0–313–28779–1 (alk. paper)
    1. Schoenberg, Arnold, 1874–1951.   I. Bailey, Walter B. (Walter
Boyce)
  ML410.S283A745   1998
  780'.92—DC21   97–41923

British Library Cataloguing in Publication Data is available.

Library of Congress Catalog Card Number: 97–41923
ISBN: 0–313–28779–1

First published in 1998

Greenwood Press, 88 Post Road West, Westport, CT 06881
An imprint of Greenwood Publishing Group, Inc.

Printed in the United States of America

The paper used in this book complies with the
Permanent Paper Standard issued by the National
Information Standards Organization (Z39.48–1984).

10 9 8 7 6 5 4 3 2 1

To the memory of the Arnold Schoenberg Institute at the University of Southern California, Los Angeles, California (1976–1997)

and with best wishes to its reincarnation as the Arnold Schoenberg Center, Vienna, Austria

Contents

Preface

Scholarly writings on musical topics are often highly specialized and can be difficult to comprehend for readers without substantial background in the subject at hand. This situation is especially true for writings on Schoenberg, which tend to be not only specialized but also technical in nature. This is an understandable consequence given the complexity of Schoenberg's music, but it only serves to further isolate his music from a potential audience; in fact, it may even be fair to assert that the understanding of Schoenberg's music has been hindered by the density of most of the writings about it.

This volume seeks to address these issues by providing nonspecialist readers with complete but general introductions to many of the key features of Schoenberg, his creative process, his music, and its influence. The intent has been to provide a thorough discussion of these issues without extensive technical terminology, a breadth of coverage instead of complete immersion into one specific aspect. Topics range from a biography and broad surveys of musical works within certain periods of Schoenberg's career to discussions of specific developments in Schoenberg's style and reports not only on Schoenberg's attitudes toward music, composition, and analysis but on others' attitudes toward Schoenberg. "Changing Views of Schoenberg" and "Schoenberg's Influence" place Schoenberg and his achievements in the context of the past and the present. The other essays provide differing points of view as each author presents his or her specialty in general terms. The authors' approaches vary, as does the technical language that each one employs to illuminate the topic at hand. But each essay presents a succinct, informed picture of an element important for the understanding of Schoenberg. For further study, there is a chronological list of works (with references to publishers), an annotated bibliography geared toward the nonspecialist, and a discography. It is hoped that this volume will provide a valuable introduction to, review of, and resource concerning Schoenberg and his music.

Acknowledgments

This volume was a long time in the making, and it is the product of many people's time and effort. I would like to thank them all for making it possible.

First and foremost, I would like to thank the contributors for their essays, which reflect so well their varied points of view and specialties. In addition to providing essays, Jerry McBride also offered valuable editorial advice, and Ethan Haimo shared his knowledge of securing permissions for the musical examples. It has been a rich experience interacting with these committed scholars.

Next, I would like to thank Wayne Schoaf and the staff of the archives of the Arnold Schoenberg Institute in Los Angeles for their generous assistance to me (and to the other authors). No question was too large or too small for their attention. We will all miss these helpful professionals. Thanks go also to Belmont Music Publishers and the Schoenberg heirs (Ronald and Lawrence Schoenberg and Nuria Schoenberg-Nono) for their generous permission to quote from published and unpublished scores and essays.

The autographers of the musical examples are also deserving of thanks: Feng Yin, who produced most of the examples for chapters 9 and 11, and Ethan Haimo, who generously provided most of the examples for chapters 6, 7, and 8. I would also like to thank Feng Yin, composer; Rick Russell, Consulting Specialist, User Services, Rice University; and Paul Orkiszewski, Music Librarian, Rice University, for their advice on the creation of the final versions of these and the other musical examples.

At Greenwood Press I would like to thank Mary M. Blair, who commissioned the project before leaving the firm; Marilyn Brownstein, Senior Editor, Humanities, who became my contact until she retired; Cynthia Harris, Executive Editor, who provided interim advice after Marilyn Brownstein's departure; and Alicia

S. Merritt, who supplied moral support and professional advice for over four years. Finally, I thank Pamela St. Clair, who took over the project when Alicia Merritt left the firm, and Lynn Zelem, Production Editor, for shepherding the project through its final stages.

Above all, I thank Nancy Gisbrecht for myriad assistances in the preparation of this book as in other aspects of life.

I

Context

1

Changing Views of Schoenberg

Walter B. Bailey

"It seems to me that a new Mozart is growing up in Vienna," effused the conservative critic Eduard Hanslick in 1898.[1] The object of Hanslick's praise was a twenty-four-year-old, largely self-taught composer named Arnold Schoenberg, whose first completed string quartet had recently been premiered through the auspices of Vienna's Composers' Society. This String Quartet in D Major was a derivative student work, but its fluidity, grace, and obvious technical fluency, combined with Schoenberg's youth, evidently brought Mozart to the reviewer's mind. Like Mozart, Schoenberg had assimilated the dominant musical trends of his day, and he was not content to stop there. Compelled by his artistic conscience, Schoenberg explored the most innovative aspects of contemporary style. As he did so, he found that not all reviewers were as attuned to his style as Hanslick had been to his early quartet. In 1905, just a few years after the premiere of the String Quartet in D Major, Viennese critic Paul Stauber called Schoenberg's symphonic poem *Pelleas und Melisande* "not music at all, but an assassination of sound, a crime against nature, doubly damnable because the 'composer' does not merely upset old notions but also wants to renounce the natural path of musical development."[2] Thus, within the first ten years of his public career, Schoenberg had experienced favorable comparison with Mozart, at one extreme, and vilification as a destructive fraud, at the other.

The dichotomy illustrated by these two reviews marked the reception of Schoenberg and his music throughout his career. He always drew a crowd of dedicated supporters and an equal number of vehement detractors, and the interaction of the two groups often led to controversy. The most famous example of this interaction was the notorious "Skandalkonzert" of 31 March 1913, when a Viennese audience rioted at a performance of works by Schoenberg and his students. "Hisses, laughter, and applause made a bedlam," wrote a critic in a

Boston newspaper, for the story was striking enough that even foreign readers found it newsworthy.

Between numbers little groups of disputants came within an inch of blows; one of the composers shouted remarks and entered into the row; the conductor went on strike; an official boxed the ears of a man who had publicly assaulted him; the police commissioner ordered the hall cleared, and the concert was stopped before the final number.[3]

Of course, Schoenberg's supporters and detractors did not always experience such dramatic, face-to-face confrontations. More often than not his supporters were free to pay homage to their master in other ways by, for example, providing him with occasional financial support, writing books and articles about Schoenberg and his music, and exercising whatever influence they had to secure performances for his music. His detractors, too, were busy behind the scenes, where they criticized Schoenberg's music and its aesthetic basis in word and in print, warned of his dangerous effect on young composers, and even condemned his religious heritage, all in the hope of keeping his music from being performed. Whether despite or because of these grass-roots efforts, Schoenberg was repeatedly validated as an important musical figure by the musical establishment of his day. His book *Theory of Harmony [Harmonielehre]* (1911) deflated the arguments of those who saw him as an ignorant eccentric; in 1925, his appointment as teacher of the master class in composition at the Prussian Academy of the Arts in Berlin awarded him one of the most prestigious teaching positions in Europe; up until his departure from Europe in 1933, his works were published soon after their composition and premiered by major ensembles in important venues; and, following his exodus from Europe, he found employment in the American university system. Similarly, his twelve-tone method and its offspring dominated establishment music for many years after his death.

So, what was all the fuss about and why, nearly fifty years after Schoenberg's death, does it still continue? Most of the controversies concerning Schoenberg revolved initially around the sound of his music; eventually it was not only the sound but how he justified and explained it historically, theoretically, and aesthetically that sustained the controversy. (His method of organizing pitch in his later works, the twelve-tone method, was a special point of contention.) The sound of Schoenberg's first mature works was striking in its time because Schoenberg tended to emphasize the most innovative aspects of turn-of-the-century musical style: chromaticism, rhythmic freedom, intensity of expression, and motivic unity. Taken together, these elements produce an admittedly complex musical style, but it was this style that Schoenberg preferred and he made no excuse for it. Brahms's progressiveness "should have stimulated composers to write music for adults," wrote Schoenberg in the essay "Brahms the Progressive."

Mature people think in complexes, and the higher their intelligence, the greater is the number of units with which they are familiar. . . . Why should it not be possible in music to say in whole complexes in a condensed form what, in the preceding epochs, had at first to be said several times with slight variations before it could be elaborated?[4]

In other words, older music, with its exact repetitions and other built-in redundancies was akin to baby talk, and Schoenberg preferred music analogous to adult speech. He went on to explain,

Repeatedly hearing things which one likes is pleasant and need not be ridiculed. There is a subconscious desire to understand better and realize more details of the beauty. But an alert and well-trained mind will demand to be told the more remote matters, the more remote consequences of the simple matters that he has already comprehended. An alert and well-trained mind refuses to listen to baby-talk and requests strongly to be spoken to in a brief and straight-forward language.[5]

Schoenberg maintained this aesthetic point of view for the rest of his life, and the surface sound of his music was always decidedly "adult" in its complexity.

The complexity in Schoenberg's music, however, was not gratuitous. Schoenberg saw his music as part of an evolution that involved not only the freeing of chromaticism from its former, decorative function, but an increase in other levels of musical complexity. In Schoenberg's view, the free use of dissonance in tonal music after Wagner, and audiences' gradual acceptance of it, was part of an evolutionary trend that eventually negated tonality in the early twentieth century. The use of chromaticism in the absence of tonality led to atonality and a musical sound even more challenging for audiences unattuned to the latest trends. This atonal style relied on extreme motivic unity and certain novel harmonic constructs as organizing forces, but it was generated initially by the composer's intuition. It sprang from Schoenberg's innermost feelings and reflected the kinds of "adult" sound that he wanted to hear, including complete or nearly complete chromaticism. The twelve-tone method eventually emerged from this free atonality as an attempt to guarantee and regularize the interaction of its chromaticism and motivic unity, that is, Schoenberg sought with the twelve-tone method to codify and then refine the sounds and processes that he had come to prefer in his atonal works. In Schoenberg's mind this was all part of an evolutionary process that freed chromaticism ("the emancipation of dissonance") and allowed it to be used structurally.

Of course, some commentators have questioned the historical basis of this evolution, and audiences have not been quick to accept atonality, but Schoenberg held hope in the belief that one day audiences would "catch up" with the advanced sensibilities of composers such as himself. Some did catch up relatively quickly, and others have since. As Ernest Newman put it after Sir Henry Wood conducted the English premiere of Schoenberg's Five Orchestra Pieces, op. 16, in 1912, "Schoenberg is not the lunatic that he is generally taken for. Could it not be that the new composer sees a logic in tonal relations which amount to chaos for the rest of us at present, but whose connection could be clear enough to us one day?''[6] Newman's assessment has been shared by numerous critics, conductors, and performers since.

Supporting Schoenberg in his belief that his music would eventually find acceptance were the historical examples of composers such as Beethoven and Wagner, who had been underappreciated during their own lives but venerated after their deaths. Clearly these composers had been ahead of their time, and audiences did eventually catch up with their musical innovations. Identifying himself with such past masters put Schoenberg in elevated company, and this assumption incensed his detractors as much as it fueled the respect of his supporters. Schoenberg was careful to point out that he was not a groundbreaking, misunderstood composer by choice but had become one out of necessity. By his own admission, it was an inner compulsion that caused Schoenberg to compose, and he felt driven by the "Supreme Commander" to follow his artistic conscience and write the kind of music he believed in. As Schoenberg revealed in a radio interview in 1931,

I cannot either think or say anything different from what my task prescribes for me. . . . As long as I am allowed to regard my thoughts and imagination as right, I cannot believe in anything else except that thoughts must be thought and expressed, even if they are not understood, and even if they never can be understood. I myself do not believe that I am so unintelligible. But let us consider: supposing unquestionably great thoughts like those of a Kant were not allowed to be thought or said, because even today sincere people must agree that they cannot follow them? Whoever God has entrusted with the task of saying something unpopular, he has also given him the possibilities of satisfying himself that there would always be others who will understand.[7]

Schoenberg's romantic self-view was formed before World War I, and it had much in common with many nineteenth-century composers' artistic orientations; but this aesthetic attitude was "out of fashion" in the interwar years, when invention was restrained by classicism, concepts such as "Gebrauchsmusik" found favor, and composers spoke more of the craft of composition than of divine inspiration. It was especially out of place after the Second World War, when rational processes dominated the musical world.

When Schoenberg discovered and began using the twelve-tone method in the 1920s, he was, in one sense, in step with the aesthetic orientation of the time. The objectivity of neoclassical trends in the 1920s shared ground with the twelve-tone method's attempt to regularize and standardize the musical sounds born earlier of intuition, and many of Schoenberg's first twelve-tone works were obviously classical in their orientation. But because of his connections with the past, some of Schoenberg's contemporaries did not view his music as topical and, in general, his aesthetics were not those of the "new objectivity." "Suddenly public opinion began to forget the emotional power of everything I had written before," Schoenberg remembered.

Pierrot lunaire, the First and Second String Quartets, *Gurrelieder*, and even *Verklärte Nacht* were forgotten, and I was called by some critics a mere constructor. By this term they wished to imply that I did not write instinctively, and that my music was dry and without emotional expression. By others, in contrast, I was accused of exactly the opposite crime: I was called an old-fashioned romanticist and my style of expression was blamed for expressing personal feelings. . . . So I seemed to unite within myself every possible contrast: I was too dry and too sweet; I was a constructor and a romanticist; I was an innovator and I was old-fashioned.[8]

In the later 1920s, he commiserated with Franz Schrecker about how the two of them had once been considered modernists and were now called romantics; the objective style of Hindemith and Stravinsky was the new modernism.[9] Later, after Schoenberg's death in 1951, he was dismissed as old-fashioned by enfant terrible Pierre Boulez, who saw Schoenberg's combination of twelve-tone pitch organization with aspects of older musical styles to be a willful misunderstanding and underuse of the potential of serial organization. But despite these complaints, Schoenberg was considered to be modern enough and appropriately rational and intellectual to appeal to the growing trend of university composer-professors who dominated the American mainstream for many years.

Whether Schoenberg was perceived as being in or out of step with contemporary trends, he always valued his connections with past music, and he used them to justify the validity of his current styles. In the essay "National Music (2)" from 1931, nearly ten years after he began to work with the twelve-tone method, Schoenberg enumerated some of the aspects of his own musical style that he had gleaned from the German tradition, including, from Bach, "Contrapuntal thinking; i.e., the art of inventing musical figures that can be used to accompany themselves; the art of producing everything from one thing and of relating figures by transformation."[10] Schoenberg valued these most German of musical features above all others, and they underlie his tonal, freely atonal, and twelve-tone compositions. Schoenberg also played up the past in his teaching. According to a number of students, Schoenberg never spoke about the twelve-tone method and used mainly classical and romantic masterworks in his teaching. He even berated students for row-counting analyses of his twelve-tone works, since they demonstrated only how the piece was made and not "what it is." "I can't say it often enough: my works are twelve-tone *compositions*, not *twelve-tone* compositions."[11] Despite these impassioned pleas, Schoenberg suffered time and time again from assessments based on the perceived complexity of the twelve-tone method and not on the sound of the music. A case in point concerns the Piano Concerto, a twelve-tone work composed in 1942 that is perhaps the most accessible and obviously traditional of any of Schoenberg's twelve-tone works. Marked by a lyrical melody and fairly obvious form, the concerto has elicited many observations about the synthesis of tonal and twelve-tone styles in Schoenberg's later works. But the reviews of the premiere were deaf to these traditional qualities. Olin Downes found it "disagreeable and unconvincing,'' and added, ''its contents would serve excellently for the purposes of the analyst. . . . [but, despite its] sincerity and craftsmanship . . . the ideas appear to have little to do with beauty or real music.''[12] Critic Robert Bagar likened it to the machine age and war plants, noting that

it is wonderfully constructed, almost challenging in its mathematical philosophy. I suppose, though, that all the shaping and equating and balancing and scientific purpose that went into its making may be considered worthy ends in themselves, the 12-tone foundations of its structure valid ones for our time. It's all abstract stuff, as it sounds, despite the brain work that went into it.[13]

Even Leopold Stokowski, who conducted the work, prefaced it by saying it was a very difficult work to grasp without study, although he regarded it as ''one of the landmarks of musical history.''[14]

Because Schoenberg's music is complex, and because he typically saw himself as fulfilling a divine mission, he and his music are frequently charged with elitism. Of course elitism, in reality, is an aspect of all art music, and it is perhaps only in the twentieth century that it is perceived as an entirely negative attribute. Even Hans Heinz Stuckenschmidt, one of Schoenberg's most important and sympathetic biographers, compared Schoenberg to Richard Strauss by observing that Schoenberg's ''musical language is hardly ever influenced by the intention of writing brilliant vocal or instrumental effects or even of making them possible. His language is dematerialized from his first works onwards and later deliberately avoids the ideals of pleasing people or general popularity.''[15] Although Stuckenschmidt's characterization of Schoenberg's music may be correct, can we assert that Schoenberg consciously tried to avoid pleasing people? This assessment seems unnecessarily harsh and unattuned to Schoenberg's goals as a composer. Schoenberg followed his inner compulsion to compose truthfully, and the result was not calculated to please anyone but Schoenberg's artistic conscience. When his music did not find its audience immediately, Schoenberg frequently reacted out of bitterness and with blunt irony. ''If it is art, it is not for the masses,'' he wrote to a magazine editor in 1945. ''And if it is for the masses, it is not art.''[16] Many years earlier he offered an equally bitter, ironic view when referring to the effect of the advancing years on the occasion of his fiftieth birthday in 1924: ''I can no longer hate as once I could. Sometimes, and this is worse still, I can even understand without feeling contempt.''[17] Linking unintelligibility with admiration, and intelligibility with contempt: what could be more elitist? And yet Schoenberg, like most musicians, had a strong desire for recognition and understanding. As he wrote to a colleague in 1947,

my music *still* goes on suffering from the fact that the musicians do not regard me as a normal, common or garden [variety] composer who expresses his more or less good and new themes and melodies in a not entirely inadequate musical language—but as a modern dissonant twelve-note experimenter. But there is nothing I long for more intensely (if for anything) than to be taken for a better sort of Tchaikovsky—for heaven's sake: a bit better, but really that's all. Or if anything more, than that people should know my tunes and whistle them.[18]

Schoenberg's detractors reacted negatively to the seriousness, complexity, atonality, and intellectual qualities of Schoenberg's music, yet these are the very qualities that he valued most. Ideally, he hoped that audiences would rise to the level of his music. He wanted to maintain his high artistic level and he wanted audience approval. Eventually, when he began to realize that audiences were not keeping up, he turned on a number of occasions to transcriptions, arrangements, and tonal works to satisfy his artist's need for public approbation, but he continued to write elevated twelve-tone works to satisfy his artistic conscience at the same time. (See, for example, the articles on Schoenberg's late tonal and twelve-tone works by Jan Maegaard and Ethan Haimo, respectively, later in this volume.)

Recent trends away from rationalism, away from complexity in music, and toward a renewed romantic aesthetic and vocabulary have launched a decline in Schoenberg's reputation in some circles. Music that is perceived to be difficult, intellectual, and constructed is now seen as unfriendly to audiences, and a more audience-driven, sensuous style is in evidence. With the rich irony that has characterized so much of the reception of Schoenberg's music, even though he was perceived as "too romantic" to appeal to the post–World War II avant-garde, he is now seen as "too intellectual" to appeal to the new romantics who emerged in opposition to that avant-garde emphasis on rational processes. For many younger composers, Schoenberg is not an issue, and even many older composers, disenfranchised in the past three or four decades by an establishment dominated by intellectual concerns, applaud Schoenberg's demise and see a more positive musical future without his influence. But a decline in Schoenberg's status is not attractive to all musicians. Even though older masters of complex styles related to Schoenberg's, such as Elliot Carter and Charles Wuorinen, have been exploring more traditionally consonant sounds in their recent works, some of them have stated their hope that the new simplicity, the new romanticism will soon pass, and that "Uncle Arnold" and the high artistic standards with which he is associated, will save contemporary music from the vapidity of the new, simplistic styles.[19]

To Schoenberg's credit, he did not teach just one style of music, but sought the highest level of musical expression in any style. He was aware of musical fashions; even in the 1940s, he observed that contemporary trends placed too much emphasis on "style" and not enough on content or, as he termed it, "idea." Certainly, Schoenberg's greatest contribution to our musical heritage is this emphasis on "idea" or musical content. As Schoenberg observed in the essay "New Music: Outmoded Music, Style and Idea," musical style might pass with time, but "an idea can never perish."[20] The challenge to the future will be to retain Schoenberg's high artistic ideals regarding musical content while remaining true to current musical trends, or, to use his words, to aspire to be, perhaps, a "better sort of Tchaikovsky" with "an alert and well-trained mind."

NOTES

1. Quoted in Malcolm MacDonald, *Schoenberg* (London: Dent, 1976), 22.

2. Paul Stauber, *Montagspresse*, 30 January 1905, quoted in Walter B. Bailey, Programmatic Elements in the Works of Schoenberg (Ann Arbor: UMI Research Press, 1984), 17.

3. Quoted in *The Berg-Schoenberg Correspondence: Selected Letters*, ed. Juliane Brand, Christopher Hailey, and Donald Harris (New York: Norton, 1987), xv.

4. Schoenberg, "Brahms the Progressive," in *Style and Idea: Selected Writings of Arnold Schoenberg*, ed. Leonard Stein, trans. Leo Black (Berkeley and Los Angeles: University of California Press, 1984), 408.

5. Ibid., 401.

6. Ernest Newman, quoted in Hans Heinz Stuckenschmidt, *Schoenberg: His Life, World, and Work*, trans. Humphrey Searle (New York: Schirmer, 1978), 177–78.

7. "Diskussion im Berliner Rundfunk (radio broadcast with Heinrich Strobel and Eberhard Preussner)" in Schoenberg, *Gesammelte Schriften I*, ed. Ivan Vojtech and trans. Gudrun Budde (Nördlingen and Reutlingen: S. Fischer, 1976), 272–282; quoted in Stuckenschmidt, *Schoenberg*, 343.

8. Schoenberg, "How One Becomes Lonely," in *Style and Idea*, 52.

9. Schoenberg, "Schrecker zum 50. Geburtstag," *Musikblätter des Anbruch* 10/3–4(1928), 82.

10. Schoenberg, "National Music (2)," in *Style and Idea*, 173.

11. Schoenberg to Rudolf Kolisch, 27 July 1932, in *Arnold Schoenberg: Letters*, ed. Erwin Stein, trans. Eithne Wilkins and Ernst Kaiser (Berkeley and Los Angeles: University of California Press, 1987), 164–165.

12. Olin Downes, *New York Times, 7* February 1944; quoted in *Arnold Schönberg 1874–1951: Lebensgeschichte in Begegnungen*, ed. Nuria Schoenberg-Nono (Klagenfurt: Ritter Klagenfurt, 1992), 391.

13. Robert Bagar, *New York World-Telegram*, 7 February 1944; quoted in *Arnold Schönberg, 1874–1951: Lebensgeschichte in Begegnungen*, 391.

14. See note 12.

15. Stuckenschmidt, *Schoenberg*, 76.

16. Schoenberg to William S. Schlamm, 26 June 1945, in *Arnold Schoenberg: Letters*, 235.

17. "On My Fiftieth Birthday: September 13, 1934," in *Style and Idea*, 24.

18. Schoenberg to Hans Rosbaud, 12 May 1947, in *Arnold Schoenberg: Letters*, 243.

19. Personal correspondence with the author.

20. Schoenberg, "New Music: Outmoded Music, Style and Idea," in *Style and Idea*, 123.

2

Biography

Walter B. Bailey

Arnold Schoenberg (1874–1951) lived in an era of great artistic upheaval, and it is customary to view his life as a series of reactions to the major aesthetic trends of his day. Schoenberg entered the world at the height of musical romanticism; he progressed to maturity during the period of spiritual and artistic idealism that preceded the First World War; and he advanced through middle and old age in the climate of rationalism that followed the war. Yet Schoenberg's music, while in tune with the changing spirit of his times, always maintained contact with the traditions of the past. Initially, he contributed to the most progressive trends within the late romantic idiom that dominated *fin-de-siècle* Vienna, but his music was firmly grounded in tonality. By 1908 Schoenberg had developed an ultraexpressive, atonal vocabulary inspired by metaphysical trends such as expressionism that were then prevalent in the arts, but this new music maintained the motivic unity that had characterized German music as far back as Bach. After World War I, from the sounds and processes embedded in his deeply intuitive, expressionistic musical style, Schoenberg extracted the twelve-tone method, which reflected the spirit of postwar rationalism by emphasizing an organic unifying method derived from the historic traditions of motivic unity and the recent trend of atonality. In all periods of his career, Schoenberg conserved the traditional values of German music, yet he superimposed innovations upon them that were in line with the artistic developments of his time.

In general, Schoenberg's musical values exemplified the highest level of German musical expression identified with the music of Bach, Beethoven, and Brahms, that is, a motivically unified, compact style. Schoenberg applied these musical values to tonal, atonal, and twelve-tone compositions alike throughout his career. As to its German-ness, Schoenberg believed in the primacy of German musical culture and saw himself not only as a participant in that culture but as the repository of its past greatness. When Schoenberg explained his new twelve-tone method to his student Josef Rufer, he declared that it would guarantee the supremacy of German music for the next hundred years. Although it is tempting to view Schoenberg's declaration as ironic in light of his Jewish heritage and the tragedies precipitated by Nazi-dominated Germany, it can be judged so only after the fact. In his musical taste and ideals, Schoenberg represented the completeness of his assimilation into Germanic culture. Well through World War I, Schoenberg thought of himself as German, and even after his gradual awakening to the traditions of his Jewish ancestors, prodded by the growing anti-Semitism of the 1920s and 1930s, he maintained a German musical style and upheld it as the best model to follow.

Although Schoenberg himself divided his career by the three major changes in his musical style, important external events also affected his life; his was an era not only of great artistic upheaval, but of great political upheaval. Foremost among the external events of his life were the two world wars and the events that led up to them, which not only made devastating interruptions in his creative work but also forced him to adjust his identity as an artist and nearly assimilated Jew in a German-dominated culture. Initially an ardent nationalist, Schoenberg served in the Austrian army during World War I but was forced to flee Europe prior to the Second World War because of his Jewish heritage.

Schoenberg's career was also influenced by his need to make a living, and this need, in combination with the artistic and political upheavals of his day, caused him to relocate a number of times. Without question, Schoenberg's life was influenced by the cities in which he lived. In many ways, Schoenberg was a product of his native Vienna, where he spent forty-six of his seventy-six years. Yet he also lived in Berlin for a dozen years and found great fame there. Eventually, despite his stature as a major musical figure in Europe, Schoenberg was forced to immigrate to the United States, where he spent the last sixteen years of his life in Los Angeles.

At the end of Schoenberg's life he was venerated in Europe and America as an important, but controversial, composer, an influential teacher, and an unswerving force in musical modernism. Many listeners were deaf to the connections between his later works and older musical traditions, and they questioned why he no longer wrote in the style of his youth. Some younger composers, most notably Pierre Boulez, were all too aware of his connections with the past and rejected him as hopelessly old-fashioned because of them. This mixed reception was frequently Schoenberg's lot throughout his career, and it shaped his often-bitter response to any criticism. But, although Schoenberg, like all composers, desired an audience's acceptance, and he believed sincerely that audiences would one day appreciate all his works, he was not obviously driven by a desire for acceptance. Instead, Schoenberg was motivated by an inner sense that what he was doing artistically was necessary and right. It is the focus of Schoenberg's artistic vision on German musical traditions that makes his music so consistent and unifies his reactions to the aesthetic changes of his lifetime.

VIENNA

Arnold Schoenberg was born in Vienna on 13 September 1874 to Jewish parents who had immigrated to the Austrian capital. His father, Samuel Schoenberg (1838–1889), was a native of Szecseny, near Brastislava, Slovakia, and had traveled to Vienna in his teens to be apprenticed to a commercial firm. His mother, Pauline Nachod (1848–1921), who came from Prague, arrived in Vienna with her parents and siblings as a young girl. Samuel and Pauline married in 1870 and Arnold was the oldest of their surviving children. He was preceded in birth by a first son, who died soon after birth, and was followed by a sister, Ottilie (1876–1954), and a brother, Heinrich (1882–1941).

The Schoenbergs lived in the Second District, also known as the Leopoldstadt, which was the traditional home of Jewish immigrants in Vienna. Within the Viennese social hierarchy, the Schoenbergs would have been seen as "Eastern Jews," a group distinct from and socially inferior to the bourgeois Jewish families who had lived in Vienna for generations. Schoenberg's father ran a shoe shop and later opened a collection agency, but he was never more than modestly successful.

Schoenberg remembered his father as an "idealistic freethinker"; he recalled his mother to be a conservative, pious traditionalist. Adding to this family dichotomy were visits from "Uncle Fritz" (Friedrich Nachod, Pauline's brother), who was well-traveled, spoke French, and shared a progressive point of view with Schoenberg's father. It is impossible to determine just how important a part religion played in Schoenberg's upbringing, but it seems to have been minimal. Schoenberg's Jewish heritage appears to have been overwhelmed by the larger German culture, which dominated the Schoenberg household as it did those of many Jewish families approaching assimilation.

Music was not of overwhelming importance to the Schoenberg family. Schoenberg referred to his father as being no more fond of music than any other Austrian who did not actively dislike it. On the other hand, his mother's family was musical and had traditionally provided cantors for Prague's main synagogue. As testimony to her family's musicality, two of her nephews later became operatic singers, as did her younger son, Heinrich. There is, however, no consistent record of music making in the Schoenberg household, and they did not own a piano.

Despite the lack of other recorded musical activity at home, Schoenberg began violin lessons at age eight and tried his hand at composition at age ten, writing short duets similar to those by Viotti and Pleyel that he played with his teacher. Eventually he began to play string chamber music with friends and wrote pieces for string trio and quartet. His only real opportunity for hearing music other than that of his own making stemmed from the varied repertory of the military bands that performed in the coffeehouses of the Prater, a park located in the Second District, to which Schoenberg and his friends could listen from outside without paying admission. Ranging from popular waltzes to excerpts from Wagner's operas, this music was Schoenberg's introduction to the concert repertory.

Schoenberg's general education supplemented his budding understanding of music. In April 1880 he began school at the local *Volksschule*, or elementary school. When he entered the *Realschule* (secondary school without classics) in 1885 he met a fellow student, Oscar Adler, who instructed him in the rudiments of music theory. Adler joined Schoenberg and one of Schoenberg's cousins to form a string trio; eventually Schoenberg bought a cello and taught himself to play it, and the group then became a quartet. Schoenberg reported that he began writing quartet movements inspired by his purchase of some Beethoven scores and schooled by the article on sonata in an encyclopedia.

At the end of December 1889, three months after Schoenberg's fifteenth birthday, his father died in an influenza epidemic that swept through Vienna. Although he had not completed his studies at the *Realschule*, Schoenberg's obligation to help support his mother and siblings forced him to leave school. His mother found him employment as an apprentice in a bank and he contributed to the family income for several years. He did not, however, neglect his musical studies.

In 1893, Schoenberg was one of several young men who founded Polyhymnia, a small amateur orchestra. To conduct its weekly meetings, the members of the ensemble—a few violinists, one violist, one cellist, and one bassist— chose Alexander von Zemlinsky, a young graduate of the Vienna Conservatory. Prior to this time Schoenberg had received no instruction in composition beyond Adler's friendly remarks and his own understanding of the scores that he had studied and played. Now Zemlinsky became his teacher, and Schoenberg later said that he owed him almost everything he knew about "the technique and problems of composition."[1]

"I had been a Brahmsian when I met Zemlinsky," wrote Schoenberg in the autobiographical essay "My Evolution." "His love embraced both Brahms and Wagner and soon thereafter I became an equally confirmed addict. No wonder the music I composed at the time mirrored the influence of both these masters, to which a flavor of Liszt, Bruckner, and perhaps also Hugo Wolf was added."[2] Several years later, Zemlinsky helped Schoenberg present his music to a public audience by recommending the String Quartet in D Major, composed in 1897, to Vienna's Composers' Society. This society, whose honorary president was Brahms, heard the quartet in 1898 first in a private concert and then later in one of its subscription concerts. A review by Eduard Hanslick observed that "a new Mozart is growing up in Vienna."[3]

Schoenberg had also found support for his work somewhat earlier. Polyhymnia awarded him his first composition prize in 1893 for the song "Schilflied," his earliest dated composition. In 1894 he and his friends played a quartet movement for the composer Joseph Labor, a student of Simon Sechter, who insisted that Schoenberg become a musician despite his lack of formal training. The critic Richard Heuberger, identified with Brahms's circle, also encouraged

Schoenberg to become a musician and suggested specifically that he write piano pieces.

In 1895, three years before the success of his D Major Quartet, Schoenberg either quit his job at the bank or lost it when the bank closed. Whatever the cause, this event allowed Schoenberg to dedicate himself to a full-time career in music. Initially this career entailed conducting small choral societies and orchestrating or making piano reductions of operettas by other composers. In addition to these activities, Schoenberg found time to compose. He composed a number of songs in the later 1890s, heard several of them performed in recital in 1898, and selected some of them to be his first published works. During this time he also composed the string quartet mentioned above, an unfinished symphonic poem, and, in 1899, during a summer vacation with Zemlinsky at Payerbach, the programmatic string sextet *Verklärte Nacht*.

In the following year he began the *Gurrelieder* with the intention of entering it in Vienna's Composers' Society's song cycle composition competition. Soon the work grew far beyond the confines of a song cycle, and it eventually became a large-scale work for soloists, speaker, choruses, and orchestra. Schoenberg had essentially completed the short score by April of 1901, and he worked on its orchestration intermittently during 1902, 1903, 1910, and 1911.

As Schoenberg dedicated himself to his musical career, he also took actions of great importance to his personal life. In 1898 he forswore his Jewish heritage and was baptized in a Protestant (Lutheran) church in Vienna. This was accomplished under the influence of his friend, the opera singer Walter Pieau, who schooled Schoenberg in the elements of Christianity. The background of this event is unknown; on at least one occasion prior to this event, Schoenberg had described himself as an "unbeliever," but later in his life he recalled that he had never been anti-or even unreligious. Although it undoubtedly had deep personal significance at the time, in the larger picture Schoenberg's conversion serves to strengthen his identification with the German culture to which he aspired.

A second major personal event in Schoenberg's life took place in 1899, when, during his vacation with Zemlinsky, Schoenberg became friendly with Zemlinsky's sister Mathilde. Some commentators have suggested that the passion of *Verklärte Nacht* and some of the songs written at this time detail the intensity of his feelings for Mathilde. They married on 7 October 1901 in the same Viennese church in which he had been baptized. Their first child, Gertrud (called Trudi), was born three months later in Berlin.

BERLIN

The inevitability of his marriage and the impending birth of his child severely challenged Schoenberg's precarious financial situation but, fortuitously, he was able to find employment with Ernst von Wolzogen's *Überbrettl* company in Berlin. Just a few weeks before Schoenberg's marriage, Wolzogen's *Überbrettl* had made its second visit to Vienna. The *Überbrettl*, or "super-theater," was designed to intermingle high artistic expression with popular entertainment; it presented serious, quality poetry in tasteful, albeit "music hall" musical settings. An outgrowth of the Parisian literary cafés of a slightly earlier age, the concept of a German literary cabaret was quite topical, as suggested by the great success of *Deutsche Chansons (Brettl-Lieder)*, a volume published in 1900 that contained poems by authors such as Wolzogen, Frank Wedekind, Detlev von Liliencron, Gustav Falke, Richard Dehmel, and Otto Julius Bierbaum. Wolzogen's *Überbrettl* had opened in Berlin in January 1901, and its success was credited not only to Wolzogen's direction but to the contribution of the conductor Waldemar Wendland, composer Bogumil Zepler, and composer-conductor Oscar Straus. A spring tour of several cities, including Vienna, had also been a success, and Wolzogen was on the verge of building his own theater in Berlin for the exclusive use of his company.

During the second tour of the *Überbrettl*, Oskar Straus was scheduled to conduct at Vienna's Carltheater, but the performance fell on Yom Kippur and Straus's wealthy Viennese uncle forbade him to take part. Therefore Straus proposed Schoenberg as his replacement, and apparently Schoenberg conducted the performance. It is not known how Straus and Schoenberg came to know each other, but there are a number of likely connections between the two. Straus (1870–1954) had been born in the same neighborhood as Schoenberg and may have been part of Schoenberg's youthful acquaintance. In addition, Zemlinsky was employed as conductor at the Carltheater, and the association may have been developed through him. At any rate, in addition to conducting in Straus's place, Schoenberg managed to play some of his own settings of poems from the *Deutsche Chansons* for Wolzogen. Schoenberg had owned this collection since Christmas 1900, and he had set several of the poems prior to meeting Wolzogen. (Although never published during his lifetime, Schoenberg's settings of texts from the *Deutsche Chansons* appeared in print as the *Brettl-Lieder* many years after his death.) Wolzogen liked Schoenberg's songs and conducting enough to offer him a job with the *Überbrettl* in Berlin, and Schoenberg accepted this offer of employment.

In December 1901, Schoenberg and his wife moved to Berlin, where his contract required his presence from 16 December 1901 to 31 July 1902. There is no record of Schoenberg's specific duties as kapellmeister; the contract makes no mention of conducting but does mention composing. However, Schoenberg remembered that only one of his works was performed at the *Überbrettl* and that its difficulty precluded a good performance. Despite the wording of the contract, Schoenberg may have conducted or prepared musical performances at the theater. Outside the *Überbrettl* Schoenberg supplemented his income by orchestrating many works for other composers.

Schoenberg's contract with the *Überbrettl* was not renewed when it ran out, at least in part because Wolzogen had resigned his directorship the previous month. Schoenberg remained in Berlin until the summer of 1903, continuing to orchestrate the music of others and following up relations with a new contact, Richard Strauss. Schoenberg was certainly familiar with Strauss's music before he moved to Berlin. But in April 1902, either Schoenberg wrote directly to Strauss, or Wolzogen, who had provided the libretto for Strauss's opera *Feuersnot*, gave him an introduction. Strauss replied by inviting Schoenberg to visit him, and, apparently the two became fairly close. During the next several years, Strauss went out of his way to help Schoenberg. Initially, he critiqued Schoenberg's *Verklärte Nacht*, and he then employed Schoenberg to copy parts for *Taillefer*, his recent work for large orchestra and chorus. In addition, Strauss recommended Schoenberg to the director of the Stern Conservatory in Berlin, where Schoenberg may have begun teaching a composition class as early as December 1902. In response to Schoenberg's poor financial circumstances, Strauss was instrumental in granting Schoenberg a fellowship of 1,000 marks from the Liszt Foundation in 1903 and again in 1904.

Strauss also introduced Schoenberg to Maeterlinck's *Pelléas et Melisande* when Schoenberg asked for his advice on selecting an appropriate text for an opera. Schoenberg did not write an opera at this time, but he used Maeterlinck's play as the basis for his first orchestral work, the tone poem *Pelléas und Melisande*. It was completed on 28 February 1903, less than a year after his first meeting with Strauss.

With the completed score of *Pelleas und Melisande* in hand, Schoenberg attempted to make contact with another influential musician in Berlin, Feruccio Busoni. Busoni, best-known as a piano virtuoso but also an innovative composer, had lived in Berlin since 1894 although he continued to tour widely. For practical and financial reasons, Busoni limited his piano repertory to the standard virtuoso works; to satisfy his dedication to modern music, he conducted orchestral concerts. He began a series of such concerts with the Berlin Philharmonic in the fall of 1902, featuring first performances of works by Elgar, Saint-Saëns, Sibelius, and Delius, among others. In the spring of 1903 Schoenberg offered *Pelleas und Melisande* to Busoni, hoping that he would include it on the series. Although Busoni asked to see the score and presumably examined it, he did not perform it. His relations with Schoenberg, however, were cordial, and they remained so in their later dealings.

Schoenberg's life in Berlin was not easy. Despite his copying work, he was always short of money, and despite his many musical contacts, he did not have many performances. One important exception was the first Berlin performance of *Verklärte Nacht*, which took place on 30 October 1902, seven months after it had been premiered in Vienna during Schoenberg's absence. This Berlin performance probably brought Schoenberg into contact with Max Marshalk, the director of the Dreililienverlag, who became Schoenberg's first publisher. In 1903 Marshalk published twelve of Schoenberg's songs as his opp. 1, 2, and 3, and *Verklärte Nacht* as op. 4.

Discouraged by the realities of life in Berlin and hoping for better prospects through his older contacts in Vienna, Schoenberg returned to Vienna. His sojourn in Berlin had brought him into contact with important composers such as Strauss and Busoni, and he had found a publisher for his works. Vienna would offer other advantages.

VIENNA II

Once Schoenberg had returned to Vienna in the late summer of 1903, Zemlinsky was one of his most important contacts. Zemlinsky's position as conductor at the Carltheater, a haven for operetta, made it possible for him to send many orchestration jobs to Schoenberg. Universal Edition hired Zemlinsky and Schoenberg to make four-hand piano arrangements of standard works such as Rossini's *The Barber of Seville*. When Dr. Eugenia Schwarzwald decided to offer music courses at her private school, she hired Zemlinsky to teach form and analysis and, at Zemlinsky's suggestion, she hired Schoenberg to teach harmony and counterpoint. In addition, the Schoenbergs rented an apartment in the same building as the Zemlinskys.

But Zemlinsky was not Schoenberg's only contact in Vienna. In the fall of 1903, the Rosé Quartet, along with members of the Vienna Philharmonic, gave a second Viennese performance of *Verklärte Nacht*, which they had premiered more than a year earlier. Because the violinist Arnold Rosé (Gustav Mahler's brother-in-law) was the leader of the Philharmonic, the quartet rehearsed in the Philharmonic's rehearsal room, and it was there that Mahler heard the work and became acquainted with Schoenberg. As a fellow conductor, Zemlinsky already knew Mahler; this connection had been strengthened in 1902 when Zemlinsky's composition pupil, Alma Maria Schindler, became Mahler's wife. Now Schoenberg became a part of Mahler's circle.

At the beginning of 1904, Zemlinsky and Schoenberg were foremost among the Viennese musicians who founded the Society of Creative Musicians, a group designed to present concerts of works by modern composers. Mahler was named honorary president, and the group sponsored seven concerts during the one year of its existence. Among the works presented was Schoenberg's *Pelleas und Melisande*, in its premiere performance; other works presented on the programs included Strauss's *Domestic Symphony*, Mahler's *Kindertotenlieder*, and compositions by Reger, Pfitzner, Zemlinsky, and several lesser-known composers.

Indirectly, it was Mahler who sent Schoenberg one of his two most famous students. Anton von Webern, a musicology student at the University of Vienna, sought advice from his professor, Guido Adler, about a composition teacher. Adler, a friend of Mahler since his childhood, consulted with Mahler, who suggested Hans Pfitzner at the Stern Conservatory in Berlin. Early in 1904 Webern and another student, Heinrich Jalowetz, went to Berlin to study with Pfitzner, but they did not stay because of Pfitzner's negative attitude toward Mahler's music. When they returned to Vienna, Adler consulted with Mahler again, who now suggested Schoenberg as a teacher. Webern showed some of his works to Schoenberg in the summer of 1904 and became his student in the fall.

Private teaching was necessary for Schoenberg, because the classes at the

Schwarzwald school had lasted only for the 1903–4 school year. Schoenberg had placed a notice in a Viennese newspaper advertising his availability as a composition teacher and through this action gained other students. Among these was Alban Berg, who began lessons in the fall after his brother had secretly sent Schoenberg some of Berg's compositions. Other private students included Heinrich Jalowetz, Erwin Stein, and Egon Wellesz.

Schoenberg's new students were all supporters of Mahler's music. Schoenberg had been aware of Mahler's music as early as the 1890s, when he was probably introduced to it by Zemlinsky. At that time Schoenberg was apparently unmoved by the music, and he remained unconvinced of Mahler's talent as a composer until he heard a performance of Mahler's Third Symphony in December 1904, more than a year after he had met him. From that point he saw Mahler as a "saint," and close friendships developed among Zemlinsky, Schoenberg, and Gustav and Alma Mahler. Mahler always supported Schoenberg's music, although he said that he sometimes did not understand it.

During the next few years, Schoenberg taught privately, composed mostly during summer vacations, and promoted performances of his works. His domestic routine was enlivened by the birth of his second child, Georg, in September 1906. In 1907, his String Quartet no. 1 (composed in 1905) and the First Chamber Symphony (composed in 1906) were premiered in Vienna. Mahler, who attended the performance of the quartet, enjoyed it greatly and recommended it to Strauss in Berlin, where it was soon performed. Apparently the audience's response to the Quartet was mixed, and the Chamber Symphony was interrupted by a variety of negative reactions. Soon thereafter, however, a recital of songs from opuses 2, 3, and 6 was very well received.

The year 1907 also saw considerable upheaval in Schoenberg's life. When Mahler resigned his positions in Vienna in preparation for his move to New York, Schoenberg and his students were stunned. Not only did Mahler's departure threaten a possible slackening of musical standards in the city, it meant the loss of support for modern music in general and, specifically, the loss of one of Schoenberg's staunchest supporters. As Schoenberg continually pushed the boundaries of musical expression, he quite naturally felt the impact of Mahler's departure. But Schoenberg's continuing search for new means of expression was no longer satisfied by music alone, and he began to paint in 1907. Soon he and his wife began to take lessons from a young Viennese artist, Richard Gerstl (1883–1908).

Gerstl, like other Viennese, had been influenced by the recent exhibition of works by Van Gogh and Gauguin in Vienna, as well as by works by the Norwegian painter Eduard Munch. History has identified Gerstl's work as protoexpressionist, and his individual vision apparently coincided to a certain degree with Schoenberg's. As a musical counterpart to that vision, Schoenberg began one of his most original musical works that spring, the String Quartet no. 2. Taken as a whole, the events of 1907 suggest that Schoenberg was searching for new means of expression in the absence of former stabilities.

Schoenberg continued this search during 1908. In that year, Gerstl moved his studio into the same building as the Schoenbergs' apartment. He painted pictures of Schoenberg, Mathilde, and their family; Zemlinsky; and Berg, and he continued to be close to the Schoenbergs and the Zemlinskys. In an unanticipated event that rocked the Schoenberg circle, Mathilde acted on her strong attraction to Gerstl and left her family to live with him that summer. She returned to Schoenberg and their children only after many requests delivered by Schoenberg's students, primarily Webern. Soon after Mathilde returned to Schoenberg, Gerstl committed suicide.

Gerstl's death in the fall of 1908 followed Schoenberg's completion of the String Quartet no. 2, which he had dedicated ''To My Wife,'' and coincided with his work on a song cycle to texts of Stefan George, the *Fifteen Songs from the Book of the Hanging Gardens*, that details metaphorically the progress and eventual failure of a love affair. Soon afterward, on 21 December, the premiere of the String Quartet no. 2 on a Rosé Quartet subscription concert precipitated a full-scale riot among the concertgoers, who hissed and laughed throughout much of the work. A second performance, sponsored by the Ansorge Verein, an organization committed to new music that had sponsored a recital of Schoenberg's songs in 1904, was politely received. Apparently the modernity of the Quartet was too much for a general audience, but well within accepted norms for an audience drawn especially to new music.

There is a very strong temptation to link the upheaval of Schoenberg's personal life with the novelty of the compositions and paintings that he created at this time. But it is also possible that the musical changes and the sudden interest in painting, as reflections of general aesthetic trends that were in the air, would have happened anyway. In terms of trends then apparent in the arts, Schoenberg's creations are closely related to expressionism. A movement evident in all the arts prior to World War I, expressionism concerned the direct depiction of the artist's or composer's deepest, most personal feelings without regard for any social norms of beauty. With a type of shock value thus built in, expressionist works were intended to jolt viewers or listeners out of their artistic complacency so that they might accept art as a spiritual rather than a commercial experience. Schoenberg may have painted because music was not enough of an outlet for his intense inner feelings; his career as a painter was short-lived, but the intensity of expression in text and music that he developed during this time remained with him for the rest of his life.

Despite the volatility of the events that occurred during 1907 and 1908, Schoenberg's musical output intensified. In 1909 he completed the *Fifteen Songs from the Book of the Hanging Gardens*, op. 15, composed the Three Piano Pieces, op. 11, the Five Pieces for Orchestra, op. 16, and the monodrama *Erwartung*, which concerns a confused female character's search for her lover in the woods late at night—is she to meet him, or has she already killed him? ''Extravagant emotion is the fever that purges the soul of impurity,'' wrote Schoenberg to Mahler in 1910, and in the same year he described his latest style as a long-sought-for ideal of expression and form that he had finally achieved only by severing all ties with a ''bygone aesthetic.''

Schoenberg's expressionistic musical style was marked by motivic and formal compression, heavy use of dissonance, and dramatic gestures. The "bygone aesthetic" from which Schoenberg sought freedom was dominated by classical tonality and conventional modes of expression. By writing what has come to be called atonal music, Schoenberg used consonant and dissonant pitch combinations equally throughout his compositions, even in important structural junctures. Thus the musical shapes that emerged from his intuition could be expressed immediately, without recourse to traditional modes of expression. But, of course, Schoenberg's musical ideas could never be completely divorced from the musical past. Although admitting that these works had sprung from his intuition, Schoenberg was pleased to observe how cogently the works were organized on a motivic basis. In fact, one view of this music sees each piece as a free development of the motives stated at its beginning, expressed outside a tonal context. But Schoenberg expected even more from his intuition, and he predicted that one day theorists would discover other levels of unity in these works and, of course, they have.[4]

To Schoenberg, the new style was inevitable despite the opposition he knew that it would inspire. "I am being forced in this direction not because my invention or technique is inadequate, nor because I am uninformed about all the other things the prevailing aesthetics demand, but [because] I am obeying an inner-compulsion, which is stronger than any up-bringing: [because] I am obeying the formative process which, being the one natural to me, is stronger than my artistic education."[5]

In 1910 and 1911, Schoenberg's compositional pace slackened dramatically. In 1910 he composed only the Three Little Pieces for Chamber Orchestra, which remained unpublished and unknown during his lifetime, the beginning of the opera *Die Glückliche Hand*, and orchestrated a small portion of the *Gurrelieder*, which had been dormant since 1902. Instead he worked on the text of *Die Glückliche Hand*, the *Theory of Harmony* (which he began in the summer of 1910 and completed in the fall of 1911), and his teaching. Teaching was of great importance to Schoenberg, and to further his reputation in this area, Emil Hertzka of Universal Edition, the Viennese publisher who had begun publishing Schoenberg's music in 1909, had requested that he write a book on harmony. The idea appealed to Schoenberg and became a focus for his ideas on teaching; later it would bolster Schoenberg's reputation as a musician and teacher, especially with those unsympathetic to his recent compositions.

Schoenberg requested and was granted a position as adjunct lecturer in theory and composition at Vienna's Royal Academy of Music and Dramatic Art in 1910; among his references for this position was Gustav Mahler, who called Schoenberg "one of those fiery spirits—of the kind bound to provoke opposition but just as certainly to add life and set things in motion—who have always had a fructifying and productive effect on other minds. And particularly when, as in the present case, this is linked with so eminent a didactic talent."[6] Because of a rumored opposition to his appointment at a higher level, Schoenberg did not seek a professorship initially but hoped that his position as lecturer would prepare the way for his eventual promotion. Despite this new position, Schoenberg was forced in the summer of 1910 to ask Mahler for a loan to cover his rent payment, and Mahler graciously sent twice the amount that Schoenberg requested.

Much of 1911 was taken up with the completion of the *Theory of Harmony*, but Schoenberg also composed the Six Little Piano Pieces, op. 19. These short pieces mark the momentous event of the year—Mahler's death. The last of the Piano Pieces is said to represent Mahler's funeral. Even after his death, Mahler continued to be an important figure in Schoenberg's life and career. He dedicated the *Theory of Harmony* to Mahler's memory; Mahler's widow, as the head of Mahler Foundation after her husband's death, saw to it that Schoenberg received several grants over a number of years; in his later life Schoenberg took every opportunity to praise Mahler.

The *Theory of Harmony* was well received when it was published, and Schoenberg's teaching was very satisfying, but neither brought much income. Schoenberg felt unappreciated in Vienna, he had been deeply moved by Mahler's death, and he wanted a change. Somewhat earlier, Webern, now living in Germany, had suggested a move to Berlin. As a preliminary move, Schoenberg and his family left Vienna for the town of Berg on the Starnberger Sea near Munich. There he met Oskar Fried, who had conducted *Pelleas und Melisande* in Berlin, the theater producer Max Reinhardt, and Otto Klemperer. He also had plans to meet Strauss and Kandinsky. With no income at all, Schoenberg relied on a gift of money collected by former and current students to tide him over this time of transition.

Kandinsky had written to Schoenberg in January 1911, after hearing a concert of Schoenberg's Second String Quartet and the Piano Pieces, op. 11, in Munich. He enjoyed the concert greatly and observed how much he had in common with Schoenberg aesthetically. From this beginning, a correspondence had developed and Schoenberg's presence in Bavaria allowed them to meet. Kandinsky found interesting parallels between Schoenberg's atonal music and his own goals of pure expression in painting; like Schoenberg's "inner compulsion" to compose in the new style, Kandinsky cited "inner necessity" as the motivating force behind his art. Presumably Schoenberg and Kandinsky shared many ideas during Schoenberg's sojourn in Bavaria.

Kandinsky and Reinhardt, who had many contacts in Berlin, actively encouraged Schoenberg to move there. Vienna without Mahler seemed bleak, and although Schoenberg speculated that a professorship at the Vienna Academy would free him from financial concern and finally acknowledge his importance, he believed that there was little chance he would actually receive such an appointment. In September 1911, he left for Berlin.

BERLIN II

Schoenberg arrived in Berlin in the fall of 1911 and found that his controversial reputation had preceded him. Although negative reports in the press added to his notoriety, Schoenberg also had important supporters in the city. Artur Schnabel, Oskar Fried, and Busoni, for example, recommended Schoenberg to the Wolff Concert Agency, which began to promote Schoenberg and his music. Various performing groups presented some of Schoenberg's earlier works in concert, and these works were well received. Schoenberg also began teaching a course in aesthetics and composition at the Stern Conservatory, where Richard Strauss had recommended him back in 1902. Strauss was now unsympathetic to Schoenberg's latest compositions, and he no longer offered him any kind of support.

Despite the publicity that accompanied his arrival in Berlin, Schoenberg had little means of generating an income. Initially he had no private students, and by the end of the year he had only two. His pay at the Stern Conservatory was based on the number of students in his course, and this number was also quite low. To remedy Schoenberg's financial distress, some of his former students took up a collection on his behalf, and patrons in Berlin granted him 2,000 marks. The generosity of these supporters allowed Schoenberg to complete the orchestration of the *Gurrelieder* in November and to compose the song "Herzgewächse," op. 20, in December.

In addition to concerning themselves with Schoenberg's finances, his former students were devising a book in his honor. Begun in the fall of 1911 by Berg and Webern, the book, simply titled *Arnold Schönberg*, contained essays of homage to Schoenberg by many of his friends and former students. It was published by R. Piper and Co. in Munich and presented to Schoenberg in February 1912.

In the same month, Schoenberg arranged for a performance of some of his recent works, including the *Fifteen Songs from the Book of the Hanging Gardens*, op. 15, the Six Little Piano Pieces, op. 19, and a two-piano, eight-hand arrangement by Webern of several of the Five Pieces for Orchestra, op. 16. Except for the members of the press, the audience accepted the new music, and Busoni's positive comments were published in a popular music magazine. Soon thereafter the prestigious Leipzig publisher Peters accepted the Five Pieces for Orchestra, op. 16. Despite the relatively low fee that he received for the work, Schoenberg was impressed with the publisher's reputation, and he used the publication of the Orchestra Pieces as a lever in his continuing efforts to receive more favorable treatment from his Viennese publisher, Universal Edition. The Five Pieces, conducted by Henry Wood, premiered in London to mixed reviews during September 1912.

Schoenberg's stay in Berlin also marked the beginning of his conducting career. In February 1912 he traveled to Prague at the invitation of Zemlinsky, who had been the musical director of the German Opera there since the fall of 1911. Schoenberg was to conduct his own *Pelleas und Melisande* and Mahler's arrangement of a Bach Suite on a program that concluded with Zemlinsky conducting a concerto. Many of Schoenberg's friends and students attended the concert, and *Pelleas* was warmly received. Later in the year Schoenberg conducted *Pelleas* in Amsterdam and St. Petersburg.

During the summer of 1912, Schoenberg composed one of his most famous works, *Pierrot lunaire*, op. 21, on a commission from the actress Albertine Zehme. Zehme, who specialized in reciting poetry to musical accompaniment, wanted Schoenberg to set a series of poems by the Belgian symbolist poet Albert Giraud (in the German translations by Otto Erich Hartleben) for spoken voice and piano. She asked Schoenberg to set the texts because she thought that his notorious musical style would suit the poetry's nightmarish tone. Schoenberg, who was normally unable to address such a specific commission because of his artistic conscience, was very taken with the poems, and he therefore took on the project. As he worked on the settings, he found that piano accompaniment alone was not sufficiently varied for his ideas, so he added a variety of instruments to the ensemble. He also employed the distinctive vocal technique of *Sprechstimme*, which required the speaker to follow specific rhythms and melodic contours, gliding from pitch to approximate pitch. The product delighted Zehme and the work was well received in Berlin and on a European tour in the fall of 1912.

In *Pierrot lunaire*, as in contemporary works such as "Herzgewächse" and *Die Glückliche Hand*, Schoenberg began to employ traditional contrapuntal and formal structures that had been absent from his first expressionistic works. In these recent compositions there are a limited number of passages of exact repetition and, especially in *Pierrot lunaire*, sophisticated canons and fugal passages. Since Schoenberg retained the free dissonance and dynamic melodic gestures of his first expressionistic works, these new techniques are not always audible, but they signal a move away from the completely intuitive structures of the works from 1908 and 1909.

The events of 1912 and 1913 forced Schoenberg to confront his attitude toward his native city. The summer of 1912 brought the long-awaited invitation to join the faculty of the Vienna Academy as Professor of Composition. Although Schoenberg was tempted to take this job, he ultimately refused it because of his experience with Vienna's negative, confining atmosphere. At the same time he began negotiations for the premiere of the *Gurrelieder* in Vienna, which would eventually take place in March 1913. The Mahler Foundation gave Schoenberg a second large grant in January 1913. This payment, along with the salaries that he had earned conducting in Amsterdam and St. Petersburg, made him more secure financially than at any previous point in his life. He traveled to Vienna for the premiere of the *Gurrelieder* in March 1913 and was pleased not only by the quality of the performance, but by the very appreciative audience. Schoenberg, however, out of his long-standing anger with Viennese audiences, did not acknowledge the audience's response. Just a few weeks later the Viennese public rekindled Schoenberg's anger when they caused an uproar that halted a concert of music by Schoenberg and others of his circle. Webern's Four Orchestra Pieces, op. 4, which opened the concert, apparently incited the audience; although the songs of Zemlinsky that followed seemed to soothe them, Schoenberg's Chamber Symphony, op. 9, upset them further, and Berg's two

Altenberg Lieder then precipitated a riot. Mahler's *Kindertotenlieder*, with which the concert was supposed to end, was not played.

After Schoenberg returned to Berlin from this disastrous performance, he resumed his routine of teaching, composing and conducting. In the fall of 1913 he completed the song "Seraphita," which would eventually be published as the first of the Four Songs for Voice and Orchestra, op. 22. He also completed the opera *Die Glückliche Hand*, which he had begun in 1910. His conducting duties involved significant travel: in early 1914 he went to London and Amsterdam to conduct the Five Orchestra Pieces; later that year he also traveled to Prague to conduct three of the Songs for Voice and Orchestra, op. 8, and to Leipzig to conduct the *Gurrelieder*.

For a number of years Schoenberg had been planning to write a large-scale dramatic work based on Honoré de Balzac's *Seraphita*, and the aspects of the plan that coincided with his interest in religion—albeit a supradenominational, spiritual religion—continued to dominate his thoughts through 1917. In the winter of 1912, he had considered combining Balzac's work with August Strindberg's *Jacob Ringt*. As he wrote to the poet Richard Dehmel in December 1912, Schoenberg was interested in depicting how modern man could rise above his earthly situation, "wrestle" with God, and become religious.[7]

Balzac's *Seraphita* popularized the religious revelations of the eighteenth-century author Emanuel Swedenborg, especially his ideas about the nature of angels. According to Swedenborg, angels were created from humans who had risen through three stages of love: love of self, love of the world, and love of God. The gradual progression of the process, similar to ideas expressed in Theosophy, anthroposophy, and Eastern religions, was an idea present not only in Schoenberg's original planned dramatic work, but in the planned but unfinished program symphony which grew out of it, in the unfinished (but performable) oratorio, *Die Jakobsleiter*, which was originally conceived as a movement of the symphony, and also in the Four Songs, op. 22.

By May 1914 this idea had evolved into an idea for a large-scale programmatic symphony. Schoenberg made a detailed outline and many musical sketches for this work, including one for a scherzo theme that incorporated all twelve tones. Setting the work aside, he and his family went to stay with Kandinsky in Murnau in Upper Bavaria during the summer. When war broke out in August, Schoenberg returned to Berlin. Most of his students had left the city, and many had volunteered for military service. For once, income from them was not crucial, since Schoenberg had received grants from various foundations. He continued to work on the Songs, op. 22, and he completed the second and third by January 1915. Also in January he wrote the text "Death-Dance of Principles," which he planned to use in the second-to-last movement of his programmatic symphony. He then made the first sketches for the text of what would eventually be known as *Die Jakobsleiter* but at the time was considered to be the final movement of the planned symphony. During the war, he would complete the last of the Songs, op. 22, abandon the planned symphony, and complete the text and much of the music for *Die Jakobsleiter*. But the war would change the European social order dramatically and tear Schoenberg from the spiritual idealism of these works. In the years following the war, not only would spirituality be seen as insupportable, but the large-scale vision carrying over from the end of the nineteenth century would be negated. Schoenberg would never finish *Die Jakobsleiter*.

VIENNA III

In April 1915 Schoenberg traveled to Vienna to conduct Mahler's arrangement of Beethoven's Ninth Symphony, financed by a wealthy friend of Mahler's widow. While in Vienna he volunteered for military service but was rejected for unspecified medical reasons; perhaps, at age 40, he was viewed as too old for military service. In September he and his family moved from Berlin to Vienna where, through the generosity of a wealthy patron, he had a rent-free apartment. When Schoenberg took a second physical examination, he was judged to be fit for active service. In December he volunteered for a one-year period and was sent away for officer's training. During this training he began to experience asthma, and friends and colleagues tried to secure his release, which was granted in October 1916. After his discharge, Schoenberg was eager to resume work on his compositions. By July 1916 he had completed the last of the Songs for Voice and Orchestra, op. 22. He also resumed work on the text of *Die Jakobsleiter*, completing it during May 1917, and he began immediately to compose the music. In the space of three months he had completed the first half of the work except for the details of orchestration, but he was called up again in September 1917. Fortunately, this tour involved lighter duties in Vienna, and Schoenberg was often at home. He was finally discharged in December 1917. Sadly his military service interrupted his work on *Die Jakobsleiter*, and although he tried on a number of occasions to pick up the thread, he was able to compose only half of the interlude that joined the two halves of the work. The second half of the text remained unset, a casualty of the war. The continued difficulty of life after the war made it impossible for Schoenberg to recapture the elevated spiritual tone of *Die Jakobsleiter*.

In 1917, before he was recalled, Schoenberg had begun to lecture on composition again at the Schwarzwald School in Vienna. Since he had no private students at the time, the Schwarzwald lectures provided his only income. The cost of living was very high in Vienna, and food was scarce. Schoenberg himself was experiencing a financial crisis, since he had lost the use of the rent-free apartment in October 1917. In recognition of the difficulties shared by everyone in the city, Schoenberg had asked that students at the Schwarzwald School pay only what they were able to afford. Once again, his former students collected money on his behalf, and Eugenia Schwarzwald, the school's organizer, solicited patrons for Schoenberg. In January 1918, after his final parting with the military, Schoenberg began a new seminar in composition at the Schwarzwald School, where he continued to teach until 1920. Because of the high cost of living in Vienna, he moved to the suburb of Mödling in April 1918 and commuted to Vienna two days a week for the seminar. As he rebuilt his private class, his students had to travel to his apartment in Mödling. His financial position was improved through gifts from patrons and a third grant from the Mahler Foundation.

Out of his experiences with his seminars at the Schwarzwald School, Schoenberg conceived of educating audiences through public rehearsals of a given musical work, knowledgeable commentary, and a final public performance. During June 1918 he used his own Chamber Symphony to this end, and the presentations were well attended and well received. For Schoenberg's second term at the Schwarzwald School, September 1918 to June 1919, he had fifty-three students. From the success of his seminar and the open rehearsals of the Chamber Symphony, Schoenberg concocted a new idea: a society that would present private concerts of representative modern works and guarantee that each piece would be well rehearsed and played more than once in a season. In November 1918 he founded this Society for Private Musical Performances, and it presented twenty-six concerts in its first (1918–19) season. Key to the society was the idea that audience members would subscribe for a season not knowing what works were to be offered on which programs. The press would not be allowed to attend, and audience members would be prohibited from expressing appreciation by applause or distaste by booing. The new society and new private students took up most of Schoenberg's time, leaving little energy for composition.

Schoenberg's activities in 1920 and 1921 demonstrated the increased recognition he was receiving. In June 1920 Schoenberg conducted the Vienna Philharmonic and the *Singverein* in two very successful performances of the *Gurrelieder*. Later that year Schoenberg was invited to stay in Holland for six months, from late September 1920 through the end of March 1921, to teach and conduct his own works, including the *Gurrelieder*. During his absence his students kept the Society for Private Musical Performances running. He also expanded and clarified the text of the *Theory of Harmony* for a second edition. In 1921, Egon Wellesz, Schoenberg's former student and a scholar in his own right, completed and had published a book about Schoenberg.

During the summer of 1920, Schoenberg began to compose again for the first time since 1917, sketching piano pieces and ensemble movements that would eventually become part of the Five Piano Pieces, op. 23, and the Serenade, op. 24. In these sketches, Schoenberg continued to explore the chromaticism and motivic conciseness that were the hallmarks of his earlier expressionistic style, yet he was clearly experimenting with techniques that would guarantee or regularize these musical qualities. As early as the 1914 sketch for the Scherzo of the unfinished programmatic symphony, Schoenberg had explored the possibilities of themes that contained all twelve chromatic pitches, thus ensuring complete chromaticism, and different permutations of those themes, such as inversions and retrogrades, which provided not only surface variety but new levels of subcutaneous motivic unity. He had pursued similar concerns in *Die Jakobsleiter* in 1917. Schoenberg continued to explore these properties in the compositions that he began during the summer of 1920 and returned to during the next two summers.

Before the war, Schoenberg had given up his usual practice of spending the summer in a resort area, but in early June he traveled to Mattsee near Salzburg to spend the summer of 1921 with his brother and his brother's family. Unfortunately this attempt to recapture the routine of prewar life soured when local residents posted signs demanding that all Jews leave the area. Schoenberg was insulted that he had to prove his Christianity to the local authorities. At first he wanted to leave and return to Vienna, but when the Vienna and Salzburg press reported the episode, he decided to find another resort area rather than return to Vienna. Schoenberg went to Traunkirchen and enjoyed the rest of the summer there. Many of his friends and pupils visited him, and he was able to compose two of the piano pieces that would eventually become part of the Suite for Piano, op. 25.

Schoenberg returned to Mödling in October and resumed his teaching schedule and work on the Society for Private Musical Performances. Unfortunately the Society folded in the middle of this, its fourth, season (fall 1921) because of inflation. He returned to Traunkirchen the next summer, where he composed the interlude to *Die Jakobsleiter*, and he also arranged a charity concert to fund new church bells for the village.

In early 1923 Schoenberg completed the formulation of the twelve-tone method that had its immediate roots in the sketches for and movements of opuses 23, 24, and 25 composed in 1920 and 1921, and this unleashed his creative powers. After a performance of the Chamber Symphony in Copenhagen in January 1923 the publisher Wilhelm Hansen negotiated a contract with Schoenberg for new works and paid him an advance. He promised the Piano Pieces, op. 23, and the Serenade, op. 24, to Hansen, but because his contract with Universal Edition in Vienna gave them first right to all that he wrote, Schoenberg also had to negotiate their release from Universal. Universal would release op. 23 and op. 24 to Hansen only if Schoenberg could deliver two other new works to them. So Schoenberg hurried to complete op. 23 and op. 24 for Hansen, and the Suite for Piano, op. 25, and the Wind Quintet, op. 26, which he had not yet begun, for Universal. He alternated work on pieces from opuses 23, 24, and 25 in February, March, and April, moving freely from an atonal to a twelve-tone technique and back in each set. He began the Quintet, which is completely twelve-tone, in April and worked on it through the summer, not completing it until the next summer (1924), which he also spent in Traunkirchen.

Kandinsky, now a teacher of painting at the recently formed Bauhaus in Weimar, wrote to Schoenberg in April 1923, encouraging him to apply for the directorship of Weimar's Music High School. But Schoenberg had heard rumors of anti-Semitic tendencies on the part of Kandinsky and the other Bauhaus masters. When Kandinsky proclaimed his innocence and suggested that one should avoid religious or nationalist identities and instead focus on being "human," Schoenberg responded (4 May 1923) with an explanation of how the war years had changed him from a "free thinker" to a very religious man.

In the fall of 1923, Schoenberg's wife Mathilde, age 46, became very ill from kidney cancer; she died in October. Schoenberg was sincerely saddened, despite the earlier troubles in their marriage. The year 1924, however, was one of rebirth for him, as he began a friendship with Gertrud Kolisch (1898–1967), the sister of the violinist Rudolf Kolisch. Schoenberg frequented Viennese night spots with his friends, and he became interested in the jazz that he heard there. Improved economic conditions in Germany had brought him more royalties, and his standard of living rose for the first time in years. He married Gertrud Kolisch, twenty-four years his junior, in October 1924, just after his fiftieth birthday.

As the pace of his personal life accelerated, so did his professional activities. During March and April of 1924 he had conducted performances of *Pierrot lunaire* for a tour of several Italian cities. In July the Serenade, op. 24, had been publicly premiered at Donaueschingen after an earlier private performance in Vienna. Schoenberg had completed the Wind Quintet, op. 26, during the summer and had dedicated it to his grandson Arnold, son of his daughter Trudi and her husband Felix Greissle, Schoenberg's former student. It was premiered in Vienna during September, for Schoenberg's fiftieth birthday. Additionally, *Erwartung* had premiered in Prague, *Die Glückliche Hand* had premiered in Vienna, and a special issue of the magazine *Musikblätter des Anbruch* had been dedicated to Schoenberg during 1924.

In January 1925 the Schoenbergs had a late honeymoon in Venice and traveled to other Italian cities to meet composers Gian Francesco Malipiero and Alfredo Casella. In April they journeyed to Barcelona for a concert of Viennese music, organized by Schoenberg's former pupil Roberto Gerhard, which included some of Schoenberg's earlier songs, the Chamber Symphony, and *Pierrot lunaire*. Schoenberg also began a new work in the spring, the Suite op. 29 (for E-flat clarinet, bass clarinet, and piano quartet), for which he had made sketches as early as the previous October. Dedicated to his new wife, the Suite's light spirit illustrates the recent changes in his life. The Schoenbergs spent the summer at Altaussee and returned to Venice for the International Society of Contemporary Music (ISCM) Festival in September, where Schoenberg conducted a performance of the Serenade. Clearly, Schoenberg was receiving more professional recognition than at any previous point in his career, and the next several years would see that recognition increase even further.

BERLIN III

Before this trip to Venice Schoenberg had been offered and had accepted a very prestigious post as teacher of the master class in composition at the Prussian Academy of the Arts, a position previously held by Busoni. This job guaranteed Schoenberg a good salary and required him to hold classes for only six months out of the year. Although his move to Berlin was delayed by appendicitis, he arrived there during January 1926. His married daughter and grown son remained in Vienna, but some of his private students followed him to Berlin.

Soon after arriving in Berlin, Schoenberg completed the Three Satires, op. 28. These choral settings of his own satirical texts were inspired by the factionalized musical politics of the day, especially those which pitted Schoenberg against Stravinsky. Specifically, the Satires were precipitated by Schoenberg's experiences at the ISCM meeting in Venice during September 1925, where the neoclassical and twelve-tone camps were firmly entrenched. Although Schoenberg insisted that he meant no harm with the Satires, texts such as ''Little Modernsky . . . Quite the Papa Bach'' and ''I hate Romantic! From tomorrow on I write only Classical'' gained him many enemies.

Schoenberg's teaching schedule in Berlin was time-consuming, but he also found time to travel, compose, and write. In the summer of 1926 Schoenberg wrote the drama *Der biblische Weg*, which is the first of many documents detailing his relationship with Judaism. In February and March 1927 he composed the Third String Quartet on a commission from the American patron Elizabeth Sprague Coolidge, and for his fifty-third birthday, in September 1927, he visited Vienna for its premiere. In the midst of his third session of master classes in Berlin (1927–28), he traveled to Paris for the premiere of the Suite, op. 29, to London for rehearsals and a performance of the *Gurrelieder*, and to Breslau for a performance of *Die Glückliche Hand*.

The only drawback to living in Berlin was the severe winter climate, which exacerbated Schoenberg's asthma. He now sought warmer, drier regions during his summer holidays so as to recover his health. In 1928, for example, the Schoenbergs traveled to the French Riviera, where Schoenberg completed the Variations for Orchestra, op. 31, an arrangement of Bach's Prelude in E-flat Major for orchestra, and the text for his Biblical opera *Moses und Aron*. Due to his continuing poor health, he did not return to Berlin in the fall but took a six-month leave of absence from his teaching position. The Variations for Orchestra was premiered in Berlin during his absence; the reception was divided, and one reviewer demanded that Schoenberg be removed from his teaching post so that he could not damage the ''guiltless youth'' that studied with him.[8]

Schoenberg's main work during this hiatus was the comic opera *Von Heute auf Morgen*, on a libretto by his wife. Because of the popularity of Ernst Krenek's *Zeitoper*, to which Schoenberg likened his new work, he was convinced of his own topical opera's potential popularity. Thus he was incensed when Universal Edition would not offer him what he considered to be an appropriately high sum for the work, and he decided to publish it himself. Although he undertook its publication with zeal, it turned out to be an expensive and unsuccessful business undertaking. It was premiered in Frankfurt in February 1930.

Schoenberg resumed his teaching position in Berlin in the fall of 1929. Among the high points of the year were performances of *Erwartung* and *Die*

Glückliche Hand at the Kroll Opera in Berlin; unfortunately the two operas were withdrawn after only a few performances.

The Schoenbergs spent the summer of 1930 in Italy, where Schoenberg finished a second scene of *Moses und Aron* in August. In the fall they returned to Berlin to resume Schoenberg's teaching schedule. Schoenberg's continuing trouble with asthma sent him to Lake Geneva for the summer of 1931, where he worked on *Moses und Aron*, completing the first act in July. Unfortunately the weather at Lake Geneva was rainy and cold for most of the summer, and a doctor warned Schoenberg against returning to Berlin. After being granted a second leave of absence from his teaching position, Schoenberg went to Barcelona. Schoenberg and his wife were frequently ill with colds and flu; his wife was also pregnant with their first child.

Schoenberg's new works continued to appear before the public. The Four Songs for Voice and Orchestra, op. 22, premiered in Frankfurt in February 1932; Schoenberg was not able to travel so he prepared a speech about the songs that was read over the radio. Despite the passage of time, the musical hostilities of the 1925 ISCM festival in Venice continued to irritate Schoenberg, and he refused that group's request for a new work for their summer festival in Vienna. Schoenberg's assistant in Berlin, Josef Rufer, conveyed the Academy's displeasure with Schoenberg's long absence from Berlin; Schoenberg was still within the letter of his contract but he now became aware of a new climate that viewed him with suspicion not only because of his music's modernity, but because of his Jewish heritage. Schoenberg finished the second act of *Moses und Aron* in March 1932, but he never completed the rest of the work. His doctors continued to advise him to stay away from northern climates during the cold months and Schoenberg sent their reports to his superiors in Berlin. A month after the birth of their first child, Nuria, in May, the Schoenbergs returned to Berlin.

Schoenberg was certainly aware of political conditions in Germany; he had been reluctant to return there from Spain and had previously sought a patron who could support him so that he would not have to do so. Unfortunately, German currency restrictions and the absence of patrons made it impossible for him to stay abroad any longer. He taught and continued to compose after he returned to Berlin. In November he began a cello concerto for Pablo Casals based on a free transcription of a preclassical work by the Viennese composer Georg Matthias Monn. But the well-received Berlin performance of his String Quartet no. 2 by the Kolisch Quartet, in October 1932, was the last performance there of any of his works until after World War II.

PARIS AND ARCACHON

In January 1933 Hitler came to power, and with him came government-sanctioned anti-Semitism. In March the president of the Prussian Academy of the Arts declared that "Jewish influences must be broken." Later that month,

Schoenberg submitted his resignation from the Academy voluntarily and asked that his contract be bought out (it ran through 30 September 1935), that he be paid the costs of returning to Vienna, and that he be given permission to take money abroad. His correspondence shows no particular concern or hurry about leaving, but when his brother-in-law Rudolf Kolisch sent a telegram from Florence suggesting the need for a ''change of air,'' the Schoenbergs left immediately for Paris, packing as if for a brief stay. Since his resignation had seemingly made no impact, Schoenberg informed the Academy from Paris in May that he was beginning his leave for that year.

The Schoenbergs stayed in Paris until the end of July. Their only reliable financial resource was Schoenberg's publisher in Vienna, since their German bank account had been blocked. In Berlin, while Schoenberg's sister and her husband closed up the Schoenberg's apartment, Furtwängler protested the removal of leading Jewish artists. Ten months earlier, Schoenberg had written to Berg about how it felt to be in Berlin ''among the swastika-swaggerers and pogromists.'' ''Today I am proud to call myself a Jew,'' he concluded, ''but I know the difficulties of really being one.'' In Paris, on 24 July 1933, Schoenberg recognized the significant changes in his life by making a formal reentry into the Jewish community, thirty-five years after his Protestant conversion.

Following his reconversion, Schoenberg moved to Arcachon near Bordeaux and intensified his search for a new teaching position. He had recently begun a new work, the Concerto for String Quartet and Orchestra, a free arrangement of a Concerto Grosso by Handel, and he continued to work on it in Arcachon. In addition, he wrote about various Jewish issues and expressed his desire that activism would ''unite Jewry in a common action.'' His reconversion was complete: ''I have definitely separated myself from whatever binds me to the Occident,'' he wrote to Webern (4 August 1933). His former students were shaken; as Berg wrote to Webern after reading Schoenberg's comments, ''Even if I regard his departure from the Occident as *humanly* possible (I don't believe it, or at least I don't regard his turning to the *Orient* as possible) there remains for me the unshakable fact of his musical works, for which there is only one description: German.''[9]

As part of the separation process, Schoenberg abandoned old-fashioned German cursive handwriting in September and began signing his name with the international spelling (''oe'' rather than ''ö''). In the following month, the Prussian Academy announced that his employment was terminated as of 31 October 1933, despite the time remaining on his contract. Although Schoenberg wanted to remain in Europe, no employment opportunities presented themselves. Instead, he began corresponding with Joseph Malkin in Boston about teaching a composition class in the newly formed Malkin Conservatory. Malkin, a cellist and member of a famous piano trio in the 1920s, proposed a salary comparable to that which Schoenberg had received from the Prussian Academy. Since there were no other possibilities, Schoenberg agreed to the post and traveled to New

York (with tickets purchased with a salary advance from Malkin) in late October. He was never to return to Europe.

BOSTON AND NEW YORK

Schoenberg was surprised to find that the Malkin Conservatory did not measure up to his idea of what constituted a conservatory. Housed in only five or six classrooms, it was quite small, and it did not even have an orchestra. In Boston, Schoenberg had only one student in the fall and a total of four in the spring. Fortunately, Malkin arranged public lectures at the New School for Social Research in New York, where Schoenberg's unique version of the English language was reported to be quite entertaining. Malkin also arranged for Schoenberg to teach students in New York, where his class was larger than in Boston.

In addition to his teaching, many events greeted Schoenberg's arrival in the United States. There was a League of Composers Concert featuring Schoenberg's music in New York, Schoenberg gave lectures on radio, and he conducted the Boston Symphony Orchestra. Schoenberg also gave a lecture on the twelve-tone method at the University of Chicago, where he was honored with a concert of chamber music.

Schoenberg taught in Boston and New York until the end of May 1934. The frequent train travel back and forth between the two cities, the winter cold, and even the East Coast's summer humidity stressed his health and exacerbated his asthma. The Schoenbergs spent the summer at a health resort in Chautauqua, New York. There Schoenberg rested, played tennis, and recovered his health. His busy schedule had prevented him from composing for most of the year, but at Chautauqua he composed the Suite in G Major for String Orchestra, a tonal piece for school orchestra, his first piece "in a key" since 1909. He also began the Violin Concerto and, although he had hoped to complete *Moses und Aron*, he was unable to do so.

Schoenberg missed his many colleagues in Europe, but he was increasingly suspicious of anyone who stayed there, even his former students Webern and Berg. He made important new American contacts such as Carl Engel at the publisher G. Schirmer, who became a trusted friend and advisor.

LOS ANGELES

Despite the cultural richness of the northeastern United States, the Schoenbergs weighed the harshness of its climate against Schoenberg's health problems and decided to try a different area of the country. In September 1934 they left for Southern California, where they lived in a furnished house in the Los Angeles suburb of Hollywood until spring 1936, when they purchased a home in the nearby suburb of Brentwood. Eventually, their belongings from Berlin arrived. The warm, dry climate agreed with them, as did the new California lifestyle. As Gertrud wrote to friends in Germany, "Everything that we call a luxury is regarded here as a necessity of life." In Los Angeles, Schoenberg dedicated himself to mastering English.

By this time Schoenberg had no intention of ever returning to Europe, since he continued to receive reports about anti-Semitism and other attacks directed against him and his music. Nevertheless, his String Quartet Concerto after Handel premiered in Prague on 26 September 1934 and was a great success. Since the Society of German Composers had dropped his membership, Schoenberg had not received any royalties for two years. As a remedy, Schoenberg tried to gain membership in the Austrian Society of Authors, Composers, and Publishers, writing to ask Berg to propose and support his bid. Despite Berg's efforts, the Austrian organization turned Schoenberg down.

In Los Angeles, Schoenberg had only a few private students and a class of ten students at the University of Southern California, where he taught during the academic year 1935–36. In general, Schoenberg was disappointed with the musical background of his American students, who lacked familiarity with the classical masterworks that he used in his teaching. Because scores were so expensive in America, he observed, it was impossible for students to form even a basic musical library, and the high price of concert and opera tickets worked similarly against the students' education.

In his ongoing search for optimal employment, Schoenberg relied heavily on Carl Engel of the publisher G. Schirmer in New York. Engel advised him on all aspects of his career and promoted his music, in addition to paying him as much as possible for his compositions. He encouraged Schoenberg to return to New York and take a position at the Juilliard School because of New York's artistic prominence and the support found there for Schoenberg's music. Schoenberg was hesitant to give up the comfort of his life in California, where it was also less expensive to live, unless Juilliard could guarantee him a position and salary that would allow him to compose for six months a year and maintain homes in California as well as New York. Despite Engel's efforts and the support of Juilliard president John Erskine, Juilliard could not meet Schoenberg's demands. Schoenberg gave up the plan in the summer of 1935 and soon thereafter signed a contract with the University of California at Los Angeles (UCLA) at a salary comparable to that which he had received from the Berlin Academy.

Schoenberg's works continued to be performed both in America and in Europe. In March 1935, Schoenberg conducted *Pierrot lunaire* and the Chamber Symphony in San Francisco and *Verklärte Nacht* and the Bach Arrangements in Los Angeles. During the same month the String Quartet Concerto after Handel was performed in New York. In October the Suite for String Orchestra was premiered in Los Angeles. Schoenberg also gave public lectures and radio interviews in Los Angeles. Other works were performed in Europe: the Cello Concerto after Monn was premiered with Emanuel Feuermann in London in December; the *Gurrelieder*, conducted by Bruno Walter, had been performed in

Vienna; and *Erwartung* was performed in Barcelona as part of the 1936 ISCM festival.

Schoenberg had maintained only minimal contact with friends and acquaintances who had remained in Europe, and their experiences and reactions to current events often proved foreign to him. When Alban Berg died in 1936, for example, Schoenberg offered to complete the orchestration of the third act of his opera *Lulu* out of generosity to the memory of his friend and former student. However, after receiving the material from the publisher, Schoenberg refused the project. Although he told Berg's widow that the task was more demanding and time-consuming than he had imagined, he actually refused the job because he was deeply offended by the depiction of a Jewish character in the libretto. He questioned others as to how Berg could have been so insensitive at a time when Jews were in such peril. "I should like to suppose that Berg has done this, difficult as it is to understand, out of thoughtlessness," Schoenberg wrote to his former pupil, Erwin Stein, "although in this period of the most extensive persecution of Jews it seems hardly credible that anyone could fail to give thought to something that gives his friends cause for thought."[10] Episodes such as this, and even unsubstantiated rumors that were reported from Europe, fueled Schoenberg's recurring suspicions about those who continued to live in Nazi-dominated Europe.

Despite a continuing sense of betrayal in Europe, Schoenberg entertained new opportunities in America. In 1936 he was approached by a representative of Irving Thalberg, a guiding force at Metro-Goldwyn-Mayer movie studios, about composing the music for the movie version of Pearl S. Buck's novel *The Good Earth*. Having heard *Verklärte Nacht* on the radio, Thalberg was convinced that Schoenberg was the right composer for the job. Schoenberg, however, was torn between the reputed high salaries that people in the movie business received, which would have allowed him to live comfortably and complete his large-scale works, and what he perceived as the generally low artistic standards of Hollywood. As a result he demanded a high salary and significant artistic control of the movie, both of which were denied.

Although he did not break into the film music market, Schoenberg settled into life in Los Angeles. He enjoyed swimming, rowing, and tennis, which he played with members of his family, new friends (including George Gershwin), and members of Los Angeles's growing émigré community. In May 1937 the Schoenberg's son Ronald was born; their second son, Lawrence, was born in 1941.

As a professor at UCLA, Schoenberg directed much of his attention to his teaching activities, including textbooks on counterpoint, harmony, and composition. Some of these texts were completed and published during Schoenberg's lifetime, and others were completed from his notes after his death.[11] Schoenberg also continued to compose. In the spring of 1936 he began work on the Fourth String Quartet, which, like the Third Quartet, was a commission from Elizabeth Sprague Coolidge, and he completed the work in July of that year. He orchestrated Brahms's Piano Quartet in G Minor between May and September 1937 and completed the Second Chamber Symphony in October 1939 for the conductor Fritz Stiedry, who performed it in New York in November 1940.

In 1937 Schirmer published a book in tribute to Schoenberg, edited by Merle Armitage and containing reprinted articles written by a number of authors between 1929 and 1935. Schoenberg was also recognized with a number of public performances and speaking invitations in several cities. The Federal Music Project Symphony Orchestra in Los Angeles, for example, performed *Pelleas und Melisande*.

In March 1938 the Nazis assumed control in Austria; later in the year there were serious pogroms against the Jews in Germany. Schoenberg's daughter and son-in-law, Trudi and Felix Greissle, emigrated to the United States, and Greissle found employment with Schirmer in New York. The Greissles advised Schoenberg not to speak out on political issues because of possible retaliation against friends and relatives who remained in Austria. Old friends wrote to Schoenberg seeking advice or letters of recommendation as they tried to relocate outside Germany and Austria. Schoenberg's music was now rarely played in Europe, since the Nazis regarded it as decadent; Schoenberg was personally targeted in a campaign against "Degenerate Music" in Düsseldorf in May 1938. These events renewed Schoenberg's reflections on his Jewish heritage. He resumed writing about plans to unite the world's Jewry that he had begun in France in 1933, and, at the invitation of a Los Angeles rabbi, he set the traditional "Kol nidre" in August–September 1938.

Schoenberg continued to receive bad news as Germany's aggression provoked war in 1939. Many of his friends and relatives, including his cousin Arthur, were sent to concentration camps. Zemlinksy moved to New York in 1938 but was unable to work because of his poor health. After the fall of France in 1940, German, Austrian, and French refugees were plentiful in Los Angeles, including Thomas Mann, Theodore Wiesengrund-Adorno, Franz and Alma Werfel, Berthold Brecht, and Hanns Eisler.

Despite a number of performances Schoenberg considered himself to be neglected in America, especially when compared with composers such as Hindemith, Bartók, Stravinsky, and even Sibelius. For example, when he spoke at the Music Teachers National Association convention in Kansas City-Missouri in 1939, he discovered that the concerts at the convention included music by Stravinsky, Ravel, and Prokofiev, but none of his own. In 1940, however, his works were programmed on a contemporary series in Los Angeles, and he conducted a recording and performance of *Pierrot lunaire*. The Violin Concerto was also premiered by Krasner and Stokowski in 1940, and Stiedry conducted the premiere of the Second Chamber Symphony the same year.

Schoenberg became a citizen of the United States in 1941, and he continued to teach, compose, and have his music performed in America. In 1941, he began the Variations on a Recitative for organ; in 1942, he composed the *Ode to Napoleon* and the Piano Concerto. *Verklärte Nacht* was presented to and well-received by new audiences as Antony Tudor's ballet *Pillar of Fire*. Schoenberg would have liked to complete *Moses und Aron* and *Die Jakobsleiter* but could not do so because of his teaching commitments and the need to compose smaller works for which he could receive commissions. Various family emergencies made him especially sensitive to money issues, and this, in turn, provoked problems in negotiating contracts with his publisher. Because Schirmer was unable to pay the high fees that Schoenberg demanded for his works, for the first time in his career his scores were not published within a few years of their composition. Fortunately Carl Engel was sensitive to Schoenberg's financial worries, and eventually new contracts were worked out.

In 1943 Schoenberg took Engel's suggestion to write an accessible piece for wind orchestra, since there were many of these ensembles in the United States. Schoenberg completed the Theme and Variations in G Minor for Wind Band, op. 43A, in August, but his publisher decided that it was too difficult to be commercially viable. Engel died the following year and, despite some differences, Schoenberg mourned him as one of his most devoted friends in America. In October the Theme and Variations for Wind Band, arranged for orchestra, was premiered by Koussevitsky and the Boston Symphony Orchestra.

Schoenberg had been preparing for his retirement from UCLA for some time, since, because of university regulations mandating retirement at age seventy, 1943–44 would be his last year. His seventieth birthday in the fall of 1944 was marked by many tributes and social occasions. Afterwards Schoenberg worked sporadically on *Die Jakobsleiter*, but his difficult financial situation made it impossible to finish either this work or *Moses und Aron* for posterity. Because he had worked at UCLA for only a short time, his monthly pension was small, and at the time of his retirement he had only two paying private pupils to augment his income. Schoenberg applied for a Guggenheim fellowship in January 1945, listing the compositions and textbooks that he planned to complete, but his application was rejected. For the rest of his life, Schoenberg had to teach privately, lecture, and take commissions to survive. On several occasions he even allowed some of his manuscripts to be auctioned in order to earn money.

The surrender of the Nazi regime in May 1945 made communication with Europe possible once again. Schoenberg soon reestablished contact with friends and former students; he was saddened to learn of Webern's death soon after the end of the war. In January 1946 he was appointed honorary president of the ISCM; in March he was invited to return to Vienna to teach and help in the ''work of reconstruction'' at the Academy, and in April this invitation was repeated by the lord mayor of Vienna. Although Schoenberg was flattered by the offer, he did not return to Europe. Instead, his former students saw to it that his music was promoted once more after the censorship of the war years. Although the influential Summer School at Darmstadt was dominated by Hindemith and Stravinsky in 1946, in 1947 it included two works by Schoenberg. The following year saw more of Schoenberg's music performed at Darmstadt, plus a lecture on the twelve-tone method by René Leibowitz. In 1949 there were additional European performances of Schoenberg's music, and he was invited to participate personally in the Summer School, although poor health forced him to decline. But even these attentions did not diminish Schoenberg's memories of the circumstances that had caused him to flee Europe. When the Second International Music Festival in Vienna had requested permission to premiere one of his works early in 1948, Schoenberg had declined, commenting that it seemed to him that works of art in Vienna were still judged from racial rather than artistic points of view, or he would have been contacted sooner after the end of the war.

Schoenberg had suffered a serious heart attack in August 1946, the most cataclysmic of the various health complaints, including asthma and diabetes, from which he suffered during his later years. While he was recovering he composed the String Trio, op. 45, which he said described his illness. It had been commissioned by Harvard University before Schoenberg's heart attack, and it was premiered at Harvard in May 1947 at a conference on music criticism. Because of Schoenberg's poor health and failing eyesight, Richard Hoffmann, a cousin of Schoenberg's wife, came from New Zealand in 1947 to be Schoenberg's pupil and secretary. By the summer of 1948 Schoenberg's health had improved enough that he could travel to the Music Academy of the West in Santa Barbara, California, to give several weeks of composition lessons.

In April 1947, the American Academy of Arts and Letters awarded Schoenberg a $1,000 prize for "outstanding achievement." In typical fashion, he responded with a letter of thanks in which he credited his opponents for his success. He was also honored by his former students' projects. Hans Stuckenschmidt, who was writing a book on Schoenberg, and Josef Rufer, who was writing a book on twelve-tone music, were in close contact with Schoenberg at the close of 1947 as they completed their projects. Schoenberg berated his other former students by letter for their irregular or complete lack of attention. Inspired by the many stories told to him by survivors of Nazi atrocities, Schoenberg composed *A Survivor from Warsaw* later in 1947, on a commission from the Koussevitzky foundation.

As had been the case throughout his life, Schoenberg's later years were marked by controversies. In 1948 Schoenberg became aware that Thomas Mann's book, *Dr. Faustus*, published in 1947, credited the twelve-tone method to its protagonist. Schoenberg had not read the book because of his deteriorating vision, but, relying on the impressions of his wife and his friends, Schoenberg concluded that his "intellectual property" had been stolen, and he was afraid that the misattribution would lessen his historical importance. Mann was greatly confused and offended by Schoenberg's response, but he finally agreed to add a note to future copies indicating that Schoenberg originated the twelve-tone method. Eventually the two made up.

In 1949, after a long period of silence, Schoenberg began composing again. In March he completed the Phantasy for Violin with Piano Accompaniment, op. 47. At about this same time he also completed *Dreimal Tausand Jahre*, op. 50A, the first of several late choral works on Jewish themes. In this same category he began but did not finish *Israel Exists Again* in September, and he completed the Hebrew setting of Psalm 130, *De Profundis*, op. 50B, in the following year. In 1950 he also began the musical setting of his recent text series *Modern Psalms*, additions to the biblical Psalms in light of contemporary experience, but he did not complete any of them. *Dreimal Tausand Jahre* and *De Profundis* were his last completed works.

Schoenberg's health was precarious, but he was pleased to be recognized by a number of organizations and individuals. In July 1949, he was named an honorary member of the Austrian Society of Dramatists and Composers. The mayor of Vienna granted him "freedom of the city" in the fall of 1950. And in April 1951, he was made honorary president of the Israel Academy of Music in Jerusalem. Despite these honors, Schoenberg realized that his music was still controversial and likely to remain so. In a letter that he sent to those who congratulated him on his seventy-sixth birthday in 1950, Schoenberg repeated a sentiment that he had stated often before: he, like Beethoven, Wagner, and Mahler, said things musically that had to be said, even if they were unpopular. But he seemed to be optimistic that his music would ultimately find its audience. It was in this frame of mind that Schoenberg died on 13 July 1951.

NOTES

1. Schoenberg, "My Evolution," in *Style and Idea*, ed. Leonard Stein, trans. Leo Black, 1975; rpt. (Berkeley and Los Angeles: University of California Press, 1984), 80.

2. Schoenberg, "My Evolution," in *Style and Idea*, 80.

3. Quoted in Malcolm MacDonald, *Schoenberg* (London: Dent, 1976), 22.

4. See chapter 11 by Bryan Simms in this volume.

5. Program notes, 14 January 1910, quoted in Willi Reich, *Schoenberg: A Critical Biography*, trans. Leo Black (New York: Praeger, 1971), 49.

6. Quoted in Reich, p. 44.

7. Schoenberg to Dehmel, 13 December 1912, quoted in Arnold Schoenberg, *Letters*, ed. Erwin Stein (Berkeley and Los Angeles: University of California Press, 1987), 35–36.

8. Hans Heinz Stuckenschmidt, *Schoenberg: His Life, World, and Work*, trans. Humphrey Searle (New York: Schirmer, 1978), 325.

9. Ibid., 368–70.

10. Quoted in George Perle, *The Operas of Alban Berg, Vol. II, Lulu* (Berkeley and Los Angeles: University of California Press, 1985), 284.

11. See chapter 12 by Leonard Stein on "Schoenberg as Teacher" in this volume.

II

Music

3

List of Works

Walter B. Bailey and Jerry McBride

INTRODUCTION

Compiling a complete list of Schoenberg's works is challenging because of the varied nature of Schoenberg's *oeuvre*. In addition to works published during his lifetime, to which Schoenberg assigned opus numbers, there are several major published works, such as the *Gurrelieder*, to which he never assigned an opus number. In addition, there are major works left unfinished by Schoenberg but performed in their incomplete state, such as the oratorio *Die Jakobsleiter* and the opera *Moses und Aron*. There are also a number of smaller works, mainly from Schoenberg's student period, that were published only after Schoenberg's death, such as the *Brettl-Lieder (Cabaret Songs)* (1901) and Piano Pieces (1894). Schoenberg also began many more works than he completed, and these fragments often provide valuable information about developments in his musical style. Finally, Schoenberg composed a number of ''occasional'' pieces for specific informal circumstances, and he also made arrangements of a variety of works for private use within his circle and for public use, either in the groundbreaking Society for Private Musical Performances or general concert venues.

The scope of Schoenberg's works is, therefore, tremendous, and it is impossible to include a complete list here. Instead, the list that follows includes all of Schoenberg's major works and many of his lesser works and fragments, especially those that are referred to in the various articles in this collection. At least one category of works is missing from the list: Schoenberg's impressive collection of canons (1905–49, published by Bärenreiter), to which he added throughout his career. The works are presented chronologically, and the list is divided by the three major stylistic changes of Schoenberg's career. The names of the publishers for each are listed after the title of the work, followed by the number of the volume in which the work appears in the *Sämtliche Werke [Complete Works]*, or where it is projected to appear when the set is complete. Only the principal publishers are listed, and no attempt has been made to include all distributors. Aside from publishing many works, Belmont Music Publishers is the primary distributor of Schoenberg's music in the United States, and they include in their catalog the publications of Universal Edition and Schott. Reprint editions have also begun to appear as Schoenberg's works enter the public domain. These editions are not listed here, but readers may find works reprinted primarily by Dover, Kalmus, and Masters Music.

The volumes in the Arnold Schönberg *Sämtliche Werke* are organized into two series (Reihe): Series A consists of a final edited version of each work that takes into account all published and unpublished source material; Series B consists of the critical notes, transcriptions of sketches, and transcriptions of alternate versions of finished works, where these exist. Each of these series is organized into eight sections (Abteilungen): I) songs, II) piano and organ music, III) stage works, IV) orchestral works, V) choral works, VI) chamber music, VII) arrangements of music by other composers, and VIII) supplements and ephemera. In the following list of works, pieces not yet published in the *Sämtliche Werke* are indicated by an asterisk. Thus, "AS III/A/9*" indicates that the work is expected to be published in Section III, Series A, Volume 9 of the *Arnold Schönberg Sämtliche Werke*.

PUBLISHER ABBREVIATIONS

AMP	Associated Music Publishers
AS	Arnold Schönberg Sämtliche Werke
AV	Ars Viva Verlag Hermann Scherchen
BB	Boelke-Bomart
B&B	Bote & Bock (recently purchased by Boosey and Hawkes)
B&H	Breitkopf & Härtel
BMP	Belmont Music Publishers
BSS	Schott
CFP	C. F. Peters
D	Dreililien
EBM	E. B. Marks
EE	E. Eulenburg
F	Faber Music
GS	G. Schirmer
H	Heinrichshofen
HWG	H. W. Gray
IMC	International Music Co.

IMP	Israeli Music Publications
LMC	Leeds Music Corp.
MCA	Music Corp. of America
NM	New Music, v. 5, no. 3
RB	Richard Birnbach
T&J	Tischer & Jagenberg
UE	Universal Edition
WUE	Wiener Urtext Edition
WH	Wilhelm Hansen

"STUDENT" WORKS, CA. 1893–CA. 1900

1893	"In hellen Träumen" (for voice and piano) (AS I/A/2)
1894	"Ein Schilflied: Drüben geht die Sonne scheiden" (for voice and piano) (AS I/A/2)
1894	Three Piano Pieces (BMP; AS II/A/4)
1895–96	"Ei, du Lütte" (for mixed choir) (BMP; AS V/A/18)
1896	Six Piano Pieces (four hands) (BMP; AS II/A/5)
1897	Gavotte and Musette (for string orchestra) (AS IV/A/9*)
1897	Scherzo in F Major (for string quartet) (BMP; AS VI/A/20)
1897	"Mädchenfrühling" (for voice and piano) (AS I/A/2)
1897	String Quartet in D Major (F; AS VI/A/20)
undated	numerous songs, including "Die Beiden," "Deinem Blick mich zu bequemen," "Eclogue," "Gedenken," "Mädchenlied," "Mädchenfrühling," "Mannesbangen," "Mein Herz das ist ein tiefer Schacht," "Nicht doch," "Waldesnacht" (F, BMP; AS I/A/1–2)

MATURE TONAL WORKS

1898	Two Songs for Voice and Piano, op. 1 (D, UE, BMP; AS I/A/1)
1899	Four Songs for Voice and Piano, op. 2 (D, BMP; AS I/A/1)
1899–1903	Six Songs for Voice and Piano, op. 3 (D, BMP; AS I/A/1)
1899	*Verklärte Nacht [Transfigured Night]*, op. 4 (for string sextet) (D, RB, IMC, UE; AS VI/A/22*); arr. for string orchestra, 1917 (UE; AS IV/A/9*); rev. 1943 (AMP, UE; AS IV/A/9*)
1900	"Gruss in die Ferne" (for baritone voice and piano) (UE; AS I/A/2)
1900–1911	*Gurrelieder* (for vocal soloists, choirs, and orchestra) (UE, BMP; AS V/A/16*)
1901	*Brettl-Lieder* (for voice and piano; also known as *Cabaret Songs*) (BMP; AS I/A/2)

1902–3	*Pelleas und Melisande*, op. 5 (symphonic poem) (UE; AS IV/A/10*)
1903–4	Six Songs for Voice and Orchestra, op. 8 (UE; AS I/A/3)
1903–5	Eight Songs for Voice and Piano, op. 6 (D, BMP; AS I/A/1)
1904–5	String Quartet no. 1 in D Minor, op. 7 (D, RB, EE, UE; AS VI/A/20)
1905	"Ein Stelldichein" (for oboe, clarinet, violin, cello, and piano; unfinished) (UE; AS VII/A/23*)
1906	Chamber Symphony no. 1 in E Major, op. 9 (UE; AS IV/A/11); op. 9b arr. for full orchestra 1922 and rev. 1935 (GS; AS IV/A/12)
1907	Two Ballads for Voice and Piano, op. 12 (UE; AS I/A/1)
1907	"Friede auf Erden," op. 13 (for mixed choir) (T&J, BSS, AMP, BMP; AS V/A/18)
1907–8	Two Songs for Voice and Piano, op. 14 (UE; AS I/A/1)
1907–8	String Quartet no. 2 in F-sharp Minor, op. 10 (UE; AS VI/A/20)

FREELY ATONAL WORKS

1908–9	*Fifteen Poems from the Book of the Hanging Gardens [15 Gedichte aus Das Buch der Hängenden Gärten]*, op. 15 (for voice and piano) (UE; AS I/A/1)
1908–9	"Am Strande" (for voice and piano) (BMP; AS I/A/1)
1909	Three Piano Pieces, op. 11 (UE, WUE, BMP; AS II/A/4)
1909	Five Orchestra Pieces, op. 16 (CFP, EE; AS IV/A/12); rev. for reduced orchestra, 1949 (CFP; AS IV/A/14)
1909	*Erwartung*, op. 17 (monodrama) (UE; AS III/A/6)
1910–13	*Die glückliche Hand*, op. 18 ("drama with music") (UE; AS III/A/6)
1910	Three Pieces for Chamber Orchestra (unfinished but performable) (BMP; AS IV/A/22*)
1911	Six Little Piano Pieces, op. 19 (UE, BMP, WUE; AS II/A/4)
1911	"Herzgewächse," op. 20 (for voice and small ensemble) (UE; AS VI/A/24*)
1911–12	Editions (basso continuo realizations) for the Denkmäler der Tonkunst in Österreich
	G. M. Monn, Symphonia a Quattro in A Major; Cello Concerto in G Minor; Harpsichord Concerto in D Major
	J. C. Mann [Monn], Divertimento in D Major
	Franz Tuma, Sinfonia a Quattro in E Minor; Partita a Tre in C Minor; Partita a Tre in A Major; Partita a Tre in G Major
1912	*Pierrot lunaire*, op. 21 (for speaker and small ensemble) (UE, BMP; AS VI/A/24*)

1912–14	Symphony (for vocal solists, choirs, and orchestra; unfinished)
1913–16	Four Songs for Voice and Orchestra, op. 22 (UE; AS I/A/3)
1914	"Der deutsche Michel" (for men's choir) (BMP; AS V/A/18)
1916	"Der eiserne Brigade" (for piano and string quartet) (UE; AS VI/A/23*)
1917–22	*Die Jakobsleiter* (oratorio for vocal soloists, choir, and orchestra; unfinished but performable) (UE, BMP; AS V/A/17; AS VII/A/29)

TWELVE-TONE AND LATE TONAL WORKS

1920–23	Five Piano Pieces, op. 23 (WH, WUE; AS II/A/4)
1920–23	Serenade, op. 24 (for baritone, clarinet, bass clarinet, mandolin, guitar, and string trio) (WH; AS VI/A/23*)
1921–23	Suite for Piano, op. 25 (WUE, UE, BMP; AS II/A/4)
1921	Various arrangements and occasional works for private use, including:

Luigi Denza, "Funiculi, funiculá" (for clarinet, mandolin, guitar, and string trio) (BMP; AS VII/A/28*)

Franz Schubert, "Serenade," D. 889 (for voice, clarinet, bassoon, mandolin, guitar, and string quartet) (BMP; AS VII/A/28*)

Johann Sioly, "Weil i a alter Drahrer bin" (for clarinet, mandolin, guitar, and string trio) (BMP; AS VII/A/28*)

Schoenberg, "Weihnachtsmusik" ("Christmas Music"; for two violins, cello, harmonium, and piano) (BMP; AS VI/A/23*)

1921	Various arrangements for the *Society for Private Musical Performances*, including:

Busoni, *Berceuse élégiaque* (arr. for flute, clarinet, harmonium, piano, and string quartet) (B&H; AS VII/A/28*)

Mahler, *The Song of the Earth* (arr. for voice, flute, clarinet, harmonium, piano, string quartet, double bass, and percussion by Schoenberg and Webern; completed by Rainer Riehn) (AS VII/A/28*)

Mahler, *Songs of a Wayfarer* (arr. for baritone, flute, clarinet, harmonium, piano, string quartet, double bass, and percussion) (AS VII/A/28*)

Reger, *A Romantic Suite*, op. 25 (arr. for flute, clarinet, harmonium [four hands], piano [four hands], and string quartet by Schoenberg and Rudolf Kolisch) (AS VII/A/28*)

Johann Strauss, *Roses from the South* (arr. for harmonium, piano, and string quartet) (BMP; AS VII/A/28*)

1922	"Gerpa" (variations for horn, two violins, piano, and harmonium; unfinished) (AS VI/A/23*)
1922	Bach-Schoenberg, Two Chorale-Preludes (arr. for orchestra)
	Komm, Gott, Schöpfer, heiliger Geist, BWV 631 (UE; AS VII/A/25)
	Schmücke dich, O liebe Seele, BWV 654 (UE; AS VII/A/25)
1923–24	Woodwind Quintet, op. 26 (UE; AS VI/A/23*)
1924–26	Suite, op. 29 (for E-flat clarinet, clarinet, bass clarinet, and piano quartet) (UE; AS VI/A/23*)
1925	Johann Strauss, *Emperor Waltz* (arr. for flute, clarinet, and piano quintet) (AS VII/A/28*)
1925	Four Pieces for Mixed Choir, op. 27 (no. 4 acc. by mandolin, clarinet, violin, and cello) (UE; AS V/A/18)
1925–26	*Three Satires* for Mixed Choir, op. 28 (no. 3 acc. by viola, cello, and piano; "Appendix" includes three canons for choir and one for string quartet) (UE; AS V/A/18)
1926	*Passacaglia* (unfinished) (AS VI/A/14*)
1926–28	Variations for Orchestra, op. 31 (UE; AS IV/A/13)
1927	String Quartet no. 3, op. 30 (UE; AS VI/A/21)
1928	Bach-Schoenberg, Prelude and Fugue in E-flat Major, BWV 552 (arr. for orchestra) (UE; AS VII/A/25)
1928–29	*Von heute auf morgen*, op. 32 (opera in one act) (AV, BSS; AS III/A/7)
1928–31	Two Piano Pieces, op. 33a (UE, WUE, BMP; AS II/A/4) and op. 33b (NM, BMP, WUE, BMP; AS II/A/4)
1929	Three Folk Song Movements (arr. for mixed choir) (CFP; AS VI/A/18)
1929	Four German Folk Songs (arr. for voice and piano) (CFP; AS I/A/1)
1929–30	Six Pieces for Men's Choir, op. 35 (B&B AMP; AS V/A/18)
1929–30	*Accompaniment to a Film Scene [Begleitungsmusik zu einer Lichtspielszene]*, op. 34 (for orchestra) (H, CFP; AS IV/A/14)
1930–32	*Moses und Aron* (opera; unfinished but performable) (BSS, EE; AS III/A/8)
1932–33	Cello Concerto after a Keyboard Concerto by Georg Matthias Monn (GS, UE; AS VII/A/27)
1933	Three Songs for Voice and Piano, op. 48 (BB; AS I/A/1)
1933	String Quartet Concerto after Handel (GS; AS VII/A/27)
1934	Suite in G Major ("in Ancient Style") for String Orchestra (GS; AS IV/A/9*)
1934–36	Violin Concerto, op. 36 (GS, UE; AS IV/A/15)
1936	String Quartet no. 4, op. 37 (GS; AS VI/A/21)

1937	Brahms-Schoenberg, Piano Quartet no. 1 in G Minor (arr. for orchestra) (BMP; AS VII/A/26)
1938	*Kol nidre*, op. 39 (for speaker, mixed choir, and orchestra) (BB, BMP; AS V/A/19)
1939	Chamber Symphony no. 2, op. 38 (begun in 1906) (GS, UE; AS IV/A/11); op. 38b arr. for 2 pianos (1942) (BMP; AS II/A/5)
1941	*Variations on a Recitative* for organ, op. 40 (HWG, BMP; AS II/A/5)
1941	Sonata for Organ (unfinished; performed as a fragment) (BMP; AS II/A/5)
1942	*Ode to Napoleon Buonaparte*, op. 41 (for speaker, piano, and string quartet; a second version with string orchestra) (GS, BMP; AS VI/A/24*)
1942	Piano Concerto, op. 42 (GS, UE, BMP; AS IV/A/15)
1943	Theme and Variations in G Minor for band, op. 43a (a second version, op. 43b, arr. for orchestra) (GS, BMP; AS IV/A/13–14)
1945	Prelude to the *Genesis* Suite, op. 44 (for mixed choir and orchestra) (BMP; AS V/A/19)
1945	*Fanfare on Motifs of Die Gurrelieder* (for brass and percussion) (unfinished; completed by Leonard Stein, 1977) (BMP; AS VI/A/23*)
1946	String Trio, op. 45 (BB, UE, BMP; AS VI/A/21)
1947	*A Survivor from Warsaw*, op. 46 (for speaker, men's choir, and orchestra) (BB, BMP, UE; AS V/A/19)
1948	Three Folk Songs, op. 49 (arr. for mixed choir) (EBM, BMP; AS V/A/19)
1949	*Phantasy for Violin with Piano Accompaniment*, op. 47 (CFP; AS VI/A/22)
1949	"Dreimal tausend Jahre," op. 50a (for mixed choir) (BSS, BMP; AS V/A/19)
1950	"De profundis" (Psalm 130), op. 50b (for mixed choir) (IMP, LMC, MCA; AS V/A/19)
1950	"Modern Psalm no. 1," op. 50c (for mixed choir, speaker and orchestra; unfinished but performable) (BSS; AS V/A/19)

4

Schoenberg's Tonal Beginnings

Walter B. Bailey

Late nineteenth-century Vienna provided an opulent array of musical riches to the interested listener; to the dedicated student of music, this wealth represented a nearly overwhelming fund of musical models. As is the case in any age, Vienna's musical "present" included the comfortingly old, the surprisingly new, the reactionary, the avant garde, and all stages in between. The Viennese classicists Haydn, Mozart, and Beethoven loomed out of the past and were deified by an increasingly conservative public. Johannes Brahms, the perceived successor to the classicists, epitomized the combination of this classical tradition and romantic innovations. From a different, hyperromantic source sprang the dramatic music of Richard Wagner along with modern devotees and followers such as Hugo Wolf, Gustav Mahler, and Richard Strauss. At the turn of the century, their music was still surprisingly controversial in Vienna; its detractors were often Brahms's supporters, and vice versa. Challenging complacent audiences and the musical status quo, the interaction of modernists and conservatives, romantics and classicists not only broadened musical horizons, but fanned the fires of major aesthetic issues concerning the meaning and perception of music. On an entirely different plane, the "light" creations of Johann Strauss and other popular composers kept the waltz city's inhabitants, regardless of their taste in more serious music, well stocked with beautiful tunes.

In Arnold Schoenberg and others of his generation (e.g., Zemlinsky, Reger, and Schrecker), Vienna found a remarkable synthesis of all that made it such a musically dynamic city. Schoenberg was among the first to consider Brahms and Wagner as equally viable models. As the heir to a refined and evolving classical tradition, Schoenberg epitomized the clarity, cohesiveness, and motivic integrity of the classical style. As a native Viennese, Schoenberg respected and loved high-quality "light" music. Finally, as a man of romantic sensibility,

Schoenberg was fired by the modernity of Strauss and Mahler and eventually became one of the major innovators of the twentieth century. This "conservative revolutionary" (to borrow the title from Willi Reich's biography of Schoenberg), one of the first composers to reconcile the conflicting strains of innovation and conservatism in nineteenth-century music, was a product of his time and place: late nineteenth-century Vienna.

Schoenberg typically divided his own musical output into three stylistic periods: he labeled the music that he wrote before 1908 as tonal; for the music that he wrote between 1908 and about 1921, Schoenberg preferred the term "totally chromatic," although "atonal," a term that Schoenberg detested, is now the accepted label; and after 1921, Schoenberg referred to his music as twelve-tone. More often than not, Schoenberg is known on the basis of the controversies surrounding his later works, but because the music of each of Schoenberg's developmental periods builds on that of its predecessor, the music of the first period is decisive for Schoenberg's later development. As Schoenberg himself was fond of recounting:

Verklärte Nacht, . . . has been heard . . . a great many times. But certainly nobody has heard it as often as I have heard this complaint: "If only he had continued to compose in this style!"

The answer I gave is perhaps surprising. I said: "I have not discontinued composing in the same style and in the same way as at the very beginning. The difference is only that I do it better now than before; it is more concentrated, more mature."[1]

Schoenberg formulated his distinctive style in compositions that are entirely consistent with the musical genres and approaches to music prevalent in the Vienna of his youth. Like almost all composers of the age, conservative, innovative, or popular, Schoenberg wrote songs for voice and piano. More than thirty songs date from Schoenberg's student years, and, of his first published works, opuses 1, 2, 3, 6, 8, 12, and 14 are vocal works. Like the classicists and Brahms, Schoenberg also wrote chamber music. In addition to some early, individual movements for string quartet, Schoenberg completed an early String Quartet in D Major (1897), the String Quartet no. 1, op. 7 (1905), the Chamber Symphony no. 1, op. 9 (1906), and the String Quartet no. 2, op. 10 (1907–8) during this time. And like the more progressive romantic composers, Schoenberg wrote programmatic instrumental works. His most popular work from his early period, the programmatic string sextet Verklärte Nacht, op. 4, dates from 1899; it was followed in 1903 by the orchestral symphonic poem Pelleas und Melisande, op. 5. The chorus Friede auf Erden, op. 13, reflects the late romantic taste for choral music, and the gigantic Gurrelieder (1899–1901), for vocal soloists, choruses, and orchestra, although not labeled as such, suggests the world of Mahler's vocal symphonies.

MUSICAL STYLE

By as early as 1899, when he completed *Verklärte Nacht*, Schoenberg had developed a mature musical language based on his understanding of past models coupled with his own unique ideas. The process by which this maturity was obtained was remarkable not only because it involved little outside guidance, but because it happened at such an accelerated pace. In well under ten years, Schoenberg evolved from a tentative beginner to a sophisticated composer.

Two important facts guided Schoenberg's acquisition of musical knowledge. First, he was largely self-taught; his formal instruction in music was limited to violin lessons as a child. The rest he gleaned from friends with more traditional musical training, from writings about music (for example, the article on sonata form in his family's encyclopedia), and, most importantly, from studying and analyzing the scores of the great masters such as Bach, Mozart, Beethoven, and Brahms. As Schoenberg later assessed it, he was able to imitate the best of whatever music he found. Second, when Schoenberg did seek advice concerning his compositions from a knowledgeable, professional musician, he turned to Alexander von Zemlinsky, who, as a product of Vienna's conservatory, was completely immersed in the Brahmsian language of the day. This Brahmsian language, which might be viewed as the summation of an intellectually rigorous German musical tradition dating back to Bach via Beethoven and Mozart, served as the basis for Schoenberg's personal musical style and provided the aesthetic measuring stick for his appreciation of all music. As Schoenberg remembered it, he had been a Brahmsian when he met Zemlinsky; Zemlinsky substantiated that tendency but encouraged him to appreciate Wagner's music as well. Then, rather suddenly, Schoenberg became aware of different models, more "modern" music as he put it, which seemed to include Wagner as well as Mahler and Strauss. He assimilated these new influences quite rapidly in the last years of the century, and it was a combination of his older, Brahmsian devotion and this new Wagnerian-inspired element that precipitated his own distinctive style.

In general, commentators agree with Schoenberg's own statements about which aspects of style he acquired from Brahms and which from Wagner. Brahms is viewed as Schoenberg's connection to classicism, to absolute instrumental music (especially chamber music), to counterpoint, and to aspects of coherence and unity in music (such as complex interrelationships among themes and motives and formal structures based on those relationships). Wagner is seen as the source of Schoenberg's extremely chromatic harmony, use of leitmotifs, preference for program music, and tendency toward overstatement (not only in terms of extreme emotion but also extended length and scope).

Regardless of the source from which it springs, what emerges in the early works is a sense of Schoenberg's own style, much of which stays with him for the remainder of his career. In the most straightforward terms this style is embodied in music that is rigorously unified and well-crafted by even the toughest academic standards, tonal but extremely chromatic, written for traditional media but conceived with the aid of programmatic influences, and traditionally beautiful but challenging to the listener because of its seriousness, complexity, and compression (i.e., the rapidity with which material is presented and the thoroughness with which it is developed). Contributing to the complexity of this music is its densely polyphonic texture, the continuous variation of its thematic materials ("developing variation"), and a "prose" style of rhythm and phrase structure that avoids periodic construction in favor of asymmetrical phrase lengths. Although specifically traceable to Brahms and Wagner, Schoenberg's style also represents a larger German tradition of cohesively structured, motivic music characterized by integrated melodic and harmonic relationships—qualities that Schoenberg would later describe as aspects of the "unity of musical space," where melody, accompaniment, harmony, and rhythm are interrelated as multidimensional expressions of a single idea. Related to Schoenberg's idea of "Grundgestalt" (see the chapter by Bryan R. Simms later in this volume), this concept presupposes that a composition's smallest units would mirror the whole work and vice versa.

STUDENT WORKS AND FIRST PUBLISHED SONGS

Schoenberg's quest for compositional fluency resulted in a large body of apprentice compositions, consisting of more than thirty songs and a number of small instrumental works. Schoenberg began composing short violin duos such as those he played with his teacher soon after he began violin lessons at age eight (1882)—original dance tunes, arrangements of popular melodies, and a set of three "Songs Without Words" survive from this era. These consonant, triadic, diatonic works are conventional compositions in a light-classical mode. They owe more to Johann Strauss, popular opera, and the music of the cafés than to "high art" music, but they are competent works nonetheless.[2]

As Schoenberg's musical strengths asserted themselves, he began to associate with more musicians, form and participate in chamber music ensembles, and write chamber music. Schoenberg reported that he began writing quartet movements inspired by his purchase of some Beethoven scores and schooled by the article on sonata from an encyclopedia. In the meantime, in 1893, he had met Alexander von Zemlinsky. "His love embraced both Brahms and Wagner and soon thereafter I became an equally confirmed addict," Schoenberg remembered. "No wonder the music I composed at the time mirrored the influence of both these masters, to which a flavor of Liszt, Bruckner, and perhaps also Hugo Wolf was added."[3]

After a succession of quartet movements and small piano pieces, Schoenberg eventually produced a String Quartet in D Major that was judged to be "good enough" to warrant a performance for Vienna's Composers' Society in 1898.[4] Apparently Schoenberg had begun the work on his own and only when it was nearly done had he shown it to Zemlinsky, who recommended extensive changes including revisions to the outer movements and completely new inner movements. Although "strongly under the influence of Brahms and Dvořák," as Schoenberg described it, this four-movement quartet is a viable work.[5] The first and last movements are decidedly Czech in flavor, with prominent folklike, pentatonic themes, and they inhabit the same sound world as quartets by Dvorak and Smetana. However, these movements, and especially the two inner movements, an Intermezzo and a Theme and Variations, are permeated with sounds and musical techniques gleaned from Schoenberg's understanding of the music of Brahms, and more generically, German instrumental music since Beethoven.[6]

In addition to these early instrumental works, Schoenberg composed songs for voice and piano, beginning as early as 1893. At least one of these songs was written for a contest and others were dedicated to singers within Schoenberg's circle. These works are quite varied in style and, as is the case with the early instrumental works, often show the influence of Brahms. "Waldesnacht" (1897) is the most obviously Brahmsian of the group, and its asymmetrical phrasing, triadic, archlike melody, and characteristic piano texture are as typical of the surface qualities of Brahms's music as Schoenberg's sophisticated introduction of chromaticism into a largely diatonic context is indicative of his mastery of the subtleties of Brahms's idiom. Other songs, including "Ein Schilflied" (1894), demonstrate Schoenberg's ability to use chromaticism to delay a clear statement of the tonic, which suggests some familiarity with Wagner. In "Ein Schilflied," following a brief suggestion of the tonic in the opening measure, Schoenberg implies the tonic but delays its return until the end of the piano postlude.[7]

After years of involvement with Brahms's style, Schoenberg experienced a new passion in the last years of the nineteenth century. Then "an almost sudden turn toward a more *progressive* manner of composing occurred," he remembered. "Mahler and Strauss had appeared on the musical scene, and so fascinating was their advent, that every musician was immediately forced to take sides, pro or contra."[8] Although fired by Mahler and Strauss, the biggest new influence apparent in Schoenberg's music was their predecessor, Wagner, and the eventual outcome of this new Wagnerian passion was the string sextet *Verklärte Nacht* (1899). The process of integrating the new, Wagnerian style with the older Brahmsian style, however, is first evidenced in some of the songs for voice and piano, later published as opuses 1 and 2, that Schoenberg composed just prior to creating *Verklärte Nacht*.

The Two Songs, op. 1 (undated, but most likely composed in 1898), are expansive compositions unlike anything Schoenberg had written before and largely unconnected with his later works. However, they demonstrate a new Wagnerian scope in Schoenberg's experience, and their lavish piano accompaniments are reminiscent of the piano reductions of Wagner's operas. They offer ready examples of a technique of musical expansion that Schoenberg gleaned, according to his own writings, from Wagner: "model and sequence." Inspired by passages such as the famous opening of the Prelude to *Tristan und Isolde*, "model and sequence'' concerns a segment of music (the model) and its repetition transposed to begin on a different scale degree (the sequence). In his later writings, Schoenberg noted that it was used by most composers and that it had the advantage of being a repetition, which aided accessibility, yet a repetition on a new scale degree, which provided a slight sense of contrast. He also noted that "composers of Brahms' school avoided not only this kind of sequence but every unchanged repetition, no matter in what region."[9] Eventually Schoenberg, siding with the Brahmsians, would disparage such obvious repetitions in his music, but it was a typical method of melodic construction in his early works.

The Four Songs, op. 2 demonstrate the integration of Schoenberg's newfound interest in Wagner with his earlier focus on Brahms. In general, these songs are as compact and even compressed as the songs of op. 1 are diffuse and expansive. Of special interest are the four poems of Richard Dehmel which Schoenberg set in 1899, three of which found their way into op. 2. Dehmel had a profound effect on Schoenberg, and Schoenberg wrote to him that by finding musical equivalents for the emotions that Dehmel's poetry elicited in him, he was able to develop a distinctive style.[10]

A primary feature of these songs is their intense motivic saturation, where just a few motives permeate an entire work; in addition they demonstrate Schoenberg's fluent handling of Wagnerian chromaticism, Brahmsian asymmetrical phrasing, and developing variation. It is difficult to determine to what degree Dehmel's poetry is responsible for these stylistic elements, but the single song of op. 2 that is not a setting of a Dehmel poem is much simpler than the three Dehmel settings. The most famous of Schoenberg's first published compositions and perhaps the most popular of all his works, *Verklärte Nacht* ("Transfigured Night"), is also based on a Dehmel poem. It was composed at the same time and demonstrates the same modern features as the songs.

VERKLÄRTE NACHT, OP. 4

Schoenberg composed the string sextet *Verklärte Nacht* during the summer of 1899, when he was vacationing with Zemlinsky at Payerbach; his manuscript is dated December of that year. Zemlinsky tried to get Vienna's Composers' Society to sponsor a performance of the sextet, just as he had procured a performance of the String Quartet in D Major in 1898, but to no avail. When voting against its acceptance, a member of the jury reportedly said that it sounded as if someone had smeared the score of *Tristan* while it was still wet.[11] It was first performed, however, at a Composers' Society concert in 1903 by the Rosé Quartet.

Verklärte Nacht was inspired by a Dehmel poem. Its five stanzas and their narrative content fit the five sections of the composition and, although it functions well as an independent piece of music, it is clear that Schoenberg based its large-scale form and succession of moods on Dehmel's poem. It describes a moonlit stroll by a man and woman in the woods. The woman reveals that she is pregnant, but not by the man. The man says that his love for the woman will transfigure the child; it will become his. The first, third, and fifth stanzas set the scene by describing the cold, moonlit scene and the couple's progress through it. The second stanza contains the woman's speech, and the fourth contains the man's speech.

These poetic divisions relate to the musical divisions of the score. The introduction, interlude, and conclusion use the same few motives; the two larger sections are more complex, involved, and symphonic in nature. Although Schoenberg, in program notes written in the 1950s, was able to associate specific lines of the poem with specific musical passages, there is also a sophisticated musical cohesiveness to the work. Much of this motivic unity, interrelationship of themes, and interrelationship of melodic and harmonic elements was consciously constructed by Schoenberg. Others, however, were products of a situation Schoenberg mentioned on a number of occasions: that if the composer did his best to unify and integrate the composition, the "Almighty" would add a number of bonuses that the composer could then discover. Schoenberg was fond of combing through his compositions after they had been completed and discovering these "unconscious" relationships that strengthened the work's unity.

In the essay "My Evolution," Schoenberg discussed *Verklärte Nacht* as a work that owed equal amounts to Brahms and Wagner. He observed that "the thematic construction is based on a Wagnerian 'model and sequence' above a roving harmony on the one hand, and on Brahms's technique of developing variation—as I call it—on the other." He credited the asymmetrical phrasing to the influence of Brahms, but he observed that "the treatment of the instruments, the manner of composition, and much of the sonority were strictly Wagnerian." Original, "Schoenbergian" elements he claimed include the extended length of some of the melodies, the sonority, "contrapuntal and motival combinations" which produce dense textures, the "semi-contrapuntal movement of the harmony and its bases against the melody," and passages of "unfixed tonality" (that he saw as premonitions of the future).[12] A closer look at three passages from *Verklärte Nacht* demonstrates some of these features.

Example 4.1, mm. 50–54, consists of the beginning of an important theme (in the first cello) from the portion of the work corresponding to the woman's speech; after this passage the theme is repeated immediately in a new orchestration and extended (mm. 55–62) before giving way to new material. It also returns later in the work, intact, and its motives permeate additional sections of the piece even when the theme is not heard in its original form. Even as an isolated excerpt, this theme illustrates Schoenberg's penchant for asymmetrical phrasing or prose-style rhythm (note that it is five measures long), for melodic construction that mixes repetition with motivic development, and for polyphonic textures even in expository sections (note the "countermelody" in the first violin and first viola).

Example 4.2, mm. 255–65, which Schoenberg cited as an example of a melody of "Schoenbergian" length, is also an illustration of what he termed de-

Example 4.1
Verklärte Nacht, op. 4, mm. 50–54, excerpt.

veloping variation. The initial motive of this important theme (from the portion of the work corresponding to the man's speech), stated in the first two measures in different rhythmic configurations, is dominated by the interval of a descending fourth followed by an ascending half step. In the third measure it is varied further: the descending fourth is answered by a rising fourth followed by a rising whole step. In the fourth measure, the two shapes are reversed in order: on the downbeat, the rising element becomes a third, which is then followed by a descending sixth, creating, essentially, a free inversion of the second measure. This newly derived figure, which features a rising element on the downbeat, is combined with the initial motive, in the rhythmic shape it took in m. 255, to dominate the continuation of the theme in mm. 259–261, where the initial motive is stated in diminution in each half-measure, with the descending fourth becoming a fifth or sixth. This new version of the motive is inverted in the first halves of mm. 262, 263, and 264. The motive, in the rhythmic shape it took in m. 256, dominates the second halves of mm. 262 and 263, and the descending scale passage with which this excerpt ends (the second half of m. 264 and m. 265) fills in the octave melodic range covered by the descending-fourth motive in mm. 255–256. Almost the entire theme, then, is generated by varied restatements of the opening motive, and developing variation becomes as important in this theme as the sequential repetition in mm. 259–261.

Elsewhere in the work there are examples of the surprising density of texture brought on by the superimposition of melodic elements. Musical texture in *Verklärte Nacht* ranges from simple homophony to dense polyphony, and these extremes of texture usually correlate with the function of the various formal sections of the work. For example, thematic expositions tend to be largely homophonic; transitions and developments typically involve polyphony. A particularly dense polyphonic passage, in the developmental section of the portion of *Verklärte Nacht* corresponding to the woman's speech (beginning in measure

Example 4.2
Verklärte Nacht, op. 4, mm. 255–265, excerpt.

161), demonstrates the level of complexity possible in this work. (See Example 4.3.) In his desire "to express the idea behind the poem," Schoenberg presented "a leitmotiv and its inversion played simultaneously." "This combination was not the product of a spontaneous inspiration but of an extramusical intention, of a cerebral reflection," Schoenberg wrote. "The technical labor which required so much time was in adding such subordinate voices as would soften the harsh frictions of this combination."[13]

In general, the harmonic language of *Verklärte Nacht* is relatively straightforward. With the exception of a few chords resulting from the intersection of various polyphonic voices (such as the passage cited above), it is possible to understand the individual chords as parts of progressions in the extended tonal language of the late nineteenth century. True to this language, the dominant is largely missing as a major structural key area, and other key areas take its place. Symmetrical tonal relationships are especially important, including those between the tonic and chords built on the half steps that surround it. For example, on the largest scale, the first half of the work (that is, the introduction, the woman's speech, and the interlude) is centered on D minor; the remainder is centered on D major. D major is approached first via E-flat, the key area of the end of the interlude; slightly later it is approached again, but via D-flat (enharmonically, C-sharp).

As the first of his instrumental works to be published, *Verklärte Nacht* holds a special place in Schoenberg's *oeuvre*. It represents a synthesis of many youthful influences, including Brahms and Wagner, and original ideas. Schoenberg was fond of pointing out that he continued to use many of the techniques found in the sextet throughout his career. In the works discussed below, aspects of motivic conciseness, harmonic complexity, prose-style rhythm, and programmatic inspiration hold constant.

Example 4.3
Verklärte Nacht, op. 4, mm. 161–162.

GURRELIEDER

Schoenberg began the work that was to become the massive, cantata-like *Gurrelieder* in 1900 as a proposed entry in a competition sponsored by Vienna's Composers' Society. In its initial form, it was a song cycle for tenor, soprano, and piano, based on selections from Danish poet Jens Peter Jacobsen's *Gurre-sange*, or ''Songs of Gurre.'' Jacobsen's epic poem, written in 1868–69 and translated into German by Robert Franz Arnold in a collection published in 1897, is based on the romantic intrigue, damnation, and implied redemption of a twelfth-century Danish king. Stories vary as to why Schoenberg never entered his work in the competition; either he finished it past the deadline or he and Zemlinsky decided that it was unlikely to win and so decided not to enter it. At any rate, he was soon inspired by his song cycle to set the complete narrative as a large-scale showpiece for an ensemble comprising five solo singers (soprano, mezzo or contralto, two tenors, bass), speaker, three four-part male choruses, eight-part mixed choir, and an orchestra of about 150 players (including eight flutes, five oboes, seven clarinets, ten horns, six trumpets, bass trumpet, six trombones, four harps, and large percussion) lasting nearly two hours. Schoenberg's *Gurrelieder* became one of the most overwhelming of all late-romantic musical compositions, and it met with great acclaim when it was finally premiered in 1913.

Even after its transformation from song cycle to gigantic concert work, Schoenberg's *Gurrelieder* had a rather complicated compositional history. He began it in March 1900 and had composed all but the final chorus of the three-part work by March 1901, when he began orchestrating it. Two years later, after a variety of interruptions, he had orchestrated up to the beginning of Part III. Then, after a long hiatus, he completed most of the orchestration in 1910; in 1911 he completed the final chorus. Part I, the majority of which was intended for the song cycle competition, comprises a prelude, the nine love songs of King Waldemar and his mistress, Tove, an orchestral interlude, and the ''Song of the Wood Dove,'' in which Tove's death at the order of Queen Helwig is reported. Part II consists of a single, brief song in which Waldemar curses God for his cruelty. Part III contains two ''Wild Hunts,'' that of the ghosts of Waldemar and his vassals, condemned to rise from their graves every night after their death, and that of the Summer Wind, which sweeps away the ghoulishness of the past and precipitates a grand, optimistic sunrise.

Each part of the *Gurrelieder* illustrates something significant of Schoenberg's style. For example, the prelude, nine songs, and interlude which comprise the majority of Part I are constructed symphonically so that motives repeat from one song to another; indeed, the interlude is an orchestral development of many of the motives prominent in the songs. Here, as in the rest of the composition, there is an internal, musical logic that guides the work and enhances the dramatic narrative. The music of Part I (as well as of Parts II and III) also illustrates Schoenberg's preference for asymmetrical phrasing and his masterful handling of the chromatic harmonic idiom that he favored at the turn of the century. Motives and melodies are often densely chromatic, as is the rapidly paced succession of chords that accompanies them or results from their intertwining. Frequently, the expected arrival of a given tonic is delayed, and this delay has an effect on the work's structure. For example, the lengthy prelude to Part I is in E-flat, as is the first song, but the E-flat triad heard at the beginning of the prelude (characteristically decorated by an added sixth, the note C) does not return until about one-third of the way into the first song, creating a sense of continuity from prelude to song. There are other instances of the avoidance of a tonic throughout the *Gurrelieder*, so many, in fact, as to be a defining characteristic of the style. There are also other indications of how thoroughly planned and integrated the work is. For example, the note C that is added so prominently to the opening E-flat major harmony predicts the importance that C, as the key in which the work ends, has for the composition as a whole. Not coincidentally, the motive from the introduction to Part I returns at the conclusion of Part III inverted.[14]

The ''Song of the Wood Dove'' is more narrative than these first, lyrical songs. It also presents a new method of tonal and formal construction: it is built around a refrain—a dissonant collection of pitches (a half-diminished seventh chord in second inversion). This refrain, despite its dissonant status, returns in the manner of the tonic in a rondo form and thus unifies the varied tonal areas of this section of Part I. Beginning with a memorable, bird-song-like triplet figure, the refrain is also distinguished by a rising and descending half-step

Example 4.4
"Song of the Wood Dove" from *Gurrelieder*, Part I, mm. 848–858; 1106–1107.

figure (G-G-flat-G); both of these figures are based on the half-diminished seventh chord. A third element, a fatalistic, cadential figure consisting of a minor triad accompanied by two timpani strikes after the beat, concludes the initial refrain elements and returns only in conjunction with the refrain's last two repetitions. (See Example 4.4.) This refrain introduces the text and accompanies its first lines; thereafter it accompanies a repeating line of text, "I flew far, sought grief, and have found much," and its distinctive melodic line. At its second repeat, it is transposed up a half step, but the other three of its four repetitions are at the original pitch level. In its final statement, the refrain is greatly expanded, and the minor-triad, timpani-strike portion of the refrain concludes Part I.

Part II, as noted earlier, consists of a brief, single song—Waldemar's curse against God. It refers to some of the motives used in the "Song of the Wood Dove," but for the most part it is dominated by two new motives. One, a succession of three chords (E-flat minor, first inversion; C half-diminished; and D half-diminished), accompanies the entry of the voice. The second is a memorable motive set to the climactic line of text "To kill a poor man's only lamb" (in the score at 2 before Rehearsal 4). This second motive is heard in the orchestra immediately following the singer's last phrase, and then its central portion is repeated in counterpoint starting on each beat of the measure for six and two-thirds measures, the last of which features the motive in diminution. (See Example 4.5.) Although this is an extreme example, it illustrates how Schoenberg used thematic material contrapuntally, even in seemingly less-significant transitional passages. Both of these motives appear prominently in this song's orchestral postlude and are heard again in Part III. The song begins and ends in B-flat minor, the key in which Part I ended, but there are few references to that key during the song.

Part III, "The Wild Hunt," consists of a series of songs and like Part I, it ends with the introduction of a new character (a narrator) who views the action from a new perspective. The first section of Part III represents the chase of Waldemar and his ghost vassals as described and commented on by Waldemar in alternation with a peasant bystander (bass voice), Klaus the Fool (tenor), and Waldemar's men. There are numerous references to motives from Part I and Part II and each solo singer maintains a distinct musical character; Klaus the Fool is the lightest of the three, offering a kind of comic relief to Waldemar's self-indulgent sorrow and rage. The choral sections are nearly always contrapuntal and occasionally canonic, and the full orchestra uses its ample resources to depict the fury of the scene.

Part III concludes with the "Wild Hunt of the Summer Wind," set initially as a melodrama for speaker and orchestra and culminating in a grand passage for mixed choir. This melodrama is Schoenberg's first use of *Sprechstimme*, the half-singing, half-speaking technique that he would use prominently in *Pierrot lunaire*, op. 21 (1912). Since Schoenberg orchestrated this section of the piece several years after orchestrating the earlier portions, it sounds significantly different. Instead of massing the orchestral forces as he had done in 1903, Schoenberg treated the orchestra in 1911 as a collection of soloists and, although the music still tends toward dense polyphony, the orchestral colors are purer and less mixed, resulting in a brighter sound appropriate for the triumphant choral sunrise with which the work concludes.

PELLEAS UND MELISANDE, OP. 5

Long before he had finished orchestrating *Gurrelieder*, Schoenberg had begun his massive symphonic poem *Pelleas und Melisande*. Early in 1902, Richard Strauss had brought Maurice Maeterlinck's play to his attention, presenting it as a possible subject for Schoenberg's first opera. (At the time, Schoenberg and Strauss did not know that Debussy was already using it as the basis of his opera, which was premiered in April 1902.) Schoenberg chose not to begin an opera at this time, but he began setting *Pelleas und Melisande* as a symphonic poem in July 1902. Maeterlinck had written his play in 1893 and a German translation was available as early as 1897. As Schoenberg later recalled, "It was around 1900 when Maurice Maeterlinck fascinated composers, stimulating them to create music to his dramatic poems. What attracted all was his art of dramatizing eternal problems of humanity in the form of fairy-tales, lending them timelessness without adhering to imitation of ancient styles."[15]

Schoenberg completed the work in 1903, and many years later he noted that the symphonic poem had "taught me to express moods and characters in precisely formulated units, a technique that my opera would perhaps not have promoted as well." At about forty-five minutes in length, the work depicts many different moods and characters and, according to Schoenberg, was "inspired entirely by Maurice Maeterlinck's wonderful drama." "It tried to mirror every detail of it," Schoenberg continued, "with only a few omissions and slight changes of the order of the scenes."[16] The story concerns the mysterious young princess Melisande, found alone in the forest by the much older prince Golaud. They marry and return to the castle of Golaud's grandfather, King Arkel, where

Example 4.5
Gurrelieder, Part II, mm. 69–77.

Melisande meets Golaud's younger half-brother, Pelleas. Her apparently inno-
cent friendship with Pelleas, with whom she shares a number of adventures,
makes Golaud jealous. Pelleas, first aware of the tension, decides to leave the
castle; when he meets Melisande to say good-bye, they suddenly realize and
express their love for one another. Golaud, overhearing them, is enraged, kills
Pelleas, and wounds Melisande. Melisande dies from her seemingly insignificant
wound after giving birth to a child. Golaud grieves but is still unsure of her
faithfulness.

Although Schoenberg's program notes for a 1950 recording of the work indicate that he associated certain musical themes with specific characters and
situations in the drama, Alban Berg's analysis of the work published in 1920
demonstrates that it is constructed symphonically, while still matching the events
of the drama.[17] It is this special structure, in which a large-scale symphonic form
helps to unify the music inspired by scenes from the drama, that is *Pelleas und
Melisande*'s most distinctive quality.

In addition to following the broad outline of the drama, the thematic basis of
Pelleas und Melisande creates a "double-function" sonata form, which, like
Liszt's Piano Sonata in B Minor, combines the elements of a single-movement
sonata form (exposition, development, recapitulation) with those of a multimove-

ment sonata cycle (first movement, scherzo, slow movement, finale). The First Movement (introduction, themes I, II, III; short developmental recapitulation) includes themes associated with the discovery of the mysterious Melisande, her marriage to Golaud, her meeting with and growing love for Pelleas, and a short developmental recapitulation of these themes. The second movement, a Scherzo with added episodes, refers to scenes where Melisande loses her wedding ring, where she leans out of the castle tower, allowing her hair to envelop Pelleas, and where Golaud confronts Pelleas with his jealousy. The third, or slow, movement, concerns the development of the themes associated with Melisande, Pelleas, and fate, which give way to a new expansive love theme. It ends with Golaud's murder of Pelleas. The Finale includes recapitulations of themes from the first and third movements, an episode depicting the death of Melisande, and additional returns of themes from the first, second, and third movements. In addition to this implied four-movement structure, the traditional aspects of sonata form (thematic contrast, development, recapitulation) are also present on a large scale. Although some of the details of Berg's deployment of this formal outline are weak, it is clearly an important aspect of the work's structure on the largest level.

In addition to the general melodic characteristics typical of Schoenberg's music at the time, such as extreme chromaticism and great breadth, the themes of Pelleas and of Melisande are frequently related to one another via motivic development and transformation. They are also combined in ways that illustrate specific dramatic situations, such as the scene where Melisande leans out of her window to speak with Pelleas (see the discussion of Example 4.6, below). Such typically Wagnerian uses of the themes permeate the score.[18]

Tonally, *Pelleas und Melisande* is based in D minor, like *Verklärte Nacht* and the later String Quartet no. 1. Secondary tonal areas are clearly related to the tonic by the cycle of thirds or fifths, and some developmental sections modulate rapidly through a variety of keys. Chromatic voice leading in all parts sometimes obscures local harmonic relationships, but harmonic goals are usually clear on a larger level. One striking tonal relationship, which mirrors the return to the tonic toward the end of *Verklärte Nacht*, concerns the arrival of the tonic, D minor, in the final section of *Pelleas und Melisande*. D minor returns twice; the first time it is preceded by C-sharp minor and the second time by E-flat minor.

The instrumentation of *Pelleas und Melisande* has been described as lavish, and it is exceeded in size only by that of the *Gurrelieder*. The orchestra comprises seventeen woodwind and eighteen brass players, eight percussion instruments, sixty-four strings, and two harps. Novelties in instrumental use include trombone glissandi, which Schoenberg took credit for inventing, to depict Golaud's jealous confrontation with Pelleas in the dank, underground vaults of the castle. (See Example 4.8, below.)

The musical texture of *Pelleas und Melisande* is frequently quite complex, as was typical of Schoenberg's music at the time. Some especially complex passages are motivated by events in the story. One such passage, of which Schoenberg was justly proud, corresponds to the scene where Melisande leans out of the castle window, allowing her hair to surround Pelleas. (See Example 4.6.) Canonic imitation in the flutes and clarinets (four voices) begins the passage and this imitation continues with the addition of the two harps (the melodic figure is based on one of Melisande's themes); to this accompaniment are added Melisande's and Pelleas's themes, appearing in counterpoint in the solo violins and cello.

There are also several passages in *Pelleas und Melisande* that feature novel sounds such as whole tone harmonies and chords based on the interval of the fourth. These sounds were beginning to appear in the works of other composers at about this time, and Schoenberg credited his first use of them to this piece. He also cited examples from *Pelleas und Melisande* in his text book *Theory of Harmony [Harmonielehre]* when he later enumerated various approaches to musical composition. The passage of quartal harmonies that Schoenberg quoted occurs at mm. 86–87. Here the novel chords accompany a fragment of Melisande's theme. (See Example 4.7.) In the first measure, a chord built on perfect fourths resolves to a minor triad (in first inversion); in the second measure, a chord built on perfect fourths resolves to a major triad (in second inversion). The whole passage serves as a transition to the first of Pelleas's themes. Schoenberg's example of whole-tone chords in his textbook is taken from the scene in the castle vaults. The chord's exotic sound, in the wind instruments, adds to the foreboding of this scene, which also feature trombone glissandi. (See Example 4.8.)

Regarding the quartal harmonies, Schoenberg observed:

The fourth chords make their first appearance in music as an impressionistic means of expression, as does apparently everything that later becomes a commonly used technical means. . . . That which is new and unusual about a new harmony occurs to the true composer only for such reasons: he must give expression to something that moves him, something new, something previously unheard-of. His successors, who continue working with it, think of it as merely a new sound, a technical device; but it is far more than that: a new sound is a symbol, discovered involuntarily, a symbol proclaiming the new man who so asserts his individuality.[19]

The individuality which asserts itself in *Pelleas und Melisande*, including references to exotic harmonies, is tempered by tradition. For each novelty that Schoenberg injects into the work, there are several traditional features. This balance between new and old is often cited as an important feature in all of Schoenberg's music, and it is certainly an important factor in Schoenberg's next major work, the First String Quartet.

STRING QUARTET NO. 1 IN D MINOR, OP. 7

Schoenberg began the String Quartet no. 1 in D Minor, op. 7, during 1904 and completed it the following year. This First String Quartet shares many traits

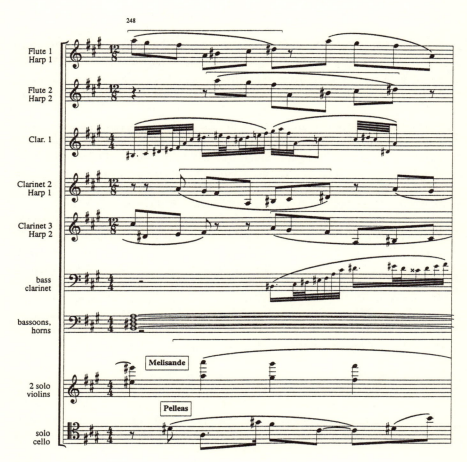

Example 4.6
Pelleas und Melisande, op. 5, mm. 248–249.

with his earlier works. It is expansive, motivically unified, formally innovative, texturally complex and, like *Verklärte Nacht* and *Pelleas und Melisande*, it is in D minor and motivated by an extra musical idea. However, Schoenberg himself believed that the quartet marked a new direction in his development.

Thereafter I abandoned program music [*sic*] and turned in the direction that was much more my own than all the preceding. It was the First String Quartet, op. 7, in which I combined all the achievements of my time (including my own) such as: the construction of extremely large forms; greatly expanded melodies based on a richly moving harmony and new chord progressions; and a contrapuntal technique that solved problems offered by superimposed, individual parts which moved freely in more remote regions of a tonality and met frequently in vagrant harmonies.[20]

Although Schoenberg claimed to have abandoned program music, the First Quartet was based on a "secret" program that he never shared with audiences or students. He did, however, allude to it to his students in later years as a rationale for the work's "extravagances of form," reflecting the mid-twentieth-century aesthetic attitude toward program music with the comment: "one does not tell such things anymore."[21] When it was finally located inside the cover of one of Schoenberg's sketchbooks, it was discovered to be not a poem or a play, but an outline of the emotional states associated with the stages of a love relationship.[22] It is keyed to the formal sections of the quartet in the way that Schoenberg later advised beginning composers to use extramusical ideas to help generate a variety of moods in their compositions. "In composing even the smallest exercises, the student should never fail to keep in mind a special character. A poem, a story, a play or a moving picture may provide the stimulus to express different moods."[23]

Although the program is keyed to the varying moods of the quartet, the work's

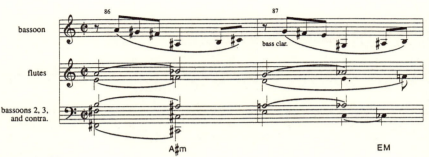

Example 4.7
Pelleas und Melisande, op. 5, mm. 86–87, excerpt.

abstract musical form is distinctive in its own right. It is a double-function sonata form of the type observed in *Pelleas und Melisande*, and at over forty-five minutes in length, the quartet is just as massive, in terms of time, as the earlier symphonic poem. The first section combines the qualities of a first movement with that of an exposition; the second matches developmental techniques with a scherzo mood; the third section is continued development in the manner of a slow movement; the final section is a recapitulatory rondo-finale followed by a coda. Although this overview outlines the form on one level, it is also true that development and thematic transformation of material introduced toward the beginning of the quartet pervades the entire work and lends it a rigorous unity.

The themes themselves are, as Schoenberg noted, "greatly expanded melodies based on a richly moving harmony and new chord progressions."[24] The first theme illustrates this expanded type of melody. It is in ternary form and extends for more than ninety measures. It begins with a dynamic statement in the first violin that spans more than two octaves; this first section continues for twenty-nine measures. The theme is then repeated and varied in other key areas and instrumentations before returning in the tonic (m. 65) to round out the ternary structure. The theme's aggressive quality has been likened to Beethoven and, indeed, Schoenberg cited Beethoven's *Eroica* Symphony as a model for the process of thematic variation (discussed below) found throughout the quartet. This theme and others in the quartet are marked by asymmetrical phrasing and prose-style rhythms. These qualities contribute to the work's complexity. (See Example 4.9.)

The theme's basis in "richly moving harmony and new chord progressions" is illustrated by reductive analysis. Schoenberg's student Alban Berg reduced the harmony of the first theme to a bare outline in an analysis designed to demonstrate the traditional underpinnings of Schoenberg's music.[25] Using only whole and half notes in a mostly four-part chorale style, Berg hoped to demonstrate that this succession of chords from the first ten measures of the quartet would be much more intelligible to listeners if it occurred at a slower tempo, as the basis, for example, of an entire slow movement. Although Berg's analysis

Example 4.8
Pelleas und Melisande, op. 5, mm. 290–292, excerpt.

demonstrates a few subsurface harmonic relationships of a traditional sort that pass too quickly to be noticed in the quartet, it more clearly demonstrates the overall harmonic complexity of the theme. Even though a dominant seventh chord is suggested in the third measure, for example, its resolution is clouded and one looks in vain for other local dominants. Instead one finds complex altered chords or even whole-tone harmonies.[26]

The contrapuntal contexts in which Schoenberg presents his themes demonstrate that the music is linear in nature and not based on any standard progression of chords. The work is almost exclusively polyphonic in texture, and only a few homophonic passages provide contrast. Schoenberg's "contrapuntal technique that solved problems offered by superimposed, individual parts which moved freely in more remote regions of a tonality and met frequently in vagrant harmonies" produces the effect of chords resulting from polyphonic melodic mo-

Example 4.9
String Quartet no. 1 in D Minor, op. 7, mm. 1–13, excerpt.

tion rather than melodies derived from harmonic progressions; that is, the harmonies result from the voice leading and not the other way around.[27]

As remarkable as the harmonic and contrapuntal languages of the quartet are, the level of motivic unity within the work is even more striking. The melodic material presented at the beginning of the quartet permeates the work in the manner of Brahms and, especially, Beethoven. As has frequently been observed, all material in the work is thematic. To cite some of the many examples of thematic transformation and development that Schoenberg liked to point out, one need look no further than the various forms taken by the transition and second theme. (See Example 4.10.) In its original form, the second theme is dominated by two ideas: a syncopated, chromatic figure that doubles back on itself (motive "x"), and a rising triplet figure (motive "y") (example 4.10a). Almost immediately, the rising triplet figure becomes the beginning of a new melody in 6/4 time (example 4.10b). Soon thereafter the syncopated figure is also treated lyrically in 6/4 (example 4.10c). It is then developed in 3/4 at a faster tempo. The theme identified with the transition is treated contrapuntally initially (example 4.10d); it returns later in a new context, transformed, as the theme of the scherzo (example 4.10e).

The music of the First String Quartet demonstrates how Schoenberg compressed and refined the musical traits of his earlier works while maintaining many connections with past traditions. He continued this process in his next major work, the Chamber Symphony no. 1.

CHAMBER SYMPHONY NO. 1 IN E MAJOR, OP. 9

Schoenberg composed the Chamber Symphony no. 1 in E Major, op. 9, in 1906. It employs many of the same qualities and techniques as *Pelleas und*

Example 4.10
String Quartet no. 1 in D Minor, op. 7, thematic transformation and development.

Melisande and the First String Quartet, but in a much more compressed manner. For example, the Chamber Symphony is cast in a single movement that combines aspects of sonata form with those of a multimovement sonata cycle, yet it is roughly half the length of the First String Quartet. It is scored for a relatively small ensemble consisting of flute, oboe, English horn, two clarinets, bassoon, contrabassoon, two horns, and string quintet, which, although larger than that of the string quartet, is much smaller than that required for *Pelleas und Melisande* and the *Gurrelieder*. In almost all respects, the First Chamber Symphony represents an intensification of the techniques found in the First String Quartet, just as that work is a refinement of techniques found in *Pelleas und Melisande*.

The form of the First Chamber Symphony comprises five integrated sections: exposition, scherzo, development, slow movement, and finale. These sections are linked by means of thematic transformation, development of earlier material, and returning themes. The scherzo and slow movement themes, for example, are derived from distinctive motives heard in the first ten measures of the work; the finale includes the return and development of themes from previous sections; and a "horn-call" motive, a melodic idea consisting of a series of perfect fourths, returns at important formal junctures. The form of each individual sec-

Example 4.11
Chamber Symphony no. 1, op. 9, mm. 4–6, excerpt.

tion is unique, yet each is characterized by returning motives and key areas. Because of the work's reduced length, it is easier for the listener to appreciate its cohesiveness and its formal contrasts.

The melodies of the chamber symphony are more compressed than those of the First String Quartet; several of them are so brief that they would best be described as motives rather than themes or melodies. Although some are as dynamic and wide in range as the first theme of the First String Quartet, others are not. In essence, Schoenberg employs a larger fund of thematic ideas in the Chamber Symphony than he had in the First String Quartet.

The quality that Schoenberg admired most in the themes of the Chamber Symphony is their close relationship to the harmonies used throughout the work. In referring to the First Chamber Symphony as the "climax" of his first period, Schoenberg noted, "Here is established a very intimate reciprocation between melody and harmony, in that both connect remote relations of the tonality into a perfect unity, draw logical consequences from the problems they attempt to solve, and simultaneously make great progress in the direction of the emancipation of the dissonance."[28]

A prime example of Schoenberg's point is the way that the horn-call motive appears not just as a melodic element, but also as a harmony, and how it returns periodically throughout the form. Fourths "do not appear here merely as melody or as a purely impressionistic chord effect; their character permeates the total harmonic structure, and they are chords like all others," noted Schoenberg in the *Theory of Harmony*. "Here the fourths, springing from an entirely different expressive urge (stormy jubilation), shape themselves into a definite horn theme, spread themselves out architectonically over the whole piece, and place their stamp on everything that happens"[29] (see Example 4.11). Example 4.7 illustrated how Schoenberg had used quartal harmonies in conjunction with triadic harmonies in *Pelleas und Melisande*, and he continued to use them in a similar manner in the Chamber Symphony. But quartal harmonies also saturate certain portions of the work completely and, most strikingly, they are realized melodically. Example 4.11 illustrates the "horn-call" melodic motive; at several places in the score (including the passage at Rehearsal nos. 77 and 78, not quoted here), this motive becomes a chord used in the context of a succession of quartal harmonies. Similarly, the sweeping first theme is notable for its derivation from the whole-tone collection, which is also used elsewhere in the work harmonically. Schoenberg appreciated that these distinctive sonorities, that is, fourths and whole-tone collections, were not used just as exotic melodic or coloristic embellishments of a traditional tonal language, but were integrated on several levels, and employed to a much higher degree in this piece than in his previous compositions.

Other aspects of harmony in the Chamber Symphony are tied in with the work's contrapuntal texture, which is frequently quite dense. Just as in the earlier instrumental works, many of the more unusual harmonies result from the intersection of several distinctive polyphonic voices. This process produces a relatively high dissonance level and a complex sense of harmony, but it does not subvert the tonal organization of the work, since cadences to traditional triads are found at major junctures in the form. In addition to complicating the harmonic language, the dense polyphonic texture of the Chamber Symphony lends it a certain urgency of mood which is compounded by the work's compressed form and themes, rapid harmonic rhythm, and high dissonance level. In many respects this sense of compression is maintained in the Second String Quartet, Schoenberg's next major work.

STRING QUARTET NO. 2 IN F-SHARP MINOR, OP. 10

Schoenberg began the String Quartet no. 2 in F-sharp Minor, op. 10, during 1907 and completed it the following year. Although it has much in common with his earlier instrumental works, it also contrasts with them sharply. Most obviously, it eschews the single-movement form of the First Chamber Symphony, the First String Quartet, and *Pelleas und Melisande* for a more traditional layout of four discrete movements, each clearly articulated according to traditional formal procedures: the first movement is cast in sonata form; the second is a scherzo; the third is a variation form; and the fourth is a second sonata form. Also by way of contrast, Schoenberg adds a singer to the ensemble for the third and fourth movements. Finally, the harmonic vocabulary of the quartet surpasses that of his earlier works. As Schoenberg described it in a famous quotation:

In this period I renounced a tonal center—a procedure incorrectly called "atonality." In the first and second movements there are many sections in which the individual parts proceed regardless of whether or not their meeting results in codified harmonies. Still, here, and also in the third and fourth movements, the key is presented distinctly at all the main dividing points of the formal organization. Yet the overwhelming multitude of dissonances cannot be balanced any longer by occasional returns to such tonal triads as represent a key. It seemed inadequate to force a movement into the Procrustean bed of tonality without supporting it by harmonic progressions that pertain to it. This was my concern, and it should have occupied the mind of all my contemporaries also. That I was the first to venture the decisive step will not be considered universally a merit—a fact I regret but have to ignore.[30]

These qualities suggest that the quartet represents a major break with Schoenberg's past, but several other aspects of the work demonstrate its connection with his previous compositions. Despite its division into four relatively short movements, Schoenberg unifies the Second String Quartet by linking the movements together through common thematic material: the second movement returns briefly to a theme from the first movement; the third movement is based on material from the second and first movements; and the fourth movement concludes with the character, if not the exact figures, of earlier movements. The unusual addition of a texted vocal part to a string quartet is a definite break with the past, but Schoenberg tempers the novelty of the voice's presence by rigorously organizing the texted movements according to the principles of absolute music. As mentioned earlier, in addition to being a setting of Stefan George's poem "Litanei," the third movement is a variation form based on motives from the two earlier movements. The fourth movement, although a moving setting of George's "Entrückung," is also a sonata form.

As a final connection to his previous works, incorporating texts into this quartet is also consistent with Schoenberg's earlier preference for programmatic references. The first line of the fourth movement, "I feel the air of another planet," has obvious correlations with the change in Schoenberg's musical style. In addition, the extramusical associations triggered by the George texts themselves are enhanced by the text associated with a musical quotation in the second movement. This "secret" program, to which Schoenberg made no overt reference, might concern the momentous musical implications of the quartet itself, or it might concern the near-breakup of Schoenberg's marriage. The George poem used in the third movement, "Litanei" ["Litany"], is a request for haven from life's woes: it concludes with the text "Kill my longing, heal my wounds, take love from me and give me your peace." The fourth movement text, "Entrückung" ["Transport"], is a depiction of spiritual elevation, a liberation from the physical world. The second movement, Scherzo, quotes the melodic line corresponding to the text "Alas, poor boy, everything is lost" from the Viennese popular song "Ach du lieber Augustin," to the accompaniment of a variety of musical figures possibly derived from the names of Schoenberg, his first wife, and her lover.[31] Whether the "loss" concerns the end of tonality, the break-up of Schoenberg's marriage, or something even more general, such as the void preceding a spiritual awakening of the type Schoenberg would experience in the coming years, this programmatic element is a connection with Schoenberg's past.

The harmonic newness of the work, although made to sound quite revolutionary by Schoenberg, is a direct outgrowth of stylistic elements in his previous works, and its novelty is countered by the clearly sectional, accessible form in which it is contained. Much of the quartet is based upon a triadic harmonic language, but it is presented in the context of a very fast harmonic rhythm; triadic writing, related to a large-scale tonal key scheme, returns at important junctures of the form. Other intermediary passages are so chromatic, so polyphonic, and so removed, tonally, from the tonic, that it is difficult if not impossible to place these portions within a key scheme. As Schoenberg noted in the previous quote, in these portions the cadence points cease to be functional and become referential. Schoenberg also observed,

The quartet played a great role in my career. However, the decisive progress toward so-called *atonality* was not yet carried out. Every one of the four movements ends with a tonic, representing the tonality. Within, one finds many sectional endings on more or less remote relatives of the key. That those endings renounce traditional cadential harmonies, does not justify the strict condemnation it had to endure. Doubtlessly, the obstacles to comprehension have to be found in the inclusion of extratonal progressions in the themes, which require clarification by remotely related harmony progressions, which are themselves obstacles to comprehension.[32]

A few examples from the quartet illustrate the salient points of its style. The first movement of the quartet, in sonata form, is in F-sharp minor, and the large-scale harmonic relations of the movement support that tonic. The first theme is stated in the tonic at the beginning of the work, but it modulates quickly through a number of keys and soon reaches F major; it returns at the beginning of the recapitulation in F major but works its way back to the tonic relatively quickly. This same theme, appearing at its original pitch level, begins the development, although there it is reharmonized to disguise its connection to the tonic. F-sharp is also stated strongly at the beginning of the coda and as the final cadence of the movement.

Harmonic contrast within the movement is not of the traditional type; it is derived instead from two different treatments of thematic material.[33] The movement begins with a theme based in triadic harmony and set in the context of a rapid harmonic rhythm that moves far-afield from the tonic (the above-mentioned motion from F-sharp minor to F major in eleven measures). The second part of the first group consists of a theme that is set in the polyphonic, chromatic context that seems to have no basis in triadic harmony. Basically, these two themes, and the processes they represent, provide the contrast within the entire movement. The first theme group is set up in a ternary arrangement: the triadic theme is followed by the chromatic theme, after which the triadic theme returns in varied form as a transition. The arrival of the second theme is prepared by a lessening of rhythmic motion, a simplification of texture, and a ritardando. The first part of the second theme group is, in essence, a transformation of the chromatic, second element of the first group and, as such, is tonally ambiguous. The second group continues with themes derived from the first theme of the first group. Since the two theme groups are so thoroughly inter-related, contrast within the movement is provided mainly by the differences between triadic and tonally ambiguous thematic treatments. In both kinds of writing, however, it is the voice-leading of the individual parts that drives the work rather than a sense of harmonic progression.

Although the texture of the first movement is generally simpler than that of the First Chamber Symphony or First String Quartet, there is still ample poly-

Example 4.12
String Quartet no. 2 in F-sharp Minor, op. 10, mm. 12–17.

phonic complexity. One type of polyphonic texture is that of the second theme from the first group. (See Example 4.12.) Such passages encompass a theme, stated here in the viola, and strong but subsidiary polyphonic accompanying lines. Other passages typically involve contrapuntal imitation as an accompaniment or as an aspect of development. At the recapitulation, for example, the viola's statement of the first theme is accompanied in the cello by the same theme in augmentation. (See Example 4.13.) In the development section there are also passages of sophisticated imitative counterpoint which, as Schoenberg observed in program notes for the quartet, "might interest a connoisseur of contrapuntal finesse."[34] The musical examples that Schoenberg cites include imitation through transposition and inversion and also invertible counterpoint. (See Examples 4.14a and 4.14b.)

The second movement is a scherzo in D minor consisting of the following sections: Scherzo, Trio and extension (which includes the famous quotation), Scherzo, Coda. The tonic returns at important formal divisions, except that the trio begins in F-sharp major and moves eventually to D major, and the return of the Scherzo begins in F-sharp major and moves rapidly to D minor. The scherzo is constructed from three motives presented in constantly differing contrapuntal arrangements; the trio includes new material, references to themes from the scherzo, the quotation of "Ach du lieber Augustin," and a reference to the second of the first-group themes from the first movement. Schoenberg noted that the composed continuation of the "Augustin" theme was transformed "so as to remind of motives and phrases of the first movement," namely the second of the first-group themes noted above (Example 4.13).[35] The harmonic language is complex, and it includes quartal and whole-tone constructions, which are also reflected in certain melodic passages.

Schoenberg wrote that he designed the third movement to "present the elaborations" that he had "restricted or omitted" in the first and second movements.

Example 4.13
String Quartet no. 2 in F-sharp Minor, op. 10, mm. 146–149.

Thus, since it serves as the "development section" of the quartet, it is appropriate that it is constructed as a set of variations on a theme fashioned upon motives gathered from the earlier two movements. Of course, it is also a setting of Stefan George's highly emotional text "Litanei." In program notes, Schoenberg noted his rationale behind the movement's structure:

In a perfect amalgamation of music with a poem, the form will follow the outline of the text. The *Leitmotif* technique of Wagner taught us how to vary such motifs and other phrases, so as to express every change of mood and character in a poem. Thematic unity and logic thus sustained, the finished product will not fail to satisfy a formalist's requirements.

Variations, because of the recurrence of one structural unit, offer such advantages. But I must confess, it was another reason which suggested this form. I was afraid the great dramatic emotionality of the poem might cause me to surpass the borderline of what should be admitted in chamber music. I expected the serious elaboration required by variation would keep me from becoming too dramatic.[36]

Schoenberg's setting of the poem is, nevertheless, quite dramatic. Yet the movement is extremely cohesive and the motives taken from the earlier movements are varied and transformed in dynamic fashion throughout. The movement is in E-flat minor, which is reiterated throughout the movement and outlined by the motive that begins the theme. This motive is stated at the same pitch in the theme and each of its five variations. The coda and postlude, in which the quoted motives are treated more freely, also begin with E-flat minor triads.

The final movement uses aspects of sonata form to provide absolute musical shape to the setting of George's "Entrückung." Exposition, Development, and Recapitulation form the backdrop for the text setting, which is introduced by an instrumental introduction and followed by an instrumental coda. The body of the movement and the coda use F-sharp major as a recurring tonal focus, al-

Example 4.14a
String Quartet no. 2 in F-sharp Minor, op. 10, mm. 106–113.

though the F-sharp triad is used more as a repeating, referential sonority than as an elegantly-prepared tonic. The introduction does not establish a key of any kind, and Schoenberg intended it as a musical illustration of the first line of the poem, "I feel the air of another planet."

[It] begins with an introduction, depicting the departure from earth to another planet. The visionary poet here foretold sensations, which perhaps soon will be affirmed. Becoming relieved from gravitation—passing through clouds into thinner and thinner air, forgetting all the troubles of life on earth—that is attempted to be illustrated in this introduction.[37]

This fourth movement is as succinct, motivically, as the earlier movements, and the motivic developments are keyed to the text. As Schoenberg put it, the development section "elaborates fractions of previous thematic material, continuously illustrating, with leitmotival technique, every expression of the poem."[38] Schoenberg also uses contrapuntal techniques to great effect in the movement, such as at the beginning of the recapitulation, where the two primary themes of the exposition are superimposed. The harmonic language, however, is less traditional than in the previous movements. Although F-sharp returns periodically, most of the work is so chromatic that there are very few harmonic progressions that pertain to F-sharp.

CONCLUSION

Clearly Schoenberg favored the musical complexity that is the hallmark of the Second String Quartet, but the density and difficulty of this music was not gratuitous. Instead Schoenberg wrote the music that he felt his artistic conscience compelled him to write. Stylistically this music is a distillation of certain traits found in his earlier works. Thus the asymmetrical phrasing and prose-style rhythms, motivic conciseness (via motivic development and transformation),

Example 4.14b
String Quartet no. 2 in F-sharp Minor, op. 10, mm. 123–129.

dense polyphonic textures, chromaticism, and linear nature that colored his earlier works now dominate. In the course of the first style period, however, the overriding importance of classical tonality gradually diminished and, although the Second String Quartet is nominally tonal, its tonality is expressed through the referential return of the tonic rather than through the elaborate, all-encompassing tonal relationships that defined earlier tonal works. In this new style, where the importance of tonality is lessened, the importance of the motive, in linear and harmonic usages, is increased. It is from this point that the second phase of Schoenberg's compositional career began.

NOTES

1. ''How One Becomes Lonely,'' in *Style and Idea: Selected Writings of Arnold Schoenberg*, ed. Leonard Stein, trans. Leo Black 1975 (Berkeley and Los Angeles: University of California Press, 1984), 30.

2. Many of these works are published in facsimile in John A. Kimmey, Jr., ed., *The Arnold Schoenberg–Hans Nachod Collection* (Detroit: Information Coordinators, 1979).

3. ''My Evolution,'' in *Style and Idea*, 80.

4. Schoenberg, ''Notes on the Four String Quartets,'' in *Schoenberg, Berg, Webern: The String Quartets: A Documentary Study*, ed. Ursula von Rauchhaupt, rev. ed. (Hamburg: Deutsche Grammophon, 1987), 32. See the following scores: Schoenberg, *String Quartet in D Major (1897)*, ed. Oliver W. Neighbour (London: Faber and Faber, 1966); Schoenberg, *Drei Klavierstücke (1894)* [Three Piano Pieces, 1894] (Los Angeles: Belmont, 1968); and Schoenberg, *Sechs Stücke für Klavier zu vier Händen (1896)* [Six Pieces for Piano, Four Hands, 1896] (Los Angeles: Belmont, 1973).

5. Schoenberg, ''Notes on the Four String Quartets,'' 33.

6. For a more complete discussion of the Quartet, see Walter Frisch, *The Early Works of Arnold Schoenberg, 1893–1908* (Berkeley: University of California Press, 1993), 32–47.

7. These songs are published: Schoenberg, *7 Early Songs*, ed. Leonard Stein (London: Faber and Faber, 1987).

8. Schoenberg, "Notes on the Four String Quartets," 33.

9. Schoenberg, *Structural Functions of Harmony*, ed. Leonard Stein, rev. ed. (New York: Norton, 1969), 125–126.

10. Schoenberg to Dehmel, 13 December 1912, in *Arnold Schoenberg: Letters*, ed. Erwin Stein, trans. Eithne Wilkins and Ernst Kaiser (Berkeley and Los Angeles University of California Press, 1987), 35. On the Dehmel-Schoenberg connection, see also Frisch, *The Early Works of Arnold Schoenberg*, 79–108.

11. Alexander Zemlinsky, "Jugenderinnerungen," in *Arnold Schönberg zum 60. Geburtstag* (Vienna: Universal, 1934), 34.

12. "My Evolution," in *Style and Idea*, 80–81.

13. "Heart and Brain in Music," in *Style and Idea*, 55–56.

14. See also Alban Berg, *Gurrelieder Guide*, trans. Mark DeVoto, *Journal of the Arnold Schoenberg Institute* 16 (1993), 24–235.

15. Schoenberg, "Foreword to a Broadcast Recording of *Pelleas and Melisande* (1950)," in *The Music of Arnold Schoenberg*, vol. 2 (New York: Columbia Records, 1963), [2].

16. Schoenberg, "Analysis: Pelleas and Melisande," program notes for the recording *Pelleas and Melisande: Symphonic Poem* (New York: Capitol, 1950).

17. Alban Berg, "Pelleas and Melisande Guide," trans. Mark DeVoto, *Journal of the Arnold Schoenberg Institute* 16 (1993), 270–292.

18. See also Berg, "Pelleas and Melisande Guide," and Frisch, *The Early Works of Arnold Schoenberg*, 160–169.

19. Schoenberg, *Theory of Harmony*, trans. Roy E. Carter (Berkeley: University of California Press, 1978), 399–400.

20. Schoenberg, "Notes on the Four String Quartets," 33.

21. Dika Newlin, *Schoenberg Remembered: Diaries and Recollections, 1938–1976* (New York: Pendragon, 1980), 192–193.

22. The program is translated in *Schoenberg, Berg, Webern*, ed. von Rauchhaupt, 236–237.

23. Schoenberg, *Fundamentals of Musical Composition*, ed. Gerald Strang and Leonard Stein (New York: St. Martin's, 1967), 94–95.

24. Schoenberg, "Notes on the Four String Quartets," 33.

25. Alban Berg, "Why Is Schoenberg's Music So Difficult to Understand?" in Willi Reich, ed. *Alban Berg*, trans. Cornelius Cardew (New York: Harcourt, Brace, and World, 1965), 189–204.

26. See also Frisch, *The Early Works of Arnold Schoenberg*, 195–201.

27. Schoenberg, "Notes on the Four String Quartets," 33.

28. "My Evolution," in *Style and Idea*, 84.

29. Schoenberg, *Theory of Harmony*, 403–404.

30. "My Evolution," in *Style and Idea*, 86.

31. Malcolm MacDonald, *Schoenberg* (London: Dent, 1976), 7.

32. Schoenberg, "Notes on the Four String Quartets," 42.

33. This view of the movement originates with Frisch, *The Early Works of Arnold Schoenberg*, 258–263.

34. Schoenberg, "Notes on the Four String Quartets," 44.

35. Ibid., 47.

36. Ibid., 50.

37. Ibid., 55.

38. Ibid., 57.

5

The Atonal Period in Schoenberg's Music

Leonard Stein

The term "atonality" has been used so extensively in twentieth-century music that it has been applied to nearly every composition that bears no key signature, that is, as an antonym to "tonality." Aware of its negative connotation, Schoenberg avoided its use as much as possible, preferring instead, "pantonal," as implying a relationship among all keys. In a general way the term, atonal, has been applied by theorists and historians to any composition that meets any of the following conditions: 1) possessing no central tonality, 2) treating its dissonances like consonances, thus requiring no preparation or resolution, 3) constructing its harmonies mainly by intervals other than thirds, that is, by nontriadic means, 4) not basing its closures, or cadences, on the usual harmonic or melodic progressions (such as subdominant, dominant, tonic). It is, of course, possible that any one of these factors can be found in tonal compositions, including the early works of Schoenberg and those of his immediate predecessors from the time of Wagner. Such symptoms as extensive chromaticism, which appear in the operas of Wagner and Richard Strauss and produces a tendency toward "perpetual" modulation, defer a tonic key for considerable lengths of time. Similar characteristics appear also in the tonal works of Schoenberg, where, in addition, there are specific examples of unresolved dissonances (for instance, in the String Quartet no. 2 in F-sharp Minor, op. 10) and of themes built out of fourth-chords (as in the Chamber Symphony no. 1 in E Major, op. 9) which tend to undermine the efficacy of tonality, thus subverting the dominating role it had acquired in the music of the preceding two centuries.

However, all of Schoenberg's compositions up through the Second Quartet and the Two Songs, op. 14, both written during 1907 and 1908, either have key signatures or end on harmonies that are analyzable within the range of tonal cadential progressions. Of course there are anomalies within these works that were confusing even to Schoenberg himself, who conceded, for example, that much of the last movement of the Second Quartet "suspends" tonality, referring to it only at certain important junctures in the composition; or that the two songs of op. 14 force tonality into what he described as a "procrustean bed," that is, into cadences which do not follow logically the buildup of fourth-chords and other nontriadic means (as in the second song), or result in what appears to be a fortuitous ending on a B-minor triad (in the first song).[1]

Schoenberg describes those passages which foretell the breakdown of tonality as examples of "unfixed" or "extended" tonality. In his article, "My Evolution," he cites "extratonal intervals" that dominate the construction of chords and regulate their succession in *Pelleas und Melisande*; he writes also of the aim to connect "remote relations of the tonality," as in the Chamber Symphony no. 1, or of the "suspension of tonality," as in the Second String Quartet.[2]

It is in the four movements of the Second Quartet that one notices most clearly the shift from strict tonality (first movement), through the dissonant chords, whole-tone scales, and nontriadic cadences in the middle movements, to the suspended tonality in the fourth movement. These nontonal tendencies are compensated for by long codas in the last two movements and by the final cadence in the fourth movement on an F-sharp major triad. Of course, the form of the quartet, as well as its harmony, is strongly affected by the Stefan George texts sung in the third and fourth movements as well as by its complicated contrapuntal style, described by Schoenberg (referring to his earlier First String Quartet) as containing instrumental parts which "changed so fast and were so advanced that the ear could not follow their meaning," thus obscuring their tonal harmonic sense.[3]

The evolution from tonality to atonality is summarized at length by Schoenberg in the preface to his lecture on twelve-tone composition:

In the last hundred years, the concept of harmony has changed tremendously through the development of chromaticism. The idea that one basic tone, the root, dominated the construction of chords and regulated their succession—the concept of tonality—had to develop first into the concept of extended tonality. Very soon it became doubtful whether such a root still remained the center to which every harmony and harmonic succession must be referred. Furthermore it became doubtful whether a tonic appearing at the beginning, at the end, or at any other point really had a constructive meaning. Richard Wagner's harmony had promoted a change in the logic and constructive power of harmony. One of its consequences was the so-called *impressionistic* use of harmonies, especially practiced by Debussy. His harmonies, without constructive meaning, often served the coloristic purpose of expressing moods and pictures. Moods and pictures, though extra-musical, thus became constructive elements, incorporated in the musical functions; they produced a sort of emotional comprehensibility. In this way, tonality was dethroned in practice, if not in theory. This alone would perhaps not have caused such a radical change in compositional technique. However, a change became necessary when there occurred simultaneously a development which ended in what I call "*the emancipation of the dissonance.*"[4]

THE PERIOD OF ATONALITY (1908–1923)

The period in which Schoenberg's atonal works flourished was one of great ferment in almost all aspects of the arts in Europe. Various new movements in art, literature and drama, including *expressionism, cubism,* and *futurism,* pervaded the quest by artists, especially younger artists, to find new means of expression and inner spirituality. Schoenberg's music of this period is usually identified, rightly or wrongly with expressionism, a term he referred to only once in his writings.[5] But he states unambiguously his own search for a new style of expression in a program note for the 1910 first performance of his *Fifteen Poems from the Book of the Hanging Gardens,* op. 15, a song cycle to the poems of Stefan George:

With the George songs I have for the first time succeeded in approaching an ideal of expressions and form which has been in my mind for many years. Until now, I lacked the strength and confidence to make it a reality. But now that I have set out along this path once and for all, I am conscious of having broken through every restriction of a bygone aesthetic; and though the goal towards which I am striving appears to me a certain one, I am, nonetheless, already feeling the resistance I shall have to overcome. . . . So it seemed a good thing to point out . . . that I am being forced in this direction not because my invention or technique is inadequate, nor because I am uninformed about all the other things the prevailing aesthetics demand, but that I am obeying an inner compulsion, which is stronger than any up-bringing: that I am obeying the formative process which, being the one natural to me, is stronger than my artistic education.[6]

Schoenberg's atonal compositions include the following works, listed here in chronological order:

Fifteen Poems from the Book of the Hanging Gardens, op. 15 (song cycle; poems by Stefan George), 1908–9

Three Piano Pieces, op. 11, February and August 1909

Five Orchestra Pieces, op. 16, May–August 1909

Erwartung, op. 17 (monodrama; text by Marie Pappenheim), August–September 1909

Die glückliche Hand, op. 18 ("Drama with Music"; text by Schoenberg), 1910–13

Three Pieces for chamber orchestra (unfinished but performable), 1910

Six Little Piano Pieces, op. 19, February and June 1911

"Herzgewächse," op. 20 (song with small ensemble accompaniment; text by Maurice Maeterlinck), December 1911

Pierrot lunaire, op. 21 (twenty-one recitations for voice with chamber ensemble; texts by Albert Giraud, German translation by Otto Erich Hartleben), 1912

Four Songs for Voice and Orchestra, op. 22 (texts by Rainer Maria Rilke and Ernest Dowson [German translation by Stefan George]), 1913–16

Die Jakobsleiter (oratorio, unfinished but performable; text by Schoenberg), 1917–22

Five Piano Pieces, op. 23, 1920–23

Serenade, op. 24 (for small ensemble), 1920–23

From this list one can see that more than half of the works were written between 1908 and 1911, with the first four compositions (opp. 15, 11, 16, and 17) being completed within the first nine months of 1909; conversely, the last five works, including the unfinished *Die Jakobsleiter*, occupied more than a decade (1912–23). Several reasons may account for this disparity: 1) Schoenberg wrote the text of the *Theory of Harmony* between 1910 and 1911, and this may have taken up nearly all of his time; 2) he was called up for army service during the First World War, and this interruption caused him to lose creative momentum; 3) Schoenberg experienced a change of attitude toward composition, from what one may call an "aesthetic of intuition" in the early works of 1909, to the more planned and systematized compositions of the later period. Thus, although it took three years to complete *Die glückliche Hand* (1910–13), the monodrama, *Erwartung*, written in a fervor of spontaneity, consumed less than a month in the summer of 1909. According to Schoenberg's own Diary of 1912, he was ready to give up composition altogether—ostensibly because it had become more difficult to find new ideas—before he received the commission to compose *Pierrot lunaire*, a project which again revived the spontaneous spirit of composition characteristic of his earlier period.[7]

The list of atonal compositions also reveals widely diversified works, extending from short piano and vocal pieces to fairly large dramatic and orchestral compositions, with several chamber works, some with voice, interspersed. However, most noticeable is the innovative character of many of these works; "experimental" is not quite the right description, although each work delves into hitherto uncharted territory of expression and form. Thus one may cite offhand the brief aphoristic piano pieces of the Six Little Piano Pieces, op. 19 (see Example 5.9), the *Klangfarbenmelodien* of the Five Orchestra Pieces, op. 16 (see Example 5.1), the up-to-date psychological dramas of opp. 17 and 18, the use of Sprechstimme in *Pierrot lunaire* (see Example 5.2), and the unconventional chamber music combinations of *Pierrot* and "Herzgewächse." Schoenberg does not employ either of the traditional chamber ensembles, the string quartet or the piano trio, during this period but invents instead a new chamber group of mixed strings and woodwinds (violin and cello; flute and clarinet) plus piano in *Pierrot lunaire*, a combination which has had a great effect on subsequent twentieth-century chamber music.

In regard to vocal treatment, Schoenberg opened new realms of possibilities, leading from the compressed lyricism of the op. 15 song cycle, through the parlando expressions of *Erwartung* and *Die glückliche Hand*, as well as the first use of a *Sprechstimme* chorus in the latter work, to the precise rhythmic and pitch-notated indications of *Sprechstimme* in the twenty-one verses of *Pierrot lunaire*. (See Examples 5.3 and 5.2.) Most of these innovations are incorporated in the chamber and orchestral songs of op. 20 and op. 22, with their unusual instrumentations, and in the unfinished oratorio, *Die Jakobsleiter*, which makes use of *Sprechstimme* in both soli and choral parts. In all of these vocal works the texts play an important form-shaping role, as the composer points out in several articles. From the expression of a heightened "stream of consciousness" (or unconsciousness) of *Erwartung* to the ironic detachment of *Pierrot lunaire* the text defines the form as well as the expressive character of the music.

Orchestral innovations, as well, support the dramatic situations of the principal stage works, underlying, for example, the hallucinatory emotions of *Erwartung* and the "color" sequence of *Die glückliche Hand*.[8] In the process the orchestra becomes a more malleable force, breaking away from the choirlike organization of the nineteenth-century orchestra to one featuring soloistic and chamberlike components which can reflect more readily the actions and expressions on the stage. This divisiveness of orchestral means is exploited in most unusual ways in the Five Orchestra Pieces, op. 16, and the Four Songs for voice and orchestra, op. 22. In the third piece of the former ("Farben"), for example, small combinations of instruments, including some hitherto considered incompatible, are required to dovetail with other combinations producing constantly changing "colors" all at the same dynamic level. (See Example 5.1.) The precision demanded here, particularly from m. 245 to m. 250, presages many of the types of writing to be found later in the works of Webern and the serial composers. As a matter of fact, the Five Orchestra Pieces were considered purely experimental by Richard Strauss and other conductors to whom Schoenberg sent copies of the score and were not performed until 1912, at which time the work was called "futuristic" and eventually required a program for better understanding. As regards the Four Songs, op. 22, each of the four songs is written for a different combination of instruments, including six clarinets playing in unison in the first piece and predominantly woodwinds and solo strings in the other songs. It is interesting to note that Schoenberg returned, more or less, to standard orchestration in his later works, such as the Variations for Orchestra, op. 31 (1926–28).

THE STAGES OF ATONALITY

Although various attempts have been made to depict progressive stages among the atonal works of Schoenberg, one can only generalize certain tendencies which characterize some of the works at any particular period according to form, content, or technique. While acknowledging the unique character of each work, the following outline may be of help in describing certain trends within these works.

Stage 1: Thematically oriented, harmonically settled around a tone center, motivically related, repeated forms (variation or recapitulative), using pedal points or ostinatos: characteristic of many of the op. 15 songs, the first two of the Three Piano Pieces, op. 11, and the first two of the Five Orchestra Pieces, op. 16. These works, dating from the first part of 1909, still exhibit some characteristics of the preceding tonal period. (See Examples 5.4, 5.5, 5.6, and 5.7.)

Stage 2: Less systematically organized, irregular and variegated phrases, constant fragmentation, nonthematic ("athematic"), and fluctuating rhythms and tempi: characteristic of the third of the Three Piano Pieces, op. 11 and of the fourth and, possibly, fifth pieces of the Five Orchestra Pieces, op. 16. (See Example 5.8.)

Stage 3: Reduction of thematic structures to their elementary form, that is, to figures and intervals in which phrase repetition is at a minimum, often referred to as "athematicism": most characteristic of the Six Little Piano Pieces, op. 19 and the Three Pieces for chamber orchestra of 1910, but also descriptive of "Herzgewächse" and certain phrase structures in *Erwartung*. (See Example 5.9.)

Stage 4: The assimilation of more systematized and regular forms, rhythms and phrase structures, associated with earlier types of composition, both tonal and atonal: characteristic of *Pierrot lunaire* and *Die Jakobsleiter*.

Stage 5: Serialized structures, which first appear in *Die Jakobsleiter*, where the basic material is based on an unordered hexachord. (See Example 5.10); later in the Five Piano Pieces, op. 23 and Serenade, op. 24, where groups of three, five, or nine tones approach the method of twelve-tone composition, whose presence may be found, finally, in the fifth piece of op. 23 and the Sonnet of op. 24. (See further chapter 6, "The Evolution of the Twelve-tone Method.")

To summarize: there is generally a movement away from thematic structure in the early atonal works, reaching its apogee in the Six Little Piano Pieces, op. 19 ("athematic"), and then gradually returning to more regulated "classical" forms in *Pierrot lunaire* and the Serenade, which also include repetitive dance forms. However, each work, as mentioned before, is unique in itself, bringing forth new devices and techniques. Some of these aspects of atonality are illustrated in the following examples:

Example 5.1
Orchestra Piece, op. 16, no. 3, mm. 1–7. *Klangfarbenmelodie* ("tone-color melody"), where subtle changes in instrumental color on fixed or slowly changing pitch structures substitute for traditional melody; achieved here by dovetailing of instrumental combinations in a canonic structure.

Example 5.2
Pierrot lunaire, "Der kranke Mond," mm. 1–9. *Sprechstimme*, a vocal technique halfway between speaking and singing.

Example 5.3
Erwartung, mm. 145–148. Disjointed parlando in the vocal part.

Example 5.4
Fifteen Poems from the Book of the Hanging Gardens, op. 15, no. 6, mm. 1–3, 17–19. Succession of dissonant parallel chords at the beginning of the song and their varied repetition at the final cadence.

Example 5.5
Piano Piece, op. 11, no. 1, mm. 1–3, 34–36. Opening Phrase and its varied repetition in
m. 34.

Example 5.6
Piano Piece, op. 11, no. 2, mm. 16 and 40. A secondary section, starting over a broken
chord on B-flat in m. 16, is repeated in m. 40 over E-flat, thus producing a V-I
relationship typical of the recapitulation of a secondary theme.

Example 5.7
Orchestra Piece, op. 16, no. 1, mm. 1–3, 46–48. The opening phrase and its later repetition over a pedal point (in the winds) and ostinatos (in the strings).

Example 5.8
Piano Piece, op. 11, no. 3, mm. 1–5. Analysis of mm. 1–5 as a "Sentence" structure, showing that even in the most fragmented ("athematic") type of composition there is always cohesion ("formgefühl") in Schoenberg's writing.[9]
© Copyright 1910 by Universal Edition AG Wien. Used by permission.

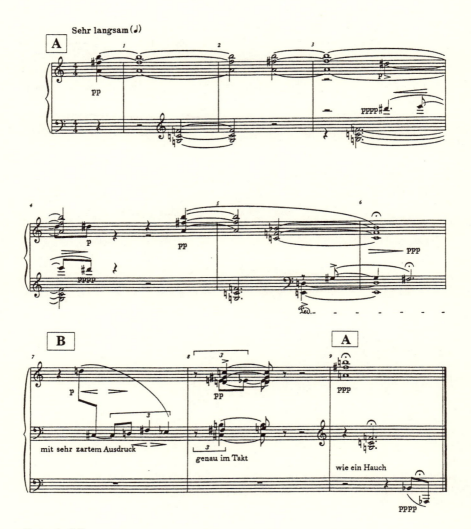

Example 5.9
Piano Piece, op. 19, no. 6. Brief, condensed, aphoristic form, yet distinctly in three parts, a-b-a.
© Copyright 1913 by Universal Edition AG Wien. Used by permission.

Example 5.10
Die Jakobsleiter, mm. 1–6. Six-note ostinato (reduction, left hand), in conjunction with
gradually building sustained chord (in reduction, right hand), comprises all twelve tones.

A CONCLUSION

"Somebody had to be Schoenberg," the composer was reported to have said.
Whether or not he was the first "atonal" composer, his explorations into this
newly discovered realm were to have the greatest effect on composers in the

twentieth century in many ways. Always offended by composers who merely used dissonances to enhance their conventional harmonies, he nevertheless felt the inevitability of "the emancipation of the dissonance," which he proclaimed in many of his writings. Dissonances, he asserted, could be understood in the same manner as consonances and could be used similarly. Yet he was always searching for new ways to use this new resource, both formally and expressively. On the formal level he sought more irregular, asymmetrical, what he called proselike types of construction. On the expressive level he delved into such matters as states of the unconscious (Erwartung), the juxtaposition of sudden changes of emotions, the role of intuition and spontaneity (as in Erwartung, the third of the Three Piano Pieces, op. 11, or the last two of the Five Orchestra Pieces, op. 16), as well as the ironies of Pierrot lunaire and the spiritual exaltations of Die Jakobsleiter. But, as he had anticipated, the path to discovering the new means was thorny and required many kinds of explorations and changes of attitudes and techniques, which occupied him throughout the years from 1909 to 1920.

It is much too facile to describe this period as one of "experiment" or as a "transitory" era between tonality and twelve-tone composition. In a way, any work may be called experimental, but to do so introduces new solutions to old problems, even though Schoenberg approached each work as something absolutely new. Nevertheless, we see in these works, despite the new techniques and devices, connections between the various compositions and even relationships to past (pre-atonal) methods. Although Schoenberg's atonal adventures pointed the way to composers who followed his examples, he did not hesitate to abandon some of his new discoveries or to improve upon others. Thus, some of the orchestral devices of the Five Orchestra Pieces, op. 16, particularly of the third piece, were eagerly embraced by later composers, but either abandoned or only subtly incorporated by Schoenberg in his later works for orchestra. On the other hand, Sprechstimme (and speech) was to play a more and more prominent role in such later works as the opera Moses und Aron and the last choral works.

In regard to the claim made by many historians that the atonal period was essentially one of "transition," leading from the tonal works up to 1908 to the first twelve-tone compositions of 1921 (single movements of the Five Piano Pieces, op. 23, and the Serenade, op. 24, and the Prelude of the Suite for Piano, op. 25), one may assert that the "extended" tonal pieces of the previous era bear a similar relationship to the atonal works as the latter do to the succeeding twelve-tone compositions. Certainly the groundwork for the period to follow was laid down by the preceding period: the "unordered" twelve-tone serialism of the atonal period (actually the full employment of the chromatic scale and the "liberation" of dissonances as well as the horizontal-vertical equivalency of musical space), as evident in such works as Die Jakobsleiter and the first four pieces of the Five Piano Pieces, op. 23, was the harbinger of the "ordered" serialism of twelve-tone music that followed. However, it is more than apparent that had Schoenberg stopped composing after 1912 (Pierrot lunaire), his position in the pantheon of the great masters and his influence on future generations of composers would still have been completely assured.

NOTES

1. "My Evolution," in *Style and Idea: Selected Writings of Arnold Schoenberg*, ed. Leonard Stein, trans. Leo Black (Berkeley and Los Angeles: University of California Press, 1984), 86.

2. Ibid., 82, 84.

3. "How One Becomes Lonely," in *Style and Idea*, 44.

4. "Composition with Twelve Tones (1)," in *Style and Idea*, 216

5. *Editor's note*: "Analysis of the Four Orchestral Songs, Opus 22," in *Perspectives on Schoenberg and Stravinsky*, rev. ed., ed. Benjamin Boretz and Edward T. Cone (New York: Norton, 1972), 25–45. The reference to Expressionism is on page 27.

6. "Foreword to the First Performance of the *Gurrelieder* and *George*-lieder (1910)," Willi Reich, *Schoenberg: A Critical Biography*, trans. Leo Black (New York: Praeger, 1971), 48–49.

7. "Schoenberg's Aesthetic of Intuition," in Joseph Henry Auner's unpublished dissertation, "Driven Out of Paradise: The Genesis of Schoenberg's Die Glückliche Hand" (The State University of New York at Stony Brook, 1991).

8. *Editor's note:* Erwartung concerns a distraught woman, alone in the forest, confused as to whether she is to meet her boyfriend, or whether she has killed him. The "color sequence" in *Die Glückliche Hand* is a series of light cues, specified by Schoenberg, that produces a gradual crescendo of color from black to yellow in order to accompany the main character's changing emotional state. It links the third and fourth scenes. Musically, this interlude is a long orchestral crescendo marked by subtly changing orchestral timbres.

9. *Editor's note*: For a definition of "Sentence Structure," see the article "Schoenberg: The Analyst and the Analyzed," by Bryan R. Simms, chapter 11 in this volume.

6

The Evolution of the Twelve-tone Method

Ethan Haimo

SERIAL ORIGINS

Any investigation into the origins and development of Schoenberg's twelve-tone method must, at some point, confront a basic problem: Where does one begin? It should quickly become apparent that no simple answer is possible. Although Schoenberg was—by temperament and habit—an innovator, he never made sudden, radical changes in his compositional method. From his earliest surviving compositional efforts in the 1890s up through his last musical utterance in 1951, we can follow a continuous, restless, transformation of his thought. This is not to say that the line of his development was straight—far from it. But we cannot find a single one of his compositions in which the majority of the stylistic features is new. This is particularly true concerning the development of the twelve-tone idea. The essential characteristics of Schoenberg's twelve-tone method emerged gradually, through a process of trial and error, refinement, and modification.

To be sure, if we were to formulate a precise definition for the twelve-tone method, the task of identifying "the beginning" might seem easier. We could define a twelve-tone composition as a work in which every note belongs to at least one statement of a twelve-tone set. But, if we begin only with works which satisfy this definition, our narrative will omit essential steps in the development of Schoenberg's twelve-tone serial method. Therefore, for a proper understanding of the evolution of Schoenberg's idea, it will be necessary to begin with works which are not entirely serial.

The Scherzo Fragment, 1914–15

In 1914, Schoenberg made plans for a massive symphony of at least five movements. Among the sketches for this never-completed work is a draft of a

Example 6.1
Scherzo Fragment, 1914, mm. 1–15.

section of the Scherzo. And as this fragment begins with a theme that has twelve tones (see Example 6.1), it serves as a logical starting point for our investigations.

The Scherzo begins with a twofold statement of a vigorous theme in the clarinets (mm. 1–2). This theme consists of precisely twelve notes in which each of the twelve tones of the chromatic scale occurs once and only once. (In twelve-tone music, we must assume that there is no meaningful difference between enharmonic equivalents. Therefore, C-sharp is the same as D-flat, E-flat the same as D-sharp, etc.) To be sure, for quite some time it had been an essential feature of Schoenberg's style to make free use of all twelve tones. However, with the exception of some passages found in *Die glückliche Hand*, op. 18, and its

sketches (1910–13), Schoenberg had never before formulated a theme or phrase that consisted of all twelve tones, with each tone appearing precisely once.

Even though the theme was carefully constructed to include all twelve tones, other collections of notes in the passage are not derived from its ordering. The accompaniment, for example, consists of a succession of three chords which are not accountable to the ordering of the twelve tones found in the theme or any of its transformations. This means, that although the theme may be twelve-tone, its accompaniment is not.

The theme and its accompaniment (mm. 1–3) are immediately repeated (mm. 3–5), and this repetition is followed by the beginning of a third statement of the theme. Before it is completed, the line changes direction, and, in mm. 8–11, we come to another reiterated theme, this one consisting of only six notes. As was the case with the accompaniment in mm. 1–5, this six-note theme cannot be derived from the ordering of the twelve-tone theme.

Not until m. 12 does the twelve-tone theme return. At that point, it is restated in its entirety in the E-flat clarinet, transposed up a perfect fourth (five half steps). Once again, the remaining parts are not directly derived from the twelve-tone theme. The punctuating accompanimental chords from mm. 1–5 return, appropriately transposed, while new voices are added in the clarinet and trumpets. So too, in the next passage, mm. 17–22, no statement of the twelve-tone theme occurs. The next complete statements of the twelve-tone theme appear in mm. 23–26, where the original form of the theme is stated simultaneously with two of its transpositions. From that point to the end of the scherzo fragment (m. 103), there are no further complete statements of the twelve-tone theme.

If a twelve-tone serial composition is a work in which a single, specific, ordering of tones serves as the basis for all of the notes in a composition, then clearly the Scherzo fragment does not even remotely qualify. The complete twelve-tone theme occurs only a few times (mm. 1–5, 12–16, 23–26)—this in a fragment of 103 measures. In most of the fragment (mm. 6–11, 17–22, 27–103) the twelve-tone theme does not appear at all, or—at best—only a portion of it is stated. Moreover, even when the twelve-tone theme occurs, it usually appears in but a single voice and does not account for all of the other notes in the relevant passage. Indeed, had we not known of Schoenberg's subsequent compositional development, there is very little in the treatment of the twelve-tone theme that would have led us to describe this as a serial composition.

Before we reject the identification of this fragment as the beginning of Schoenberg's twelve-tone method, however, we should recognize that some features of the Scherzo mark a significant departure from his previous compositional procedures and that these new features will take on increasing importance in the years to come. Moreover, there is some evidence that permits us to infer that Schoenberg had begun to formulate some of the fundamental ideas that would eventually prove to be essential aspects of the twelve-tone method.

One of the most obvious signs of his future path of development is Schoenberg's use of a transposed version of the twelve-tone theme in mm. 12–14 and the suggestion that he was considering using inversions of the theme as well. Although no inversion of the twelve-tone theme actually occurs in the fragment itself, there are, nevertheless, clear indications that suggest he was thinking in terms of the inversion in mm. 32–35 (see Example 6.2).

In this passage we see a repeated eight-note theme, first stated in clarinets 1 and 2, and answered in canon by the piccolo, flute, and other clarinets at the time interval of one quarter note. This eight-note theme is clearly derived from the twelve-tone theme. Schoenberg has retained the first five notes of the theme in their original order, retained—but reordered—the last three notes, and excised the sixth through ninth notes. The four excised tones (E-F-B-C) are not omitted entirely from the passage, but (initially in retrograde order) appear in mm. 33–35 in another line, played by the glockenspiel, xylophone, and celesta.

From a preparatory sketch page, we can reconstruct some of the compositional reasoning that seems to have led Schoenberg to excise those four notes from the twelve-tone theme. As we can see from a transcription of part of that sketch (Example 6.3), when Schoenberg wrote out the theme and its inversion, he

Example 6.2
Scherzo, mm. 32–35.

noticed an interesting property: the sixth through ninth notes of the theme (E-F-B-C) occur in reverse order (C-B-F-E) in the inversion. Schoenberg marked this relationship with a bracket. (In fact, five notes are held invariant, but he seems to have been interested in exploiting only the four.) What Schoenberg has done here is to make a first tentative step toward the exploitation of what would become a fundamental aspect of his treatment of the twelve-tone system—what theorists have named ''invariance.'' Twelve-tone invariance can be defined simply as some musical relationship (e.g., a pair of pitch classes)[1] that is held in common between two different forms of the same set. In the present case, Schoenberg worked with two specific forms of the original twelve-tone theme—the theme itself and that inversion which begins with the same opening pitch class (D). As Schoenberg noticed, this particular inversion holds a four-note segment, E-F-B-C (the sixth through ninth notes of the twelve-tone theme), invariant but in retrograde order. Therefore, we can deduce that the eight-note theme was formulated in order to exploit the property of the twelve-tone theme that holds a segment invariant in the inversional form.

Since this is a never-completed fragment, we do not know precisely how Schoenberg would have used the invariant property in the Scherzo itself, had

Example 6.3
Scherzo, excerpt from sketch.

he finished the work. Nevertheless, its presence in this sketch demonstrates that one of the most important features of Schoenberg's serial technique can be traced back to this earliest surviving layer of his twelve-tone writing.

The sketch pages associated with this fragment demonstrate the emergence of another idea that will be essential for the development of the twelve-tone serial idea. One of the most important features that distinguishes the twelve-tone method from its historical forerunners was the treatment of the twelve-tone set as an abstract referential idea, not merely as a concrete theme. From the 1914 Scherzo fragment itself there is no real evidence to show that Schoenberg's conception of the twelve-tone theme differed from the treatment of themes in the compositions of his predecessors. Every time the twelve-tone theme is stated, it is with precisely the same contour, rhythm, metric placement, and articulation.

But in an associated sketch, there are indications that suggest Schoenberg was making a tentative first step toward the treatment of the twelve-tone set as an abstract, referential idea and not merely as a concrete theme (see Example 6.4).

In this sketch, he takes the twelve-tone set and restates it as a succession of three-note chords, serving as the accompaniment for another linear statement of the twelve-tone theme. This suggests that the chordal and the linear versions of the theme may best be described as two different realizations of a single, abstract referential idea—a specific ordering of the twelve tones.

Obviously, repetition, inversion, retrograde, transposition, and their combinations are operations that had existed in music long before Schoenberg. But there is something fundamentally different about the way in which Schoenberg came to treat and think of these operations in his twelve-tone method. In earlier centuries, a restatement of a theme (or a transposition or inversion, etc., of that theme) that did not preserve the rhythm and contour of the original would not have been considered closely related to the original and surely would not have been thought of as a repetition (or transposition, etc.). Serial operations, by contrast, have no such presupposition of preservation of rhythm, contour, register, or anything else—except for interval order.

In the continuity draft of the Scherzo, all of the statements of the twelve-tone theme conform to the historically determined idea of thematic repetition or trans-

Example 6.4
Scherzo, excerpt from sketch.

position. There is nothing in that fragment that would cause us to describe its thematic treatment as different from the way in which these operations functioned at any prior point in musical history. But the sketch transcribed in Example 6.4 (and other, similar sketches) indicates clearly the birth of a new kind of musical idea, one in which a particular ordering of tones would become the referential basis for an unlimited range of specific realizations. Therefore, in Schoenberg's serial music, the set upon which the composition is based does not predetermine the registral placement of the pitches, nor their dynamics, nor their rhythm.

The sketch transcribed in Example 6.4 also presents us with an early attempt to regulate the way in which one might combine different twelve-tone set forms. Schoenberg stated the twelve-tone theme at its original pitch level, with its familiar rhythm, meter, and contour. He then added an accompaniment formed from a rotated version of the twelve-tone set, segmented into trichords.[2]

By beginning the accompaniment before the entry of the theme, and by rotating the trichords in the accompaniment, Schoenberg has ensured that there will be no octave duplications between the melody and its accompaniment. For all of its slightness, therefore, this seemingly simple sketch has some important implications. In it we see Schoenberg manipulating his material in order to avoid octave duplications, thereby taking the first steps to systematizing harmonic relationships between set forms.

The Scherzo is a fragmentary sketch of a never-completed movement from a never-completed symphony. Nevertheless, it occupies an extremely important place in the evolution of Schoenberg's twelve-tone idea. By the later standards of Schoenberg's works, we would scarcely classify the Scherzo as a twelve-tone serial composition, but it is here that the beginning of the twelve-tone revolution can properly be said to begin. The significance of the Scherzo does not lie merely in the fact that its principal theme used all twelve tones—other composers had taken that step long before Schoenberg. Rather, by exploring ways to make entire passages accountable to a twelve-tone set, by beginning to recognize and exploit the idea of invariance, by starting to think of the twelve-tone theme as an abstract referential idea, and by experimenting with ways to regulate the combination of different set forms, Schoenberg had

Example 6.5
Die Jakobsleiter, hexachordal themes mm. 1–2, 29–30, 37–41.

begun a transformation in his thought, taking the first steps toward becoming a serial composer.

Die Jakobsleiter

In Schoenberg's own recollections, *Die Jakobsleiter* was identified as the next step in his development as a twelve-tone composer.[3] This massive (but never completed) oratorio had originally been intended as the final movement of the symphony of which the Scherzo was to have been the second movement.

Die Jakobsleiter, like the Scherzo, begins with the careful and deliberate exposition of all twelve tones. The composition opens with a vigorous, reiterated, six-note figure (C-sharp, D, F, E, G-sharp, G), stated in the lower strings. The remaining six tones that complete the chromatic are gradually added in the winds in mm. 2–6 (see Example 5.10).

Although *Die Jakobsleiter* begins with the careful exposition of all twelve tones, the work is not based on a twelve-tone theme, even to the extent the Scherzo had been. Instead, as Schoenberg remarked: "I had contrived the plan to provide for unity—which was always my main motive: to build all of the main themes of the whole oratorio from a row of six tones—C-sharp, D, E, F, G, A-flat."[4] Thus *Die Jakobsleiter* (and a number of other of Schoenberg's early serial works) is based on something other than a *twelve*-tone series. Indeed, only at the end of the period under discussion did Schoenberg settle upon the approach that a serial composition would be based solely on a twelve-tone set.

Moreover, in this work, Schoenberg did not attempt to restrict himself to one specific ordering of his set. Instead, he treated the six pitch-classes of the opening ostinato as a source collection from which a wide variety of different themes were drawn. Several of the many themes derived from the hexachord appear in Example 6.5. The first two excerpts present themes that use the original version of the hexachord while the last uses a transposition.

The use of a single hexachord as the source from which many of the principal themes of the oratorio were formed marks another important stage in the evolution of the serial idea. By forming so many disparate events from the same hexachord, Schoenberg began to confront the problem of deriving an entire composition from a single, referential idea.

But, as Schoenberg quickly realized, it was not easy to reconcile his desire for unity (which was always his "main motive") with his concern for variety. At this point in his development, he apparently felt that he could not write a composition in which every note was derived from the six-note row and also produce sufficiently varied material. Instead, as in many of the works to follow in the next few years, Schoenberg attempted to find a balance between variety and adherence to serial ordering. Thus, themes and motives derived from the opening hexachord account for only a small fraction of the music of this massive fragment. Indeed, even when hexachordally derived themes do occur, they generally do so merely as a line in one or more of the voices. The accompaniment frequently has little or nothing to do with the referential hexachord. And, as was the case with the Scherzo, for long stretches of music, no themes or motives derived from the hexachord appear at all.

Yet in *Die Jakobsleiter*, we find the emergence of another important idea: the treatment of the original transposition of a set as a stable point of reference. Although a number of different transpositions of the six-tone set occur in the course of the oratorio, the opening version of the hexachord returns again and again as a point of arrival or resolution akin to the tonic region in a tonal composition. This idea, though much modified, was to be a central feature in Schoenberg's large-scale planning of his serial compositions.

The 1914–15 Scherzo and *Die Jakobsleiter* are not the only incomplete works from 1914–20 in which incipient serial procedures are present. In a fragment of a piano piece (1918) and a string septet (also 1918), and in some other fragments from this period, serial passages and sketches can be found. Clearly the idea of serial ordering was beginning to take on increasing importance in Schoenberg's compositional thought. Through 1919, however, no composition had been completed in which serial ordering played a central role. Schoenberg was, as he stated, "still at this time far away from the methodical application of a set."[5] Nevertheless, the serial revolution was under way.

EARLY SERIAL TECHNIQUES

An Analysis of op. 23, no. 2

The economic and social chaos that followed World War I were sufficient to put a virtual halt to Schoenberg's compositional production in the years 1918–19. Not until the summer of 1920, when Schoenberg vacationed at Traunkirchen, did he again find conditions conducive for creative artistic work. During that summer and over the course of the next three years Schoenberg began and eventually completed three sets of small compositions, the Five Piano Pieces, op. 23, the *Serenade*, op. 24, and the Suite for Piano, op. 25. It is in these works that Schoenberg's serial idea finally took hold.

In the period of his work on opp. 23–25 Schoenberg learned how to write a composition in which all of the notes are derived from a single serial ordering. Of course, it would not have been hard for Schoenberg (or anyone else) to write a limited, pedantic, compositional exercise in which all of the notes in the piece were accountable to a set. The problem was learning how to do so in such a manner that the result was a convincing work of music and not a stiff technical exercise.

Rather than survey all of the different compositions in opp. 23 and 24, we will look at one composition in some detail. Of course, as every one of his compositions is unique in some manner, some features of this example will not be typical of other compositions from the period. Similarly, we will not see some procedures that appear only in other works. But these disadvantages should be more than outweighed by the advantages of studying a single work in some detail. For our example, we will examine the Piano Piece, op. 23, no. 2 (see Example 6.6).

The opening phrase in the right hand in m. 1 constitutes a nine-tone referential musical idea that will be manipulated in the course of the composition. We will designate the level of its transposition in its first appearance P-0.

For many, the terminology and symbols that theorists use to describe serial music, its operations, and its relationships are forbidding, effectively deterring nonexperts from approaching the repertoire or the literature about it. In this and the following two chapters, every attempt will be made to explain Schoenberg's procedures using as little jargon as is possible. But at some point it is simply inefficient to avoid altogether at least some of the technical terms.

We will designate the first complete appearance of a set in Schoenberg's serial compositions as P-0. This simply means that the first appearance of the set is the prime form ("P"), and since it is at the original pitch level (not transposed), we indicate that fact with the "0" (zero). Thus, "P-0" means the prime form of the set at its original pitch level (untransposed). "P-1" means the prime form, transposed up a half step, "P-2" means the prime form, transposed up two half steps, and so on. It is important to remember that since a "set" is not the same thing as a "theme," registral relationships are not predetermined, and, in the actual compositional realization, up a half step (C to C-sharp) can mean down eleven half steps, up thirteen half steps, and so forth.

If we label the first phrase in the right hand P-0, then we can see that in the twenty-three measures of the composition, several other statements of P-0 occur: mm. 7, 10, 14, 20, 22. In addition to these six statements of P-0, other forms of the set appear in the movement. In mm. 10–11, several transpositions of the original set form occur: P-0 is followed immediately by P-7, P-2, and P-9. To complete the listing of the appearances of statements of the set in this composition, we see that in mm. 18–19, there are three set forms in polyphony in each measure. In m. 18, reading from the top voice down to the bottom voice we find I-1, I-9, and I-5; in m. 19, I-3, I-7, and I-11. "I" indicates that the set-form employed is an inversion of the prime form.

As was the case with the prime forms, so too here, the second part of the label indicates how many half steps the inversion has been transposed. I-0 simply indicates the form of the inversion that has the same beginning note as the original prime form (in this case, that would be D), then I-1 is a transposition up a half step, I-2 a transposition up two half steps, and so forth.

Here, as with both the Scherzo and *Die Jakobsleiter*, a significant feature of the compositional structure of this Piano Piece is the relatively limited number of appearances of the nine-tone set. No complete statement of the set occurs in mm. 2–6, 8–9, 15–17, 21—that is, in most of the piece. Even in measures where set statements occur, not all of the voices are part of set statements.

The relatively limited use of the set in op. 23, no. 2 is typical of most of the works from this period. At this stage in the development of the serial idea, Schoenberg did not yet feel that it was possible, or even desirable, to construct his composition so that every single note in every single voice from the beginning of the piece to the end was a member of some statement of a set form. Instead, Schoenberg normally intersperses freely composed, nonserial passages between statements of the set.

Schoenberg's unwillingness to restrict himself exclusively to statements of the set is highly revealing. It indicates that in the early days of his serial period Schoenberg seems to have thought of serial ordering as inherently limiting, incapable of permitting him sufficient freedom of expression. When we look carefully at the nonserial passages, it is possible to deduce what compositional aims Schoenberg seems to have felt incapable of accomplishing by serial means.

For example, the brief phrase in m. 2 is not a statement of the nine-tone set, but the phrase is clearly derived from that set. Schoenberg takes the opening phrase, drops the first four notes, then states the fifth through eighth tones of the set in their original register, continuing on to replace the final note of the phrase (D-flat) with a G-flat—which is the same tone as the fourth note of the original set, stated an octave higher than its original appearance in m. 1. In effect, the modified restatement in m. 2 is an ad hoc, informal variation of the phrase in m. 1—a paradigmatic example of what Schoenberg meant by "developing variation."[6]

The phrase that begins in m. 3 continues this process. The first five notes (A, B, C-sharp, C, B-flat) of this phrase are not equivalent to any segment of the referential set but are a rearrangement of the last four tones of the set, with the addition of a new tone (C) that had not been in the opening set-statement.

The nonserial passages in op. 23, no. 2 suggest how Schoenberg viewed serial ordering at this stage of his development. To Schoenberg around 1920, the serial idea was something that imparted potential unity and order. It was used to form a variety of statements of important themes all of which had as their common denominator the systematic use of a single referential ordering. But Schoenberg did not regard serial ordering as flexible enough to be usable in more than a

Example 6.6
Piano Piece, op. 23, no. 2.

few limited passages. He did not yet see how it would be possible to write a composition that adhered strictly to serial ordering while at the same time was capable of replicating the extraordinarily flexible process of developing variation that had been a hallmark of his compositional method.

At the same time that the sporadic use of the referential set in op. 23, no. 2 demonstrates how tentative his serial thinking was during this period, it is also possible to see the nascent development of a number of the techniques that eventually would permit Schoenberg to follow the set yet write as freely as before. A close examination of some of these features will help us understand how it was that Schoenberg would eventually resolve the paradox of serial organization and developing variation.

Perhaps the single most important technique Schoenberg developed during this period, can be seen by his treatment of the opening nine-note idea. In the course of the composition, the passage in the right hand in m. 1 functions as an abstract, referential nine-tone series, and not merely as a concrete "theme." Of course, we had already seen the first steps in this direction in the preparatory sketches for the Scherzo. Nonetheless, in the continuity draft in the Scherzo, the set was still treated throughout as a concrete theme, always with precisely the same rhythm, contour, and metric placement. In op. 23, no. 2, and in other compositions from this period, the set is no longer seen merely as a specific theme. Rather, it has become the source of a wide variety of remarkably different compositional manifestations. Compare, for example, m. 1 with the beginning of m. 7. Unlike the Scherzo, here the two statements of P-0 could not reasonably be regarded as two statements of the same "theme." The relative registral placement of the notes (the contour) and the metric placement are completely different in the two statements. Instead both of these passages are better thought of as specific realizations of an abstract, referential, compositional idea: an ordered succession of intervals. The development of the idea that a set was not a theme was one of the most essential steps in the evolution of his method. Once Schoenberg freed himself from the narrow interpretation of the set as a concrete theme, it would become possible for him to produce an extraordinary variety of musical events from a single ordering of tones. This step was indispensable for him to be able to write a composition in which all events related back to a single referential ordering.

Another problem that Schoenberg would have to face if he would be able to construct an entire composition from a single set is the issue of polyphony. That is, how is it possible to generate all of the voices of a composition from a single serial ordering? In several passages in op. 23, no. 2, we find some preliminary solutions to this problem.

In m. 1, the nine-tone set statement appears in the right hand. This line is accompanied, in the left hand, by a three-note statement: C-sharp, A-flat, A. Although this statement is not a segment of the nine-tone set, it is related to and derived from that set. What Schoenberg has done is to extract the third note from each group of three tones of the set to produce the collection A-flat, A, D-flat, which, in turn, provides the pitch material for the accompaniment.

Simple though this accompaniment is, it constitutes an important step in the evolution of the serial idea. The accompaniment is not freely written, nor is it totally unrelated to the referential set in the right hand. Rather it is derived from it in a systematic (if somewhat simplistic) manner, and it is presented so as to avoid octave relationships between the principal line and its accompaniment.

Another solution to the problem of serial polyphony appears in mm. 18–19. In each of these two measures, Schoenberg presents three set forms, stated in layers. Unlike m. 1 and elsewhere, all of the notes in these two measures are members of set forms. If Schoenberg wanted all of the notes of a composition to be members of at least one set-form, then he needed to develop strategies that might regulate the combination of different set forms. Schoenberg realized that it would be necessary to establish criteria to determine which set forms could be combined together. In these two measures we can see some of the first steps he took to develop those strategies and establish those criteria.

In both measures, the three set-forms chosen are separated from one another by the same interval of transposition—four half steps. In m. 18, I-1 appears in the top layer, I-5 in the middle, and I-9 at the bottom; in m. 19, I-3, I-7, and I-11. The choice of the intervals of transposition and the pacing of the combinations were carefully calculated so as to produce some specific compositional results.

Schoenberg divided each of the statements of the nine-tone set into three segments of three elements each, with one trichord from each set appearing within each half-note beat in the measure. As a result of the intervallic properties of these specific trichords (none of which include the interval class of four half steps) and the intervals chosen for transposition (which are all four half steps), Schoenberg ensures that at no point will there be any pitch duplications between the trichords.

In a number of places in his writings, when Schoenberg discussed his twelve-tone music, he indicated that one of his principal concerns was to avoid octaves between voices:

To double is to emphasize, and an emphasized tone could be interpreted as a root, or even as a tonic; the consequences of such an interpretation must be avoided. Even a slight reminiscence of the former tonal harmony would be disturbing, because it would create false expectations of consequences and continuations. The use of a tonic is deceiving if it is not based on *all* the relationships of tonality.[7]

Schoenberg's procedures in mm. 18–19 show some of his earliest solutions for the problem of how to combine different set forms together in different voices while avoiding octave relationships between the voices. In effect, Schoenberg has calculated which combinations were possible in response to properties of the set (in this case, the absence of any interval of four half steps within any of the trichords dictates the transposition of four half steps; no octaves will result). The specific details would change in the next few years, but the essence of the solution is present here: a prerequisite for determining which set forms could be combined was the desire to avoid any possibility of octave (or unison) repetitions.

The passage in mm. 18–19 is significant as well for the reappearance of a feature we have already encountered in the Scherzo, one that is in the process of becoming a significant component of Schoenberg's serial writing—invariance of segments between different set forms. For example, in m. 18 in the uppermost stratum, the second trichord (in beat two) presents the pitch classes B, B-flat, A-flat. In the following beat, the final trichord of the lowest voice states the pitch classes B-flat, B, G-sharp. Unlike the Scherzo where only a four-note segment was held invariant between P-0 and I-0, in the present case, each of the last two trichords of each set form appear in one of the other set forms. The middle trichord of the middle voice, F-sharp, E, G, also occurs as the last trichord of the top voice; the middle trichord of the bottom voice, E-flat, D, C, appears as the final trichord of the middle voice.

Schoenberg's experiments with invariance, as seen in mm. 18–19, became one of the principal avenues through which he developed the techniques that eventually permitted him to feel capable of writing with "fluency" while at the same time adhering strictly to the series. Schoenberg employed invariance to effect a reconciliation of serial ordering with developing variation. Let us recall that in m. 2 Schoenberg abandoned the set in order to construct a passage that was a free, ad hoc, flexible reformulation and variation of m. 1. In passages like m. 18, Schoenberg developed techniques that permitted him to accomplish the same task—but through purely serial methods. The second and third beats of m. 18, (and also of m. 19) are serially related to one another. At the same time, however, they are variants of one another, much the same way that m. 2 is a variant of m. 1. In m. 18, the middle trichord in the top voice has the ordering B, B-flat, A-flat. But in the bottom voice, the ordering of these same three pitch classes is different: B-flat, B, G-sharp. At one and the same time, the last trichord of the bottom voice is a transposition of the last trichords of the upper two voices and a varied repetition of the middle trichord of the top voice.

REFINEMENTS OF SERIAL TECHNIQUES

Op. 23, no. 2, and the other compositions from the period of Schoenberg's compositional activity in the summer of 1920 paved the way for the serial method to become a viable compositional approach. In this important period of his career, he established many of the basic procedures that—when refined and polished—would eventually permit him to construct an entire composition from a single set, while retaining the flexibility that characterized his earlier compositional efforts.

As Schoenberg gained experience with his method in the years 1920–23, certain trends began to emerge. He gradually became comfortable enough with the serial idea to consider using it in larger stretches of the compositions. And by the end of this period, when he had finished opp. 23–25, he had finally made the decision that it was possible for him to base an entire composition on a twelve-tone set and that every note in every voice in the composition should be a member of at least one set-form. The experience he had gained, particularly in learning how to reconcile serial ordering and developing variation, permitted him to take this step. As a result, from the Woodwind Quintet, op. 26 (begun April 1923) onward, with only occasional exceptions, Schoenberg's compositions would be twelve-tone, serial works.

For Schoenberg, the decision to base all of his compositions on sets with twelve-tones (as opposed to the generally smaller sets in opp. 23–25) may be traced to the merging of two central concerns. On the one hand, Schoenberg attempted to learn how to make all events in the composition have as their origin a referential ordering of tones—a set. On the other hand, he was interested in a regular circulation of twelve tones, trying—in the absence of a tonal center—to avoid unwanted or unintended emphasis on any one of the twelve tones. By the end of his work on opp. 23–25, having learned how to make a set account for all of the notes of a composition, Schoenberg came to the realization that a twelve-tone set would permit him to pursue both goals simultaneously.

During the next few years, Schoenberg's twelve-tone technique would develop and change at an almost vertiginous pace. In only a few short years, scarcely a single feature of his method would remain unchanged. As a result it is not possible for us to examine a single composition in the hope that it might be representative of this period. Nor, in the interests of space, is it feasible to analyze every composition with the kind of detail that was devoted to op. 23, no. 2. Therefore, in the following, we will examine one or two of the most significant features from some of the compositions from op. 25–32, attempting to show what were some of Schoenberg's principal concerns as he refined his use of the twelve-tone method.

Polyphony and Meter in the Suite, op. 25

The Suite, op. 25, was begun in the summer of 1921 but not finished until 1923. Given the convoluted chronology of his works during this period (Schoenberg interrupted almost every composition he wrote in 1920–23 at least once), the Suite represents several layers of his thinking. In 1921, Schoenberg wrote the entire Prelude and a few measures of the Intermezzo. Two years later he returned to the work, finished the Intermezzo, and wrote the remaining movements. We will concern ourselves here only with the last period of work on this composition.

When Schoenberg returned to complete the Suite in 1923, he changed his overall conception of the work to a neo-Baroque Suite. The two movements already in existence were renamed Prelude and Intermezzo, while the movements begun in 1923 were all modeled in some manner on baroque dance movements: Gavotte, Menuett and Trio, Musette, Gigue. Dance movements normally receive their characteristic identity from their metric organization and tempo. If

Example 6.7a
Suite for Piano, op. 25, Gavotte, mm. 1–3.
© Copyright 1925 by Universal Edition AG Wien. Used by permission.

Schoenberg was to be able to create a meter that was not arbitrary or heavy-handed, he needed to address the problem of how to relate serial organization to meter. Perhaps his interest in addressing this problem was one of the motivations for his writing a series of dance movements. Whatever the motivation, Schoenberg faced the problem of serial meter in the Suite, op. 25, formulating some solutions that would serve as the basis of his method in the years that followed (see Example 6.7).

In the example we can see two different solutions to the problem of meter in serial music. In the first few measures of the Gavotte (Example 6.7a) Schoenberg has produced the upbeat-to-downbeat, 2/2 meter by making the final note of four of the first five tetrachords arrive on the beat. In the right hand this regularity is reinforced by the identity of the closing interval—in each case a tritone.

In the Gigue (Example 6.7b), Schoenberg explored another possible way to coordinate the meter and the set structure. At the beginning of the movement, Schoenberg forms the meter through the harmonic rhythm of the twelve-tone set. In the first thirteen measures, Schoenberg presents a statement of the set within each of the measures. This equation of twelve-tone collection and metric units would eventually become one of the standard means for the formation of twelve-tone meter. Schoenberg's usual method—as here—was to establish a regular pattern of harmonic rhythm at the beginning of the movement. Once established, however, Schoenberg generally used that meter as a norm from which he would deviate, usually returning to the norm at the end of the composition or at the beginning of the next major section. Although the most common practice would be for Schoenberg to state a twelve-tone collection within a measure, frequently Schoenberg would divide the set into its component hexachords and have the harmonic rhythm of the hexachord determine the meter.

Some of the specific solutions Schoenberg devised for op. 25 would not remain a part of his compositional arsenal in the years that followed. But if we look past the specific details, we can see op. 25 as an extended attempt to make the twelve-tone set account for multiple compositional dimensions: not only the

Example 6.7b
Suite for Piano, op. 25, Gigue, mm. 1–4.

themes, but the harmony and the meter. In coming years the details would change, but Schoenberg persisted in expanding the ways in which the twelve-tone set could function as the basic idea of the composition.

Melodic Variety, Extracted Lines, and Form in the Woodwind Quintet, op. 26

The Woodwind Quintet, op. 26, was begun in 1923 and finished in 1924. As early as the first sketches for the Serenade, op. 24 (in 1920), Schoenberg had experimented with the idea of basing an entire multimovement work on a single set. Although this plan was eventually abandoned for op. 24, he did carry it through in op. 25. The Quintet, op. 26, continued this line of thought: all four movements of the Quintet are based upon a single twelve-tone set.

The decision to base an entire composition on a single set would seem to be an obvious logical consequence of Schoenberg's interest in making the set function as the referential idea for the entire composition. Clearly, what better way would there be to aspire to unity than to base different movements of the same composition on the same set? However, this quickly presented Schoenberg with a serious compositional challenge—melodic variety. And that, in turn, was related to how Schoenberg was addressing the problem of polyphonic combinations.

As we have seen, up to this point in his development of the serial idea, Schoenberg frequently generated polyphony by layering of set forms. Two voices required two set forms, three voices required three forms, and so forth. Other methods of producing a polyphonic complex were used, but the layering of set forms was the most common single method.

This presented Schoenberg with some interesting compositional problems. If the normative means of presenting the set was as a line, and if there were four or more lines, continuously in operation, and if—for reasons of unity—all four movements of a piece were derived from the same twelve-tone set, then there arose the very real danger of an unacceptable level of redundancy. Schoenberg

a. Oboe, 2nd mvt, mm. 1-7

b. Bassoon, 2nd mvt., mm. 19-24

Example 6.8
Woodwind Quintet, op. 26.

clearly worried that he simply would not be able to produce a sufficiently varied arsenal of different melodic figures, even given his use of inversions, retrogrades, transpositions, and their retrogrades. This was particularly true at the beginnings of phrases, for if all phrases began with the first element of the set and the set was stated only as a line, then there would only be two possible interval classes with which a phrase could begin—in this case a minor third (and its inversion) or a major third (and its inversion).

In order to address this problem, Schoenberg employed the technique of rotation. Instead of stating the set in linear form, beginning with the first tone of the set and continuing on to the last tone, Schoenberg also would begin some linear statements at various other points in the set, continuing on past the end of the set and on through the tones at the beginning of the set (see Example 6.8). By these means, Schoenberg was able to achieve some variety, while still retaining the set as the referential basis for the composition.

The technique of rotation had appeared in some earlier works (the Sonnet of op. 24, for example), and its use in the Woodwind Quintet, op. 26, and the Suite, op. 29, might give the impression that Schoenberg had settled upon a satisfactory means by which he could achieve the variety he needed while retaining the unity he wanted. However, rotation would not remain one of Schoenberg's techniques for long. Rather, in the Quintet we can see early stages in the development of the very technique that would make rotation unnecessary.

The third movement of the Quintet begins with a duet between the horn and bassoon. Unlike many other passages in the Quintet, the polyphony here is not generated by assigning a single set-form to each line. Instead, in mm. 1–7, each set statement is divided between the two instruments, with the horn assigned four notes from each set form, the bassoon eight (see Example 6.9).

In the horn line, over the three statements of P-0, all twelve tones are stated.

Example 6.9
Woodwind Quintet, op. 26, third movement, mm. 1–7.

But this twelve-tone statement is not one of the forms of the referential twelve-tone set of the Quintet. Schoenberg has created a subsidiary twelve-tone set—a new line with a new set of intervals—that is derived from the referential twelve-tone line of the composition.

The significance of this method of generating subsidiary lines goes far beyond its function of providing additional (and virtually limitless) sources of melodic variety, freeing Schoenberg from the necessity of resorting to the relatively crude technique of rotation. That, certainly, was an important, even essential aspect of this new method of presenting the twelve-tone set.

But if the extracted lines were arbitrary, if the tones were chosen without any particular rhyme or reason, then clearly unity would scarcely be enhanced by this method. Schoenberg's solution at the beginning of the third movement of op. 26 demonstrates that he had begun to think very carefully of how he should structure the lines that were formed by the conjunction of elements that are not adjacent in the set. In coming years he would not restrict himself to the formalized, symmetrical plan we see in this passage. In some cases—as here—Schoenberg would extract all twelve tones for a secondary line. In other cases, he did not limit himself solely to twelve-tone lines but would produce smaller, specific combinations of tones that would play some essential role in the developmental process. Clearly, with this tool, he could extract melodic units of any size, eventually permitting him to reproduce—seemingly effortlessly—the kind of flexible developing variation that had been an essential aspect of his earlier style.

Another important accomplishment of the Quintet is its contribution to addressing the problem of twelve-tone form. Schoenberg had noted that in his posttonal but preserial compositions, he had tended to write either very short compositions, or to base the form of his compositions on a text. Between 1908 and 1920, the only purely instrumental compositions Schoenberg completed were the Piano Pieces, opp. 11 and 19, and the Orchestra Pieces, op. 16, all three of which were collections of short movements.

It cannot be happenstance that Schoenberg's interest in writing neoclassic forms (dance movements, sonata forms, rondos, etc.) surfaced at the same time as the development of the twelve-tone method. There seems to have been a significant change in his aesthetic outlook between *Erwartung*, op. 17, and the early twelve-tone works—a change from a style that had forsworn virtually all traditional compositional techniques of musical organization (even recurring themes) to the very highly organized and structured techniques of twelve-tone, serial music. Thus, neoclassicism and the twelve-tone technique may have been (at least initially) two sides of the same aesthetic coin.

In the Quintet, Schoenberg devised some of the fundamental techniques that would characterize his approach to form throughout his twelve-tone period. Although many of the specific details would change, the basic approach to form established in the Quintet would remain the same throughout his twelve-tone period.

Simply put, in Schoenberg's larger twelve-tone compositions formal regions are characterized by and delineated through, their set-form content. Normally, the opening section of a serial composition is characterized by means of a carefully limited, temporally stressed, group of set-forms. This group of forms establishes a referential region, somewhat analogous in Schoenberg's thinking, to the tonic key in a tonal composition. Subsidiary sections were characterized by the use of contrasting groups of set forms. Schoenberg used the stability of the opening referential group of sets to establish a structural, formal dynamic: the move away from this referential region creates formal instability, which is resolved only with the return of the referential group of set forms at the end of the movement, effecting closure.

The first movement of the Quintet is organized as a sonata form, with a clearly identifiable exposition, development section, recapitulation, and coda. The exposition begins with clear linear statements of a limited number of set forms: P-0, R-0, and I-0. At the same time, the accompaniment consists entirely of partitioned statements of these same set forms. Throughout the first twenty-three measures of the composition, only these set-forms are used (plus RI-0). What Schoenberg has done is to establish a referential collection of set forms. By virtue of both temporal emphasis and their placement at the beginning and ending of the composition, these forms are treated as functionally similar to the tonic region in a tonal composition. Having established the referential region,

Schoenberg then moves to the second theme group. That group, which begins at m. 42 with a contrasting theme, consists primarily of the set forms I-4 and I-9. Here, as will be the case in all of his larger twelve-tone compositions, Schoenberg has not relied solely on surface features to provide the differentiation between sections. Formal sections of the composition are characterized not only by their themes, texture, and tempo, but by their twelve-tone content as well. It should be no surprise then, that the collection of set forms (P-0, I-0, and their retrogrades) with which the movement began, returns only with the recapitulation, thereby serving to delineate the reprise and to permit closure— precisely as we might expect given the analogy to tonal form.

Hexachord Inversional Combinatoriality, Aggregates, Harmony, and Form

In Schoenberg's earliest twelve-tone works, there was no systematic method for determining how set forms should be combined. Rather, he would make various ad hoc combinations, depending on the circumstances. The one constant seemed to be his concern to avoid octave relationships between voices (as we saw in op. 23, no. 2). During the period between the end of his work on the Quintet and the Variations for Orchestra, op. 31, Schoenberg gradually devised a systematic basis for the combination of set forms in his twelve-tone music. This compositional discovery was perhaps the single most significant step in the development of his mature twelve-tone method.

Schoenberg gradually came to the conclusion that the sets he would use in his twelve-tone compositions had to have a very specific property. That is, if a form of the set was combined with a specific transposition of the inversion, the combination of pitch classes in the corresponding hexachord would consist of all twelve tones, an aggregate. (An aggregate is a collection of all twelve tones, without regard to order.) This property can best be visualized with an example. Let us take the set of Schoenberg's Variations for Orchestra, op. 31 (see Example 6.10).

In the example it can be seen that the first six elements of the set (the first hexachord) are the pitch classes, B-flat, E, F-sharp, E-flat, F, A. In the transposition of the inversion down a minor third (i.e., I-9), the first hexachord includes G, C-sharp, B, D, C, A-flat. When the first hexachord of P-0 is counterpointed opposite the first hexachord of I-9, all twelve pitch classes result—an aggregate. By corollary, when the second hexachord of P-0 is combined with the second hexachord of I-9, another aggregate results. To put this another way, the first hexachord of P-0 has the same pitch-class content as the second hexachord of I-9, and that is the case with the remaining pair of hexachords as well.

The property we see here is called "hexachord inversional combinatoriality" because it produces aggregates by the combination of hexachords of inversionally related set forms. There are other kinds of combinatoriality (transpositional,

Example 6.10
Variations for Orchestra, op. 31, set.

retrograde, tetrachordal, and so forth), but Schoenberg rarely exploited anything other than hexachord inversional combinatoriality in his works.

IH combinatoriality (as this property will now be abbreviated) has many interesting consequences for twelve-tone harmony. The IH combinatorial property results only when the two halves of the set are inversionally equivalent to one another. Therefore, when Schoenberg makes the division of the set into hexachords the actual surface compositional norm (as he does from approximately 1928 onward), the harmonic equivalence of the fundamental building blocks is not some irrelevant theoretical property, but a compositional reality that is consistently reiterated and stressed on the surface.

Moreover, IH combinatoriality gave Schoenberg a consistent, systematic basis for the combination of set forms in polyphony. A set could be combined with its inversionally related combinatorial counterpart with confidence that no octave relationships would result, as long as the corresponding hexachords were in alignment. This, in turn, meant that aggregates would result in several dimensions, between sets and within them.

One can trace Schoenberg's gradual discovery of the compositional potential of IH combinatoriality in his early twelve-tone works. The set of op. 25 was IH combinatorial, but in its first manifestation (1921) was divided principally into tetrachords; the set of op. 26 was IH combinatorial, frequently divided into hexachords, but was not combined with its IH combinatorial counterpart; several of the sets used in op. 27 were IH combinatorial, were divided into hexachords, and were used in conjunction with their IH-combinatorial counterparts, but the hexachords were not aligned so as to produce aggregates. Finally, in the little cantata, *Der neue Klassizismus*, op. 28, no. 3, Schoenberg combined all these features: its set is IH combinatorial; the normative division of set forms is into hexachords; set forms are normally combined with their inversionally related, combinatorial counterparts; and the corresponding hexachords are carefully aligned so as to produce aggregates.

Once Schoenberg settled upon IH combinatoriality as the criterion for set construction and combination, he also discovered a way in which this could effect the formal structure. With IH combinatoriality, Schoenberg now had a systematic basis for the determination of what set forms to use to establish regions. Unlike op. 26, where, to some extent, these decisions were ad hoc, Schoenberg was now able to chart a path of formal development through a composition, moving from a group of set forms, whose members were all related to one another by IH combinatoriality, to other such groups, and eventually, back to the original group to conclude the movement. For example, in op. 28, no. 3, P-0, I-5 and their retrogrades are the only set forms used in the first fifty-one measures of the composition (nearly a third of the work). These four set forms (P-0, I-5, R-0, and RI-5) have only two hexachords (in terms of pitch-class content). None of the other forty-four transpositions, inversions, retrogrades, and retrograde inversions of the set has this pair of hexachords. In effect, Schoenberg has established a referential hexachordal level for the composition, a norm he treats as somewhat analogous to the tonic region in a tonal composition. When Schoenberg first moves away from his opening region (m. 52), it is to another IH-combinatorial group of set forms: I-0, P-7 and their retrogrades. To conclude the movement, he returns to the opening region of set forms.

For all of these reasons, IH combinatoriality becomes an essential feature of Schoenberg's twelve-tone music from 1928 onward. Its effects extended from the harmonic equivalence of the hexachords to the structure of the form.

Multiple Sets, Limited Linear Presentations, Partitioning

In the String Quartet no. 3, op. 30 (1927), Schoenberg perfected another technique that would become an essential feature of his twelve-tone writing. In his earliest twelve-tone works, the normative method for the statement of a set form was as a line in a single voice. As we have seen, this presented Schoenberg with some compositional problems—in particular, melodic redundancy. One of Schoenberg's favored solutions to this problem was rotation. In op. 30, as in other compositions from this period, Schoenberg attempted to provide more melodic variety by another method: by using several different sets, instead of a single set.

Paradoxically however, in the same composition in which Schoenberg was using three different sets, he was also developing the very compositional techniques that would make multiple sets (and rotation) unnecessary. It is in the String Quartet no. 3 (and in the Variations for Orchestra, op. 31, which in typical Schoenbergian chronology both preceded and followed op. 30) that Schoenberg perfected the compositional techniques that permitted him to draw themes from the set with sufficient flexibility that he would have no need of multiple orderings.

This can best be illustrated by recognizing, that—in contrast to Schoenberg's prior twelve-tone works—linear statements of the set are an extreme rarity in op. 30. With the exception of the third movement, straightforward linear presentations of set forms are limited to a few strategic locations. In the first movement, for example, there are no purely linear presentations of the set in the first sixty-one measures, a profound contrast to the procedures for set statement in earlier twelve-tone compositions. This careful limitation on linear statements is to become the norm in Schoenberg's twelve-tone music.

Instead of linear statements of the set, Schoenberg divides the sets into segments and distributes the segments in different instruments—this is called "partitioning." For example, as we see in Example 6.11, a complete statement of the set occurs in each measure (with some obvious implications for the meter). But unlike the normative method in earlier twelve-tone works, here the four voices are not produced by layering four different set forms. Instead, in each measure Schoenberg presents a complete statement of a set form. The twelve tones of the set are distributed as follows: three each in the first violin and cello, four in the second violin, and two in the viola.

This example illustrates some other features that will take on increasing importance in Schoenberg's style. In the first violin, the principal voice, the combination of the groups of three notes from the four local set forms exhausts the chromatic: all twelve tones occur in this line. This is further evidence that the aggregate has become an essential building block of the compositional surface, articulated (as here) simultaneously in several dimensions.

Another feature that is of central importance is the pattern of how the notes are partitioned. As can be seen in the example, in the two disjunct pairs of adjacent set forms, precisely the same order numbers appear in the same lines. When two set forms are partitioned in precisely the same way, we will refer to this as "isomorphic partitioning." One of the most immediate consequences of isomorphic partitioning is the exploitation of invariant properties—in this case, we can see the inversional equivalence of the intervallic patterns. This inversional equivalence becomes an essential technique of Schoenberg's mature twelve-tone method, one which will be discussed in greater detail in the coming chapter.

By 1928, with the completion of the Variations for Orchestra, op. 31, Schoenberg's twelve-tone method was no longer a tentative experiment; it had become a powerful compositional system, used with assurance and freedom. Schoenberg had taught himself how to write with the fluency he had enjoyed in his earlier works. He had begun in 1914 with only the most tentative notion of how he might make serial ordering anything more than an occasional device, neither necessarily present, nor if present, of anything other than local significance. Gradually, between 1914 and 1928, Schoenberg learned how to manipulate the serial idea in such a way that it could be far more than a dry, academic, compositional technique. He had learned how to make the serial idea an abstract source of ideas, reconcile serial ordering and developing variation, produce invariants, make all voices accountable to the referential order, control the meter, shape the form, and above all, to write with a combination of fluency and strictness, order and inspiration, structure and expression. Having reached this stage, it is possible for us now to examine in some detail how Schoenberg used his mature twelve-tone technique in a composition. The next chapter, therefore, will be an in-depth look at one of Schoenberg's most significant twelve-tone

Example 6.11
String Quartet no. 3, op. 30, first movement, mm. 1–4.

compositions, his String Quartet no. 4, op. 37, written when he had achieved full mastery over his method.

NOTES

1. The term ''pitch class'' denotes the class of pitches related by octave equivalence. Thus, for instance, any C, regardless of registral placement, is a member of pitch class C. Enharmonic spellings are without significance: C, B-sharp, and D-double-flat are members of the same pitch class.

2. Rotation is discussed in more detail in the next chapter. See also Ex. 6.8 and the corresponding discussion.

3. ''Composition with Twelve Tones (2),'' in *Style and Idea: Selected writings of Arnold Schoenberg*, ed. Leonard Stein, trans. by Leo Black (Berkeley and Los Angeles: University of California Press, 1984), 247–248.

4. ''Composition with Twelve Tones (2),'' 247.

5. ''Composition with Twelve Tones (2),'' 248.

6. In an essay entitled ''Bach,'' Schoenberg described ''developing variation'' as follows: ''Music of the homophonic-melodic style of composition, that is, music with a main theme, accompanied by and based on harmony, produces its material by, as I call it, *developing variation*. This means that variation of the features of a basic unit produces all the thematic formulations which provide for fluency, contrasts, variety, logic and unity, on the one hand, and character, mood, expression, and every needed differentiation, on the other hand—thus elaborating the idea of the piece.'' *Style and Idea*, 397.

7. ''Composition with Twelve Tones,'' 219.

7

The Mature Twelve-tone Method

Ethan Haimo

With the completion of his Variations for Orchestra, op. 31 (1928), Schoenberg had settled upon an integrated group of technical and stylistic features that would characterize his use of the twelve-tone method for the remainder of his career. The very consistency of his compositional approach after 1928 is—by itself— implicit evidence that Schoenberg felt he had found a persuasive set of answers to the stubborn compositional problems he had faced ever since he had first ventured beyond the borders of tonality, twenty years earlier.

Schoenberg's mature twelve-tone method was relatively stable, involving the common use of a substantial number of procedures in a large number of compositions spanning a long stretch of his career (from the late 1920s to 1951). This is not to state that Schoenberg ceased to experiment with different ideas during this (or any other) period in his career (and we will examine some of the interesting ideas he explored in his late twelve-tone works in the next chapter). But it is clear that one can speak of a significant body of compositional ideas which are common to virtually all of Schoenberg's post-1928 twelve-tone works. This includes many of his most significant twelve-tone compositions: the operas *Von Heute auf Morgen* and *Moses und Aron*, the Concertos for Violin (op. 36) and Piano (op. 42), the Piano Pieces, op. 33a and 33b, the *Accompaniment to a Film Scene*, op. 34, the String Quartet no. 4, op. 37, the String Trio, op. 45, the *Phantasy for Violin with Piano Accompaniment*, op. 47, the Three Songs, op. 48, the Prelude to the *Genesis* Suite, op. 44, the *Ode to Napoleon Buonaparte*, op. 41, the *Survivor from Warsaw*, op. 46, and a number of other shorter compositions.

Therefore, it will be most logical for us to examine in detail a single representative work from Schoenberg's mature twelve-tone compositions. Although virtually every work by Schoenberg has some unique feature that distinguishes it from any other of his compositions, it is still possible to find enough common ground in the mature twelve-tone compositions to permit the analysis of a single work to serve as an efficient and useful introduction to Schoenberg's twelve-tone method from this period. For our example, we will discuss the String Quartet, no. 4, op. 37 (1936). After a general introduction to the work as a whole, we will confine our remarks to the first movement.

Like many—though not all—of Schoenberg's twelve-tone compositions, the large-scale formal structure of the String Quartet no. 4 can be described as neoclassic in that Schoenberg constructed both the overall multimovement plan as well as the specific forms of the individual movements with clear references to eighteenth- and nineteenth-century formal antecedents. Indeed, for listeners who are approaching Schoenberg's twelve-tone compositions for the first time, these references to the past represent a good avenue for getting acquainted with the composition. That said, however, the neoclassical forms of the String Quartet no. 4 are not simplistic twelve-tone recreations of textbook models of tonal forms. For example, although the first movement is clearly a kind of sonata form, it does not possess some of the features normally described as most characteristic of classical sonata form—notably, the second group is not transposed back to the "tonic" (i.e., the original hexachordal level) in the recapitulation. So too, while the second movement pays obvious debts to minuet-trio (or scherzo-trio) genres, the third movement to lyrical slow movements, and the last movement to culmination finales, none is a straightforward translation into twelve-tone terms of an ossified textbook definition of eighteenth- or nineteenth-century formal types. Moreover, Schoenberg's tendency to base his twelve-tone works on prior formal models was not limited solely to formal patterns from the classical era. For example, the Piano Piece, op. 33a, recalls the romantic character piece, the 1923 layer of the Suite, op. 25 reinterprets baroque dance-form models, the opera *Moses und Aron* owes much to the Wagnerian music drama, the Prelude to the *Genesis* Suite, op. 44 includes a quasi-fugue, and so forth. Regardless of the specific historical reference, Schoenberg takes great pains to make sure that the formal structure is not arbitrarily grafted onto the pitch language, lacking meaningful connections between the form and the twelve-tone syntax. Nor, as indicated, does he ever treat the forms and genres from the past as museum pieces, incapable of being touched or altered. As a result, Schoenberg's approach to form might well be described as a synthesis of progressive and retrospective elements, borrowing formal types and genres from prior centuries but recasting them in twelve-tone terms, never treating them as fixed, immutable ideas, and never sacrificing the consistency of the twelve-tone logic for the form.

If that is an accurate description of Schoenberg's form, one might make a similar generalization about Schoenberg's approach to the texture of his musical surface. On the one hand, Schoenberg's twelve-tone compositions, such as the String Quartet no. 4 make full use of the variety of colors, sounds, and rhythms that were seen as innovative in the first half of this century. In the quartet, his frequent recourse to harmonics, tremolos, pizzicatti, sul ponticello, and other coloristic devices, like his inimitable orchestration and instrumentation in other works, are—in the context of the time in which the work was written—progressive elements. So too, the free prose rhythms that often contradict or obscure the written meter were regarded—in their day—as modern, and even today frequently serve as a barrier to listeners unfamiliar with (or unsympathetic to) the idioms of the first half of the twentieth century. On the other hand, in many ways the texture of his twelve-tone works is rather conventional and conservative, generally articulating the musical surface into two strands: a principal line (usually marked *Hauptstimme*, i.e., "principal voice") supported by an accompaniment. In addition, Schoenberg generally maintains a referential meter within each movement, with local rhythms clearly articulating the beats. Thus, in the formal, rhythmic, orchestrational, and textural domains, Schoenberg's twelve-tone music is a synthesis of what might be called progressive and retrospective elements. As Carl Dahlhaus put it:

This tendency to make use of what he had done earlier in his career at a time when musical conditions had changed so much as to make such a retrograde step seem impossible was extremely characteristic of a Schoenberg in whom musically revolutionary and conservative traits cancelled each other out.[1]

The first movement begins with a clear linear statement of the referential twelve-tone set in the first violin, the *Hauptstimme* (see Example 7.1). In this statement, all twelve tones are presented in succession, with no duplications other than immediate repetitions. As per the conventions described in the previous chapter, we will designate this first statement of the twelve-tone set P-0.

At the end of m. 6, the *Hauptstimme* migrates to the second violin which proceeds to state another set form, this one a transposition of the inversion: I-5. Here too, all twelve tones are stated with no duplications other than one immediate repetition. This is followed by a further statement of a complete set form in the first violin: R-0 (mm. 10–15). Finally to close out this opening section of the movement with its linear presentations of the set, the cello states I-5 in mm. 17–21. Taken as a whole, therefore, Schoenberg has employed only three of the forty-eight possible set forms in mm. 1–21: P-0, I-5, and R-0. (These set forms are also used to construct the accompaniment in these measures— more on this issue below).

In these measures we see a paradigmatic example of Schoenberg's confrontation with one of the basic problems of twelve-tone music. This problem might be formulated as a series of simple questions: Of the forty-eight possible set forms, which forms can or should one use in a composition? What set forms should go together in counterpoint, or in immediate succession, or within a section of the work? What governs the long-range succession of set forms that are used in the course of the composition?

In mm. 1–21 we can see how Schoenberg answers at least some of these

Example 7.1
String Quartet no. 4, op. 37, first movement, mm. 1–22.

questions. His decision to use P-0, I-5, R-0 in these measures stems from a specific property Schoenberg composed into the twelve-tone set of op. 37—IH combinatoriality. The first hexachord of P-0 includes the following six pitch classes: A, B-flat, C-sharp, D, E-flat, F. Let us designate this particular collection of six tones, regardless of the order, Ha-0 (i.e., Hexachord 'a' at the original level of transposition). The second hexachord of P-0 contains the following tones: C, B, A-flat, G, F-sharp, E. Let us designate this particular collection of six tones, regardless of the order, Hb-0 (i.e., Hexachord 'b' at the original level of transposition).

As we have seen, in mm. 6–9, the second violin presents I-5. Its first six tones (G, A-flat, C, B, E, F-sharp) form hexachord Hb-0, while its second six tones (F, A, C-sharp, D, E-flat, B-flat) produce hexachord Ha-0. For the set of the String Quartet no. 4, there are four and only four set forms which have hexachords Ha-0 and Hb-0: P-0, I-5, R-0, and RI-5. Schoenberg exploits this property as the fundamental criterion that determines which set forms will appear together in any given section of the composition. In mm. 1–31, only these four set forms (P-0, I-5, R-0 and RI-5) appear. Throughout the rest of the movement, Schoenberg proceeds by groups of IH combinatorially related set forms. For example, in m. 32, Schoenberg first moves away from the opening group of set forms and introduces a new set form: I-10 (mm. 32–34). This new set form does not appear in isolation. Rather, I-10 appears in a section that includes the three other set forms that have the same hexachordal content as I-10: P-5, R-5, and RI-10. (We designate their hexachords Ha-5 and Hb-5). In mm. 32–41, these four set forms and only these four set forms appear.

Schoenberg has exploited the property of IH-combinatoriality as the determinant that governs his local choice of set forms. We know that when P-0 appears, it will do so together with, counterpointed against, or adjacent to I-5, R-0, and RI-5. Similarly, when P-1 appears, it will be stated with I-6, R-1, and RI-6; P-2 will appear with I-7, R-2, and RI-7, and so forth.

It is important to recognize that the IH-combinatorial property of Schoenberg's set would be virtually irrelevant were there not a normative subdivision of the set into two hexachords on the musical surface. Without that subdivision, all of the essential properties of IH combinatoriality (the inversional equivalence of the two hexachords, the ability to create aggregates when IH combinatorially related forms were combined, the invariance of the content of the hexachords of IH combinatorially related forms) would not be realized or realizable. However, as we can see from the treatment of the linear statements of themes in mm. 1–21 (and will see frequently in the measures to come), the subdivision of the set into hexachords is a practical reality that is constantly restated and reinforced on the musical surface. For example, in m. 3, Schoenberg marks off the second hexachord from the first by the rhythmic repetition. In m. 8, the only rest within the thematic statement in the second violin is placed to divide the set into its component hexachords. Indeed, throughout the movement and the quartet as a whole, the hexachordal division is the normative means of articulating the set. This is not to say that no other subdivisions appear, receiving local (sometimes extensive) emphasis. Frequently the hexachordal division of the set is limited to one dimension, while other subdivisions of the surface yield different, nonhexachordal divisions of the twelve tones. Notwithstanding the frequent use of nonhexachordal divisions of the set that occur in the course of a composition, the hexachordal division is unquestionably the norm in Schoenberg's mature twelve-tone works.

To this point, we have examined only the principal lines in mm. 1–21 in which there were linear statements of three set forms. But what of the accompaniment? From where does its material stem? What criteria have guided Schoenberg's hand in his choice of material?

If we look at the first measure of the quartet (and the first beat of the second measure), we can see that the accompaniment is formed from three trichords: F, D-sharp, B-flat; C, E, A-flat; B, G, F-sharp. These three trichords accompany the first trichord of the linear statement of the set (D, C-sharp, A), stated in the first violin.

The three trichords in the accompaniment, together with the opening trichord in the first violin include all twelve tones—an aggregate—but Schoenberg has not randomly distributed the nine tones of the accompaniment into the three chords. Rather, each chord is a three-tone segment from P-0. If we label the four discrete trichords of P-0 ''a,'' ''b,'' ''c,'' and ''d,'' then ''a'' is stated in the first violin while ''b,'' ''c,'' and ''d'' appear in succession in the accompaniment. Even before the set has been stated in complete form as a line in the first violin, it has been anticipated by the conjunction of the unfolding principal voice and its accompaniment.

In m. 2, the principal line continues on to the second trichord of P-0 (''b''), while the set is completed in the accompaniment (trichords ''c,'' ''d,'' ''a''); the third trichord of P-0 (''c,'' m. 5) is accompanied by trichords ''d,'' ''a,'' and ''b''; the linear statement of P-0 is completed in mm. 4–6 (trichord ''d''), with trichords ''a,'' ''b,'' and ''c'' in the accompaniment.

The procedure by which Schoenberg generated the accompaniment in m. 1 for the opening statement of P-0 is followed throughout the opening, expository section of the movement (mm. 1–21). For each trichord that appears in the linear statements of the twelve-tone sets in the principal line, the remaining three trichords that complete the operative set form are stated as chords in the accompaniment. As a result, the referential twelve-tone set appears simultaneously in two dimensions. On the one hand, the set is stated in its most unambiguous form—as a linear succession of tones, presented in a single instrument as the principal line. On the other hand, another, less rigorously ordered version of that same twelve-tone set results from the intersection of the trichordal segments of the principal line together with the relevant accompaniment. Here is one (but by no means the only) method that Schoenberg employed to produce a complete musical structure, with all elements on the surface members of at least one twelve-tone set. The notes in the principal lines play two roles. They are components of the gradually unfolding statements of the twelve-tone set occurring in the principal line; at the same time, each trichord is a component of the local statements of the twelve-tone set. The twelve-tone set appears as a two-dimensional musical idea, creating a hierarchical twelve-tone structure.

As we have seen, in the opening, expository section of the movement (mm. 1–21), Schoenberg has formed the themes in the principal lines from a succession of linear statements of the set. The practice of presenting a linear-thematic statement of the twelve-tone set at or very near the beginning of the composition is a common feature of Schoenberg's mature twelve-tone method. (However, not infrequently, as in the Variations for Orchestra, op. 31, and in *Moses und Aron*, the first linear-thematic statement does not occur at the very beginning of the work but follows a clearly articulated introduction.) Often—as here—Schoenberg begins the composition not just with a single statement of the referential set, but with all or most of the group of four IH combinatorially related set forms. After the initial linear statements of the referential twelve-tone set, linear statements are not the norm and instead tend to be reserved for the articulation of important structural points in the work. In the present case, after the linear-thematic statements of the set in mm. 1–21 (and further statements in mm. 21–24 in which the linear presentation of the set is gradually fragmented), there are no more purely linear statements of the set until m. 63—nearly forty measures later.

If the set is not stated in linear form in a single part, then clearly it will have to be divided up (partitioned) into segments which are then assigned to different lines—that is "polyphonic partitioning." For example, if one were writing a duet, one could place one tone from the set in one voice and the remaining eleven in the other voice. Or, one could place two tones in the top voice, and ten in the other, or three in one, nine in the other, and so forth. There are seventy-seven different ways a twelve-tone set can be partitioned, ranging from all twelve tones in a single line (as we saw in the principal line in the opening twenty-one measures of the movement), through six possible duets, twelve three-voice partitions, seventeen four-voice partitions, on to a single twelve-voice partition of the twelve-tone set (a twelve-tone chord).

This is a large number of possibilities. But even this does not begin to give a comprehensive picture of the vast number of potential compositional realizations of the seventy-seven possible partitions of a twelve-tone set. For example, as stated above, six of the seventy-seven partitions divide the set into two segments (for our purposes, two voices): $1 + 11$ (i.e., one tone in one voice, eleven in the other), $2 + 10$, $3 + 9$, $4 + 8$, $5 + 7$, and $6 + 6$. There are twelve possible specific compositional realizations of the first of these partitions alone (i.e., the single tone in the top voice could be the first note of the twelve-tone set, or the second, or the third, etc., with the remaining eleven tones assigned to the lower voice). There are sixty-five possible compositional realizations of the $2 + 10$ partitioning (i.e., the two tones assigned to the upper voice could be the first two tones of the set, or they could be the first and third, of the first and fourth, the first and fifth . . . the first and twelfth, the second and third, etc.). There are 220 possible compositional realizations of the 3 + 9 partitioning, and so forth. Each specific order-number realization of each of the seventy-seven partitions will yield a different succession of intervals within the segments.

Clearly there are more than enough possible compositional realizations of partitions for a composer to use. The problem is not the possible number of choices but how to determine which partitioning and which order number patterns should be selected and why.

For example, let us say that we divide the twelve-tone set into two six-element segments and assign six tones each to two voices. If we were to do this by assigning the first six tones (the first hexachord) to one voice and the remaining six tones (the second hexachord) to the other voice, then this particular realization of the 6 + 6 partitioning might seem reasonable enough, a logical extension of the twelve-tone serial idea.

But what if the six tones assigned to the top voice were not successive elements from the set? What if Schoenberg were not to pick the first six tones (order positions 0, 1, 2, 3, 4, 5) and assign them to the top voice but were instead to pick some other combination of tones? For example, what if he were to extract order positions 0, 4, 5, 6, 10, and 11 and place those in the top voice while order positions 1, 2, 3, 7, 8, and 9 were assigned to the lower voice? (And this is but one of 231 different ways of dividing a twelve-tone set into two hexachords.) Partitions of this sort should prompt us to ask some fundamental musical questions. Why this particular succession of order numbers and not another? By extracting tones (for example, order positions 0 and 4) that were not adjacent in the twelve-tone set, Schoenberg has formed strong surface relationships between elements that were not conjoined in the set. What compositional purposes did Schoenberg have in making these connections?

The partitioning described above is precisely the pattern Schoenberg uses in m. 25, the very first place in the quartet where strictly linear statements of the set are abandoned and where partitioned set forms are first used (see Example 7.2). In m. 25, P-0 is stated as a duet between the second violin and the viola. Six tones are assigned to each instrument: D, F, E-flat, E, F-sharp, and B in the second violin (order positions 0, 4, 5, 6, 10, and 11), while the remaining six tones (C-sharp, A, B-flat, C, A-flat, and G) appear in the viola (order positions 1, 2, 3, 7, 8, 9).

As we have seen, there are many possible extractions that Schoenberg could have made of six tones (231 pairs of hexachords). Why did he choose this particular pair of hexachords?

To suggest a possible answer for this question, we need to look past m. 25 to m. 26. In m. 26, Schoenberg continues the duet in the second violin and viola with a statement of I-5. Here too, the set form is not stated as a single line. Instead, as was the case with P-0, Schoenberg extracts six tones from the set (order positions 0, 4, 5, 6, 10, and 11) and assigns them to the second violin, while the remaining tones of the set (order positions 1, 2, 3, 7, 8, and 9) appear

Example 7.2
String Quartet no. 4, op. 37, first movement, mm. 23–31.

in the viola. For two successive set-form statements, Schoenberg has used precisely the same partitioning. We call this procedure "isomorphic partitioning."

One of the most obvious results of the isomorphic partitioning of inversionally related set forms is that equivalent extracted segments are also inversions of one another. When we look at the second violin's line in m. 25, for example, we see that it rises three half steps, then descends two half steps, rises a half step, and so on. Correspondingly, in m. 26 in the same instrument we see a precise inversion of this pattern, which—*pace* some of the criticism that has been directed at the twelve-tone method—is easily and immediately audible.

Still the question remains—why this particular partitioning? Of the many possible ways in which the twelve tones could be divided between two instruments, why did Schoenberg choose to place order numbers 0, 4, 5, 6, 10, and 11 in the second violin and the remaining six tones in the viola?

In order to begin to answer this question, let us look first at the viola line. In m. 25, there are two trichordal figures, separated by a rest: C-sharp, A, B-flat; C, A-flat, G. In m. 26, the two trichords are A-flat, C, B; A, C-sharp, D.

Even if we were unaware of the twelve-tone structure of these two measures, a simple analysis of the passage would reveal some obvious pitch-class connections. In m. 25, the first trichord in the viola has two tones (C-sharp and A) that are retained in the second trichord of m. 26. Similarly, the second trichord in m. 25 has two tones (C and A-flat) that are retained in the first trichord in m. 26. To emphasize this connection, Schoenberg keeps the invariant tones in the same register.

Having noticed these relationships, it should be easy to see a corresponding pair of connections in the second violin. There are two trichords in the second violin in m. 25 (D, F, E-flat and E, F-sharp, B) and two in m. 26 (G, E, F-sharp and F, E-flat, B-flat). Each of the trichords in m. 26 holds invariant two tones from one of the trichords in m. 25. As was the case with the viola, so too here, Schoenberg emphasizes the connections between the invariant tones by holding them fixed in register.

As we have seen in the previous chapter, one of the most important steps during the evolution of Schoenberg's mature twelve-tone method, was the reconciliation of developing variation and serial order. For Schoenberg, developing variation had long been an essential component of his compositional method. It was a principle of composition he saw and admired in the works of his illustrious predecessors. In his so-called "free atonal" works, the technique of developing variation was used in an informal, ad hoc manner, with thematic ideas subjected to a continuous and flexible process of variation and transformation.

The treatment of the trichords in mm. 25 and 26 of the String Quartet no. 4 is a textbook example of what developing variation meant to Schoenberg in a serial context. We can see a sophisticated network of relationships between the passages. Each trichord in m. 26 in the viola (or the second violin) relates in two different ways to the antecedent trichords in the preceding measure. The first trichord in the viola in m. 26 (A-flat, C, B) is an inversion of the first trichord in the same instrument m. 25. But at the same time it holds two tones of the immediately preceding trichord fixed in register (C and A-flat), this time proceeding to a different third tone (B instead of G). Thus, in short, Schoenberg seems to have chosen particular partitionings of his set in order to allow a clearly audible musical relationship (varied repetition) to emerge.

Another feature of the partitioning used in mm. 25–26 merits attention because it is a common feature of Schoenberg's twelve-tone works. In our description of this partitioning, we have used the twelve order numbers ranging from zero to eleven. If instead, the order numbers begin at zero for each hexachord and extend only to five, the correspondences between the hexachords are obvious: in both cases, the hexachordal order numbers are 0 4 5 for the second violin and 1 2 3 for the viola. In other words, Schoenberg has chosen a partitioning that is symmetrical at the hexachord. Perhaps one motivation for the symmetrical order number scheme was the desire to project the parallel rhythmic structure of mm. 25 and 26, where the second half of each measure has the identical rhythmic shape as the first. At the same time, however, we must recognize that Schoenberg was fascinated throughout his life by numerology and numerical symmetries. Complicated and recondite numerical symmetries often occur even where there is no easy method of perceiving those symmetries through aural means.

Another symmetrical partitioning is also used for the next group of partitioned set forms. In mm. 27–28, the first and second violins state P-0 and I-5 in succession. For both set forms, the first violin states order positions 0, 1, 5, 6, 7, 11, while the second violin states order positions 2, 3, 4, 8, 9, 10. If we view the order numbers in terms of the hexachords (as we did for mm. 25–26) we find that both times the first violin states hexachordal order positions 0, 1, 5 while the second violin states order positions 2, 3, 4.

As we have just seen in mm. 25–26 (Example 7.2, above), the specific partitioning chosen, when applied to both P-0 and I-5, resulted in every trichord of P-0 sharing two pitch classes with one trichord in the same instrument in I-5. In mm. 27–28, however, Schoenberg's partitioning results not just in near identity; the partitioning produces complete invariance of the pitch-class content of the trichords between P-0 and I-5. For example, the first trichord in the first violin (D, C-sharp, D-sharp), returns as the last trichord in the second violin in m. 27; the second trichord in the first violin (E, C, B), appears as the first trichord in m. 27 in the second violin, and so forth. Although the content of the trichords is held fixed, the order of their elements is not. For example, the first trichord in the second violin in m. 27 has the pitch-class succession A, B-flat, F. When this trichord returns in the first violin in m. 28, it has the order F, A, B-flat. Thus, even when the pitch-class content is preserved in toto, Schoenberg does not produce a literal repetition; instead the order of the elements in the collection is changed, another facet of Schoenberg's serial developing variation.

In passages that are related by developing variation, a later event is a varied and altered repetition of a prior event. For it to be so heard, it must hold some aspects of the original passage fixed while altering others. The two passages we have seen present prototypical examples of Schoenberg's most common techniques of serial developing variation. In the first case, some, but not all, of the pitch elements of one collection are held fixed and a new tone is added to the fixed elements. In the second case, all the elements of a collection are held fixed, but their order is varied. Another important feature of mm. 27–28 can be seen in the upper two voices. In both the first and second violin in these two measures, all twelve tones—aggregates—appear within each line, formed by the conjunction of six tones from two local set forms. This produces a clear twelve-tone hierarchy, with the notes functioning in several dimensions. Each note is simultaneously a member of a partitioned set form, an element of an aggregate formed by the combination of several set forms, and an element of an unfolding linear aggregate.

We have already seen that Schoenberg constructed the order number pattern for his partitioning for both mm. 25–26 and the upper two parts in mm. 27–28 in such a manner that the order-number pattern of the first hexachord was replicated in the second hexachord. The similarities between these two partitioning patterns go well beyond their common use of symmetries. We should recall that the partitioning of the top voice of m. 25 extracted order positions 0, 4, 5, 6, 10, and 11 from P-0. The extracted order numbers of the top voice in m. 27 is 0, 1, 5, 6, 7, 11. As we can see in Example 7.3, these two order-number patterns are retrogrades of one another. Indeed, had we not adopted the practice of describing retrogrades with the order numbers descending from 11 to 0, then the connection would be quite obvious. If we begin the retrograde with 0, then the order number pattern for R-0 in the first violin in m. 29 is 0, 1, 5, 6, 7, 11— exactly the same as m. 27. Taken as a whole, therefore, the order number symmetries in mm. 25–31 are not only extensive, they are comprehensive—both partitions are symmetrical at the hexachord, and together, the partitions are mirror symmetries of one another. And as the partitions discussed are the only partitions used between mm. 25–31, we can see how Schoenberg has constructed the entire section from related order number and partitioning patterns.

When we turn our attention to the lower voices in m. 27, we find that P-0 in the violins is accompanied in the viola and cello by I-5. Similarly, in m. 28, when I-5 is stated in the top two instruments, P-0 occurs in the lower parts. As this is the first place in the composition where Schoenberg combines two different set forms together, and as the procedure employed here is normative in his mature twelve-tone works, it is essential that we understand the rationale for this compositional decision.

By combining P-0 with I-5 and by aligning the corresponding hexachords opposite one another in the same half of the measure, Schoenberg has ensured that aggregates will result between each polyphonically combined pair of hexachords. In the first half of m. 27, the first hexachord of P-0 in the upper two

A. The order number pattern in mm. 25–26:

```
0                        4 5 6                10 11
         1 2 3                    7 8 9
```

B. The order number pattern in mm. 27–28:

```
0 1                      5 6 7                   11
         2 3 4                   8 9 10
```

C. Our convention is to describe retrogrades with the numbers descending from 11 to 0. Thus, the order numbers of R-0 in m. 29 would be:

```
11 10                    6 5 4                    0
         9 8 7                   3 2 1
```

   (See A. above)

D. But if we had adopted the opposite convention and begun the retrograde with 0, the result would be:

```
0 1                      5 6 7                   11
         2 3 4                   8 9 10
```

   (See B. above.)

Example 7.3
String Quartet no. 4, op. 37, partitioning and order numbers, mm. 25–28.

lines includes the pitch classes D, C-sharp, A, B-flat, F, E-flat—that is, Ha-0. The remaining six tones that complete the aggregate are provided by the first hexachord of I-5 which is stated in the lower two parts (i.e., Hb-0).

Throughout Schoenberg's mature twelve-tone period, a given set form would normally be combined polyphonically only with its IH combinatorially related counterpart—precisely as we see in mm. 27–28. As the division of the set into hexachords is the norm, one essential consequence of combining IH combinatorially related set forms and aligning the corresponding hexachords with one another is the creation of aggregates.

Of course, there are other ways for Schoenberg to create aggregates by the polyphonic combination of two set forms. Schoenberg could, for example, have combined P-0 with R-0 (or I-5 with RI-5). In such a case aggregates could also have been created between the set forms. This would be retrograde combinatoriality (and when one combines a set form with its own retrograde, it is not dependent on any particular property of the set nor is it limited to hexachords; retrograde combinatoriality will result in any set when complementary segments of the set are juxtaposed directly opposite one another).

However, with the exception of the second movement of the String Quartet no. 3, op. 30, Schoenberg never made extensive use of this kind of combinatoriality. Perhaps he was concerned to avoid the near-octaves that will always result at the joint between the two hexachords. As Schoenberg had stated that one of the reasons he was interested in combinatoriality was his concern to avoid octaves, it might make sense that he would wish to avoid the near-octaves that result from retrograde combinatoriality. However, another reason for his preference for hexachord-inversional combinatoriality might relate to specific harmonic consistencies that result from the juxtaposition of inversionally related set forms. This can be seen clearly in Example 7.2. The first dyad that is struck in m. 27 includes D in the first violin, G in the viola. In the second half of m. 27, this same dyad appears between the second violin and the cello (beat four). So too, the second note of P-0 (C-sharp—in the first violin in m. 27) occurs opposite the corresponding element of I-5 (A-flat, in the cello). In the second half of m. 27 this same pair of pitch classes occurs between the second violin and the cello. It is a property of twelve-tone inversion that under odd transpositions of the inversion (i.e., I-1, I-3, I-5, etc.), six pairs of pitch classes will be formed between notes in corresponding positions of their set forms. Therefore, when a given pitch "x" in the prime version of a set form occurs opposite its counterpart in the inversion "y," then when "y" occurs in the prime form, "x" will appear in the corresponding position in the inversion. Schoenberg's recognition and exploitation of this property may be one of the reasons for his preference for IH combinatoriality.

For the remainder of this passage, up to the significant change in texture that takes place at the end of m. 31, Schoenberg uses only the partitioning patterns that had been introduced in mm. 25 and 27; he uses only the set forms P-0, I-5, and their retrogrades. In m. 29, for example, R-0 occurs in the top two voices, using the order number pattern from m. 25, while RI-5 is stated in the bottom voices, using the order number pattern first introduced in m. 27. From both the perspective of the set forms chosen and the order-number patterns used, this is a highly integrated and concise use of material. Although there are, literally, hundreds of possible realizations of the seventy-seven partitions, Schoenberg restricts himself to a carefully limited group of partitions, both in the individual sections of the work as well as in the work as a whole.

For the first thirty-one measures of the composition, Schoenberg restricts himself only to four set forms: P-0, I-5, and their retrogrades (i.e., the initial IH combinatorially related group of set forms). In many ways, therefore, the opening IH-combinatorial group of set forms functions as a metaphor for the tonic—providing an opening, referential, temporally stressed group of set forms which employ but a single pair of hexachords. This opening group of set forms and their associated hexachords is treated as the referential base from which Schoenberg will move and to which he will return, functioning to articulate the large-scale form of the work by providing a comprehensible pitch basis for the form. Continuing with the analogy to tonality, Schoenberg normally departs from the opening, referential group of forms, proceeding through a number of different hexachordal levels, before returning at the end of the composition back to the original level, thereby effecting an obvious and easily perceptible closure, analogous to the return to the tonic key at the end of a tonal composition.

In its rough outlines Schoenberg's treatment of twelve-tone form should be obvious enough. The details, however, are more recondite. We can best focus on the problem by asking similar questions to those we asked with regards to Schoenberg's choices of partitioning and order-number extractions. Upon leaving an area which was characterized by the use of a group of four set forms, to what area can or should one proceed? What compositional aims direct Schoenberg's choice of hexachordal levels?

This problem surfaces immediately at the end of m. 31. At that point, Schoenberg introduces a new group of set forms and abandons the forms used to this point. In mm. 31–34, I-10 is first presented, followed by P-5 opposite I-10 in mm. 35–37, R-5 and RI-10 in mm. 37–40, and so forth. From the end of m. 31 until m. 42 (where a new group of set forms is introduced), Schoenberg uses only P-5, I-10, and their retrogrades—an IH-combinatorial group of set forms. If we assign the opening group of forms (P-0, I-5, and their retrogrades) the designation CC-0 (combinatorial complex at the original level of transposition) which indicates that only the hexachords Ha-0 and Hb-0 are used, then the group of set forms that is used in mm. 31–42 will be called CC-5, this time with hexachords Ha-5 and Hb-5 (see Example 7.4).

Why this particular hexachordal level, this particular group of set forms? Why did Schoenberg follow CC-0 with CC-5? We know very well what were the criteria Schoenberg used to choose set forms to go together on the local level in his mature twelve-tone works—IH combinatoriality. But we have by no means been as successful in identifying Schoenberg's motivations for the large-scale progression of twelve-tone regions. Can we suggest an answer here?

In much of the analytical literature where this problem has been addressed, the tendency has been to compare the linear versions of the set forms used in one area with the linear versions of the set forms used in the new area, with the comparison designed to show what adjacencies or other segments are held invariant between the set forms. In the present case, such a search would not be particularly rewarding. To be sure, the linear versions of P-0/I-5 and P-5/I-10 have some segments in common, but the relationships are not particularly extensive or striking. In any event, the presence of invariant segments between these set forms is, to some degree, irrelevant, for neither P-5 nor I-10 appear in a straightforward linear presentation anywhere in the passage. Similarly the most recent statements of P-0 and I-5 were not linear, but partitioned presentations. Therefore the motivation for the specific choice of P-5/I-10 might not be best deduced from a comparison of the linear versions of set forms.

When we actually look at mm. 31–37 and examine the statement of I-10 (mm. 31–34) and the following polyphonic combination of P-5 and I-10 (mm. 35–37), we are apt to be even more puzzled. If we compare these statements with the opening region, we do not find that the connections are particularly strong. For example, the opening dyad in the cello in mm. 31–32 (C, D-flat) conjoins two pitches that were never closely associated anywhere in the first thirty-one measures. So too, next dyads F, E in the viola, B, A in the second

Example 7.4
String Quartet no. 4, op. 37, first movement, mm. 31–37.

violin, and B-flat, D in the first violin, juxtapose pitch classes that were not so juxtaposed in the first section of the movement. It seems as if P-5/I-10 is not particularly closely related to, nor does it follow obviously from, the P-0/I-5 region.

I believe that this is precisely what Schoenberg was trying to articulate—a substantial disjunction between the opening combinatorial region and the new region, a disjunction that was emphasized by the extreme textural and motivic contrast between the beginning of m. 31 and its end. When the new region first begins, Schoenberg seems to be stressing differences, emphasizing the lack of

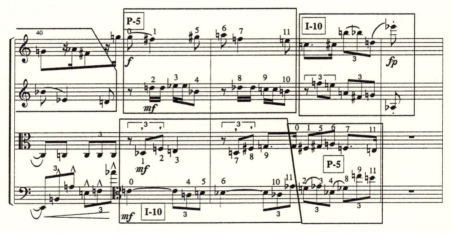

Example 7.5
String Quartet no. 4, op. 37, first movement, mm. 37–42.

connection between the P-0/I-5 region (CC-0) and the new region beginning at the end of m. 31 (CC-5).

Schoenberg resolves the thesis/antithesis of the apparently incompatible combinatorial regions with an interesting synthesis in the passage beginning in m. 38 (see Example 7.5). In these measures, P-5 and I-10 appear in familiar partitioning—Schoenberg restates these forms using precisely the partitioning that had been used for P-0 and I-5 in mm. 25–31: the 0, 1, 5, 6, 7, 11 and 2, 3, 4, 8, 9, 10 order-number patterns (and their retrogrades) are virtually the only patterns used. With this familiar partitioning we finally see that the connections between P-0/I-5 and P-5/I-10 are quite significant. For example, if we look at the first violin in mm. 40–41, we see that it is a restatement of the same part from m. 27, transposed up five half steps. Whereas linear statements of P-0/I-5 and P-5/I-10 shared very few significant invariant relationships, statements of these same two groups of sets, partitioned in this particular manner produces near-identity of the opposite hexachords. In m. 27, the hexachord produced in first violin presents the pitch classes D, C-sharp, D-sharp, E, C, and B; in mm. 41–42, five of these tones are held fixed in I-10—an easily audible instance of serial developing variation.

In the opening forty-one measures we can retrace an interesting developmental process involving a series of interrelated compositional decisions. Schoenberg presents P-0/I-5, at the beginning of the work, stating these set forms as lines, thereby establishing an unambiguous referential ordering of the set and a referential group of set forms. He next delves deep into the structure of these sets to produce interesting relationships that are revealed only by a specific partitioning, one that was chosen from hundreds of alternatives. He then moves to a new region that seems not to have close relationships with the original region. Finally he reveals that the regions are indeed related by applying the same partitioning to the new region, thereby uncovering a significant array of invariant/developmental relationships.

Although there are hundreds of possible partitionings and order-number extractions, Schoenberg has been highly concise in his use of different partitionings of the twelve-tone set in the first forty-one measures. Measures 1–21 use only linear statements accompanied by trichords. Mm. 25–31 and 37–41 use only the related partitioning described above in Example 7.3. The few remaining measures (21–24 and 31–36) act as transitions (cf. first violin, mm. 35–37 and mm. 37–40). This concision is characteristic of Schoenberg's application of the twelve-tone method. Normally speaking, within a twelve-tone composition, Schoenberg employs a carefully limited arsenal of partitionings and order-number extractions, with each pattern chosen because of important invariant, developmental, or variational relationships that it reveals.

Beginning in m. 42, Schoenberg presents a new combinatorial complex of sets (CC-2: P-2, I-7 and their retrogrades) associated at first with an order number pattern not previously seen in the composition. In mm. 42–44, I-7 and RI-7 appear in succession with the second violin (the *Hauptstimme*) stating order positions 0, 1, 2, 6, 7, 8 from I-7, then 11, 10, 9, 5, 4, 3 from RI-7 (see Example 7.6).

This passage exhibits many of the features we have seen in previous passages. Once again, the order numbers are symmetrical at the hexachord: the order-number pattern for both hexachords is 0, 1, 2. It is also retrograde symmetrical: if we adopt the convention of numbering the retrograde from 0 to 11, and not from 11 to 0, then the order number pattern of mm. 43–44 in the second violin is identical to the previous measure: 0, 1, 2, 6, 7, 8. Moreover, as we have seen in other passages (notably mm. 27–28), all twelve tones—an aggregate—appear

Example 7.6
String Quartet no. 4, op. 37, first movement, mm. 42–44 and mm. 53–58.

in the principal voice in mm. 42–44 (and, by corollary, in the two accompanying parts), the combination of six elements each from two local set forms, thus creating a clear two-dimensional twelve-tone fabric, with each tone in the second violin a member of a local, partitioned set form, and an unfolding, higher-level aggregate that subsumes the two local set statements.

And there is much more to this passage. If we look at the first and last six tones of the second violin's line, we find that these two hexachords are harmonically equivalent to the hexachord of the referential twelve-tone set of the quartet. That is, these two six-note collections are transpositions of hexachords Ha and Hb. Indeed, the collection of the first six tones (A, B-flat, D, G, B, D-sharp) is precisely the collection we will find in the first hexachord in I-8 and R-3 and the second hexachords of P-3 and RI-8 (i.e., Hb-3). Obviously the second six tones in the principal voice and both six-tone collections in the accompaniment are also equivalent to the hexachord of the set. At one and the same time, Schoenberg presents partitioned statements of I-7 and RI-7, unfolds long-range aggregates in the principal voice and the accompaniment and constructs transpositions of the referential hexachord by the conjunction of non-adjacent elements of the set.

There are still other remarkable features of this partitioning that Schoenberg reveals through his composing out of their properties on an even larger scale. In m. 55, after moving quickly through CC-8 in mm. 50–54, Schoenberg begins a new area: CC-4. At this point, the 0, 1, 2, 6, 7, 8 partitioning returns for the first time since it was used in mm. 42–44. The principal line is now in the cello, which—as before—unfolds an aggregate over two local set-form statements, with each of the local hexachords transpositions of Ha and Hb. When we look at the specific pitch-class content of the hexachords of the cello line in m. 55, we find that they are precisely equivalent in content to the hexachords that occurred in the parallel passage in mm. 42–44: C, E, G-sharp, C-sharp, E-sharp, F-sharp is the same collection of tones we saw in the mm. 43–44 in the second violin, mm. 42–43 in the accompaniment, and so forth.

But even this remarkable connection is not the final word on this particular pattern. In the second movement, the 0, 1, 2, 6, 7, 8 and 3, 4, 5, 9, 10, 11 order-number extractions are used to form one of the central ideas of the movement—appearing for the first time in mm. 290–91 and dominating much of the movement. Thus, Schoenberg has taken an idea that appears first in the initial movement and uses it as one of the principal ideas of a later movement. This, in turn, is a specific manifestation of an important general concept. In Schoenberg's mature twelve-tone music, multimovement works are normally based upon a single referential set. Coming, as Schoenberg did, out of a musical culture and tradition that frequently portrayed ''unity'' or ''organic unity'' as absolute musical values, it is not surprising to find Schoenberg stressing the virtues of unity in his compositions and attempting to realize that unity in twelve-tone works by the use of a single referential set. To be sure, in a number of his earlier twelve-tone works (even works as late as *Von Heute auf Morgen*, op. 32 [1928]),

Schoenberg—concerned that he might not be able to generate sufficient melodic variety from a single ordering—used several different variants of a set (the String Quartet no. 3, op. 30, uses three different ordering variants of the last seven tones of the set). With the development of his skills in partitioning and isomorphic partitioning and the concomitant decline in the frequency with which the twelve-tone set was stated as a line, Schoenberg allayed his concerns about the potential redundancy of the twelve-tone set and ceased to feel the need for subsidiary orderings of the set.

In Schoenberg's mature twelve-tone works, linear statements of the set are used very rarely and are instead reserved for important structural points in the form. In the String Quartet no. 4, after the initial statements of the set in mm. 1–21, no further such statements appear until m. 63, where a complete, linear statement of I-0 appears in the first violin. After dramatic changes in tempo and texture, this is followed by a succession of statements of set forms from the P-7/I-0 region. Unlike mm. 1–21, where a single linear set statement was accompanied by rotated trichords of the same set form, here there are duets of linear set statements, with added chordal figures in the accompaniment. In mm. 69–71, I-0 appears in the viola, answered at a slower pace by the cello. In mm. 72–75, I-0 is stated in the first violin, answered this time by P-7 in the cello. Finally, this section concludes with a statement of R-7 in the first violin in mm. 75–78, answered by RI-0 in the cello.

With the arrival of these linear statements of the set, we have come to an important point in the formal structure of the movement—the second theme group of the sonata form. In the exposition, Schoenberg has chosen two essential points of the formal structure for his use of linear statements—the contrasting first and second themes.

The set forms chosen for the second theme are P-7/I-0, that is, set forms from CC-7. This choice of set forms for the second theme is not happenstance. In his twelve-tone works, Schoenberg frequently treated I-0 as a counterpart to P-0. In his early twelve-tone compositions, he frequently expressed the pairing of these two set forms by combining P-0 and I-0 polyphonically. In his mature works, such a combination was no longer possible, since P-0 and I-0 can never be combined to produce aggregates between corresponding hexachords. Instead, Schoenberg tends to reserve I-0 for an important subsidiary role in the composition (like the second theme of a sonata form exposition).

In the opening sections of the composition, as we have seen, the set was normatively divided into trichords and hexachords. In the second theme area, a new division of the twelve tones makes its first appearance in this movement: the division into four-tone segments—tetrachords. This is not to say that every set statement in the second theme area is divided into tetrachords (any more than every statement in the first theme region was divided into hexachords), but it is a frequent subdivision in this section.

The division of the set into tetrachords reveals another interesting feature of the set of the String Quartet no. 4. The second and third tetrachords are inver-

Example 7.7
String Quartet no. 4, op. 37, set, invariant tetrachords.

sionally equivalent to one another, and the first tetrachord is a symmetrical
tetrachord, with one of its centers of symmetry identical to the center of symmetry between the two other, inversionally related tetrachords. Therefore there
exists an inversion where the three tetrachords will be preserved, though the
internal order within the tetrachords will change, and the second and third tetrachords will switch positions. For I-0, the set form that initiates the area of
tetrachordal subdivisions, the set form that holds its three tetrachords invariant
is P-5 (see Example 7.7). For P-7, the other set form in this region, the form
that shares the same tetrachords is I-2.

Although Schoenberg's set possesses the property of tetrachordal invariance
under a transposition of the inversion, Schoenberg does not seem to exploit this
property directly in the first movement. Among other things, he rarely subdivides
the set into its disjunct tetrachords, and without this subdivision the property of
tetrachordal invariance under inversion effectively disappears as a practical musical reality. Compare, for example, the statement of P-0 in mm. 1–6 to that of
I-7 in mm. 42–43. Although the linear statements of these two set forms have
the same three tetrachords, the actual distribution of the notes in mm. 42–43
attenuates any easy musical realization or perception of this property. Perhaps
this should be understood as a kind of cautionary tale—Schoenberg does not
always exploit every aspect of every twelve-tone property of his sets.

Although Schoenberg does not stress the tetrachordal invariance property of
his set in a stark, simplistic manner, it would be an overstatement to assert that
he did not recognize or exploit any aspect of this property. To cite a simple
example, we can see that when I-0 is stated in mm. 62–63 in the first violin,

divided into tetrachords, it is possible to hear a fairly clear connection with at least one previous statement of P-5. In mm. 35–37, in the upper two instruments, P-5, while not stressing the tetrachords, certainly does not contradict them, thereby permitting I-0 (in mm. 62–63) to be heard as a variant of P-5 (in mm. 35–37).

Having looked in detail at but a few measures, we cannot lay claim to have analyzed this movement in its entirety. Nor was that our purpose. Instead, our analyses were designed to serve as an introduction to the methodology of Schoenberg's twelve-tone technique and to identify some of the significant analytical questions that might be asked when approaching this repertoire. That said, however, we have in fact discussed a substantial proportion of the specific twelve-tone patterns used in this movement and even in the remaining three movements. This is so because of Schoenberg's concise treatment of his material. For example, at the beginning of the development section, there is a linear statement of the set (once again, linear statements are reserved for a crucial point in the form), this time I-3 in the cello. In the upper parts, we hear the constant reiteration of the partitioning that were introduced in mm. 25–26 and discussed at length above. (These patterns also return in the final movement.) Similarly, beginning in m. 116, there is a long section based on the division of the set that first appeared in m. 35 (order positions 0, 1, 4, 5, 6, 7, 10, 11, another symmetrical partitioning). In short, because of careful limitations on his use of material, for many of Schoenberg's twelve-tone works, a study of the first third or so of a movement will frequently address many of the significant twelve-tone ideas used in the entire movement.

Given Schoenberg's commitment (at least at this stage in his career) to the notion of unity, it should not surprise us that the patterns and ideas presented in the first half of the composition are not abandoned, but rather return numerous times in the course of the movement. Therefore, instead of continuing with a blow-by-blow analysis of this movement, we can conclude our analysis of op. 37 with a discussion of the form of the first movement.

As was mentioned above, in its broadest outlines, the first movement can profitably be analyzed as a twelve-tone reinterpretation of late-eighteenth- or early-nineteenth-century sonata forms. We must remember that in Schoenberg's time, the view of sonata form that was most prevalent (that of Adolph Bernhard Marx and his intellectual heirs) often called "textbook" sonata form, emphasized the role of themes—particularly the opposition of contrasting principal themes—in the articulation of the form. It should come as little surprise then to see that Schoenberg's twelve-tone sonata form relies heavily on thematic opposition. The aggressive first theme (mm. 1–21) is set off against the more lyrical second theme (mm. 66–78), and this opposition is supported by clear textural changes, entirely in keeping with the prevalent view of sonata form (though Schoenberg—ever the organicist—does transform his opening theme into the accompaniment of the second theme, cf. m. 2, first violin with m. 66, cello).

In the past half-century, Marx's views of sonata form have been much criticized (though not always justifiably) for a variety of reasons: because his description does not account for the extraordinary variety of eighteenth-century sonata forms, because he did not place enough emphasis on the tonal aspects of the form, and because the view he promulgated took insufficient consideration of the ''organic'' structure of tonal form (or so theorist Heinrich Schenker claimed). Historically, analytically, and musicologically accurate or not, the textbook view of sonata form constituted an important element in the formation of Schoenberg's view of classical forms. Indeed, as Schoenberg was largely an autodidact, his first acquaintance of any sort with a description of sonata form was through an encyclopedia article based on the Marxian view of sonata form.

In its defense, even though its emphasis may have been on the themes, the textbook view of sonata form does stress the important role of tonality in form, prescribing a secondary key to go along with the contrasting second theme. Schoenberg seems to have seen the twelve-tone system as a substitute for tonality and as a means of recreating the role tonal structure played in formal construction, so it should not strike us as surprising that the second theme group in this sonata form uses a complex of set forms other than those with which the work began and, comparatively speaking, remains there for some time. This is a translation of the idea of modulation in a tonal context to a twelve-tone environment.

In the textbook view of sonata form, the development section was often seen as the site for the extensive development of the themes and motives laid down in the exposition, and as a harmonically unstable region, passing quickly through a succession of keys, frequently extending (in the nineteenth century, at least) to keys most remote from the original tonic. Schoenberg adapts that idea for his development section (mm. 95–164), manipulating the thematic and motivic elements that had been presented in the exposition while touching on a number of different combinatorial complexes of set forms.

In the textbook description of sonata form, the prominent return of the principal theme (usually, but not always) in the tonic was identified as the most crucial marker for the beginning of the recapitulation. (Since World War II, owing to the rediscovery of so much previously unknown music from the late eighteenth century it has emerged that there was far more variety at this point in the form than was generally recognized in Schoenberg's time.) In any event, in the nineteenth century, the return of the theme in the *tonic* was not treated as an inviolable norm—one need only recall some of the sonata forms of Schubert that begin the recapitulation in the subdominant.

Given the precedents of Schubert and others, we should not be particularly surprised to see the recapitulation in Schoenberg's quartet begins, not with a return of the principal theme with the original complex of set forms (P-0/I-5 and their retrogrades), but with the opening theme restated in the P-6/I-11 region. As was stressed earlier, Schoenberg did not regard the forms of the classical era as incapable of extension or elaboration but felt free to treat them as living ideas, subject to further artistic development.

There have been a number of suggestions to explain Schoenberg's choice of

Example 7.8
String Quartet no. 4, op. 37, set forms.

CC-6 (P-6, I-11 and their retrogrades) for the beginning of the recapitulation. Perhaps the most persuasive explanation points to the fact that when the corresponding dyads of P-0 and I-5 are combined, the resultant tetrachords are identical to the tetrachords produced when the corresponding dyads of P-6 and I-11 are combined (see Example 7.8). However, Schoenberg hardly emphasizes or isolates the invariant tetrachords, making the connection very difficult to hear (particularly given the long span of time separating the two passages). Perhaps another, more persuasive explanation will be forthcoming as this work continues to be the subject of careful study.

Most theories of sonata form—whether they emphasize its thematic or the tonal aspects—stress the importance of completing the movement in the same key in which it began, thereby effecting closure. It is entirely in keeping with the parallels Schoenberg articulated with tonal models that this quartet movement concludes by returning to the twelve-tone equivalent of the tonic—the opening complex of set forms with which the movement began, P-0/I-5 and their retrogrades. Much like a late-eighteenth-century tonal sonata form, Schoenberg has constructed an easily heard and obvious sense of large-scale resolution in his twelve-tone sonata form by returning to the opening hexachordal level at the end of the movement.

Schoenberg's twelve-tone method has been much criticized, particularly by those who have seen it as a mechanistic, mathematical, and unmusical method of note generation, a system that is viewed as unforgivingly and dictatorially inflexible in its demand that every note adhere to a preexistent ordering of the twelve tones. If the analysis and discussion in this chapter has shown anything, it should have demonstrated that Schoenberg's twelve-tone music was anything but inflexible or mechanistic. In Schoenberg's mature twelve-tone works, his method was not limited to the production of twelve-tone themes. Rather he learned how to manipulate the abstract ordering of twelve tones to produce a broad range of musical ideas, from the phrase to the meter to the form. As such, Schoenberg's twelve-tone method represents an intensely musical effort to address the many problems posed by the abandonment of tonality.

NOTE

1. "Schoenberg and Programme Music," in *Schoenberg and the New Music: Essays*, trans. Derrick Puffett and Alfred Clayton (Cambridge and New York: Cambridge University Press, 1987), 102.

8

The Late Twelve-tone Compositions

Ethan Haimo

In a number of important respects, Schoenberg's late twelve-tone works (which we will define to be the twelve-tone compositions from *Ode to Napoleon Buonaparte*, op. 41, onward) do not differ significantly from their predecessors. The essential features that we saw as characteristic of his mature twelve-tone works are also prominent in Schoenberg's late twelve-tone works: hexachord inversional combinatoriality, set forms related by invariance, form articulated through hexachordal levels, isomorphic partitioning, limited use of linear set statements, and so forth. This might suggest that it would be more confusing than helpful to isolate Schoenberg's later twelve-tone works and define them as a separate period.

Moreover, by artistic temperament and philosophical belief, Schoenberg was committed to the notion of progress in the arts. As a result virtually every one of his compositions included an innovation of some sort—be it the use of a tone poem in a chamber work in *Verklärte Nacht*, the color chord in the Five Orchestra Pieces, op. 16, the vocal range and unusual ensemble in "Herzgewächse," op. 20, the Sprechstimme and differing instrumental combinations of *Pierrot lunaire*, op. 21, the aphoristic dimensions of the Six Little Piano Pieces, op. 19, the monodrama of *Erwartung*, the twelve-tone method in opp. 23–25, the gigantic scope and orchestration of *Gurrelieder*, the addition of the voice in the String Quartet no. 2, and so forth. For a composer who was so concerned with innovation and change, it might seem either arbitrary or tautological to mark off the late twelve-tone works as a special category. *Of course* Schoenberg's late twelve-tone works are different from their predecessors—but that is a truism for all of Schoenberg's works. Furthermore, Schoenberg's compositional output began to decline markedly in the 1940s. To be sure, throughout his career his productivity had been erratic, with great bursts of compositional activity followed by long fallow stretches. But in the 1940s, Schoenberg's health began to deteriorate, particularly his eyesight. As a result, there was a precipitous decline in the quantity of his creative work, particularly in the latter half of the decade. Not only did he write fewer compositions in the 1940s, but they tended to be shorter works. Therefore, perhaps one ought to be hesitant to make generalizations about the late twelve-tone works given the relatively small size of the sample available for analysis.

Having made these disclaimers, however, there are some very convincing reasons for us to think of Schoenberg's late twelve-tone works as constituting a specific period in Schoenberg's twelve-tone output, a period in which there were a number of important concerns and trends that either were not present in earlier works, or if present, were not prominent. In the late twelve-tone works, three general stylistic features become increasingly significant: (1) the interest and willingness to make explicit triadic and tonal references, suggesting some kind of reconciliation between serialism and tonality; (2) a heightened tendency to exploit symmetrical relationships; (3) the growing treatment of the hexachord as a harmonic unit, with the concomitant diminishing of the importance of a single serial ordering. Not every one of the late twelve-tone compositions makes use of all three of these stylistic features in equal measure, but as most of those works employ more than one of these features, we might well be justified as describing the late twelve-tone works as constituting a specific period in Schoenberg's work. Rather than examine a single work—as we did in the last chapter— or follow an evolutionary path of development—as we did in the chapter on the origins of the twelve-tone method, we will describe the principal trends of Schoenberg's late twelve-tone period by discussing aspects of three compositions: *Ode to Napoleon Buonaparte*, op. 41, the Concerto for Piano and Orchestra, op. 42, and the String Trio, op. 45.

ODE TO NAPOLEON BUONAPARTE, OP. 41 (1942)

Schoenberg's *Ode to Napoleon Buonaparte*, op. 41, is a setting of Lord Byron's lengthy ode on the humbled Napoleon and the evanescence of fame and glory. Although Byron's ode is formed from nineteen strophes of nine lines each (generally of eight and six syllables cast in iambic rhythms), Schoenberg's setting is entirely through-composed, without any literal repetitions of sections (though there are many passages that are obvious transformations of one another), or any clearly classifiable formal shape. A striking feature of Schoenberg's setting (and a challenge for the performers) is the frequency with which there are dramatic changes in tempo and texture—but Schoenberg did not make such changes congruent with the beginnings and endings of the strophes. Indeed, he allowed himself complete freedom to regroup the poetic lines, with his musical subdivisions frequently cutting across the boundaries of Byron's stanzas.

Schoenberg, ever the innovator, chose a unique ensemble for his setting— piano, string quartet, and reciter, undoubtedly the first time that such a combination had been employed. Unlike *Pierrot lunaire* (which also called for a 're-citer'), Schoenberg did not notate the vocal line with specific pitches (regardless of how they were meant to be performed) but used a single reference line for the reciter's staff with the general contour of the vocal line indicated by the placement of the notes with respect to that reference line. Byron's dramatic rhetoric and effusive language is matched by Schoenberg's setting, which strains the dynamic and registral resources of the ensemble, and results in a thick, nervous musical surface.

In the period of the evolution of the twelve-tone method and during the mature period itself a prominent feature of Schoenberg's twelve-tone works was the avoidance of explicit tonal references. Vertical combinations resulting in triads were carefully avoided, and Schoenberg generally refrained from extensive emphasis on any single pitch or pitch class. With occasional exceptions, he constructed his twelve-tone sets so that triads would not result from the succession of any three adjacent tones from the set, or from combinations of corresponding elements in combinatorially related set forms. Tonal references that did occur were tongue in cheek (like the folk tune in the Suite, op. 29), or were designed to pay homage to a prior composer (Bach, as in the case of the Variations for Orchestra, op. 31), or were dictated by practical performance considerations (the 6 Pieces for Men's Choir, op. 35, were originally intended for a workers' choir). Schoenberg also avoided octaves, determining the combination of set forms so that the same tones would not appear juxtaposed opposite one another (this was his stated reason for the use of IH combinatoriality), and avoided orchestrational doubling at the octave, not even permitting the contrabass to double the cello at the octave.

But Schoenberg made it clear that in his later twelve-tone music he was much less concerned about avoiding tonal references. In 1946, in an addendum to his essay "Composition with Twelve Tones (1)," Schoenberg contrasted his earlier twelve-tone works with the more recent compositions:

In the course of about the last ten years, some of the strictness of the rules concerning octave doubling and prominent appearances of fundamental chords of harmony have been loosened to some degree.

At first it became clear that such single events could not change the style of non-tonality into tonality. There remained still those characteristic melodies, rhythms, phrasings and other formal devices which were born simultaneously with the style of freedom of the dissonances.[1]

There is ample evidence to support Schoenberg's contention that, with a few exceptions, he normally avoided triadic or tonal references in his earlier serial compositions. But, in approximately 1940, explicit tonal and triadic features begin to appear in his twelve-tone works. And from that point onward, such references become common features of Schoenberg's late twelve-tone works.

For those who believe in a straight line of musical evolutionary development, it might seem odd that Schoenberg turned to the use of tonal references and that he did so at this point in his career. Suddenly—or so it might seem—the most prominent advocate of a musical method that did not depend on tonality (and a method which had been billed by some of its partisans as the evolutionary successor to tonality) began to write compositions with some reconciliation of the ideas of serialism and tonality.

Although Schoenberg never completely abandoned writing tonal works of one sort or another at any point in the more than thirty years from the time he first ventured beyond the frontiers of tonality until the composition of the *Ode to Napoleon* in 1942, there are no major tonal works in the first two decades that followed his first steps past tonality. Instead most of Schoenberg's tonal activity was concentrated in his pedagogy. Interestingly enough, we find that as a teacher of composition, he never formally taught atonality or serial composition but rather began the instruction of all of his students with the traditional disciplines of tonal harmony and counterpoint. Furthermore, he wrote textbooks on harmony and counterpoint but never wrote, or even seriously considered writing, a textbook on twelve-tone composition.

Although Schoenberg's interest in tonal ideas may never have been completely extinguished, there is no question but that at the beginning of his atonal period, such activities were a relatively minor part of his serious creative work. By contrast we see that in the 1930s he becomes progressively more involved in tonal projects that he wished to be considered as serious works, even giving some of them opus numbers—which had not been the case since the beginning of his atonal period some twenty years earlier. For example, one of the choral works from op. 35 ("Verbundenheit" [1929]) is tonal (another, "Glück" is quasitonal) as is *Kol nidre*, op. 39 (1938). He also wrote a tonal Suite in G Major for string orchestra (1934), returned to and completed his second Chamber Symphony, op. 38 (begun 1906, completed 1939), and wrote variation/arrangements of works by Handel, Monn, and Brahms (1932–33, 1933, and 1937, respectively) as well as arrangements of folk melodies. Finally, the composition that immediately preceded the *Ode* was his *Variations on a Recitative* for organ, op. 40 (1941), also a tonal composition, as is the Theme and Variations in G Minor for Band, op. 43a.

Given this background, the tonal aspects of Schoenberg's *Ode to Napoleon Buonaparte* should not appear to be either unexpected or unconnected with other important strands in Schoenberg's compositional thought. The complete picture of his activity as a composer and a teacher in the 1930s and early 1940s shows an increasing interest in returning to tonal ideas as an outlet for his serious creative thoughts and a desire to find still further ways of manipulating tonality or, at least, new ways to structure tonal elements and idioms.

The twelve-tone set Schoenberg used in the *Ode* was designed to facilitate tonal references. But, unlike his sets since *Die Jakobsleiter* of 1917, he does not hold to a single ordering of the twelve tones (or even to a limited group of orderings, as in the String Quartet no. 3 and *Von Heute auf Morgen*) for the set

Example 8.1
Ode to Napoleon Buonaparte, op. 41, hexachords.

of the *Ode*. Instead of a unique ordering of the twelve tones, the *Ode* is based
on a pair of symmetrical hexachords which are used as source collections. The
twelve tone set of the *Ode* is based upon a source hexachord of which the
following is one of its four possible collections: C, C-sharp, E, F, G-sharp, A.

Because the source hexachord excludes three intervals (2, 6, and 10 half steps)
and is symmetrical (in several ways, as we will discuss), there are only four
distinct possible versions of the hexachord, which we will label A, B, C, and
D (see Example 8.1). Because of the symmetry of the collection, any hexachord
relates to any other hexachord as a transposition or inversion or retrograde (or
combination of these operations). Given the symmetry of the collection, and
given that Schoenberg does not always combine different hexachords to produce
aggregates, one might argue that the referential idea of the *Ode* is not so much
a twelve-tone set as it is the source hexachord, two transformations of which
can be (but are not always) combined into a twelve-tone complex. Each of the
four distinct transpositions of the source hexachord can be combined uniquely
with only one of the remaining hexachords to produce an aggregate. Therefore
the four transpositions can produce only two distinct twelve-tone 'sets': A + B
and C + D. Correspondingly, there are only two possible hexachordal levels,
as half of the set forms share the same pairs of hexachords.

As can be seen in Example 8.2, the source hexachord of the *Ode* is symmetrical around a number of axes. This has some interesting consequences.
When the hexachord is partitioned into trichordal segments, it always is the case
that whatever trichord is partitioned out of the hexachord will leave a complementary trichord which is inversionally or transpositionally equivalent to the
first extracted trichord. Thus, if the trichord C, C-sharp, E is extracted from the
first hexachord, the remaining tones from the hexachord, F, G-sharp, A are
inversionally equivalent to the first trichord.

Given Schoenberg's interest in effecting a reconciliation of tonal and twelve-
tone elements, it is significant that one can partition a number of major, minor,
and augmented triads out of each hexachord. From the ''A'' hexachord (C, C-
sharp, E, F, G-sharp, A), one can extract the following six major and minor
triads: A major, A minor, F major, F minor, D-flat major, and D-flat minor.
There are also two augmented triads embedded in this hexachord: A, C-sharp,
F and C, E, G-sharp. (See Example 8.3.) As each of the four hexachords contains

Example 8.2
Ode to Napoleon Buonaparte, op. 41, hexachordal centers of symmetry.

six different major and minor triads, the four different collections can produce all twelve major and all twelve minor triads.

Thus, the structure of this hexachord permits Schoenberg to make extensive use of triads simply by dividing the hexachord into two trichordal segments, each of which is a triad. For example, if one were to extract the C-sharp minor triad from the "A" hexachord, this would mean that the F major triad would complete the hexachord. In mm. 19–21, the piano part states the "A" hexachord. (See Example 8.4.) In the right hand, Schoenberg arpeggiates the C-sharp minor triad while the left hand presents the F major triad. Such partitionings, which result in pairs of triads, are a constant theme in this work.

Although in a number of places in the work, triads literally saturate the surface of the *Ode*, and although the composition ends with a clear E-flat major triad, the question inevitably arises as to whether it is a tonal composition. Clearly, the answer will depend on one's definition of tonality. If one believes that it is sufficient for a composition to be defined as tonal when it concludes with a clear triad and has frequent triadic references or statements in the course of the work, then one might well argue that the *Ode* is indeed tonal. Some analysts, have indeed remarked that the work is an E-flat composition.

To the present writer, this definition does not seem persuasive. Triads abound, but there is never any feeling of goal-directed harmonic progression, nor of a single tone and its associated triad achieving a referential status. What one hears, again and again, is a characteristic harmonic/serial theme: a succession of two

Example 8.3
Ode to Napoleon Buonaparte, op. 41, triads extracted from the hexachord.

different triadic types (major and minor) whose roots are a major third apart—C major to A-flat minor, or C-sharp major to A minor, and so forth.

In his harmony textbook, *Structural Functions of Harmony*, written during the last years of his life (and approximately contemporaneously with the *Ode*), Schoenberg clearly differentiated between harmonic progressions which can establish a tonality and successions which do not:

A *succession* is aimless; a *progression* aims for a definite goal. . . .

A *progression* has the function of establishing or contradicting a tonality. The combination of harmonies of which a progression consists depends on its purpose—whether it is establishment, modulation, transition, contrast, or reaffirmation.

A *succession* of chords may be *functionless*, neither expressing an unmistakable tonality nor requiring a definite continuation. Such successions are frequently used in descriptive music.[2]

It would seem that from Schoenberg's own definition of tonality and his description of the different types of harmonic progressions, the *Ode to Napoleon Buonaparte* is not tonal. Its triads do not form harmonic progressions as much as they are harmonic successions—perhaps, most precisely, functionless harmonic successions. (If so, is it happenstance that the *Ode* seems to be a reasonable candidate for the designation "descriptive" music?)

In the *Ode*, although there is no single ordering of the twelve tones that holds for the entire work, it is not the case that Schoenberg had abandoned the principle of serial ordering altogether. However, the role of serial ordering is comparatively limited in this piece. Instead, Schoenberg tends to construct passages

Example 8.4
Ode to Napoleon Buonaparte, op. 41, mm. 19–21.

in which the six elements of a hexachord will occur, but frequently with multiple repetitions. For example, in m. 33 in the strings, every note belongs to the ''A'' hexachord. In its function, this passage is much like a simple expansion of a triad in tonal music. The free repetition of the tones demonstrates that they function not so much as ordered elements, but as components of a larger harmonic unit—the hexachord.

One feature of this work that is atypical of Schoenberg's usual twelve-tone approach is the inconsistency in forming aggregates by combining complementary hexachords. If Schoenberg wished to form aggregates, he would combine only hexachords ''A'' with ''B'' and ''C'' with ''D.'' Frequently he does precisely that. However, there are many instances in the *Ode* where ''A'' is not combined with ''B,'' but with ''C'' or ''D'' instead. Given the structure of the source hexachord, when the ''A'' hexachord is combined with either ''C'' or ''D,'' it shares three pitch classes in common with each—an augmented triad. Schoenberg's willingness to make such nonaggregate producing combinations in the *Ode* may be related to his interest in making explicit use of familiar tonal elements with his concomitant lack of concern with octave doubling.

In some respects the *Ode to Napoleon Buonaparte*, op. 41, might seem to be a cul de sac in Schoenberg's overall serial development. No other completed twelve-tone work has the degree of explicit use of tonal elements that the *Ode* has. Nor does any other twelve-tone work have so little emphasis on serial ordering as does this composition. And certainly no other post-1928 twelve-tone work places so little stress on aggregate production by hexachordal combinatoriality.

But if we look at the larger picture of Schoenberg's stylistic development, both the triadic references and the treatment of the hexachord as a harmonic unit are essential features of many of Schoenberg's later twelve-tone works. Their use might be particularly intense in the *Ode*, but this must be seen in the broader context of his compositional interests in the 1940s.

PIANO CONCERTO, OP. 42 (1942)

Schoenberg's Piano Concerto, written in 1942, was premiered in 1944 by Edward Steuermann, piano, with Leopold Stokowski conducting the National Broadcasting Symphony Orchestra. It is a typically Schoenbergian paradox that the Concerto places much more emphasis on elements borrowed from tonality than had been typical of Schoenberg's works a decade earlier, while at the same time, is cast in a form that owes much less to classical tonal forms than those twelve-tone works from the late 1920s and early 1930s which avoided surface references to tonality.

In terms of its form, the Piano Concerto reaches back to Schoenberg's own past (and the latter half of the nineteenth century) for its models and not to the tonal forms of the classical and early romantic eras. Much like the String Quartet no. 1, op. 7, and the Chamber Symphony no. 1, op. 9 (written nearly forty years earlier), the Piano Concerto is cast as an "all-in-one" movement, suggesting both a multimovement work and a single, cyclical musical form. Moreover, as another aspect of its indebtedness to the Romantic era, Schoenberg composed the Concerto with a program in mind, a kind of autobiographical description of the effect of the Nazis' rise to power on Schoenberg's life. In a sketch for this work, he attached programmatic designations to the themes of the principal sections of the concerto. The first section of the work, with its gentle theme, was to depict "Life was so easy." At m. 176, with its dramatic change of tempo and character, the program stated: "Suddenly hatred broke out." Still later, "A grave situation was created," and finally "But life goes on."

In one important respect, the Piano Concerto reveals a significant change in Schoenberg's compositional technique. In all of his twelve-tone orchestral compositions up to this point, Schoenberg had scrupulously avoided orchestrational octave doubling of any sort, restricting himself only to unison doubling. Indeed, he went so far as to make no use of the traditional practice of doubling at the octave on two registral extremes: the flute is not doubled by the piccolo an octave higher, nor is the cello by the bass an octave lower. In the Piano Concerto, however, Schoenberg abandons this orchestrational limitation. Octave doubling is used freely throughout this work.

It might be tempting to dismiss this change as trivial or cosmetic, but this must not be seen merely as a superficial change in orchestrational technique. Orchestration—at least in Schoenberg's hands—is never separate from com-

Example 8.5
Piano Concerto, op. 42, set.

positional structure. That Schoenberg chose to avoid orchestrational doubling in earlier twelve-tone orchestral works and to permit it in the Piano Concerto is not an arbitrary decision, divorced from the compositional process. Rather, it stems from that very process—and in this instance, it is the extensive emphasis on tonal elements that permits, or perhaps more accurately, dictates the orchestrational octave doubling.

Compared to the *Ode to Napoleon Buonaparte*, the explicit use of tonal elements is much less prominent in the Piano Concerto. The set of the Concerto does not have quite so many obvious possibilities for the extraction of tonal elements, certainly not the multiple pairs of triads that can be extracted from each hexachord in the *Ode*. But, compared with the Violin Concerto of six years earlier (or, for that matter, most of Schoenberg's twelve-tone compositions before 1940), the set of the Piano Concerto makes possible the exploitation of elements of tonal syntax, and these possibilities are not avoided in the piece itself.

For example, a number of segments of the set of the Piano Concerto are equivalent to segments of diatonic (or, in two cases, whole-tone) scales. The first four notes of the original version of the set (as stated by the piano in mm. 1–8) are from the B-flat major collection; order positions 1–5 comprise most of the F-major collection; order positions 2–5 are from the C major collection; order positions 4–7 are a segment of the whole-tone scale; order positions 6–10 include most of the A-major collection; order positions 8–11 could belong to the D major collection or the whole-tone scale. In short, every single tone in the set belongs to at least one segment that could be used to make references to elements of tonal syntax (see Example 8.5).

The treatment of the set in the composition demonstrates clearly that the inclusion of tonal segments within the set was not happenstance; nor did Schoenberg make any attempt to hide these and other tonal references. It is not only the linear statements of the set that often seem to imply that the collection of a given key is going to hold sway. The way in which Schoenberg partitions the set and the manner in which he combines different set forms often produces moments that sound similar to passages that might have come from a tonal composition, or that seem—for a moment—as if they are about to be transformed into a rather straightforward reminiscence of tonal language.

It is in this context that we should understand the change in orchestration practice in this concerto. As Schoenberg was now interested in including tonal elements in this twelve-tone works, he had no motivation whatsoever to avoid the octave doubling that, at one point, had seemed to him something that needed to be avoided, because it might seem to be a "disturbing" reminiscence of tonal vocabulary and syntax.

In addition to its tonal emphases, the Piano Concerto also demonstrates that the treatment of the hexachord as a harmonic unit and the frequent use of symmetrical relationships were not isolated features of the *Ode*, but were part of a larger set of compositional and stylistic concerns in Schoenberg's late twelve-tone music.

For example, in the opening measures, the right hand presents the original version of the referential twelve-tone set in a linear statement. The accompaniment, in the left hand, is not, however, derivable from any strict ordering of the twelve-tone set. The first three notes are order positions 3–5 of P-0, but the next three notes (m. 2) are order positions 5, 0, 2, and in m. 3, we hear order positions 2, 1, 3. (Note that these repetitions do not cross the boundary line of the hexachord.) Clearly the presumably referential ordering of the twelve-tone set is subsidiary to the treatment of the hexachord as a harmonic unit in the accompaniment in mm. 1–3. This feature is also characteristic of mm. 4–8, where the second hexachord of P-0 in the melody (right hand) is accompanied by elements of that same hexachord, freely restated, with multiple repetitions, generally designed to add most or all of the complementary tones of the hexachord to the dyads in the right hand (see Example 8.6).

Symmetrical relationships also play an important part in the Concerto. To be sure, unlike the *Ode*, the set of the Concerto is not based on a multiply symmetrical hexachord. (Because of the property of IH combinatoriality the two hexachords are inversionally symmetrical to one another, as is the case for virtually all of Schoenberg's twelve-tone sets.) Therefore there are no symmetrical extractions of equivalent trichords from the source hexachord. But Schoenberg makes increasing use of formations of notes in which he draws equally from the IH combinatorially related hexachords. For example, the piano part in mm. 64–65 presents three ascending tetrachordal flourishes which, in their total pitch-class content include all twelve tones stated in a linear succession (see Example 8.7).

If one compares this ordering of the twelve tones with the twelve-tone set of the Concerto, one sees that this particular ordering is not one of the forty-eight set forms. Instead, what Schoenberg has done is to take two tones from the second hexachord of the prime form (P-2) and follow these with the two corresponding tones of the IH combinatorially related form (I-7). As each flourish comprises two tones from P-2 and two from I-7, the resultant tetrachords are symmetrical, and all the resultant tetrachords share the same axis of symmetry.

It is this kind of symmetry, resulting from the combination of corresponding tones from inversionally related set forms, and not the symmetry built into the hexachord of the set itself (as in the *Ode*), that is the most predominant strain in Schoenberg's later twelve-tone works. To be sure, this kind of symmetrical relationship is not appearing for the first time. One can find very similar passages

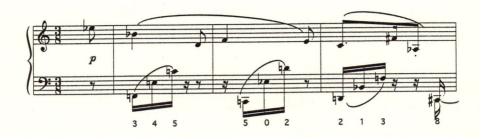

Example 8.6
Piano Concerto, mm. 1–7.

in earlier works. But what we do see is an intensification of Schoenberg's interest in symmetry and a willingness to mix the elements from inversionally related sets together in such a manner that there is no clear differentiation (by dynamics, orchestration, register, etc.) between the elements derived from the different set forms.

In its frequent, but restrained, references to tonal elements, its normative treatment of the hexachord as a harmonic unit, and its formation of symmetrical collections by combining corresponding elements of inversionally related set forms, the Piano Concerto is very much in the mainstream of Schoenberg's late twelve-tone style.

STRING TRIO, OP. 45 (1946)

Schoenberg's String Trio was completed in September 1946, written as a result of a commission from Harvard University. Although—like the Piano Concerto—it is cast in a single movement to be played without a break, it is clearly subdivided into five sections: Part 1, mm. 1–51; First Episode, mm. 52–132; Part 2, mm. 133–179; Second Episode, mm. 180–207; Part 3, mm. 208–293. The Trio has long been regarded as one of the most complicated of Schoenberg's twelve-tone works. To the listener, particularly the first-time listener, the surface of the Trio presents numerous challenges to easy comprehensibility, particularly

I-7, second hexachord 6 7   8 9   10 11

P-2, second hexachord   7 6   9 8   10 11

Example 8.7
Piano Concerto, op. 42, piano part, mm. 64–65.

given the sharp juxtaposition of colors, the violent contrasts in register and dynamics, the frequent use of false harmonics and tremolos, and the free over-lapping of the lines. At the same time, the Trio has challenged many theorists, who have found its twelve-tone structure difficult to follow. Much of the diffi-culty that has attended the understanding of the Trio and deciphering its twelve-tone structure stems from the fact that it is not based on a single twelve-tone set (and, indeed, one of its sets has more than twelve notes). Moreover, to add to its complications, the sets that are used are rarely stated as single lines and are also frequently mixed together with their combinatorial counterparts, with no clear instrumental or registral differentiation of the set forms.

To a large extent, the Trio is based on two related sets—an eighteen-note set and a twelve-tone set. But even these two orderings do not exhaust the serial resources used in the work, for Schoenberg makes use of still other orderings. However, although other twelve-tone orderings do occur in the course of the Trio—as we will see—they might best be understood as derived from one of the original sets.

Although the Trio makes use of different sets, it bears very little resemblance to the procedures that led to multiple orderings in his early twelve-tone works. Perhaps, Schoenberg was willing to use multiple sets in the 1940s because he was no longer concerned about what he saw as the possibilities for tonal im-plications that might result from a repeated tone being interpreted as a tonic. But in addition, the use of different sets in the Trio is probably directly related to one of the principal features of his late twelve-tone style: the treatment of the source hexachord as the fundamental unit of musical structure and progres-sion—a feature we have already examined in the *Ode* and the Piano Concerto. We can see this most clearly when we look at the two basic sets (paired with their combinatorial complements) used most extensively by Schoenberg in the Trio (see Example 8.8). For clarity, we will refer to the two sets as follows: P-0 [18] means the original form of the eighteen note set; P-0 [12] means the original form of the twelve-tone set.

As can be seen in the example, Schoenberg does not randomly choose dif-

P-0 [18]

I-5 [18]

P-0 [12]

I-5 [12]

Example 8.8
String Trio, p. 45, sets.

ferent twelve-tone (or eighteen-note) sets. Rather, the source hexachords of all three hexachords of the eighteen-note set and both of the hexachords of the twelve-tone set are harmonically equivalent. Thus, if we apply the label "A" to the collection of six tones that appears in the first hexachord of P-0 [18], we can see that the first hexachord and third hexachords of P-0 [18], the second hexachord of I-5 [18], the first hexachord of P-0 [12] and the second hexachord of I-5 [12], all have precisely the same collection of tones: C-sharp, D, E-flat, E, A, B-flat. And, with one exception, each of these hexachords presents a different ordering of those six tones (the first hexachords of P-0 [18] and P-0 [12] share the same ordering). Thus, we can hear the different versions of this hexachord as variations of one another, with a common set of tones, presented in a variety of orderings.

In the Trio, Schoenberg supports the clear demarcation of the sections with his choice of sets. In the opening section, Part 1, he uses, exclusively, the eighteen-note set. In the first Episode, after a brief lead-in, the twelve-tone set is used—again exclusively. Part 2 (mm. 133–79) returns to the eighteen-note set. The Second Episode is based on a new ordering (which will be discussed below), derived from the twelve-tone set. Finally, Part 3, which functions as a clear recapitulation (with many measure-for-measure repetitions of passages from Part 1 and the first Episode) includes both the eighteen-note set (for its recapitulation of material from Part 1) and the twelve-tone set (for its recapitulation of passages from the first Episode).

As we have seen, Schoenberg's use of different sets in the Trio is not so much the reemergence of a technique that had been abandoned more than a decade earlier as much as it is a manifestation of something quite different, something which ties into one of the important stylistic strands of his late serial music: the treatment of the source hexachord (and not the ordered twelve-tone set) as the fundamental building block of musical structure. But the desire to have multiple different orderings of the referential hexachord might have led Schoenberg to use multiple twelve-tone sets, not an eighteen-note set. Why did Schoenberg employ one set with three hexachords in the Trio? An explanation might be deduced from mm. 12–17 (see Example 8.9).

As can be seen in the example, Schoenberg presents P-0 [18] in mm. 12–14, followed by RI-5 [18] in mm. 15–17. As is customary for Schoenberg's post-1926 twelve-tone works, the set forms are not presented as lines, but are stated in polyphony, partitioned between the three instruments.

Of particular importance is the line in the violin. As can be seen, the violin presents two notes from each hexachord. As there are three hexachords (eighteen notes) in the set, over the course of the two set statements, twelve notes appear in the violin. Schoenberg has carefully controlled the extraction of tones so that all twelve tones are presented in this line—an aggregate. This is a familiar procedure, with its roots reaching back to almost the beginning of Schoenberg's twelve-tone period. The result is a clear twelve-tone hierarchy with each note in the violin line a component element of two aggregates and two hexachords. On one hand, each note belongs to a local, partitioned hexachord, each of which (until the end of the passage) spans exactly a measure. At the same time, the elements of the violin line are also components of the gradually unfolding aggregate which subsumes the local presentations of the hexachord.

Thus, Schoenberg's use of an eighteen-note set was designed not only to permit multiple orderings of the source hexachord but also to permit a middle-ground aggregate to be formed by the partitioning out of two elements from each hexachord of the two combinatorially related sets, P-0 [18] and I-5 [18]. And the specific twelve-tone ordering that results is also hardly arbitrary. Rather, the line divides into two chromatic hexachords (B, C, C-sharp, D, D-sharp, E and its complement). And although the chromatic hexachord is not equivalent to the source hexachord which lies at the foundation of the Trio, the chromatic hexachord (and tetrachord) is a frequent harmonic motto in the Trio.

The method by which Schoenberg extracted the two tones from each hexachord is itself intimately connected to another essential strand in his late twelve-tone thinking. If we assign order numbers to the elements of each hexachord of P-0 [18] and RI-5 [18] and begin each hexachord with zero (or five for retrogrades), an interesting consistency emerges. As can be seen from Example 8.9, Schoenberg has extracted precisely the same order positions out of each hexachord to produce the aggregate in the violin. In each case, hexachordal order positions 0 and 5 are placed in the violin—itself a symmetrical division of the hexachord. (It should not escape the reader's attention that Schoenberg had to construct his eighteen-note set in a very special way to produce the property

Example 8.9
String Trio, op. 45, mm. 12–17. (Note: Notation simplified to clarify pitch. Those notes marked with (o) are produced through natural or artificial harmonics in the original score.)

that the three hexachords would be either IH combinatorially related or identical and that the first and last elements of every hexachord would yield an aggregate.)

Obviously, the extraction of the first and last order positions of each hexachord also yields a multiply symmetrical division of the eighteen-note set. This, of course, is entirely in keeping with an important feature of Schoenberg's works from this period. As we have seen in our discussions of the *Ode* and the Piano Concerto, symmetrical relationships had begun to play an extremely significant role in Schoenberg's late twelve-tone works.

It should be emphasized that Schoenberg's interest in symmetrical relationships, although important for much of his career, began to take on increasing importance in his later years. Schoenberg's interest in the manipulation of order numbers and his concern to extend symmetrical relationships to this dimension, had long been an important feature of his twelve-tone writing (as we saw in the analysis of the Fourth String Quartet), and it would be a distortion of the historical record to suggest that such ideas surfaced only in his late works. But in his late twelve-tone compositions, this aspect of his treatment of the material begins to take on even more prominence. In the Trio, the partitionings are frequently designed to be symmetrical at the hexachord—not the pitch-class collections, but the order numbers. One example of many should suffice. Beginning in m. 86, P-8 [12] is partitioned between the top two instruments with the following order numbers assigned to the violin: 0, 1, 3, 5, 6, 7, 9, 11. If one rewrites this sequence of order numbers so that each hexachord begins with zero, the symmetrical nature of the partitioning becomes clear: 0, 1, 3, 5 is the hexachordal order numbering of both hexachords.

Schoenberg also used a hexachordally symmetrical means of generating the subsidiary twelve-tone ordering that appears for the first time in the Second Episode. Beginning in mm. 184, Schoenberg employs an apparently new twelve-tone set (using, of course, the same source hexachord as was used for the twelve-tone and eighteen-note sets). But this new twelve-tone set is derived by a fairly simple process from the twelve-tone set. Example 8.10 shows how Schoenberg derived his new set. As can be seen from the example, he took the order numbers of each hexachord of the twelve-tone set of the first episode and restated them in a new ordering: 0, 2, 3, 1, 4, 5.

Symmetrical relationships in the Trio are hardly limited to order-position extractions. Indeed, the nature of the symmetries in the Trio are such that it is impossible in much of the work to discriminate the individual set forms that are employed from one another. The opening measures of the work are a case in point (see Example 8.11).

In m. 1, the first hexachord of P-0 [18] is combined with the equivalent hexachord from I-5 [18] to produce an aggregate. But, unlike in many of Schoenberg's earlier twelve-tone works, the two inversionally related set forms are not clearly differentiated by register or instrumentation. Instead, the notes of the two set forms are inextricably intertwined. For instance, the cello has a total of four different pitch classes in m. 1—order positions 1 and 4 from both

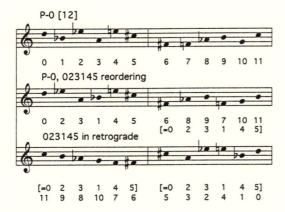

Example 8.10
String Trio, op. 45, set reorderings based on order numbers.

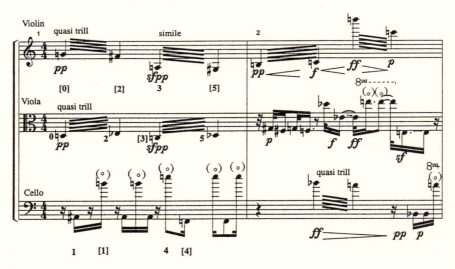

Example 8.11
String Trio, mm. 1–2. Note: Bracketed order numbers belong to I-5; nonbracketed order numbers belong to P-0. Note: notation simplified to clarify pitch. Those notes marked with (o) are produced through natural or artificial harmonics in the original score.

P-0 and I-5. As we have seen in the similar passage from the Piano Concerto, the pairing of equivalent order positions from I-related set forms produces symmetrical pitch structures. In the Trio, symmetrical pitch-class collections abound because of the kind of procedures we see in m. 1.

Although its references to tonal elements are far more restrained than those of the *Ode*, the Trio is by no means devoid of such references. And certainly by comparison with the twelve-tone works of the 1930s, where tonal references were studiously avoided, the Trio is quite obvious in its willingness to employ tonal elements. This can be seen not only in the clear triadic outline provided by order positions 3–5 of both of the principal sets of the Trio, but also—as in the Piano Concerto—in Schoenberg's treatment of the orchestration: octave doublings are a prominent characteristic of the Trio (e.g., m. 5).

It has been said that each of his compositions "fulfilled a uniquely innovatory stage in Schoenberg's voyage of musical discovery."[3] In the case of the Trio it is easy to identify some of its most singular features—most obviously, the use of several sets, one of which included eighteen notes. But at the same time it is not a paradox to state that although the Trio is unique, it shares many essential characteristics with other of Schoenberg's late twelve-tone works: the treatment of the source hexachord as the fundamental building block of musical structure, the pervasive use of symmetrical relationships, both pitch and order number, and the unabashed willingness to try to interleave elements of tonal syntax into the context of a twelve-tone serial composition.

NOTES

1. "Composition with Twelve Tones (1)," in *Style and Idea: Selected Writings of Arnold Schoenberg*, ed. Leonard Stein, trans. Leo Black (Berkeley and Los Angeles: University of California Press, 1984), 244.

2. *Structural Functions of Harmony*, rev. ed. (New York: W. W. Norton, 1969), 1.

3. Milton Babbitt, "Three Essays on Schoenberg," in Benjamin Boretz and Edward Cone (ed.), *Perspectives on Schoenberg and Stravinsky*, rev. ed. (New York: W. W. Norton, 1972), 53.

9

Schoenberg's Late Tonal Works

Jan Maegaard

THE BACKGROUND

Among the great innovators of European music in the first half of the twentieth century, we must include Arnold Schoenberg, Béla Bartók, Igor Stravinsky, Anton Webern, and Alban Berg. They were born within a surprisingly short span of time, 1874–85. A late-romantic tonal style invariably governs their early works, such as Schoenberg's *Verklärte Nacht* (1899), Bartók's *Kossuth* (1903), Webern's *Im Sommerwind* (1904), Berg's *Seven Early Songs* (1905–8), and Stravinsky's *Four Studies for Piano* (1908). These composers not only "knew" how to handle tonality in an advanced manner, they actually had it in their bones. From this point of departure they all found ways to free themselves from the ties of tonality.

Stravinsky's contribution to the stylistic turmoil of the 1920s was the establishment of a dissonant style related to tonality, but not governed by it. Bartók, after his "atonal adventure" 1918–20,[1] found a way to utilize basic elements of folk music in a highly sophisticated fabric of tonal/nontonal texture. Still, the most radical effort to create a new tonal logic was made by Schoenberg when, in the early 1920s, he laid down the basic principles of dodecaphonic technique. Berg and Webern followed him immediately, each in his own distinctive way, and even Stravinsky adopted the method in his own way in works after 1953. Between 1930 and 1960 a great number of composers did likewise, and so twelve-tone technique became accepted as a practical way of composing nontonal music.

However, Schoenberg, the originator of the dodecaphonic technique, was the only one who continued to occupy himself with tonality, both practically and theoretically. In fact his interest in tonality continued even during the formative years of his atonal style and his "method of composing with twelve notes related only to one another," as he called the twelve-tone technique. Not only was his teaching invariably based upon tonal principles, as laid down in his book *Theory of Harmony* (1911), but he wrote a surprising number of tonal compositions and arrangements during the time from 1910 to 1933, considering the music Schoenberg has become famous for having created during those years. Examples of tonal works include the Chamber Symphony no. 2, op. 38 (begun in 1906, but not finished until 1939), a few works related to the First World War,[2] and some chamber music intended for private performance by the family.[3] Later in the 1920s Schoenberg sketched a piece of incidental music, "Prozessionsmusik," for a play he had written, *Der biblische Weg.*

In 1911–12 Schoenberg arranged music by Matthias Georg Monn (1717–50) and his brother Johann Christoph Mann [Monn] (1726–82) for *Denkmäler der Tonkunst in Österreich*, vol. 19, no. 2. He also prepared music by Franz Tuma (1704–74), but it was not published in Schoenberg's lifetime. He orchestrated songs by Beethoven, Carl Loewe, and Schubert for the singer Julia Culp, and during the war he began the orchestration of two grenadier marches, but they were not completed. After the war Schoenberg arranged two waltzes by Johann Strauss, Jr.[4] In 1922 he orchestrated two organ chorales by J. S. Bach, *Komm Gott, Schöpfer, heiliger Geist* and *Schmücke dich, o liebe Seele*, and he arranged his own "Lied der Waldtaube" ("The Wood Dove's Song") from *Gurrelieder* for an ensemble similar to that of the First Chamber Symphony for a concert in Copenhagen in January of 1923 where that work was also performed. In 1928 came the orchestration of the Prelude and Triple Fugue in E-flat Major from Bach's *Clavierübung III*. Finally arrangements of six German folk songs for mixed choir, voice with piano, or both were commissioned by Peters in Leipzig and written in 1929. They appeared in *Volksliederbuch für die Jugend* in 1930.

None of the tonal compositions and arrangements so far mentioned show any sign of a wish to break new ground. But this situation changed in the late 1920s. Already in 1925 Schoenberg sketched a piano piece in B minor, which he never completed, in which he used chords and combinations of chords not belonging to traditional harmony. Besides triads, chords built of fourths are plentiful, and more often than not chords are connected, not as root progressions in the usual sense, but according to chromatic relations between individual tones. A cadence to D major at the end of the first part of this piece is an example of that kind of harmony (see Example 9.1). This use of chords built of fourths chromatically combined is only one device among several already known from works originating in 1906–7, when Schoenberg was working his way out of tonality, e.g., from the Chamber Symphony no. 1 in E Major, op. 9 and the Two Songs, op. 14. Such chords had more or less given way to other kinds of chords as atonality took over, but were now reintroduced in association with tonality.

A little later, during 1929–30, Schoenberg composed Six Pieces for Men's Choir, op. 35, of which only four are dodecaphonic; nos. 4 and 6 are not. These two are "tonal," but each in a different sense from the pieces just mentioned.

Example 9.1
Unfinished Piano Piece in B Minor (1925), mm. 20–22.

Judging from how it sounds, no. 4, "Glück" (Happiness), might as well have been dodecaphonic. Dissonances are plentiful and sharp and rarely resolve. In addition, the difficulties of intonation are as acute as in the atonal songs. Still, a flavor of A-flat major is present. Still more interesting, however, is no. 6, a two-stanza song entitled "Verbundenheit" (Obligation), the first of the songs to be composed. Here the chords are mostly triadic, and the tonality of F major/ D minor is unmistakable. Striking is the fact that the voice parts of the second stanza are actually inversions of the voice parts of the first stanza. In the second stanza, tenor 1 sings the inversion of the first stanza's bass 1, while tenor 2 and bass 2 sing the inversions of their own previous parts, and bass 1 sings the inversion of tenor 1. This alone is complicated counterpoint; but what makes it specifically significant is the fact that the parts are not inverted in the manner of tonal counterpoint, that is, according to the steps of a diatonic scale, but that the intervals are the exact inversions of the intervals of the previous stanza with reference, not to the scale of any key, but to the chromatic scale. This is basically a nontonal device applied to a tonal texture. Example 9.2 shows the beginning and the ending of the two stanzas. The first stanza starts in F major and goes to the relative minor in m. 6; at the end (mm. 16–18) it aims at a cadence in F major which at the last moment changes into D major. The chords of the second stanza are unusual in a tonal context. They are not combined by the same tonal logic as those of the first stanza. Instead, they are combined by the inversional logic of the voice leading, a logic directly imported from the texture of dodecaphonic music. Only after these attempts to reconcile tonality and dodecaphony did Schoenberg compose the remaining four songs in a purely dodecaphonic manner.

It seems that these attempts at a fusion of tonal and atonal practices did not fully satisfy Schoenberg, for the tendencies observed in the piano piece in B minor appear even more strikingly in a fragmentary work for violin and piano from 1930. Here the harmony is dominated by chords built of fourths—now both perfect fourths and perfect and augmented fourths combined, the latter being a chord structure typical of his atonal harmony. But still the key is D major. Here it seems that Schoenberg is aiming at a tonal or quasitonal style to go along with, rather than to blend with, the style of his dodecaphonic music.

Example 9.2
"Verbundenheit," op. 35, no. 6, mm. 1–6, 16–18, 19–24, 34–36.

Finally, in 1933 he sketched (but never completed) a piano concerto clearly written in the key of D major.

In addition to harmonic changes in original compositions, there are also changes in some of the arrangements from that period. The Cello Concerto and String Quartet Concerto, both from 1933, are not merely faithful reproductions of the music to be arranged, namely Matthias Georg Monn's Harpsichord Concerto in D Major and Handel's Concerto Grosso, op. 6, no. 7, but rather are composed "in freier Umgestaltung" (in a free arrangement) as is specified in the title. Whereas Schoenberg remained as faithful to the model as he could in the Bach arrangements, in these works he felt free to change the music and substantially add to it. In addition, he lent to it an instrumental flavor and a virtuosity far removed from the style of the eighteenth century. For example, in the finale of the Cello Concerto he added a cheerful "Spanish" section—with kind regards to Pablo Casals, whom he wanted to perform it.

All these works and arrangements testify to a wish to work creatively with tonality, rather than merely treating it in the traditional fashion. The reason for this may well be seen in light of political developments in Germany at the time. The Nazis were gaining power, and their almost spiteful attitude toward what they termed "entartete Kunst" (degenerate art)—meaning among other things modern art—was no secret. Schoenberg, who since 1926 had been living in Berlin as a professor of composition at the Prussian Academy of the Arts, had to face the fact that there would be no room for his atonal music in Germany in the near future. This was clearly indicated by the hostile reception of his Variations for Orchestra, op. 31, and the opera *Von heute auf morgen* in 1928 and 1930 in Berlin and Frankfurt am Main. So, if Schoenberg wanted to go on working as a composer, his activities had to be undertaken along different lines. When we consider the compositions mentioned above, it appears that he was looking for a way to deal with tonality without compromising himself as a composer. However, although tonality came to play an important role in Schoenberg's music at this time, he did not abandon composing dodecaphonic music. On the contrary, his opera *Moses und Aron*, which may well be regarded as his greatest achievement, was created in exactly these years, 1930–32. Not intended for immediate performance, this music was composed with a better future in mind.

THE AMERICAN YEARS

Schoenberg's situation, upon his arrival in the United States in October 1933, has been characterized as "homeless and speechless."[5] He had been reluctant to leave his spiritual home, which was the German-speaking part of Europe, but his Jewish extraction had left him no choice after Hitler had come to power in January of 1933. At that time Schoenberg fled to Paris and there reconverted to the Mosaic faith. As an exile he looked for positions in France, Turkey, and the Soviet Union. Although America was not his first choice, this was where he found an opening, which he gratefully accepted.

Schoenberg's creative output during his American years can be looked upon in two ways: either as something quite different from what he might have composed back in Europe, had conditions allowed for it, or as a further development of tendencies already present during his tenure in Berlin. Considering his tonal works, the latter point of view is the more fruitful, particularly in reference to the original compositions of that period.

Original Compositions

In this category we find two works written for didactic purposes, the Suite in G Major (in "Ancient Style") for string orchestra (1934) and the Theme and Variations in G Minor for band, op. 43 (1943), together with *Kol nidre*, op. 39 (1938), the completion of the Chamber Symphony no. 2, op. 38 (1939), and the *Variations on a Recitative* for organ, op. 40 (1941).

Suite in G Major ("in Ancient Style"). The didactic works form a small group of their own. During a stay in Chautauqua, New York, in the summer of 1934, Schoenberg met Martin Bernstein, a young double bass player and the director of a student orchestra at New York University. Bernstein informed Schoenberg of the numerous student orchestras at colleges and universities all over the States and their need for a suitable repertoire. The idea of writing music for such a purpose thrilled him, and by the end of the year the Suite was composed. In a preface, intended for the score but never published, he wrote:

I became convinced that every composer—especially every modern composer, and I above all—should be interested in encouraging such efforts. For here, a new spiritual and intellectual basis can be created for art; here young people can be given the opportunity of learning about the new fields of expression and the means suitable for these.[6]

This issue may also have had a polemic point. In a circular letter written to friends later that year, Schoenberg touched on the information he had received concerning student orchestras and their needs:

It has convinced me that the fight against this infamous conservatism has to begin here. And so this piece will simply be an example of those progresses which are possible in tonality when you are a true musician and know your trade: a true preparation as regards harmony, but also melody, counterpoint and technique. . . . [7]

By the term "infamous conservatism" Schoenberg was no doubt referring to the so-called *Gebrauchsmusik* (functional music) which had its heyday in Germany in the late 1920s with Paul Hindemith and Fritz Jöde as its leading figures (although Hindemith rejected the term). Schoenberg had absolutely no sympathy with that trend. In his view music did not have to be simplistic in order to be pedagogical. He explained the task he set for himself in these words:

Without harming the students by a premature dose of "Atonality Poison," I had to prepare them, using harmony which leads to modern feelings, for modern performance technique. Fingerings, bowings, phrasing, intonation, dynamics, rhythm—all this should be developed without the introduction of insuperable difficulties. But modern intonation, contrapuntal technique, and phrase-formation were also to be emphasized, so that the student might gradually come to realize that "melody" does not consist only of those primitive, unvaried, symmetrical structures which are the delight of mediocrity in all countries and among all peoples. Already here there are higher forms, which belong to a higher order of art not only technically, but also, and especially, spiritually.[8]

The formal layout of the Suite more or less follows a conventional pattern in that an overture is followed by a slow movement and three dance movements: Menuett, Gavotte, and Gigue. The disposition of keys also reflects tradition, since the main key of G major governs the first, third, and fifth movements, whereas E minor and B flat major, the relative minor of the tonic and the relative major of the tonic minor, are chosen for the second and fourth movements. Furthermore each movement in some way refers to well-known patterns, formally and rhythmically and, in a few cases, with respect to modulation. But otherwise the music is composed quite freely within the framework of an expanded harmony and highly developed counterpoint somewhat reminiscent of the style of Max Reger, a composer whom Schoenberg admired and who, in his late works, absorbed classical patterns into a late-romantic idiom. This, according to Schoenberg, had to be the point of departure toward a more advanced music not governed by the regulations of tonality. Therefore the composition is actually not as simple as one might expect from a "Suite 'in Ancient Style' in G major'' written for pedagogical purposes. Rather advanced devices of string technique, full command of rhythmic complexities, and intonation strictly conforming with equal temperament are called for as prerequisites of a successful performance.

Although the Suite turned out to be technically too demanding for many college orchestras, it was still very didactic in terms of compositional technique, and Schoenberg apparently used it for that purpose. In her recollections, Dika Newlin has reported several occasions between 1939 and 1941 when this work was discussed in class at UCLA.[9]

Theme and Variations. The other didactic work is the Theme and Variations in G Minor for band, op. 43, composed nine years later, in July–August 1943. Schoenberg was notified by his friend Carl Engel, director of the Schirmer Edition, that high schools were looking for band music other than marches and arrangements. Again Schoenberg set out, eager to fill the need. Whether this work was ever used for teaching analysis and composition is not apparent from any source that I know; but the music would certainly be well suited for the purpose. Although it was composed less than one year before Schoenberg's retirement from UCLA, he still may have used it in his private teaching after retirement. In addition to composing the Theme and Variations for band he also arranged it for symphony orchestra so that it might reach a wider audience. The work was published simultaneously in both versions as op. 43a and 43b. In terms of compositional technique, this music is even more sophisticated than the movements of the Suite and, as we shall see, Schoenberg was proud of it.

A theme of twenty-one measures is followed by seven variations and a finale. The variations are like those developed by Max Reger during the years before World War I: the first variations follow the theme rather closely, whereas the later ones appear as symphonic elaborations upon elements from the theme. After variation 2 there is an adagio which is a fantasy on a detail from the theme. It is succeeded by three even more independent character pieces: a waltz, a canon, and a fugue. In these variations new musical ideas are introduced while the accompanying parts elaborate upon reminiscences of the theme. In variation 5, the canon, a long melody, is played by the first clarinet together with its inversion played by the baritone. Here again, we find Schoenberg applying exact intervallic inversion rather than inversion according to the scale of the key. This device, which we observed in the two successive stanzas of ''Verbundenheit'' (Example 9.2) is here applied simultaneously to create a canon which is then imbedded in a web of accompanying parts—a true masterpiece of counterpoint. The seventh variation is again a fantasy on an element from the theme, now directly preparing for the finale. Regardless of how much each variation deviates from the theme, all of them strictly adhere to the theme's structure and dimensions. All are twenty-one or forty-two measures long, and we may notice that the number of variations, seven, relates beautifully to these proportions.

The finale is longer. Where Max Reger would have set a crowning fugue, Schoenberg writes a finale composed of several short contrasting sections, perhaps after the model of the finales from Mozart's operas. It is a summary of various ideas from the theme and variations ending in a hilarious clash, from which the concluding G major chord emerges. One should not disregard the humor of this effect.

Since the work is not twelve-tone, Schoenberg did not count it among his main achievements. But still he admired the work, as he told Fritz Reiner, the conductor:

It is one of those works that one writes in order to enjoy one's own virtuosity and, in addition, to give a group of amateurs—in this case, wind bands—something better to play. . . . As far as technique is concerned it is a masterpiece, and I believe it is also original, and I know it is also inspired. Not only because I cannot write even ten measures without inspiration, but I really wrote the piece with great pleasure.[10]

Kol nidre. Among the tonal compositions not written for didactic purposes *Kol nidre* was the first to be composed, in August–September 1938. This work is significantly different from any other work by Schoenberg. Among his religious works it stands out for being the only one written for a liturgical purpose. The text, which belongs to Yom Kippur, the feast of atonement, holds a special position among the texts of the Mosaic liturgy. It says, ''All vows which we may have made and with which we may have taken upon ourselves religious commitments which have turned out to be impossible to fulfill, those we repent, and we declare them null and void.'' This is how the late chief rabbi Marcus Melchior of Copenhagen translated the Aramaic text to me. Schoenberg, the newly reconverted member of the Jewish congregation, undoubtedly entertained a desire to pay a tribute to its ceremonies by his musical interpretation of this famous text.

Kol nidre is a cantata of about thirteen minutes for speaker (rabbi), chorus, and symphony orchestra. The text was reformulated by Schoenberg in collaboration with the rabbi Dr. Jacob Sonderling of Los Angeles, who also contributed an additional, introductory text. In this it is told that at in beginning God said, "Let there be light," whereupon a flame broke out. God crushed it to atoms, and myriad sparks are hidden in the world. But only the meek and modest can see them. It leads to a traditional formula which allows the breakers of the law to partake of the prayer: "A light is sown for the pious, a light is sown for the repenting sinner." Then follows the main text—reformulated and with commentary—performed by the rabbi and the chorus in alternation. A renewed statement of repentance concludes the work.

From the holdings of the Schoenberg Archives it appears that the composer spent a great deal of effort studying both the text and the music of the "Kol nidre." The interpretation of the text is known to have caused controversy. On the surface it seems to say that any oath and vow you have made can be annulled, if only you turn up at Yom Kippur and ask for it. But that is not the true meaning. Schoenberg came to the following conclusion:

I assume that at the time when these words were used for the first time, everybody understood them perfectly: Whenever under the pressure of persecution a Jew was forced to make oaths, vows and promises counter to his inherited belief in our religious principles, he was allowed to repent them and to declare them null and void. Thus he was allowed to pray with the community as a Jew among Jews. This seems to me the very idea of atonement: purgation through repentance.[11]

This interpretation conforms with that of chief rabbi Marcus Melchior, who explained to me that the text deals solely with the relationship between God and man, not with relationships among humans.

The melody associated with this text is assumed to go back to the Middle Ages. So close is this association that at times and places where it was not advisable for Jews to recite the text for fear of persecution, the melody alone was sung without the words, as a valid expression of the "Kol nidre." But this melody caused Schoenberg trouble. In a letter to the composer Paul Dessau he explained that it was not really a melody, but a collection of similar "flourishes" that appeared in varying orders, and that it was truly monophonic and not based in harmony or polyphony. "I chose the phrases that a number of versions had in common, and put them into a reasonable order."[12]

One can well understand that this medieval chant, consisting of melodic formulas loosely compiled and handed down in various shapes, troubled Schoenberg, who was not familiar either with the history of old music or with synagogical practice through the ages. So he put parts of it together "in a reasonable order" so as to make it constitute a firm, choralelike form. But there was no doubt in his mind as to what kind of music he wanted to make out of it—and what he did not want it to sound like. In his letter to Dessau he continues: "One of my main tasks was to vitriolize out the 'cello sentimentality of Bruch and others, and to bestow upon this DECREE the dignity of a law, of an 'edict.' " And he refers specifically to mm. 58–63, where the "Kol nidre" text is first introduced, as "at least no sentimental minor-key stuff."[13] (See Example 9.3.)

The melody is played in unison as a *cantus firmus* by the woodwinds. The harmony is played by the brass section in short strokes of chords ending on an extended fifth G/D—an excellent example of the kind of tonality Schoenberg cultivated in his later years. A chromatic counterpoint is performed by the strings in octaves. Along with this the rabbi recites the text in fixed rhythms, but without any indication of pitch—all of it kept on a low dynamic level. To say that all sentimentality has been "vitriolized out" is no exaggeration, nor could one deny that the strictly controlled texture and orchestration lend to the statement "the dignity of an edict."

The work was actually premiered at Yom Kippur on 4 October 1938 under Schoenberg's direction, but not in the synagogue. It seems that it never found its way into the liturgy as Schoenberg had wished. In the letter to Paul Dessau quoted earlier he wrote, "It is too bad that people . . . , from a ritual and musical standpoint, refuse to accept the piece for use in the synagogue. I think it would be very effective both in the synagogue and in the concert hall."[14] It has been pointed out that the reason that it has not been used liturgically is that such lavish music, so well known in the Christian church, is not common practice in the Mosaic liturgy. In this connection one should bear in mind that by 1898 Schoenberg had converted to the Protestant faith[15] and therefore was far more familiar with Christian church music than with the Jewish. Nevertheless, the question of its fitness for liturgical purposes notwithstanding, *Kol nidre* is one of the truly remarkable achievements of Schoenberg's American years.

Chamber Symphony no. 2. The composition of the Chamber Symphony no. 2 in E flat Minor was begun in 1906, right after the completion of the Chamber Symphony no. 1 in E Major for fifteen solo instruments, a pioneering work on Schoenberg's road out of tonality. In this and the following year, 145 measures of one movement and about 100 measures of another were composed. He then embarked on other projects in which his new atonal style was created.

In 1910 and 1911 Schoenberg completed the orchestration of the late-romantic *Gurrelieder* composed in 1901–2. This may have caused him to resume work on the Second Chamber Symphony in 1911. But at that time only about fifty measures were added to the second movement and the work was again put aside. Then, during World War I, in 1916, Schoenberg resumed work on the second movement. At this time he was working on the text for a large oratorio, *Die Jakobsleiter* (Jacob's Ladder), dealing with matters of life, death, and reincarnation. Now he wrote a text "Wendepunkt" (Turning Point) which was to be recited along with the music of the Chamber Symphony, and he sketched some

Example 9.3
Kol nidre, op. 39, mm. 58–63.

music for that section. Although both text and music were later abandoned, it is interesting to see the direction Schoenberg imagined the work to take at this point. The text says:

To proceed on this road was not possible. A beam of light had illuminated a sorrow both general and special. Depending not only on its constitution, but also on the caprices of external happenstances, a soul is as unable to respond insensibly to a stroke of luck as it was before to misfortune.

In a sudden change it reacts with cheerful delight, then rises in powerful buoyancy, dreams of blissful fulfillments, sees itself as victor, rushes on, feels its power increase ever more, and—deceiving itself to believe it can own a world which it considers to be its possession already—gathers everything in its power in order to gain in a powerful effort a realm above this world. What would need to happen by necessity comes about by chance: just when the accumulated power is expected to burst out, it fails; a small but deceitful occurrence—a grain of dust in the clock-work—is capable of obstructing its unfolding.

Sorrow follows upon the collapse. It is at first of a specific, then also of a general nature. Proceeding from the external event, the soul believes at first to find the explanation there, and then looks for it in its own constitution. That is the true and perfect completion of this collapse. But it does not mean an end, it is, on the contrary, a beginning: a new road to salvation appears, the only one, the eternal one. To find it was the purpose of all previous experience.[16]

Schoenberg had a disposition for turning concepts around in order to make them look like paradoxes, or to reveal the paradoxes actually inherent in them. Also, he rejoiced in making statements appear to mean the opposite of what they actually meant. An early example of this is found in the prospectus of the Vereinigung schaffender Tonkünstler (Society of Creative Musicians) of 1904. Here one finds the statement that "a composition must not be the Ninth Symphony [i.e., by Beethoven] in order to be misunderstood."[17] The implication is that even lesser works, though still worthwhile music, may well have to wait some time for the appreciation they deserve. And as late as 1950 Schoenberg told Josef Rufer in a letter that "not everything that does not shine is not gold,"[18] implying that some detail of the music which does not immediately appear as thematic ("golden") may well turn out so after all. In the case of "Turning Point" it is told that luck is as dangerous as misfortune. But having had this experience and found the explanation within yourself, you have gained more than you lost by the collapse; for only when the luck has been lost does it truly become that which it was actually never before.

It is not known whether this notion was associated with the Second Chamber Symphony at any time prior to 1916. We must, therefore, assume that it was a new idea at that time. One can only guess what impact it would have had on the work, had the idea of the melodrama been carried through.

Finally, after the completion of *Kol nidre* in 1938, the Chamber Symphony was taken up again, and this time it was carried to an end, although undoubtedly in a way different from how Schoenberg had imagined it in the beginning. From the outset it was conceived as music for eighteen solo instruments, not unlike the First Chamber Symphony; but the final version is scored for a small symphony orchestra. There was a practical reason for this. In 1937 Fritz Stiedry, the conductor, had settled in New York, and there he was active in forming a society of New Friends of Music. This comprised a small orchestra of which he undertook the direction. He wanted to perform music by Schoenberg and, if possible, conduct a first performance. Stiedry communicated with the composer concerning the matter, and so Schoenberg completed the work and scored it for Stiedry's orchestra.

Most of the first movement had been written in 1907, so only twenty measures needed to be added as a conclusion. This is sinister music in a slow tempo, strangely consonant as compared to the First Chamber Symphony, and very chromatic. For the second movement he went back to the 150 measures of the 1911 version and added another 150 measures. This is very lively music in G major. The contrast is so striking that it is difficult to foresee how the two movements can possibly belong to the same work. The gay and dancing opening theme returns several times in a rondolike manner, with more singing ideas in between. However, after some time this clear-cut formal design seems to dwindle, giving way to a development of ever more complicated variants of the thematic material. As a listener, one may almost feel let down by the composer—''Where does this go?''—until one realizes that a return of the mood of the first movement has been prepared. That is Schoenberg's *coup de surprise* in this music: as if hit by a stroke of lightning (reminiscence of the collapse?), the music sinks back into the darkness of the first movement, and there it remains until the end. In retrospect it appears to be a perfectly logical consequence of the foregoing development.

Of course one can hear stylistic differences within a work composed over a span of more than thirty years—particularly at the end of the first movement one can clearly distinguish the ending composed in 1939 from the main part—still, the diverging elements have been juxtaposed and combined in such a way that it almost lends increased significance to the composition. Fritz Stiedry wanted a third movement to conclude the Chamber Symphony, and Schoenberg started to work on it but abandoned it after 130 measures—presumably realizing that it would be felt as an addition rather than as an integral part of the work.

Variations on a Recitative. The third work in this group of original compositions is Schoenberg's greatest solo instrumental work and the only one he completed for organ.

Schoenberg was in no way a connoisseur of the organ, and this was actually the first time he composed music for that instrument. However, already at the beginning of the century—in 1906 or 1907, according to his own estimation—he started to write an article ''Die Zukunft der Orgel'' (The Future of the Organ) in which he advanced the viewpoint that at the beginning of the twentieth century one had to consider the organ an obsolete instrument. He saw a disproportion between the huge size of it and the fact that it was played by just one performer, and between its wealth of possible colors and the fact that these can only be treated in a rather stiff manner. And he found that the organ was more apt to glorify the performer than to serve the interests of the composer.

Unfortunately this article exists only as a fragment, and in its two pages Schoenberg never explains what kind of future he actually foresaw for the organ.[19] Late in his life, however, he found an opportunity to develop his ideas. In a letter dated 10 May 1949 to Dr. Werner David, who prompted the first Berlin performance of Schoenberg's Variations by the organist Manfred Gräter in December 1948, Schoenberg sketched the kind of organ he felt would meet the demands of a modern composer. The instrument he envisioned was small, one and a half times as big as a portable typewriter, having two to six stops, each of which, however, should cover the entire range of seven to eight octaves and all dynamic levels. For larger organs he imagined two to four performers and the possibility of adding a corresponding number of manuals. Significantly he added, "This is, naturally, a fantasy of the future, but who knows if we are so far from it."[20] So Schoenberg was perfectly aware that the instrument he imagined had little to do with organs the way they actually are. However, it cannot but strike the modern observer to see how close this fantasy comes to the electronic organs of today.

It appears from correspondence between Schoenberg and William Strickland, the general editor of the Contemporary Organ Series published by the H. W. Gray Co. in New York, that at the beginning of August 1941 Schoenberg was invited to contribute a composition to the series. Immediately he started to compose a dodecaphonic sonata. But at the same time he wrote to Strickland asking for further information about the size and character of the composition they wanted from him, mentioning the possibilities of a sonata, a set of variations, a set of smaller pieces, or a suite.[21] In his reply Strickland called for the set of variations, and three days later, on 25 August Schoenberg set out to compose the *Variations on a Recitative* in D minor, thus abandoning the idea of the dodecaphonic sonata.[22] This decision is interesting, not so much in that Schoenberg took the editor's advice, but because the two works are so widely different. The part of the sonata he had already composed when he decided on the variations, is enough for us to form an impression of the music. In its crisp and clear-cut style it somehow anticipates a dodecaphonic work he was to compose a year later, namely the Piano Concerto. Although, as we shall see, this work does contain hints of tonality, there are few distinct references to its particular style in the Variations. We must conclude, therefore, that in 1941, when he set out to write a piece for organ, Schoenberg considered at least two styles as equally appealing.

As indicated in the title, the theme is a "recitative." It appears as a monophonic statement in the low register. The way it is constructed and treated in the variations is of particular interest, if you are looking for the reason that Schoenberg expressed himself equally freely—and equally willingly—in differ-

Example 9.4
Variations on a Recitative, op. 40, mm. 1–11.

ent styles. Although the recitative represents a perfectly rounded-off arch form, it is not a self-contained theme, as one might expect from "theme and variations"; rather it exposes a number of ideas to be developed later on. It divides into seven (keep this number in mind!) small sections of either three, four, or six notes (see Example 9.4). In the first three sections of the theme the idea of a rising interval followed by a smaller one in the opposite direction is exposed and developed. I: D, A, G-sharp; II: the same plus F-sharp, B, A-sharp; III: D-sharp, F-sharp, E, D, C-sharp, G-sharp. The remaining sections are all concerned with the scalewise falling motion from the top point, C-sharp, to the end on the low D, which was also the starting point. The theme spans a major seventh and contains all the twelve tones of the chromatic scale. Due to its beginning and conclusion, D stands out as the tonic; but the key of D minor is not spelled out tonally.

Three elements of this melodic line have been worked out in particular and given prominence: 1. The idea of the falling half step which generates the opening of the first variation (see Example 9.5a) and permeates the entire work. 2. An important motif is derived from section III by way of octave displacement of individual tones (see Example 9.5b). This appears in the seventh variation. 3. Of even greater importance, however, is another, slightly different motif (see Example 9.5c) which appears already in the bass line of the first variation. Its connection with section III is looser, and therefore less convincing, than was the case with Example 9.5b. The way it appears to have been constructed is also quite different: if one takes the first notes of mm. 2, 4, 6, 8 and 10, it becomes apparent that they constitute this motif: D, D-sharp, F-sharp, B, E; the last one followed by the second note of that measure.[23] This way of deriving a motif from a thematic source is far from normal tonal organization, but it is very close to dodecaphonic thinking in that the motif emerges from a systematic selection from a series of tones which, in this case, is taken as an abstract phenomenon, just like a twelve-tone series.

As we have seen, the theme comprises eleven measures, so one should not

Example 9.5
Variations on a Recitative, op. 40, motivic shapes.

be surprised to find that it is followed by ten variations of exactly the same structure. Together with the theme this makes eleven sections, total. But one variation, no. 6, actually contains twenty-two measures, so in themselves the variations comprise eleven times eleven measures. Considering that the recitative consists of seven sections in eleven measures, it can hardly be altogether coincidental that the finale turns out to comprise seventy-seven measures. Total: 132 + 77 = 209 measures.[24] These simple relations define the structural framework of the entire composition.

The variations are constructed in a very strict way, not only because of their number of measures but also in that the tones of the recitative are sounded as a more or less hidden *cantus firmus* throughout each of them. The beginnings of the first two variations are shown in Example 9.6 with the tones of the *cantus firmus* marked by numbers. Although this *cantus firmus* is well hidden and hardly discernible to the listening ear in the first variation, it appears quite prominently in the bass of the second. This compositional technique is strikingly similar to the one Schoenberg applied in his Variations for Orchestra, op. 31, composed during 1926–28 in a strictly dodecaphonic manner. Here the twelve-tone series serves as a *cantus firmus* throughout the variations like the theme of a *passacaglia*.[25] The way Schoenberg adopted this technique in op. 31, the twelve-tone series constitutes the backbone of the composition. The point is that in this respect the theme of the *Variations on a Recitative* is treated like the twelve-tone series of the earlier work.

The finale is a kind of freely structured mirror fugue, ending with a coda. The theme of the fugue is easily recognizable as consisting of the first nine tones of the recitative, sections I and II. Against the fugal expositions and alternating with them are heard many of the motives from the preceding variations. As the movement develops the theme seems to get lost in the wilderness of other motives, not unlike the way the theme ''got lost'' in the second movement of the Second Chamber Symphony. However, in this case it reappears forcefully near the end. The closing measures show a cadence in which the key of D major is powerfully exposed and confirmed (see Example 9.7).

The way tonality is handled in this work is still less governed by the harmonic functions of the key than was the case in *Kol nidre*. Instead, it is more permeated

Example 9.6
Variations on a Recitative, op. 40, mm. 12–14, 23–25.

by devices otherwise associated with the twelve-tone technique than in any other tonal work. In spite of the lack of harmonic functions and presence of dodecaphonic devices, it does not sound "atonal" the way the dodecaphonic works do. This cannot be simply accounted for by the ever-occurring return to D as a gravitational center; one has to look at the texture to find a fuller explanation. When Schoenberg was thinking "in terms of tonality" he had the music of late romanticism, with its warm colors and rather thick texture, in mind, whereas his thinking "in terms of atonality" after 1920 was far more governed by the sparse and poignant, almost neoclassicistic texture of his dodecaphonic works. These two basic conceptions of how music should sound were apparently equally alive in his mind during the latter part of his career. The Variations were conceived within the framework of tonal music and sound tonal, although several technical procedures developed in dodecaphonic music were carried over and applied in the musical texture.

It is obvious that such a heavy impact of dodecaphonic devices on several

Example 9.7
Variations on a Recitative, op. 40, mm. 206–210.

compositional levels is bound to lend to the Variations a particular flavor of suspended or suppressed tonality and, therefore, to raise doubts in the mind as to whether this music is in fact tonal at all. As already noted, the theme, although having its firm footing on D, does not make the key of D minor explicit. Both in the variations and in the finale one finds that the tones are most often combined according to procedures not dependent on the conventions of tonality, but rather on devices of atonal counterpoint, so one may wonder whether the glorious ending on a D major triad is only just a postulate. It is certainly not. Rather it releases a tension and clarifies a doubt which was there from the beginning. George Rochberg has described this tension by saying that ''no single beat, main or subdivided, escapes harmonic change. The musical result is a kind of chromatic *perpetuum mobile*; the acoustic result is an opaque harmonic noise of an often intolerable density,'' and he sees in the music images of great pain and expressions of human suffering.[26] This, of course, is an interpretation open to doubt; but it reflects perfectly the bewilderment this music may cause in the observer's mind. It should be added, however, that the confusion is released at the end, not by the D major chord itself, but by the way it is approached, namely not as the result of a tonal cadence, but by way of chromatic progressions in connection with strong thematic references (see Example 9.7). The half-step motif inherent in the theme and spelled out in the first variation reigns in the upper parts, while the tones of the very start, the fundamental idea of the entire composition, are powerfully sounded in the bass. This, again, is a basically atonal way of creating a cadence, but it can be used for tonal purposes without loss of its inner logic, and thus give the composer the opportunity to resolve what during the foregoing 207 measures was seemingly one huge dissonance into a huge consonance at the end. Looked upon in this way it is beyond doubt that the Variations is a tonal work, albeit in a very special way. In 1947 Schoenberg expressed a similar view in a letter to René Leibowitz: ''The harmony of the Organ Variations fills the gap between my Chamber Symphony and the 'dissonant' music. Many unexploited possibilities are to be found therein.''[27]

It is surprising to find that Schoenberg's own attitude to the work seems to have been somewhat ambiguous. He "would have made the theme better, if he had thought longer," he is reported to have said, maybe referring to the fact that the work was actually composed at great speed during seven weeks from August to October 1941.[28] Also, Schoenberg is said to have characterized the finale as a succession of "small variations of two to four measures.''[29]

After long and frustrating negotiations with the publisher, the Variations eventually came out in 1947, edited and supplied with directions of registration by Carl Weinrich, organist at Princeton University, who had also premiered the work in April 1944 in New York. But Schoenberg was not happy with the edition. In the preface to the score Weinrich quotes from a letter to him by Schoenberg: "I write always the pitch I want to hear . . . I am not very fond of unnecessary doublings in octaves. I would like to have such doubling avoided if clearness and transparency can be achieved without addition of octaves.''[30] His dissatisfaction with the edition he expressed in the letter to Werner David quoted earlier: "The registration of my Organ Variations is apparently completely designed for the Princeton University organ. This does not suit me, and so many people complain about it.''[31] He goes on to criticize the edition. According to Glenn Watkins, Schoenberg's judgment is, however, too harsh, because he, as a nonorganist, did not fully understand Weinrich's very complicated directions.[32] The first recording of the composition was made by Marilyn Mason shortly after Schoenberg's death.[33] Her suggestions for registration, which were worked out in collaboration with the composer, have only recently been published.[34] They are much simpler than those by Weinrich. The original score was not published until 1973, when it appeared in the Collected Works.[35]

Arrangements

Besides the original compositions, Schoenberg wrote a number of arrangements during the American years, including the orchestration of Brahms's Piano Quartet no. 1 in G Minor, op. 25, and new settings of three of the six German folk songs which had appeared in the *Volksliederbuch für die Jugend* in 1930.

The Brahms orchestration. This was made in 1937, while Schoenberg was still working on the dodecaphonic Violin Concerto, op. 36. It is like the Bach orchestrations of 1922 and 1928 in that it remains strictly faithful to the model. Prior to a performance in San Francisco, Schoenberg wrote to Alfred A. Frankenstein of the San Francisco *Chronicle* and stated as his motivation for having made the orchestration that he loved the piece, that it was seldom performed and, when so, that it was then badly played, "because the better the pianist, the louder he plays and you hear nothing from the strings.''[36] Thus Schoenberg wanted to spell out the music, so to speak, so that everything might come out clearly, and he was certainly the right person to do so. From his early youth he had loved Brahms's music, and had played it as a chamber musician on viola and cello. Throughout his teaching career he had used the older composer's scores for analysis and as models for composition. And in 1933, on the occasion of the one hundredth anniversary of Brahms's birth, he gave a lecture "Brahms the Progressive," which has become famous, not only for its rather unorthodox view of Brahms' historical position as a "progressive" composer, but also for its deep insight into his music.[37]

The two composers are closer in time than one might perhaps immediately imagine. Schoenberg was almost twenty-three years old when Brahms died, and there is no doubt that he had often seen Brahms in the streets and concert halls of Vienna; so he may well have thought of him as a contemporary, as a composer of twenty-three years in 1992 might have thought of Olivier Messiaen. This may well account for an otherwise almost odd statement in his letter to Frankenstein. Among his intentions in writing the orchestration he mentions: "To remain strictly in the style of Brahms and not to go further than he himself would have gone if he had lived today." Of course, had Brahms lived at the time this letter was written, he would have been 106 years old. Still, Schoenberg might well have been his pupil. He also mentions that he had been careful not to violate any of the laws which Brahms obeyed and "which are only known to musicians educated in his environment."[38] Therefore, compositionally, nothing new is contributed by Schoenberg in this score. One can listen to it as a true Brahms composition, and in addition admire Schoenberg's lucid orchestral rendering.

Three Folk Songs, op. 49. These three settings were composed in 1948, when Schoenberg was seventy-four years old, and published the following year as op. 49 by Edward B. Marks in New York. Two of the songs, which in the earlier set had only appeared as solo songs with piano, were now given an interpretation for choir a cappella: "Der Mai tritt ein mit Freuden" and "Mein Herz in steten Treuen." The third one, "Es gingen zwei Gespielen gut," had previously been arranged both as solo with piano and for mixed choir a cappella; it was now given a new choral setting. All three arrangements are different from the earlier ones. The melodies originate in the fifteenth and early sixteenth centuries. They are modal, that is, they do not conform with the conventions of major and minor, and they diverge rhythmically in that they swerve between double and triple meter. Schoenberg has taken these characteristics as a challenge and has interpreted them in his own late-romantic tonal style. The outcome is three beautiful, but stylistically rather elusive, arrangements. As mentioned earlier in connection with *Kol nidre*, Schoenberg never occupied himself much with music before the time of J. S. Bach. His musical imagination remained within the realm of tonal and posttonal composition; it is therefore interesting to see how he went along with music before 1700. In *Kol nidre* a highly personal original masterwork came out of the encounter; in the case of the folk songs there was less he could or would allow himself to do in order to give them a significant personal stamp.

Between Tonality and Atonality

Since we have seen how strongly experiences from atonal writing can make themselves felt in some of the tonal works, particularly in the *Variations on a Recitative*, it might be interesting to investigate whether the reverse procedure, tonal implications in otherwise atonal works, is also to be found. Particularly two works are worth mentioning in this connection: *Ode to Napoleon Buonaparte*, op. 41, and the Piano Concerto, op. 42. Both were composed in 1942.

Ode to Napoleon Buonaparte. This work, written for recitation and piano quintet (also piano and string orchestra), is set to a passionately contemptuous text by Lord Byron. It is a wartime composition in that the derision of Napoleon could easily be understood as aiming at Hitler, whereas the true and far from ironical homage to George Washington at the end might well call to mind the name of Franklin D. Roosevelt, then president of the United States. Such political implications are likely—and in Schoenberg's mind they were certainly very likely—to remind one of Beethoven's Third Symphony, *Eroica,* which was at first conceived as an homage to Napoleon, at a time when Beethoven still thought of him as a hero of freedom. As is well known, Beethoven tore up the dedication in 1804, when Napoleon had himself proclaimed emperor.[39] Since Beethoven, the key of that symphony, E-flat major, has often been chosen by composers to express the heroic.

The basic twelve-tone series of the *Ode* is constructed and treated in a most special way, since it seems to have been designed to create chords rather than melodic lines. The first six tones produce a major and a minor triad on C-sharp, A, and F; the notes of the second part of the series produce exactly the same pattern one whole step higher. Together this accounts for triads on F, G, A, B, C-sharp, and E-flat; these tones form a whole-tone scale. If triads are built on each tone, they can be linked one to the next by way of three chromatic relations (see Example 9.8a). Similarly, four-part chords may be produced and connected by way of two pairs of common notes and two chromatic relations (see Example 9.8b). These are exactly the kinds of chords and chord combinations that one can observe in the otherwise tonal compositions. They are exploited throughout the work, and they allow for an ending on an E-flat major triad. Still, the *Ode* cannot be counted among Schoenberg's tonal works; but it is an example of how the dodecaphonic technique can be bent toward a texture in which tonal implications are lurking.

Piano Concerto. As already mentioned, the more truly dodecaphonic Piano Concerto seems to develop tendencies already discernible in the dodecaphonic Organ Sonata, which was abandoned in favor of the Variations. Neither the twelve-tone series nor the actual texture of the Piano Concerto contains the same kind of tonal implications as was the case in the *Ode*. Still, hints at tonality are certainly present, particularly in the melodic and rhythmic structures. Let us consider the first eight measures of the opening theme, played by the soloist, as shown in Example 9.9 together with the basic series. This is a regular dodeca-

Example 9.8
Ode to Napoleon Buonaparte, op. 41, series and chord derivations.

phonic texture in which the melody follows the series 1–12, only repeating the tones 9–10–11 in preparation of the cadence mm. 7–8, while in the accompaniment such sections of the series which are not occupied by the melody are applied. This allows for the transparent dissonant texture—no use of pedal!— known from many other dodecaphonic works. The reason for calling attention to it in this connection is that the melody, as taken by itself, has characteristics reminiscent of classical construction. It is exposed as a singing melodic line, and it appears in the metrical shape of four-plus-four measures, known from countless classical, and therefore tonal, melodies. The only irregularity is that in the second half the metrical units are pressed together to three times ⅔ rather than three times ⅜ in mm. 5–6. Therefore the ending is reached in m. 7 rather than in m. 8. But the phrase is not cut off for that reason, since the final tone is correspondingly prolonged.

Perhaps even more surprising is the fact that this melody might actually be harmonized in C minor with temporary cadences on the subdominant (IV) in m. 4 and on the dominant (V) in mm. 7–8. For the sake of demonstration one such late-romantic harmonic interpretation is shown in Example 9.10. The fact that it is possible—and even quite easily so—to harmonize the melody according to classic-romantic conventions shows that dodecaphonic thinking and atonal texture do not necessarily exclude traditional thinking in terms of phrasing and form. All through the Piano Concerto one finds patterns more or less reminiscent

Example 9.9
Piano Concerto, op. 42, series and mm. 1–8.

of classical models. And the ending, though strictly dodecaphonic, more than suggests C major.

Composing as Usual

As the dodecaphonic technique was introduced by Schoenberg in the 1920s, everybody felt that it meant a break with the past, and this was to remain the prevailing view for the next three or four decades. Schoenberg himself opposed it, sometimes angrily, as in a famous letter to Nicolas Slonimsky, the lexicographer: "I personally hate to be called a revolutionist, which I am not."[40] Even in matters of compositional technique he repeatedly stressed the continuity of his creative development. In an unpublished article, "Wiesengrund," he recalls an event "a few years after the First World War" when he invited friends and acquaintances to his home to inform them of his new way of composing according to a twelve-tone series: "At the end I formulated my most important thesis: One follows the series, but otherwise composes as usual."[41]

It took a long time until musicians and musicologists recognized the truth of

Example 9.10
Piano Concerto, first theme reharmonized in C Minor.

that thesis. Meanwhile Schoenberg had again shocked the musical world by apparently being unfaithful to his own principles, in compositions such as those under consideration here. Opponents exulted in what to them appeared as a fallback to convention, while his adherents felt let down by the very person whom they worshipped as a pioneer of contemporary music. Of course both parties were wrong as looked upon from Schoenberg's standpoint. He felt that he had expressed himself equally genuinely in the early works, the in-between atonal works, the dodecaphonic, and the late tonal works. Still, he was aware that the recent tonal music might appear as stylistically inconsistent with his development as a composer.

In 1948 Schoenberg was persuaded by his former pupil Josef Rufer to explain himself in a statement, "On revient toujours," in Rufer's and H. H. Stuckenschmidt's magazine *Stimmen*. Here he refers to composers of music in a basically homophonic style, from Haydn to Wagner and Brahms, who often included counterpoint more or less after the model of J. S. Bach in their compositions, without wondering whether this was right or wrong. They might have been driven by a desire to carry out something in the older style, something which they knew they could carry out well in their own more progressive style. He points out that sometimes one prefers the cart and horse to the faster automobile. And he explains that after having composed his First Chamber Symphony (in 1906) he felt that now he had found his style; however, "My destiny had forced me in this direction. . . . But a longing to return to the older style was always vigorous in me; and from time to time I had to yield to that urge. This is how and why I sometimes write tonal music. To me stylistic differences of this nature are not of special importance. I do not know which of my compositions are better; I like them all, because I liked them when I wrote them."[42]

Another article by Schoenberg in that issue of *Stimmen* offers a more technical explanation: Continuity in classical music depends mainly on the unifying effects of structural devices such as rhythm, motifs, phrases, and constant reference in everything that happens melodically and harmonically to the tonal center, the tonic. And he continues:

Renouncement of the unifying power of the tonic still leaves all the other factors in operation. . . . The method of composing with twelve tones substitutes for the order produced by permanent reference to tonal centers an order according to which, every unit of a piece being a derivative of the tonal relations in a basic set of twelve tones, the 'Grundgestalt' is coherent because of this permanent reference to the basic set.[43]

So, Schoenberg believed that in dodecaphonic music one unifying device, namely, tonality, was replaced by another unifying device, the twelve-tone series. Otherwise, the music remained basically similar to how it used to be. In dealing with this question one must remember that both unifying devices represent a legality according to which the tones are organized. The main difference is that whereas tonality represents a general legality common to a huge repertoire of music, the twelve-tone series, or basic set, represents a specific legality governing only the behavior of the music in that particular composition, or part of it, to which it belongs. So, to Schoenberg the act of composing dodecaphonic music was just different from composing tonal music in that one respect. One could not, however, expect his contemporaries to see this closeness, since the sounding results of the two techniques are often so vastly different; but on the other hand, one can well understand that Schoenberg felt that he was doing basically the same thing, whether he composed tonal or dodecaphonic music.

Therefore, rather than asking how in his late years he could occasionally write tonal music, it would perhaps be more legitimate to ask why he occasionally shaped his dodecaphonic music in a way so closely conforming with tonal conventions, why occasionally both the formal design and the details of melodic construction were given a stylistic appearance almost in contradiction to the harmony of the music, such as we have seen particularly in the Piano Concerto. The chronology of Schoenberg's compositions from 1934 until his death in 1951 may give at any rate part of the answer to that question. (See Table 9.1, Chronology of Works, 1934–1950.) In the left column are listed the works considered in this essay, in the right column other works composed during that period. Sketches are not listed, but a few incomplete works have been included.

Chronologically the didactic works, the Suite and Band Variations, and the Three Folk Songs are determined by suggestions from outside; they are tasks he undertook as a professional composer. If they are left out of consideration,

Table 9.1
Chronology of Works, 1934–1950

Year	Works Considered in this Essay	Other Works from the Period
1934	Sept. 11 - Dec. 26: Suite in G Major "in Ancient Style"	Sept. 11: Violin Concerto, op. 36, first mvt. completed
1935		May 5: *Moses und Aron*, text to Act III completed
1936		April 27 - July 26: Fourth String Quartet, op. 37 Nov. 23: Violin Concerto completed
1937	May 5 - Sept. 19: Brahms Orchestration	Feb.: Symphony begun (but never completed)
1938	Aug. 1 - Sept. 22: *Kol nidre*, op. 39	
1939	Aug. - Oct. 21: Chamber Symph. no. 2, op. 38, completed Nov. 5: third mvt. of op. 38 begun (but never completed)	
1940	Jan.: op. 38, third mvt. abandoned	
1941	May 24: Sonata for Organ begun (but never completed) Aug. 25 - Oct. 12: *Variations on a Recitative*, op. 40	
1942	Jan.: Chamber Symphony arr. for piano, 4 hands March 12 - June 12: *Ode to Napoleon*, op. 41 July 10 - Dec. 29: Piano Concerto, op. 42	
1943	Aug. 24: Theme and Variations in G Minor, op. 43 completed	
1944		Oct. 21: *Die Jakobsleiter*, revision attempted
1945		Sept. 21: Prelude to the *Genesis* Suite. op. 44, completed
1946		Aug. 20 - Sept. 23: String Trio, op. 45 Oct. 10: *Survivor from Warsaw*, op. 46, begun
1947		Aug. 23: *Survivor from Warsaw* completed
1948	June 24 - 26: Three Folk Songs, op. 49	
1949		March 3 - 30: *Phantasy for Violin*, op. 47 Apr. 20: "Dreimal tausend Jahre," op. 50A
1950		July 2: "De profundis," op. 50B Oct. 2: "Modern Psalm, " op. 50C (never completed)

it appears that the rest of the works we have been dealing with form a closed group within the years 1937–42, and that no other work was composed during that time. Prior to 1937 we find two major works, the Violin Concerto and the Fourth String Quartet, and the outline of what should have become a large symphony, all of them dodecaphonic. Stylistically these works differ in some ways from those prior to 1934, but that is not our concern. Let it suffice to say that they somehow prepare for Schoenberg's occupation with the tonal music of the following group. The intense work on Brahms's Piano Quartet leads directly to the concentrated composition of the three big tonal works, 1938–41. The only "disruption" of this series of tonal works is the fragmentary Organ Sonata, which was abandoned after less than three weeks in favor of the Variations. These are immediately followed by the two dodecaphonic works, the *Ode* and the Piano Concerto, in which relations to tonal composition are particularly clearly spelled out. During 1943 and 1944 Schoenberg composed very little, and from 1945 onwards—with the exception of the commissioned op. 49—the output is strictly dodecaphonic, with no distinct references to tonal writing. On the contrary, in opp. 44–47 and op. 50a–c (op. 48 was composed in 1933) the transparent and poignant style which Schoenberg cultivated in the Berlin years and more or less gave up in opp. 36 and 37, is reintroduced and further developed to conclude his lifework.

The question above, how Schoenberg could make tonal implications so clearly felt in the otherwise dodecaphonic works opp. 41 and 42 might be answered by reference to the previous work, op. 40, in which dodecaphonic implications make themselves equally clearly felt in an otherwise tonal work. During this time, 1938–42, Schoenberg seems to have found himself in a kind of no-man's-land governed by two different but not necessarily contradictory legalities, as described above. These works constitute his conclusive argument against accusations of being a composer of two split personalities, and for his position that the demands of a specific legality, the twelve-tone series, do not necessarily exclude the general legality of tonal relations from being implied. "To me, stylistic differences are not important," he told his readers in the statement quoted above. In these scores we see why. At the time they were written Schoenberg was composing "as usual," whether the music was tonal or not. Thus the dialectics of these compositions allows a deep insight in his musical mind.

Conclusion

As stated earlier, Schoenberg's American works may be looked upon in two ways, either as being different from what he might have composed had he not been forced out of his natural environment, or as a follow-up of the development he had entered upon at the time he left Europe. The latter point of view was chosen for our approach to the works under consideration here. But the former way to see it may also yield some insight.

"Homeless and speechless" were the words used by Stuckenschmidt to characterize Schoenberg's situation when he arrived in America, and they were well chosen. Upon his arrival in 1934, Schoenberg found himself in environments radically different from the ones he was used to. Beyond welcome receptions and cocktail parties, there was little American society could offer him, other than the teaching position at the Malkin Conservatory in Boston that he had accepted. From being a famous, albeit controversial, figure in music he now became just another emigrant composer seeking shelter in the United States. From holding the highly honored office as professor of composition at the Prussian Academy of the Arts, he now became a teacher of elementary music theory at a small private music school. He was bound to teach, since this was the only way he could make a living. Actually he was one of the great music teachers of this century, and he loved to teach. But when he arrived in his new homeland his command of English was so poor that he could hardly make himself understood by his students.

Also the administration of musical life was different from what he was used to, entirely dependent, as it was, on supply and demand. Whereas European concert institutions and theaters were most often public entertainments, the American ones were private institutions, and therefore they had to be run in a commercial way. As a composer one had to go out and sell one's product to the market. And since the institutions were totally dependent on public attendance, they would not buy one's product if the public did not want to hear it. Schoenberg was almost helpless in that situation, and it took him some time to figure out how things worked. 1935 appears to be one of the least fertile years of his career. On top of that, he had to realize that his health could not stand the climate on the East Coast, so he felt compelled to move to the warm, dry, and stable climate of Los Angeles and try to make a start for himself there. In California, however, even fewer people knew who Schoenberg was, or wanted to perform and listen to his music.

Elizabeth Sprague Coolidge, the wealthy patroness of new chamber music who had earlier awarded a prize to his Third String Quartet of 1927, performed the role of a saving angel for Schoenberg at this point. In 1936 she commissioned a new string quartet from him. Immediately he interrupted work on the Violin Concerto, which he had started two years earlier, and composed the new string quartet in three months. In a letter to Mrs. Coolidge of August 1936 he tells that he has finished the Fourth String Quartet and says: "I am very content with the work and think it will be much more pleasant than the third. But—I believe always so."[44]

In spite of the little added remark, it seems reasonable to interpret this as an indication that he was now more attentive to the public reception of his music than before. At any rate, the new string quartet definitely has a more "pleasant" sound than the Third. Thereafter, work on the Violin Concerto was resumed and concluded in November of that year. From here on Schoenberg entered the period of preoccupation mainly with tonal music, starting with the Brahms orchestration. Although the following three tonal works do continue tendencies that were present in his music before the emigration, one could hardly deny that his development at this time took a course that was influenced by his new surroundings and different from what one might have expected, had he had the opportunity to stay in a Europe not tormented by nazism and racist persecution of Jews.

Less predictable was what happened after 1943. The year 1944 was as empty as 1935. But thereafter, now seventy years old and retired from his teaching position at UCLA, Schoenberg seems to have turned his back on the tonal/ nontonal dialectics of the past eight years and concentrated on the creation of purely nontonal dodecaphonic masterworks. These, unfortunately, do not have their place in this essay.

NOTES

1. Jan Maegaard, "Bartók und das Atonale," *Jahrbuch Peters 1981/82* (Leipzig: Peters, 1985), 30–42.

2. The chorus "Der deutsche Michel" (1914) and "Die eiserne Brigade" for piano quintet (1916).

3. "Weihnachtsmusik" for two violins, cello, piano, and harmonium (1921) and the incomplete "Gerpa" (1922)–the title refers to Georg, Schoenberg's son, and "Papa"— for two players on violins, horn, piano, and harmonium.

4. *Roses from the South (Rosen aus dem Süden)* for string quartet, piano, and harmonium (played at a gala evening for the Society for Private Musical Performances in Vienna, 1921) and *Emperor Waltz (Kaiserwalzer)*, for flute, clarinet, string quartet, and piano (arranged for a concert of chamber music, including *Pierrot lunaire*, in Spain, 1925).

5. H. H. Stuckenschmidt, *Schoenberg: His Life, World, and Work*, trans. Humphrey Searle (New York: Schirmer, 1978), 365.

6. Josef Rufer, *The Works of Arnold Schoenberg: A Catalogue of His Compositions, Writings, and Paintings*, trans. Dika Newlin (London: Faber and Faber, 1962), 64.

7. *Arnold Schönberg Gedenkausstellung, 1874*, ed. Ernst Hillmar (Vienna: Universal, 1974), 334. Translations of German texts are by the author unless otherwise indicated.

8. Rufer, *The Works of Arnold Schoenberg*, 81.

9. Dika Newlin, *Schoenberg Remembered: Diaries and Recollections (1938–76)* (New York: Pendragon, 1980), 17, 65, 203.

10. Rufer, *The Works of Arnold Schoenberg*, 72.

11. Quotation from a typewritten statement among Schoenberg's sketches. Archives of the Arnold Schoenberg Institute, Los Angeles: C44. First published in *Arnold Schönberg: Sämtliche Werke*, part V, series B, vol. 19 (Mainz: Schott, 1977), xii.

12. *Arnold Schoenberg Letters*, ed. Erwin Stein, trans. Eithne Wilkins and Ernst Kaiser (Berkeley and Los Angeles: University of California Press, 1987), 213. It appears that Schoenberg studied at least five renderings of the melody, cf. *Arnold Schönberg: Sämtliche Werke*, part V, series B, vol. 19, 13–14.

13. Stein, *Letters*, 213.

14. Ibid.

15. Stuckenschmidt, *Schoenberg*, 34.

16. Schoenberg, "Wendepunkt," handwritten text in the Archives of the Arnold Schoenberg Institute, Sk 305–306.

17. Quoted in Willi Reich, *Schoenberg: A Critical Biography*, trans. Leo Black (New York: Praeger, 1971), 17.

18. Josef Rufer, *Composition with Twelve Notes Related Only to One Another*, trans. Humphrey Searle (1954; rpt., Westport, Greenwood, 1979), 105.

19. I am grateful to Ms. Andrea Herreshoff of the Arnold Schoenberg Institute for having provided me with a copy of the manuscript.

20. Rufer, *The Works of Arnold Schoenberg*, 68.

21. Paul S. Hesselink, "Variations on a Recitative, op. 40: Corrrespondence from the Schoenberg Legacy," *Journal of the Arnold Schoenberg Institute* 7/2 (November 1983), 142.

22. Ibid., 143.

23. Glenn E. Watkins was the first to make this observation, in his "Schoenberg and the Organ," *Perspectives of New Music* 4/1 (Fall/Winter 1965), 119–135.

24. The fact that 210 measures are counted in the printed score can be explained by a cadenza leading from the tenth variation to the finale. It has been counted as a measure, whereas it is actually a large extension of the last measure of the tenth variation.

25. The "passacaglia" has its roots in the Renaissance: a bass line is presented and followed by a number of variations, all of them in combination with the same bass line, which may even sometimes be transferred to an upper part.

26. George Rochberg in *The Music of Arnold Schoenberg*, vol. 7 (CBS M2S 767), col. 6.

27. Stein, *Letters*, 248.

28. Robert U. Nelson, "Schoenberg's Variation Seminar," *Musical Quarterly* 50/2 (1964), 159.

29. Ibid., 160.

30. Schoenberg, *Variations on a Recitative*, ed. Carl Weinrich (N.p.: H. W. Gray Co., 1947).

31. Rufer, *The Works of Arnold Schoenberg*, 68.

32. Watkins, "Schoenberg," 121.

33. Esoteric ES 507 (1951?).

34. Jan Maegaard, "Schoenberg's Organ Variations: How Should They Sound?" in *The Organ Department, School of Music, the University of Michigan: Reflections, 1947–1997*, pp. 128–131. Ann Arbor: University of Michigan School of Music, 1997.

35. *Schönberg: Sämtliche Werke*, part II, series A, vol. 5, ed. Christian Martin Schmidt (Mainz: Schott, 1973), 3–38.

36. Stein, *Letters*, 207.

37. Schoenberg, "Brahms the Progressive," in *Style and Idea: Selected Writings of Arnold Schoenberg*, ed. Leonard Stein, trans. Leo Black (Berkeley and Los Angeles: University of California Press, 1984), 398–441.

38. Stein, *Letters*, 208.

39. For further details, see Carl Dahlhaus, *Ludwig van Beethoven: Approaches to His Music*, trans Mary Whittall (Oxford: Clarendon, 1991), 19–27.

40. Niclolas Slonimsky, *Music Since 1900* (New York: Norton, 1938), 575.

41. "Artikel und Essays 133," Archives of the Arnold Schoenberg Institute.

42. Schoenberg, "On revient toujours," in *Style and Idea*, 109–110.

43. Schoenberg, "My Evolution," in *Style and Idea*, 87, 91.

44. Stein, *Letters*, 200.

III

Legacy

10

Schoenberg's Theory of Composition

Patricia Carpenter

> Music is not a kind of entertainment, but a musical poet's or thinker's presentation of musical ideas.[1]

> I myself consider the totality of a piece as the *idea*: the idea which its creator wanted to present.[2]

"I am more a composer," Schoenberg declared, "than a theorist. When I compose I try to forget all theories and I continue composing only after having freed my mind of them. . . . I am sure that a mind trained in musical logic will not fail even if it is not conscious of everything it does."[3]

He characterized his thought *about* music in similar terms, observing that he had never produced a theory and its scientific formulation but was interested rather in the clarification of musical events. He takes the point of view of the composer, he says, toward a theory of composition, which has nothing to do with "scientific" theory.[4] He thereby distinguishes between a formalized body of knowledge, *Wissenschaft*, and a method of instruction, a *Kompositionlehre*.

To establish a unified theory of composition was Schoenberg's lifelong goal. In 1911, after finishing his *Harmoniehehre*, he wrote to his editor, "I would perhaps be ready to draw up a contract for my entire activities as a writer on music."[5] Projecting books on counterpoint, instrumentation, a preliminary study of form, form and analysis, and finally a theory of form, he continued, "All of these books are textbooks or teaching aids. They form in their entirety . . . a comprehensive work."[6] This endeavor was a thread throughout his writings on music.

[Harmony,] the theory of counterpoint, and theory of form mainly serve pedagogical purposes. . . . the individual disciplines completely lack even a truly theoretical basis emanating from other external criteria. On the whole, the consequence is that three different disciplines, which together should constitute the theory of composition, in reality fall apart because they lack a common point of view.[7]

He proposed to establish a unified theory by viewing the whole of theory with a perspective that emanates from its essence, thus integrating the several disciplines into a unified theory of composition.

His primary concern was the essence of the musical composition, what it *is*, rather than how it is made. In a well-known letter to Rudolf Kolisch, written 27 July 1932, Schoenberg observes:

You have rightly worked out the row of my string quartet correctly . . . But do you think that one's any better off for knowing it? . . . I can't utter too many warnings against overrating these analyses, since after all they only lead to what I have always been dead against: seeing how it is *done*; whereas I have always helped people to see: what it *is!* . . . The only sort of analysis there can be any question of for me is one which throws the idea into relief and shows how it is presented and worked out. It goes without saying that in doing this one mustn't overlook artistic subtleties.[8]

His theory of composition comprises an extensive body of techniques for "how it is done"—how to shape a musical work so as to articulate an idea—techniques that are harmonic, motivic, contrapuntal, and dodecaphonic. The idea itself, he believed, was largely a matter of inspiration. The focus of this chapter is not the technical aspects of his theory, but rather its underlying basis.

Schoenberg depicts his own process of composition in a passage comparing divine and human creation. A human creator begins with an inspiration; he laboriously materializes his vision, his idea, so that it becomes a comprehensible message "to whom it may concern."

Alas, human creators, if they be granted a vision, must travel the long path between vision and accomplishment; a hard road where, driven out of paradise, even geniuses must reap their harvest in the sweat of their brows.

Alas, it is one thing to envision in a creative instant of inspiration and it is another thing to materialize one's vision by painstakingly connecting details until they fuse into a kind of organism.

Alas, suppose it becomes an organism, a homunculus or a robot, and possesses some of the spontaneity of a vision; it remains yet another thing to organize this form so that it becomes a comprehensible message "to whom it may concern."[9]

These aspects of his creative process—inspiration, materialization, and idea—constitute the ground of his theory of composition.

INSPIRATION

In a sense inspiration *is* idea: the idea that strikes like lightning *[Einfall]*, "a lightning-like appearance of extraordinary duration, which dissipates slowly and ends only a long time after it has fulfilled its purpose."[10] Schoenberg described himself as a creature of inspiration, who composed and painted by instinct, who arrived at the appropriate musical expressive resources by intuition, without outward intention.[11] When asked to explain his method of work, he answered,

I see the work as a whole first. Then I compose the details. In working them out, I always lose something. This cannot be avoided. There is always some loss when we materialize. But there is a compensating gain in vitality. We all have technical difficulties, which arise, not from inability to handle the material, but from some inherent quality in the idea. And it is this idea, this first thought, that must dictate the structure and the texture of the work.[12]

He describes that first thought as an "unnameable sense of a sounding and moving space, of a form with characteristic relationships."[13] He urged his students to wait for an idea, and to try to conceive the whole all at once.

A composer must not compose two or eight or sixteen measures today and again tomorrow and so on until the work seems to be finished, but should conceive a composition as a totality, in one single act of inspiration. Intoxicated by his idea, he should write down as much as he could, not caring for little details. They could be added, or carried out later.[14]

AN ORGANIC WHOLE

A work of art, Schoenberg maintains, is created as a whole, all at once, like every living being. "Art does not depend upon the single component part alone; therefore, music does not depend upon the theme. For the work of art, like every living thing, is conceived as a whole—just like a child, whose arm or leg is not conceived separately."[15] The composer's inspiration is not the theme, but the totality.

A real composer does not compose merely one or more themes, but a whole piece. In an apple tree's blossoms, even in the bud, the whole future apple is present in all its details—they have only to mature, to grow, to become the apple, the apple tree, and its power of reproduction. Similarly, a real composer's musical conception, like the physical, is one single act, comprising the totality of the product.[16]

With this view of the artwork, Schoenberg ascribes to the venerable tradition of organicism. In the nineteenth century proponents of organicism disinguished two kinds of form: mechanical form achieved by imposing rules from without and organic form achieved by a process analogous to natural growth.

Form is mechanical when it is imparted to any material through an external force, merely as an accidental addition, without reference to its character. . . . Organic form, on the contrary, is innate; it unfolds itself from within, and reaches its determination simultaneously with the fullest development of the seed. . . . In the fine arts, just as in the province of nature—the supreme artist—all genuine forms are organic.[17]

Schoenberg also contrasts these two kinds of form. In art the construct is not a mechanical one, like a clock, but an image which is like an organism in its vital unity.[18] Of the several qualities attributed to the artwork in this tradition, some characterize Schoenberg's thought. One is the notion of a "homogeneous phenomenon," in which an essential substance pervades every part.

The work of art is a homogeneous phenomenon, like a human body, for example: wherever one cuts the same thing comes out. From the body, the life-giving principle, blood; from work of art, what one finds is always in some way characteristic, somehow contains its entire essence, and can teach everything that is worth knowing.[19]

The artwork conceived as an organism is a gestalt, a functional whole the properties of which cannot be derived from the sum of its parts. Schoenberg expresses this as follows: "Above all (perhaps always) a piece of music is an *articulated organism*, whose organs, members, carry out specific functions in regard to both their own external effect and their mutual relations."[20] Such a whole cannot be built up from its parts; the whole is prior to the parts. Because the whole is prior, Schoenberg denies the popular view that no part of the work can be omitted without destroying the whole: "An organism can do without some of its members without ceasing to live. It merely becomes incapable of carrying out individual functions. But in the long run no limb is able to live if it is separated from its organism."[21]

Schoenberg also denies that the artwork grows from a seed:

An attempt to recognize and define the musical idea stands in clear contradiction to the sentimental poeticising notion that a composition might arise from the motive as a germ of the whole, as a plant grows from a seed. This is a childish notion, quite apart from the fact that it neither questions nor answers the problem that next arises: where does the seed come from, and what is it?[22]

This notion, he says, ignores the achievement of the creator.

Natural and organic processes are not unconditionally comparable to human activities. A house, for example, does not come into being through independent growth of a germ, but rather by brick being laid upon brick. . . . Every human activity, in so far as it is not exclusively instinctive, proceeds according to a plan.[23]

Just as one cannot build a house without a plan, one cannot compose a work without the idea. An organic work is a totality because its creator, by virtue of his creative imagination, has fused its elements into a single entity, with a unity that is more than a sum of its parts. The true artwork is a realization of the artist's vision. It was conceived as a whole in a single act.

Here is the basis for Schoenberg's concept of form: a musical composition is a functional organic whole that presents the vision of its creator.

FORM

A musical form materializes a vision. Schoenberg's theory of form begins with the musical "body." "The form of a composition is achieved because (1) a body exists, and because (2) the members exercise different functions and are created for these functions."[24] His theory is a theory of formal functions. He defines presentation *[Darstellung]* as the "presentation of an object to a spectator in such a way that he perceives its composite parts as if in functional motion."[25] The parts of the whole, like the organs and limbs of the living organism, exercise their specific functions.

He distinguishes limbs of a biological body from parts of an inanimate object.

True members that function, even though they may be at rest, are found only in organisms; here they are activated not by energy resulting from an inner driving power but as a result of their organic membership in a living being, and are independent of both it and of each other. . . . The difference between members and parts can best be explained as follows: If I cut up a whole (for example, a loaf of bread), I get parts. But I will never obtain members in this way. Members are parts that are equipped, formed and used for a special function.[26]

The heart of Schoenberg's theory is a body of specific techniques, harmonic and motivic, for shaping of the parts, or members, of a piece to carry out specific formal functions.

My pupils will be able to confirm the fact that, in teaching, it was my chief endeavour to make clear to them the difference between the formative potentialities of principal and secondary subjects, introductions, transitions, and codas and they will remember that I always maintained that most of the composers of today are able to write only introductions, able only to place one thing next to another.[27]

Form articulates a work in such a way as to make it comprehensible, that is, to allow it to be grasped as a whole.

Our way of taking in music proves to be, for the most part, the comprehension of parts, and only a very precise knowledge of the whole, and of all its parts and their functions, enables a particular few among us to comprehend a totality. The conception of the maker, however, proceeds from the whole. He creates from a vision of the whole in which parts function in a specific way, move, change—in short, live.[28]

THE UNITY OF FORM AND CONTENT

Form is the material presentation that makes evident the idea and its elaboration. As the presentation of an idea, a musical composition is a concrete unity of form and content. "For that is how it is in the real work of art: everything gives the impression of having come first, because everything was born at the same moment. Feeling is already form, the idea is already the word."[29] I emphasize that form in this sense is not a schema abstracted from the work or, in Schoenberg's words, not "a solid and inflexible body like a mold in which to cast material."[30] Form, rather, is the concrete embodiment of a content. The form of a work materializes the idea; it is the "outside" of the "inside":

In music we assume that the components of . . . an idea are expressed as melodic or (harmonic) progressions. That is correct, insofar as it concerns the visible or audible in music that can be perceived by the senses; it is correct only by analogy for that which makes up the actual content of a musical idea. . . . we may still assume that, as in any well-built organism . . . the form and articulation manifested by the notes corresponds to the inner nature of the idea and its movement, as ridges and hollows of our bodies are determined by the position of internal organs.[31]

The purpose of form so conceived is the articulation of the work in such a way as to make the idea comprehensible to the listener.

Form in the arts, and especially in music, aims primarily at comprehensibility. The relaxation which a satisfied listener experiences when he can follow an idea, its development, and the reasons for such development is closely related, psychologically speaking, to a feeling of beauty. Thus, artistic value demands comprehensibility, not only for intellectual, but also for emotional satisfaction. However, the creator's *idea* has to be presented, whatever the *mood* he is impelled to evoke.[32]

Two principles—comprehensibility and coherence—are the ground for Schoenberg's theory of musical form. This is so, he says, because of the difficulties inherent in the nature of the musical object, an aural object unfolding in time. Especially in music it is the listener who must put together the whole. "The effort of the composer is solely for the purpose of making the idea comprehensible to the listener. For the latter's sake the artist must divide the whole into its parts, into surveyable parts, and then add them together again into a complete whole now conceivable in spite of hampering details."[33] One can comprehend only what one can keep in mind. Man's mental limitations prevent him from grasping anything which is too extended. Thus appropriate subdivision facilitates understanding and determines the form. The organization of a piece helps the listener keep the idea in mind, to follow its development, its growth, its elaboration, its fate. "If you have been taught to provide your themes with limits, to distinguish principal and subordinate ideas, to combine fluency with lucidity, to divide distinctly into parts what cannot be conceived undivided, you will know how to make use of these earmarks in masterpieces as symbols to remember."[34]

Comprehensibility depends on coherence, which is based on the similarity of common parts. "Just as certain smallest parts . . . are repeated in each of two connected elements and thereby form a bridge between difference by means of sameness, so all coherence . . . is based on the repetition of certain common smaller parts, even in larger forms and even in the very largest."[35]

Coherence effects a quality of the whole that infuses all the parts. But the unity of the work derives from its organic nature. Schoenberg proposes that to symbolize the construction of a musical form one might think of a living body that is whole and centrally controlled, that puts forth a certain number of limbs by means of which it is capable of exercising its life function. In music, he says, only the whole itself is that central body. The cohesive force of such a whole comes from an inner energy, an inner necessity—in Schoenberg's terms, it is centrally controlled.[36] The inner force that gives the tonal body its life is for Schoenberg the musical idea that body materializes. Ultimately then a work is a whole because it presents coherently and completely an idea.

THE MUSICAL IDEA

Traditionally, the "idea" in music was understood to be the theme or melody of a composition. Schoenberg began with this meaning, but vastly broadened it. Perhaps his best-known statement is in his essay, "New Music, Old Music, Style and Idea," written in 1946:

In its most common meaning, the term idea is used as a synonym for theme, melody, phrase or motive. I myself consider the totality of a piece as the *idea*: the idea which its creator wanted to present. But because of the lack of better terms I am forced to define the term idea in the following manner:

Every tone which is added to a beginning tone makes the meaning of that tone doubtful. If, for instance, G follows after C, the ear may not be sure whether this expresses C major or G major, or even F major or E minor; and the addition of other tones may or may not clarify this problem. In this manner there is produced a state of unrest or imbalance which grows throughout most of the piece and is enforced further by similar functions of the rhythm. The method by which balance is restored seems to me the real idea of the composition.[37]

This passage epitomizes Schoenberg's concept of tonality. By tonality he meant not merely a certain collection of pitches, but more significantly a dynamic centricity. The concept of tonality, he says,

coincides to a certain extent with that of the key, in so far as it refers not merely to the relation of the tones with one another, but much more to the particular way in which all tones relate to a fundamental tone, especially the fundamental tone of the scale, whereby tonality is always comprehended in the sense of a particular scale.[38]

Tonality is a field of forces, centered on the fundamental.

Schoenberg's basic assumption concerning tonality is the movement he took to be inherent in the fundamental. He believed that unrest is inherent in the very material of music.

The primitive ear hears the tone as irreducible, but physics recognizes it to be complex. In the meantime, however, musicians discovered that it is *capable of continuation*, i.e., that *movement is latent in it*. That problems are concealed in it, problems that clash with one another, that the tone lives and seeks to propagate itself.[39]

This inherent movement in the tone becomes the starting point for the elaboration in *Harmonielehre*: "If C is taken as the midpoint, then its situation can be described by reference to two forces, one which pulls downward, toward F, the other upward, toward G."[40] He likens this situation to that of a man hanging by his hands from a beam and exerting his own force against the force of gravity. He pulls on the beam just as gravity pulls him, and in the same direction. But the effect is that his force *works against* the force of gravity, and so in this way one is justified in speaking of the two opposing forces.[41]

I think this somewhat desperate image embodies Schoenberg's notion of tonality: it represents the dynamic play of forces within the musical work. The opposing forces constitute a balanced set of forces: those close to or having the potential to move toward the tonic are termed "centripetal," those far from or moving away from it "centrifugal."

Schoenberg viewed tonality as a necessary conflict, a battlefield upon which the struggle between centripetal and centrifugal forces is played out. For example, he explains the basic I–IV–V–I cadence (and he considers a piece to be an extended cadence) in terms of conflicting forces: a statement, challenge, contradiction and confirmation.[42] The statement of the IV after a I not only functions in the tonic but also has the potential to act as a challenger, to become a tonic on its own. The introduction of V with its inherent natural 7th degree, however, contradicts any power of IV and instead confirms the tonic.

Every chord, he says, . . . that is set beside the principal tone has at least as much tendency to lead away from it as to return to it. And if life, if a work of art is to emerge, then we must engage in this movement-generating conflict. The tonality must be placed in danger of losing its sovereignity; the appetites for independence and the tendencies toward mutiny must be given opportunity to activate themselves; one must grant them their victories, not begrudging them an occasional expansion of territory. For a ruler can only take pleasure in ruling live subjects; and live subjects will attack and plunder.[43]

This "movement-generating conflict" is the life-giving force of the musical work.

Schoenberg often uses a political metaphor in regard to tonality: key areas in a piece are at war with another and ultimately at war with the ruling tonic. One of the best expressions of this occurs at the beginning of the study of modulation in *Harmonielehre*.

We can assume that tonality is a function of the fundamental tone, that is, everything that makes up tonality emanates from that tone and refers back to it. But, even though it does refer back, that which emanates from the tone has a life of its own—within certain limits; it is dependent, but to a certain degree also independent. What is closest to the fundamental has the most affinity with it, what is more remote, less affinity. If, roaming over the domain of the fundamental, we follow the traces of its influence, we soon reach those boundaries where the attraction of the tonal center is weaker, where the power of the ruler gives way and the right of self-determination of the half-free can under certain circumstances provoke upheavals and changes in the constitution of the entire structure. . . . This activity, a reflection of our own human enterprise, is what causes us to perceive as life what we create as art.[44]

This is a metaphor for Schoenberg's concept of "monotonality." Ultimately he conceived of tonality as comprising all pitches, chords, and key areas, all related to one another and to the centric key area: "Every digression from the tonic is considered to be still within the tonality, whether directly or indirectly, closely or remotely related . . . there is only one tonality in a piece."[45] Tonality is a configuration of functions or forces, defined by scale degrees, each related to a single tonal center in a specific way. That relation gives to each pitch, chord, key area, to each event, its particular function.

Those elements of "unrest" or "imbalance" which, to use Schoenberg's political metaphor, challenge the sovereignty of the tonic he termed the problem. "Every succession of tones produces unrest, conflict, problems. . . . Every musical form can be considered as an attempt to treat this unrest either by halting or limiting it, or by solving the problem."[46] He defined the musical idea in these terms.

Through the connection of tones of different pitch, duration and stress (intensity??), an unrest comes into being: a state of rest is placed in question through a contrast. From this unrest a motion proceeds, which after the attainment of a *climax* will again lead to a state of rest or to a . . . new kind of consolidation that is equivalent to a state of rest.[47]

In each work the particular way in which the presentation and resolution of the problem is carried out is the musical idea of the work. If, as he says more generally, the *totality* of the piece is the idea, he would seem to mean the process by which the challenge to the tonic is concretely manifested and coherently sustained across the work, and by which its conflicting elements are finally assimilated into the tonic.

Each composition raises a question, puts up a problem which in the course of the piece has to be answered, resolved, carried through. It has to be carried through many contradictory situations; it has to be developed by drawing conclusions from what it postulates . . . and all this might lead to a conclusion, a *pronunciamento*.[48]

The musical idea, in a tonal work, thus constitutes the total dynamic of the work, the totality of forces striving toward balance.

COMPOSITION WITH TWELVE TONES RELATED ONLY TO ONE ANOTHER

Following Schoenberg, as he works through his notions of the musical idea, what he means by it and its function in tonal music ultimately seems clear. How he conceives it in twelve-tone music is not so clear.

His studies of twelve-tone composition and of the musical idea were vitally connected. His concept of the musical idea served both to differentiate his ideas of tonal and twelve-tone composition and to establish their continuity. The first essays on both appeared in 1923. Two are the earliest essays on his new method. In the first of these, "New Music," he wrote: "Five tones have been drawn into composition in a way not called upon before—*that is all*. This does not call for any new laws. The first thing to be done is to find the form in which the laws of earlier art can be applied to the new."[49] In the series of *Gedanke* manuscripts, written between 1923 and 1936, Schoenberg seemed to be formulating the laws of earlier art in ways which might be applied to new forms.

The second of these essays, written 9 May, 1923, makes explicit the connection between his investigations of the musical idea and twelve-tone composition. Schoenberg attributes his new method to an unconscious urge to try out new resources and to produce with them alone a compact, lucid and comprehensive presentation of the musical idea. In light of the musical idea, he reinterprets the Western musical tradition, thereby demonstrating the continuity of his new method. The most important assumption of that new method, he says, is a new conception of the musical idea. "The weightiest assumption behind twelve-tone composition is this thesis: Whatever sounds together (harmonies, chords, the result of part-writing) plays its part in expression and in presentation of the musical idea in just the same way as does all that sounds successively (motive, shape, phrase, sentence, melody, etc.), and it is equally subject to the law of comprehensibility."[50] From this assumption he draws a distinction that changed his view of the history of Western music: the real contrast, he concludes, is between contrapuntal and homophonic musical art. "This law," he says, "which I was the first to utter and accord its true significance, has the following results." He distinguishes three kinds of the presentation of the musical idea, relating to three ways of structuring musical space. In homophonic forms, for the sake of the development of the principal part, a certain economy governs the harmony, which allows it to exert a decisive influence on the development of the structure. In polyphonic music, motivic shapes, themes, phrases and the like never succeed in stretching beyond a certain length. They are never developed, never split off new shapes and are seldom varied. Development takes place through alteration of the mutual relation to each other of the various components. In twelve-tone composition the relationship of the twelve tones to each other develops on the basis of a particular prescribed order (the motive), determined by the inspiration (the idea!). In twelve-tone composition, he continues, the matter under discussion is in fact the succession of tones mentioned, whose comprehensibility as a musical idea is independent of whether its components are made audible one after the other or more or less simultaneously.[51]

In yet a third essay written in 1923, Schoenberg comments on the task of twelve-tone composition:

With the renunciation of the formal advantages inherent in tonal cohesion, presentation of the idea has become rather harder; it lacks the external rounding-off and self-containedness that this simple and natural principle of composition brought about better than did any of the others used alongside it. . . . For in a key, opposites are at work, binding together. Practically the whole thing consists exclusively of opposites, and this gives the strong effect of cohesion. To find means of replacing this is the task of *the theory of twelve-tone composition.*[52]

In one of the *Gedanke* manuscripts two years later he takes up this task. The manuscript begins: "The question of tonality can only be judged according to the laws of presentation of the musical idea." Schoenberg explains those laws as follows:

Compositions executed tonally proceed in every sense so as to bring every occurring tone into a direct or indirect relationship to the fundamental tone, and their technique tries to bring this relationship to such an expression that doubt about how a tone is related can never last for a long time.

Not only is the individual tone treated in this way, but so too are all series of tones, all harmonies, and all progressions of harmonies.[53]

Composition with twelve tones, he continues, is not involved with the tonal problem. "Composition with twelve tones related only to one another . . . *presupposes the knowledge of these relationships*, and does not see in them a problem still to be solved and worked out."[54] Schoenberg compares twelve-tone composition, which works with entire complexes in music, to the way in which language works with comprehensive concepts whose range and meaning are assumed to be generally known. When a certain knowledge can be presupposed, he says, one speaks in complexes of concepts that include the phenomenon and everything connected with it. In music there can only be the question whether the ear, whether the musical understanding, is capable of grasping these relationships and drawing the consequences from them as it does from long-familiar relationships.[55]

In this 1925 essay, Schoenberg returns to his notion of the different uses of musical space. "The principle I established," he says, "is valid here: 1) Harmonies are not under discussion. 2) Use of the musical space aims at accelerating the presentation of the idea.'' He goes on to describe the two situations, the listener confronting familiar or new relationships. In a homophonically organized space, he says, one relationship that must be immediately recognized is that between chord and passing phenomenon. But in the new twelve-tone music vertical and horizontal dimensions are perceived as the same: ''simultaneity is only an extremely rapid succession, . . . [which] is to be grasped in the same way as horizontal succession.''

Is it possible, he asks, to invent a technique that makes the comprehension of the ''vertical succession of tones'' as easy as that of the horizontal, for which we have more time?[56] One such technique he proposes is composition with twelve tones related only to one another. ''Relationships are fixed once and for all. . . . Everything not grasped on first hearing is more accessible to the understanding by frequent repetition and diverse presentation.''[57]

In his 1941 essay on composition with twelve tones, he has greatly refined his concept of the musical space, which now represents the musical totality in either tonal or twelve-tone composition. His concept of the unity of the musical space, he says, is a conclusion that followed from his assumption that music is the presentation of musical ideas:

The two-or-more-dimensional space in which musical ideas are presented is a unit. Though the elements of these ideas appear separate and independent to the eye and the ear, they reveal their true meaning only through their co-operation, even as no single word alone can express a thought without relation to other words. . . . A musical idea, accordingly, though consisting of melody, rhythm, and harmony, is neither the one nor the other alone, but all three together. The elements of a musical idea are partly incorporated in the horizontal plane as successive sounds, and partly in the vertical plane as simultaneous sounds.[58]

Schoenberg maintained that that the process of composition with twelve tones was not somehow different than any other composition. In 1923, when he disclosed his new method to his students he told them to use the method, but to compose as they always had. Although compositional problems and techniques drastically changed during the course of his career, his fundamental theory of composition did not.

NOTES

1. Arnold Schoenberg, ''Composition with Twelve Tones (1),'' (1941), in *Style and Idea: Selected Writings of Arnold Schoenberg*, ed. Leonard Stein, trans. Leo Black (Berkeley and Los Angeles: University of California Press, 1984) (hereafter *SI*), 220.

2. Arnold Schoenberg, ''New Music, Outmoded Music, Style and Idea'' (1946), in *SI*, 122–23.

3. Arnold Schoenberg, ''My Evolution,'' (1949), in *SI*, 91.

4. The letter, in the collection of the Library of Congress, is described in H. H.

Stuckenschmidt, *Arnold Schoenberg: His Life, World, and Work*, trans. Humphrey Searle (New York: Schirmer Books, 1978) (hereafter Stuckenschmidt), 385.

5. Letter to Emil Herzka. Text and trans. in Bryan Simms's review, "Arnold Schoenberg, *Theory of Harmony* tr. by Roy E. Carter," *Music Theory Spectrum* 4 (1982): 160 (hereafter Simms).

6. Ibid.

7. Arnold Schoenberg, *Der musikalische Gedanke; seine Darstellung und Durchfuehrung* [The Musical Idea; Its Presentation and Elaboration], trans. Charlotte Cross (unpublished, undated) [hereafter *Gedanke* manuscript #11].

8. Arnold Schoenberg *Letters*, ed. Erwin Stein, trans. Eithne Wilkins and Ernst Kaiser (Berkeley and Los Angeles: University of California Press, 1987), 164–65.

9. Arnold Schoenberg, "Composition with Twelve Tones (1)," (1941), in *SI*, 214–15.

10. Arnold Schoenberg, "Inspiration," trans. Wayne Shoaf, in *Tenth Anniversary Bulletin* (Arnold Schoenberg Institute, 1987), 3, 7.

11. An interview with José Rodrigues for Merle Armitage, ed., *Schoenberg* (New York: Schirmer, 1937), excerpted in Stuckenschmidt, 419.

12. Ibid.

13. A letter to Dr. Julius Bahle, described in Willi Reich, *Schoenberg: A Critical Biography* (New York, Washington: Praeger Publishers, 1971) (hereafter Reich), 257f.

14. Arnold Schoenberg, "The Blessing of the Dressing," (1948), in *SI*, 385.

15. Arnold Schoenberg, "Gustav Mahler," (1912, 1948), in *SI*, 458.

16. Arnold Schoenberg, "Folkloristic Symphonies," (1947), in *SI*, 163.

17. A. W. Schlegel, *Vorlesungen über dramatische Kunst und Literatur* [Lectures on Dramatic Art and Literature] (Leipzig, 1809–1811).

18. Arnold Schoenberg, *The Musical Idea and the Logic, Technique, and Art of Its Presentation*, ed. trans., and with commentary by Patricia Carpenter and Severine Neff (New York: Columbia University Press, 1995) (hereafter *Gedanke* manuscript #10), 118–19.

19. Arnold Schoenberg, *Gedanke* manuscript #11.

20. Arnold Schoenberg, *Gedanke* manuscript #10, 118–19.

21. Ibid., 119–20.

22. Ibid., 108–9.

23. Ibid.

24. Arnold Schoenberg, "Tonality and Form," (1925), in *SI*, 257.

25. Letter to Adolph Weiss, December 1, 1931. Text and trans. in Simms.

26. *Gedanke* manuscript #10, 118–19.

27. Arnold Schoenberg, "Tonality and Form," (1925), in *SI*, 255.

28. *Gedanke* manuscript #10, 124–25.

29. Arnold Schoenberg, "Problems in Teaching Art," (1911), in *SI*, 369.

30. Arnold Schoenberg, "Form," unpublished fragment in the Archives of the Arnold Schoenberg Institute, Los Angeles.

31. Arnold Schoenberg, *Harmonielehre* (Vienna: Universal, rev. ed. 1922), trans. Roy E. Carter, *Arnold Schoenberg, Theory of Harmony* (Berkeley: University of California Press, 1978) (hereafter *HL*), 289.

32. Arnold Schoenberg, "Composition with Twelve Tones (1)," (1941), in *SI*, 215.

33. Arnold Schoenberg, "Problems of Harmony," (1934), in *SI*, 285.

34. Arnold Schoenberg, "Eartraining Through Composition," (1939), in *SI*, 381.

35. Arnold Schoenberg, *Der musikalische Gedanke, seine Darstellung und Durchführung* [The Musical Idea, Its Presentation and Elaboration], unpublished manuscript, July 6, 1925, trans. Charlotte Cross.

36. *Gedanke* manuscript #10, 120–22, 126–27.

37. Arnold Schoenberg, "New Music, Outmoded Music, Style and Idea," (1946), in *SI*, 122–23.

38. Arnold Schoenberg, "Problems of Harmony," (1934), in *SI*, 270.

39. *HL*, 313.

40. *HL*, 24.

41. Ibid.

42. *Gedanke* manuscript #10, 310–11.

43. *HL*, 151–52.

44. Ibid., 150.

45. Arnold Schoenberg, *Structural Functions of Harmony*, rev. ed. (New York: W. W. Norton, 1969), 19.

46. Arnold Schoenberg, *Fundamentals of Composition*, ed. Gerald Strang and Leonard Stein (New York: St. Martin's Press, 1967), 102.

47. *Gedanke* manuscript #10, 102–3.

48. Jean and Jesper Christensen, *From Arnold Schoenberg's Literary Legacy: A Catalogue of Neglected Items* (Warren, MI: Harmonie Park Press, 1988), 99.

49. Arnold Schoenberg, "New Music," (1923), in *SI*, 137.

50. Arnold Schoenberg, "Twelve-Tone Composition," (1923), in *SI*, 207f.

51. Ibid.

52. Arnold Schoenberg, "Hauer's Theories," (1923), in *SI*, 209.

53. Arnold Schoenberg, *zu: Darstellung d. Gedankens* [On: Presentation of the Idea], 12 November 1925, unpublished manuscript, trans. Charlotte Cross (hereafter *Gedanke* manuscript #3).

54. Ibid.

55. Ibid.

56. Ibid.

57. Ibid.

58. Arnold Schoenberg, "Composition with Twelve Tones (1)," (1941), in *SI*, 221.

11

Schoenberg: The Analyst and the Analyzed

Bryan R. Simms

Musical analysis was an important matter for Schoenberg. It was a crucial step in his teaching of composition and a useful way to introduce his music to the general public. It was an activity that he sometimes engaged in as a pastime or, more importantly, to help him to overcome an artistic stumbling block. Increasingly in his theoretical writings he resorted to analysis to illustrate common features of structure that he had deduced from musical masterpieces from Bach to Mahler, finding in these works principles of musical expression that seemed to provide reliable guidelines for the future. In his study of these masterpieces, Schoenberg developed several highly original analytic insights that have been continuously reused and refined by technical writers to the present day. Although Schoenberg rarely turned to his own music for analytic examples, the applicability of his structural precepts to his own compositions is evident.

In this article I will discuss four of Schoenberg's principal ideas concerning musical structure and its analysis—basic shape, developing variation, liquidation, and sentence form. I will then briefly trace the influence of these concepts on subsequent writers and turn finally to a survey of general trends in the analysis of Schoenberg's own music, emphasizing the composer's posttonal works.

Schoenberg valued musical analysis primarily for its role in compositional pedagogy. His student Paul Pisk summarized its position in Schoenberg's highly systematic approach to teaching:

Schoenberg's instruction of advanced students in composition was given in two directions. First correction of actual student work, secondly analysis of masterpieces. The first consisted in minute examination of every detail (''Where does this come from?'' ''What use did you make of this motive or chord?''). . . . Problems in unity or overall organization of the piece were detected and solutions attempted. For this purpose the second aspect, analysis, was brought in. Only materials which had immediate bearing on the student's pieces were used as examples. For contrapuntal devices (and others, of course) Bach, for architectural clarity, Mozart, and for manipulation of material (developmental techniques) Beethoven and Brahms. But very often less known compositions of other masters were analyzed if their content had relation to the student's work. For devices in romantic harmony, Wagner, Bruckner, and Mahler were used, the latter especially as master of variation and transformation of musical ideas. The author does not recall one instance in which Schoenberg would have used his own music as examples for the general student.[1]

It is clear from Pisk's account that Schoenberg did not consider analysis to be an independent study. Its purpose was to reveal the techniques of the great composers of the past, to show their solutions to important compositional problems, and to establish models of compositional procedure that were endowed with timeless and axiomatic significance. Given this circumscribed and decidedly practical use for analysis, it is understandable that Schoenberg cast his analytic eye primarily upon the great masters of the eighteenth and nineteenth centuries, rather than at the more experimental music of his contemporaries.

Schoenberg's theoretical writings, like his exercises in analysis, are directed to the student of composition. His first such treatise was the *Harmonielehre* (1911, revised 1922). This was to be the initial volume in a cycle of pedagogical writings on composition. In a letter to Emil Hertzka dated 23 July 1911, Schoenberg outlined a plan by which the harmony book would be followed by volumes on counterpoint, instrumentation, and form. "All of these books are textbooks or teaching aids," he wrote. "In their entirety they form an aesthetic of music, under which title I intend to write a . . . comprehensive work."[2]

Schoenberg's formulation of a *Kompositionslehre* entered a new phase as the ideas leading to twelve-tone composition crystallized in his thinking. In 1917 he returned to his earlier plan for a multipartite theory of composition and outlined a series of studies on counterpoint, instrumentation, and form, which he prefaced with a new study concerning coherence in music. This introductory discipline, in which Schoenberg planned to study the ways in which musical masterpieces achieved an organic unity, was elaborated upon in a lengthy although incomplete manuscript titled "Der musikalische Gedanke und die Logik, Technik und Kunst seiner Darstellung" ("The Musical Idea and the Logic, Technique, and Art of Its Presentation"), written shortly after Schoenberg immigrated to the United States in 1933. But Schoenberg's teaching in America quickly diverted his attention to a more practical and rudimentary level of study. During the late 1930s and 1940s he wrote elementary books on harmony *(Structural Functions of Harmony)*, counterpoint *(Preliminary Exercises in Counterpoint)*, and form *(Fundamentals of Musical Composition)*. These were directed at the "average student of the [American] universities, who has no special talent for composing or for music at all." All three texts appeared posthumously in editions completed by his students Leonard Stein and Gerald Strang.

A comparison of all of these projects with the *Harmonielehre* shows an ever-increasing emphasis on analysis. Explorations of existing musical literature are scarcely found at all in the *Harmonielehre* of 1911, they gradually appear in the fragmentary texts and outlines from 1917 until the mid-1930s, and they emerge as a central undertaking in the textbooks of the American period. The musical examples of the *Harmonielehre*—concise and abstract chordal progressions—are almost all composed by Schoenberg himself. "I have omitted harmonic analyses in this book," he wrote, "because I consider them superfluous."

Analysis is more a test the author uses for the correctness of his theory than an advantage for the pupil. I do not deny that it would benefit the pupil to account for the harmonic procedure in masterworks. But to do this the way it should be done, i.e., by examining the harmonic structure of an entire work and the significance of the individual chords and chord progressions, would be impossible within the limits of a harmony course. Yet, anything else is relatively pointless.[3]

By contrast, both *Structural Functions of Harmony* and *Fundamentals of Musical Composition* are filled with musical examples from Bach to Brahms, which are now brought forward, as Schoenberg wrote in the frontmatter to *Structural Functions*, because they are "necessary for illustrating and clarifying every problem."

Schoenberg based his analytic ideas in these and other writings upon a general theory of musical structure that he considered universally valid. A great work of music was a logical, fluent, and coherent discourse. It was intensely unified in its materials such that any passage had an organic connection with any other passage. But it was also filled with contrast, variety, and a constant infusion of new elements. Its ultimate purpose was to express an important idea. "Musical images," he wrote, "the themes, shapes, melodies, episodes, follow one another like turns of fate in a life-story—diverse but still logical, and always linked: one grows out of another."[4]

By a close and largely independent study of the tonal repertory, Schoenberg found common formal principles that the great composers had used to create this "diverse but still logical" discourse. One of the most important of these, both for Schoenberg and for later writers, was the idea of the *Grundgestalt* ("basic shape"). He began to use this concept in his teaching at about the same time that he formulated the twelve-tone idea, but it was never clearly elucidated in his published writings. For this reason the present-day understanding of basic shape is due primarily to the recollections of his students.

It was first enunciated in print by Erwin Stein in his article "Neue Formprinzipien" (1924), in which it is discussed solely in the context of twelve-tone composition in its early stages. Stein defines a basic shape as a "melodic" motive, devoid of rhythm, which contains up to twelve different pitches and which is normally encountered at the beginning of a serialized piece. If a basic shape has fewer than twelve notes, then the work may have several basic shapes.

Stein gives examples from Schoenberg's Opp. 23, 24, and 25, from which two passages are reproduced in Example 1. In the first measure of Schoenberg's Piano Piece, Op. 23, No. 4 (Example 11.1a), Stein finds three basic shapes. The first three measures of the Prelude of the Piano Suite, Op. 25 (Example 1b), also contain three basic shapes, and here the pitch contents of all three together form an aggregate of the twelve tones.

According to Stein, a basic shape is distinct from what Schoenberg later called the "basic set" of a twelve-tone work, that is, the fundamental ordering of all twelve pitch classes. The basic shape is much closer to a sounding musical entity: indeed, Stein describes it as a special type of motive, differing from a conventional motive primarily in its lack of rhythm. He wrote:

The most significant feature of the new method is the introduction of a succession of notes, a *basic shape*, as Schoenberg calls it, which carries the form of a piece. . . . The basic shape consists of several notes whose melodic structure (i.e., the relation between whose intervals) is binding upon the entire piece. The rhythm, however, is free. . . . The basic shape is the law of the piece concerned. It is not the theme but only its raw material. It is a motif in the most literal and original sense of the word, being the motive power of all melodic and harmonic happenings. Only, we have to remember that it is but a defined melodic shape without rhythmic articulation (whence we have called it a melodic motif) and that it is not the smallest possible entity, but can be split up into further motifs.[5]

The basic shapes of a work, says Stein, are subject to an ongoing process of variation by which they can be inverted, transposed, stated in retrograde, presented as chords, split apart and recombined, and expanded by the interpolation of foreign tones. The organic connection of the basic shape to the ensuing substance of a work is all the more intense.

Stein's account of the basic shape in a twelve-tone work agrees in general with Schoenberg's few statements about it. In his article "Rückblick" (1949), Schoenberg alludes to the unifying capacity of the basic shape, noting also that a twelve-tone basic shape contains a fundamental or referential order of tones that is analogous to the referential function of key in earlier music. Schoenberg writes:

The method of composition with twelve tones replaces the order that was [earlier] produced by constant reference to a tonal center with another type of order according to which every self-contained section [of a piece] stems from the pitch relations within a twelve-tone "basic shape." Every section is placed in a comprehensible interrelationship with all other sections because they relate continuously to the same basic shape.[6]

Schoenberg also viewed basic shape as central to the unity of music from the tonal repertory. In his essay "Linear Counterpoint" (1931), he writes:

Example 11.1
Piano Piece, op. 23, no. 4, m. 1 (A); Suite for Piano, op. 25, Prelude, mm. 1–3 (B).
Schoenberg Suite für Klavier, op. 25, movement I
Copyright 1925 by Universal Edition / Copyright renewed / All Rights Reserved
Used in the territory of Canada by permission of European American Music Distributors Corporation, sole U.S. and Canadian agent for Universal Edition. Reprinted also by permission of Belmont Music Publishers, Pacific Palisades, CA 90272.

Whatever happens in a piece of music is nothing but the endless reshaping of a "basic shape." . . . I say a piece of music is a picturebook consisting of a series of shapes, which for all their variety still (a) always cohere with one another, (b) are presented as variations (in keeping with the idea) of a basic shape, the various characters and forms arising from the fact that variation is carried out in a number of different ways; the method of presentation used can either "unfold" or "develop."[7]

Schoenberg's more general application of the term is expanded upon in Erwin Stein's book *Form and Performance* (1962), a work that directly reflects Schoenberg's teaching. "We shall use the term *shape*," Stein writes, "for any group of notes that is felt as belonging together and makes musical sense. A shape makes sense by virtue of its distinctive tonal and rhythmical features."[8] Stein's examples of shapes in this more general context show each of them to be complexes of intervals, rhythms, meters, textures, harmonies, and key, not just the simple melodic contours that defined twelve-tone shapes. The most elemental shape—by implication the "basic" one—is encountered at the outset of a work. Most simply, says Stein, it is a phrase made by the juxtaposition of two motives. The second motive is a variation of the first, but it also contains some striking difference or "antithesis" in comparison with the first. "Our examples, taken from various periods, styles and types of music, show how at the beginning of a piece two or more groups of notes are juxtaposed. The principle, though differently applied, remains the same: music gains shape by antithesis."[9] Stein concludes that a work has many shapes, connected with one another by an ongoing process of varied recurrence into which new or contrasting elements are constantly infused. The shape encountered at the outset is basic in that it functions as a progenitor for all that come after it.

Josef Rufer, like Stein, recalled the basic shape as a phrase encountered at the beginning of a work, which formed the model through the process of variation for subsequent shapes and substance. A basic shape, says Rufer, consists of a conjunction of two or more motives, and in length it lies between a motive and a theme. He writes: "A *shape* or *phrase* consists in the *fixed* juxtaposition, the fixed shaping, of one or more motives with their (varied) repetitions. It extends normally for 2 to 3 measures with only *one* good (i.e., strong) metric unit."[10]

Also like Stein, Rufer suggests that the basic shape is a prototype for an entire work: it contains the germinal motivic elements (intervals and rhythms), meter, key, and harmony. Echoing Stein's discussion, Rufer held that the material derived from a basic shape will embody "connected antithesis," that is, it will be connected to the original shape by variation and also antithetical in its incorporation of new or contrasting features.

The notion of basic shape is closely allied with a process that Schoenberg termed "developing variation" *(entwickelnde Variation)*. This is the means by which a basic shape comes to underlie all other materials (especially themes) of a composition. He did not exhaustively enumerate the ways that a shape can be varied, but the examples given in his many discussions of the subject emphasize the thematic dimension, showing rhythmic or metric changes, diminution and augmentation, extension or contraction, and inversion, transposition, or retrograde statement as possibilities. Another common variational device is the recomposition of a submotivic element from the basic shape, such as a single interval or rhythmic particle. But regardless of how the basic idea is varied, the resultant shape will contain elements of both contrast and sameness in comparison to earlier shapes. He writes in the outline "Zusammenhang, Kontrapunkt, Instrumentation, Formenlehre" (1917):

One can distinguish *two methods of varying* a motive.

With the first usually the changes virtually seem to have nothing more than an *ornamental* purpose; they appear in order to create variety and often disappear without a trace. . . .

The second can be termed *developing variation*. The changes proceed more or less directly toward the goal of allowing new ideas to arise.[11]

In modern works of high artistic value, Schoenberg wrote, developing variation entirely replaces direct or sequential repetition of themes as a generator of form. Schoenberg held J. S. Bach to be the originator of developing variation, which then characterized the "homophonic-melodic" idiom of the classical and romantic periods.

"Liquidation" *(Liquidieren)* was Schoenberg's term for a special developmental technique that led to the conclusion of a theme, shape, or section. Schoenberg described it in *Fundamentals of Musical Composition*:

Liquidation consists in gradually eliminating characteristic features [of a motive], until only uncharacteristic ones remain, which no longer demand a continuation. Often only residues remain, which have little in common with the basic motive. . . . The purpose of liquidation is to counteract the tendency toward unlimited extension.[12]

Schoenberg saw liquidation as a means for making musical discourse varied and fluent. It was a way of turning that discourse in a new direction, ending one line of thought and introducing a new subject. He speaks to these aspects in his essay "Connection of Musical Ideas":

One of the most important functions of the changing of features [of the basic shape] is the production of *liquidation*. By producing at least a preliminary end to a section it makes the appearance of a new idea a reasonable, if not necessary, event. A liquidation is often carried out unto the entire elimination of all features. No wonder that in such a case the entrance of a terrifically strong *contrast* does not violate the feeling of balance. It is as if everything began anew.

A liquidation can, at one point or another, cease to eliminate; instead it can begin to develop and add new features. It then will have changed into a *transition*.[13]

Example 11.2
Beethoven, Piano Sonata in F Minor, op. 2, no. 1, first movement, mm. 1–20.

As Schoenberg observed, liquidations are especially appropriate in transitional passages, although they can also appear toward the end of themes, sequences, or developments. An example cited in *Fundamentals of Musical Composition* is the main theme of the first movement of Beethoven's Piano Sonata in F minor, Op. 2, No. 1 (Example 11.2). The theme begins with a basic shape (a phrase) in mm. 1–2. This consists of two melodic motives—the arpeggiated figure in m. 1 and the ornamented scalewise descending minor third in m. 2. The phrase is repeated sequentially over a dominant harmony in the next two measures.

The concluding four measures of the theme contain a development which involves liquidation. The liquidation is seen in two phenomena: the first, which Schoenberg called "reduction," occurs in mm. 5–6, as the basic shape is reduced to the motive of m. 2. The second occurs in mm. 7–8, where the descending third of m. 2 is concatenated into a descending scale from B-flat to E. In Schoenbergian terms, the descending third is a "characteristic feature" of the motive of m. 2; in mm. 7–8 this feature is made into an uncharacteristic "residue" that does not demand further development. The transition (mm. 9–20) also involves liquidation. The transition begins with a straightforward repetition of the basic shape, reharmonized over a minor dominant chord. Liquidation in the form of reduction then returns in mm. 11–14, followed by a thrice-stated cadential figure that is again a neutral scalar residue of the descending third.

The main theme of this movement is also an example of a melodic prototype that Schoenberg called a "sentence" *(Satz)*. This term has a long history in writings on musical form, but the way that it is used by Schoenberg is highly original.[14] In its simplest manifestation, as in the eight-measure example from Beethoven's Op. 2, No. 1, a sentence has two parts. It begins with a four-measure unit consisting of a two-measure phrase stated over the tonic harmony and a sequential repetition of this phrase over the dominant harmony. In the remaining four measures, motives from the opening phrase are developed and liquidated, leading to a clear cadence on the dominant (as in this example), tonic, or mediant harmonies.

Schoenberg postulated sentence form as one of two archetypes for strict melodic presentation in works by the great masters. The other is period form, which consists normatively of four equal phrases. The first two (together forming the "antecedent") are contrasting in character, and they end in a weak cadence. The final two (the "consequent") consist of a repetition of the first phrase, then a cadential phrase bringing the form to a firm cadence on the tonic, dominant, or mediant harmonies.

Although earlier writers showed a passing awareness of these two prototypes, Schoenberg was the first to call clear attention to their differences and to underscore their importance in the construction of classical themes. They are evidence of yet another of the composer's analytic insights stemming from a profound knowledge of the tonal repertory.

Schoenberg held that the strict presentation of themes in the classical literature normally used sentence or period form, either one of which could be compounded into longer patterns such as the small ternary form (A B A'). The sentence was a more advanced structure than the period: "The sentence is a higher form of construction than the period," Schoenberg wrote. "It not only makes a statement of an idea, but at once starts a kind of development. Since development is the driving force of musical construction, to begin it at once indicates forethought."[15] In the nineteenth and early twentieth centuries, he said, composers continued to use period and sentence forms, only with greater freedom.

The concepts of basic shape, developing variation, liquidation, and sentence form were quickly taken up by later writers. Following Erwin Stein's discussion of the twelve-tone basic shape in 1924 (see above), this notion was adopted by other writers from Schoenberg's circle who were seeking to explain the twelve-tone method. The concept was put to another use in Zofia Lissa's 1935 article "Geschichtliche Vorform der Zwölftontechnik."[16] Lissa begins by paraphrasing Stein's description of a basic shape as a source of thematic relations in a twelve-tone piece. She finds a historical precedent for it in Scriabin's use of a "harmonic center" *(Klangzentrum)* in his late music. The harmonic center normally consists of six notes, changeable from piece to piece, which establish a fixed total intervallic content for pitch structures of the composition, but not a fixed linear ordering. The harmonic center is applied primarily in the construction of chords, which appear as transpositions or component parts of the *Klangzentrum*.

Following World War II, Schoenberg's ideas of basic shape and developing variations became even more widespread in the technical literature on music. This development was no doubt stimulated by compositional trends of the same period, which stressed deep structure and an intense interconnectedness of all elements in a composition. It was also provoked by a zeitgeist in which relatively abstruse mathematical models were applied to music theory and, in the United States, in which there occurred a remarkable revival of interest in the systematic theories of Heinrich Schenker. The extension of Schoenberg's ideas of basic shape and developing variation as a system for analysis was carried on by numerous writers, especially in England and the United States. Only a few of them can be mentioned here.

Although he does not use Schoenberg's terminology or even mention Schoenberg by name, it is likely that Rudolph Reti's study *The Thematic Process in Music* (1951) was inspired by Schoenberg's ideas. Reti's theory is that all themes in a musical masterpiece—even in a multimovement work—share distinctive motivic similarities ranging from straightforward transformation to subtle affinity. The pitch succession of some motives even governs large-scale tonal plan. Reti identifies the central idea of a composition as a "basic pattern"—plainly comparable to Schoenberg's basic shape—whose development ensures an intense thematic unity that Reti considered the hallmark of great music.

Josef Rufer's book *Komposition mit zwölf Tönen* (1952), unlike Reti's, is overtly based on Schoenberg's ideas.[17] But like Reti, Rufer emphasizes the power of a few initial motives in a composition to unify all of its major themes in all movements. Rufer uses Beethoven's Piano Sonata in C Minor, Op. 10, No. 1, as an example. The basic shape, which Rufer sees as the source of all later themes, consists of the conjunction of two motives first presented in mm. 1–4 of the first movement. Rufer's interpretation, like Reti's, is strongly oriented toward identifying a common intervallic source for diverse thematic phenomena. The two writers share a tendency, also present in Schoenberg, to confer motivic status on phenomena as small as a single interval, detached from how that interval might conform to the underlying harmony or to other contextual factors.

A more comprehensive interpretation of Schoenberg's idea of basic shape is found in David Epstein's *Beyond Orpheus* (1979). For Epstein a basic shape may be either a motivic complex or an abstract entity:

The *Grundgestalt* denotes a configuration of musical elements that is significant to the form and structure of a work and is manifested throughout the work in differing guises and on various structural levels. In these appearances certain intrinsic features are retained, but are varied or disguised by means of embellishments, elaborations, interpolations, and/or contractions of elements.[18]

Part of the basic shape of Mozart's Symphony in G Minor, K. 555, for example, is a figure that descends diatonically through the interval of a fifth. This figure does not appear literally in the piece, but instead underlies various themes, beginning with the main theme of the first movement and continuing through numerous other thematic "recontextualizations." Epstein's use of abstract structural phenomena, plainly inspired by the writings of Schenker, is generally unlike Schoenberg, who tended to conceive of a musical entity primarily on a foreground level, as a discourse evolving through time, rather than as a multilayered structure in which abstract forms control the musical foreground.

In the last fifteen years analyses using Schoenberg's concepts of basic shape and developing variations have continued to multiply, primarily among writers in the United States.[19] This increased interest reflects a general search among American theorists for more diverse viewpoints about musical structure and a departure from an earlier tendency to follow some single, well-established analytic procedure (such as that of Schenker). Accordingly, the "doctrinaire" interpretation of Schoenberg's notions by students such as Erwin Stein and Josef Rufer has been made more eclectic and systematic.

This broadening of approach is evident in Walter Frisch's *Brahms and the Principle of Developing Variation* (1984). Frisch's purpose is to trace the adoption of motivic development in Brahms's music, using Schoenberg's concept of developing variation as a guide. He expands upon Schoenberg in his consideration of developmental practices within large sections of music, rather than looking, as Schoenberg did in his writings, only at brief phrases or single themes. The notion of basic shape is not central to Frisch's method. Instead, the writer finds Brahms's early works characterized by thematic transformation rather than developing variation. A transformation is a process in which the entire contour of a theme is preserved despite changes in other factors. Only later in Brahms's career, says Frisch, does the composer begin to unify large sections or entire multimovement works by ongoing motivic development.

Schoenberg's insight into the melodic prototype called the sentence has also received increased attention in recent years. The sentence archetype was plainly emphasized in Schoenberg's teaching, as it reappears in the writings of many of his students. Its importance was stressed, for example, in Anton Webern's lectures of 1932–33, published posthumously under the title *The Path to the*

New Music. Webern's discussion of sentence form is very much akin to Schoenberg's in *Fundamentals of Musical Composition*, except that Webern draws on
a wider range of examples, from works by Bach to Schoenberg himself. Webern
writes:

The period and the eight-bar sentence are at their purest in Bach; in his predecessors we
find only traces of them. And these two forms are the basic element, the basis of all
thematic structure in the classics and of everything further that has occurred in music
down to our time. It's a long development, and it's often hard to make out those basic
elements. But everything can be traced back to them.[20]

Sentence form, among other Schoenbergian concepts, plays a central role in
Erwin Ratz's *Einführung in die musikalische Formenlehre* (1951). Ratz had been
a student of Schoenberg from 1917 until 1925 and, afterward, an associate of
Webern. His conception of musical structure is clearly indebted to Schoenberg:

Form is the sensory manifestation of an idea. Through form an idea takes on a visible
or audible shape. Through it an idea passes from its spiritual reality, outside of space
and time, into the material world of space and time. . . . The smallest groups [i.e., basic
motives], which are the points of origin for the formal structure, can occupy one or more
measures. In them the special character of a particular piece or of a distinct formal
segment is largely established and further events are predetermined as in a seed.[21]

As with Schoenberg, Ratz held that Bach's music epitomized both a polyphonic
treatment of themes as well as the modern homophonic principle. The difference
was that the theme in polyphonic music did not evolve by motivic variation, as
it did in homophonic music. Ratz's overall intention is to show that Bach's
Two-and Three-Part Inventions also contain forms that were associated with the
homophonic principle, forms most perfectly encountered later in the music of
Beethoven.

The most basic such forms were the period and the sentence. About the latter
Ratz writes:

The eight-measure sentence (2 × 2) + 4 consists of a two-measure phrase, its repetition,
and a four-measure development whose essence it is for some of the motives introduced
in the two-measure phrase to be dropped, producing an intensification and acceleration
of the musical presentation. As a rule there also occurs in the developmental phrase an
acceleration of harmonic motion.[22]

William Caplin further explores the phenomenon of the sentence in his article
"Funktionale Komponenten im achttaktigen Satz."[23] Using evidence from
works by Haydn, Mozart, and Beethoven, Caplin defines three "formal functions" in the eight-measure sentence: presentation (which normally occurs in
the first four measures), continuation, and cadence (together occupying the second four measures). He does not use Schoenberg's idea of liquidation, and he

puts more emphasis than Schoenberg on the role of harmony in the definition of phrase function.

Although Schoenberg did not theorize extensively about the structure of post-tonal music, his conception of such works as diverse and coherent remained unchanged. He continued to find classical forms in this repertory, including *Grundgestalten*, motivic variations, sentences, and periods. These traditional features were stressed in his two most extensive analyses of his posttonal works: radio lectures in 1931 and 1932 concerning his Variations for Orchestra, Op. 31, and Orchestral Songs, Op. 22.[24] In the lecture on the Variations, Schoenberg emphasized the congruence of this twelve-tone work with the classical variations genre of earlier composers. The theme (mm. 34–57), he says, is an example of small ternary form, of which the A section (mm. 34–45) is an irregular period. The theme is entirely constructed from developing variations of motives from the opening basic shape in mm. 34–35.

The nine variations that follow the theme are also based on classical models. Schoenberg described them as both character variations—each establishing its own distinctive character—and "formal" variations in which each develops the ternary form and characteristic motivic ideas from the theme. Also like the classical prototype, each variation uses a "motive of variation," a figure usually derived from the theme itself that serves as the motivic basis for that variation. The composer is almost entirely silent on the relation between twelve-tone elements and form.

The lecture on the Orchestral Songs, Op. 22, is similar in its emphasis upon the traditional unifying power of motivic development. The basic motive of the first song, "Seraphita," for example, is a three-note figure consisting of a minor second and a minor third. This motive is varied by reversing the order of the two intervals, inverting them, expanding them to a major second and major third, stating them in different directions, interpolating foreign tones, or embedding the three-note figure into other shapes. Here the process of developing variations differs from the classical model only in that the brevity of the songs does not allow for full-blown expansion. The basic motives and their variants appear instead as a "hall of mirrors." They are ever present in all parts of the musical texture rather than being confined to a succession of varied thematic recurrences.

Schoenberg admitted to a break with the past only in the areas of harmony and tonality. In the *Harmonielehre* he spoke of an "aversion to recalling even remotely the traditional chords" in his current music, and in the essay "My Evolution" he notes that such works "renounced a tonal centre." These strikingly innovative features were products of the "emancipation of dissonance," a term that he began using as early as in the *Harmonielehre* in 1911.[25] Later he explained:

The term *emancipation of the dissonance* refers to its [dissonance's] comprehensibility, which is considered equivalent to the consonance's comprehensibility. A style based on this premise treats dissonances like consonances and renounces a tonal centre.[26]

But the harmonic logic of Schoenberg's works characterized by the emancipation of dissonance was nowhere coherently explored in the composer's writings. In the *Harmonielehre* he alludes to counterpoint and voice leading as sources of harmony in the new style; elsewhere in this book he attributes the logic of chords to the unconscious or instinctive powers of the great artist. "Laws apparently prevail here," he concluded. "What they are, I do not know. Perhaps I shall know in a few years. Perhaps someone after me will find them. For the present the most we can do is describe."[27]

Given a harmonic language whose structure baffled even the composer, it is not surprising that other writers have approached nontonal music in the most diverse ways. In order to illuminate the leading trends in specialized writing on Schoenberg's "atonal" music (a term that Schoenberg rejected on semantic grounds), it will be useful to survey the literature concerning a prominent atonal work. Schoenberg's Piano Piece, Op. 11, No. 1, is a likely candidate. It has proved to be Schoenberg's most often analyzed piece, and the writings about it strikingly show the difficulties that exist in revealing its organization.

The reasons for the great attention accorded to Op. 11, No. 1, are plain enough. The Three Piano Pieces of Op. 11, composed in February and August 1909, are among the earliest works in the new style. They were the first nontonal pieces by Schoenberg to be published (in October 1910), whereupon they quickly attracted the attention of musicians throughout the world. The first piece of the set—very different from the third piece or from other atonal music composed later in 1909 and 1910—clearly exhibits traditional features. The texture and surface design suggest a piano character piece in the style of Brahms, and there is a large amount of motivic and thematic recurrence, taking the form of simple repetition, sequence, and continuous variation.

But Schoenberg's statement that a tonal center was renounced in his new manner has proved controversial. In fact, the most detailed early studies of the work rejected Schoenberg's viewpoint, holding that tonality was still present in the piece, albeit in a freer manner than before.[28] The first major analysis of Op. 11 was by Hugo Leichtentritt, in the third edition of his *Musikalische Formenlehre* (1927). According to Leichtentritt's view, a key is firmly evident in the melodic dimension of the work, only disguised by the octave displacement of tones. Both lines and chords suggest a polytonal organization in which keys change rapidly, often overriding one another. G major, says Leichtentritt, is the central key. The harmonies do not strongly reinforce the reigning keys due to alteration and unresolved dissonances, but neither do they dispel the sense of tonality. The author also notes other resemblances to traditional music, including regular eight-bar phrasing and a "Wagnerian melos," which conform to and reinforce a tonal reading.

Leichtentritt's interpretation of Op. 11 was extended and made more systematic in Edwin von der Nüll's *Moderne Harmonik* (1932). Nüll put forward a general harmonic theory for music composed after about 1910 by Bartók, Stravinsky, and Schoenberg. These composers, he said, use "expanded tonality"

Example 11.3
Piano Piece, op. 11, no. 1, mm. 1–3.

rather than atonality. Their music is based harmonically and melodically on centric tones, it uses diatonic scales expanded by chromatic notes, and it contains functional chords that result from either modal mixture (i.e., conflations of major and minor forms of a common triad) or "simultaneous bitonality" (i.e., conflations of common chords from two keys). Unresolved embellishing tones and coloristic effects are also pertinent to the new style, which Nüll believed to be a reaction against the anarchic experimentation of the years before 1910.

Nüll found Op. 11, No. 1, to be in the key of "Ee" (E major merged with E minor). The tonic chord (E G G♯ B) is laid out melodically in mm. 1–3 (Example 11.3). It is supported in m. 2 by the chord G♭, F B, which Nüll interpreted as an inverted and altered dominant triad on the root B. The dominant remains in m. 3, but with an altered root in the bass (B♭, representing B) and a seventh (A) and enharmonic ninth (D♭) above it. Nüll found functional harmonic relations to be temporarily suspended in the passage beginning in m. 12, where they are overridden by coloristic effects (*Klangstil*). Schoenberg's passing use of fourth chords was also attributed to timbral rather than to functional purposes. Nüll concluded:

Regardless of what opinion one entertains, one thing is clear. The analysis reveals a structurally controlled layout in both the small and large dimensions. Clearly recognizable tonal relations in every measure make it incomprehensible that people can think that they are doing justice to the laws of such music by blithely applying the empty word "atonal."[29]

Writers to the present day continue to find tonality in this piece and in Schoenberg's other ostensibly "posttonal" works. In his book *Arnold Schönberg: Drei Klavierstücke Op. 11* (1969), Reinhold Brinkmann interprets the first piece as alternating between the keys of E and E♭, thus an example of Schoenberg's concept of "fluctuating tonality" (*schwebende Tonalität*).[30] In Brinkmann's view, the form of the piece is governed by a succession of thematically strict passages, all based on variants of themes and motives first heard in mm. 1–11 and contrasting passages devoid of theme, which he calls *Auflösungszone* (a term borrowed from Adorno) or *exterritoriale Zone*. The thematic passages are freely in the key of E, the latter in E♭. These tonic pitches are expressed, he says, primarily through the boundary points of lines and by the support of tones a fifth above and a fifth below. Parts of the underlying chords are susceptible to a tonal interpretation, but other parts (such as bass tones) conflict with such a reading. "Tonal and atonal elements are played off against each other," he writes, "always in a balance, at least in the vertical dimension."[31]

Tonal interpretations of works such as Op. 11, No. 1, receive little or no support in Schoenberg's writings. To be sure, the composer often enunciated the idea that his nontonal music possessed some principle of coherence that was analogous to that of tonality, and he rejected the term "atonal" as illogical. But he was always clear that key did not exist in his artistic music after 1908 and that he had banished traditional elements from his new harmonic language. In a note tipped into his personal copy of Nüll's *Moderne Harmonik*, Schoenberg writes:

This book could just as well have been written twenty-five years ago. It is the typical "symptom research," which leads to a theory of "symptom generation." Nothing could be more irrelevant than the contrived argument that the ostensibly *"atonal"* is still *"tonal."* . . . In particular he in no way recognizes the organic relation between melody and harmony.[32]

But the problems in creating a theory of harmony that does not make reference to tonal music are inherently complex. We can see some of them by examining again the opening measures of Op. 11, No. 1 (Example 11.3). Although this passage uses a familiar homophonic texture in which a melodic line is accompanied by chords, it is not at all clear how the harmonies should be identified. Does the first chord (m. 2) have three notes, or does it also contain the G, A, or F from the theme? Since Schoenberg emphasized the "organic relation between melody and harmony" in the new style (see above), to what extent does the theme itself embody a harmonic entity? Do the harmonies undergo developing variations in a manner akin to motives, and, if so, by what principles are varied harmonies related to one another?

Virtually all writers who have taken an atonal approach to the piece have sought to define classes of related chords. In his *Harmonielehre* (1925) the Czech theorist Bruno Weigl suggested that chords that have the same vertical succession of intervals when their notes are brought within an octave above the bass are functionally equivalent. In other words, a chord spelled C E F from bottom to top is equivalent to any three-note chord whose upper tones form a major third and perfect fourth with its bass. If the chord is inverted, placing E, for example, in the bass, an entirely new chord type results. Weigl illustrates his system by analyzing a chordal succession in mm. 12–13 from Schoenberg's Op. 11, No. 2 (Example 11.4). Weigl writes:

The first chord, the five-note figure B♭ C♯ F G♭ A, sounds like the first inversion of a neighbor five-note chord consisting of a major triad [on G♭], major 7th, and augmented

9th. The second chord, the six-note figure G A♭, B♭, C D♭, F, is like a neighbor six-note chord consisting of a four-note chord having a diminished triad [on G] and minor 7th added to a minor triad whose fundamental is the seventh [F] of the six-note chord.[33]

Obviously, Weigl does not succeed in finding a musical context that supports his theory of chord equivalence. His intention is solely to characterize the intervallic makeup of chords and to draw analogies with tonal harmonies. Schoenberg was apparently unimpressed, dismissing Weigl's system as "totally idiotic" in a marginal comment that he added to his personal copy of Weigl's *Harmonielehre*.

A principle of equivalence that is more sensitive to similarities in sound and context among ostensibly different chords was suggested by Josef Matthias Hauer in his theory of "tropes." These, according to Hauer's earliest formulation in the article "Sphärenmusik" (*Melos*, 1922), are referential collections of six different pitch classes; they were intended to facilitate a composer's construction of twelve-tone melodies. In Hauer's system the notes of a trope can be presented compositionally in any order and in any transposition. In this sense a trope identifies a class of equivalent six-note collections in a musical foreground. Although Hauer never used tropes as a general analytic tool, his concept pointed to the idea of combining the operations of transposition and reordering as a principle of relatedness among atonal harmonies.

Schoenberg's twelve-tone method suggested mirror forms, or "inversions," as another such operation. According to his classic formulation of the twelve-tone method, a tone row is closely akin to another row whose intervals are octave inversions of the intervals in the original form. This notion of inversion can also be applied to harmonies outside of twelve-tone music. Using the example of the chord C E F, an inversion can be produced by replacing the notes above the bass with tones that create intervals that are octave inversions of the original ones. An inversion of the sample trichord is created if its major third (C to E) and perfect fourth (C to F) are replaced by a minor sixth (C to A♭) and a perfect fifth (C to G)—rendering the collection C G A♭ as the inversion of C E F. Howard Hanson was the first to advance this notion of inversion (which he called "involution") as a principle of equivalence in the analysis of atonal

Example 11.4
Piano Piece, op. 11, no. 2, mm. 12–13.

chords.[34] By allowing for equivalence by any combination of transposition, reordering, or involution of tones, Hanson reduced the number of distinct harmonic "forms" to little more than 200.

Hanson also noted a more abstract principle of relation between two collections of notes. It can be illustrated by considering two four-note collections: C C♯ E F♯ and C C♯ D♯ G. Although these two cannot be made identical by any combination of transposition, reordering, or inversion, they are closely related since they share an identical total intervallic content. This is the number of times that each interval class is formed when every note in the chord is paired off with every remaining tone. In both of these tetrachords, the six interval classes (i.e., minor second to tritone) can each be created exactly once, for which reason the two pitch collections are often called "all-interval" tetrachords. In his theory of pitch-class sets, Allen Forte referred to the connection between such harmonies as the "z" relation.

Forte's "set theory" was the first extensive analytic application of these principles of harmonic relatedness. In Forte's approach, collections of notes ("sets") are represented by integers, which facilitates identifying their varied recurrences. A straightforward application of set theory is found in Forte's analysis of Op. 11, No. 1, in his article entitled "The Magical Kaleidoscope."[35] Forte asserts that the recurrent themes and motivic particles of the work influence only its superficial form. A higher level of structure is governed by varied and interlocking recurrences of a relatively small number of sets. These coincide only in passing with the traditional phenomena of lines and chords, appearing instead as constellations of notes that are generally adjacent but spread throughout the musical texture. They are identifiable primarily by their recurrence. Forte writes:

The coherence of Op. 11/1 as well as its special elusive quality are provided by the dynamic and kaleidoscopic transformations beneath what appears to be a conventional musical surface composed of themes and motives. These transformations create an interlocking of protean musical configurations that forms a multi-leveled and many-faceted object, a kind of structure that Schoenberg introduced for the first time, in an extended way, in this composition, a structure determined by processes unique in music, processes that far transcend the venerable principle *unitas in varietate*.[36]

His analysis of Op. 11, No. 1, attaches special importance to six-note sets. An example is seen by comparing the opening theme to the opening of a developmental passage at m. 34 (Example 11.3 above and Example 11.5). The two passages are related thematically, as the top line in 34–36 contains a variation of the theme from mm. 1–3 a tritone higher. The parallelism of the two passages is also more subtly reinforced, observes Forte, by the notes in m. 34 alone (B♭ C D♭ D E F). This set is related to that embodied by the opening theme (E F G G♯ A B, displayed here in a compact scalewise order) by a combination of inversion, transposition, and reordering. Both sets are members

Example 11.5
Piano Piece, op. 11, no. 1, mm. 34–36.

of the same "set class" and, like all sets within this class, both have the same total intervallic content.

Many z-related sets are also revealed by Forte's analysis. Measure 12 begins a passage which, in surface design, contrasts strongly with the foregoing thematic exposition. But continuity is promoted beneath the musical surface by the recurrence of sets. The second six notes in m. 12 belong to the same set class as the figure in m. 7 (Example 11.6). Furthermore, the first six notes are z-related to the second six. This means that although they are not equivalent by transposition, inversion, or reordering, they still share the same total intervallic content (each has three minor seconds, two major seconds, four minor thirds, two major thirds, two fourths, and two tritones).

In the theories of Hanson and Forte, any collection of tones, regardless of size or makeup, can form an atonal harmony. Other theorists have postulated that only certain categories of chords—fourth chords, symmetrical chords, or small intervallic cells, for example—have primary significance. The theory of atonal harmony set forth by Jan Maegaard in his *Studien zur Entwicklung des dodekaphonen Satzes bei Arnold Schönberg* (1972) is of the latter type since it downplays the importance of all larger chords. In Maegaard's theory, all possible chords are placed into seven categories based on some general audible characteristic. All larger chords, for example, are of the same type, designated by the letter *M*, since Maegaard holds them to be similar in sound regardless of their intervallic makeup.

The primary sense of the system is to characterize chords by perceptible and conceivable harmonic criteria. Thus I confidently place all chords with many tones under the single rubric *M*, because the perceptible and conceivable harmonic features of such chords are usually little different. Granted they are distinguishable by density, but this comes as much from their spacing as from their number of tones. A nine-note chord can strike the ear as denser than an eleven noter. Conceivability falls off markedly as the number of notes increases.[37]

Maegaard's harmonic analysis of Op. 11, No. 1, aims at identifying the type to which its smaller chords belong. The pitch content of lines is also categorized

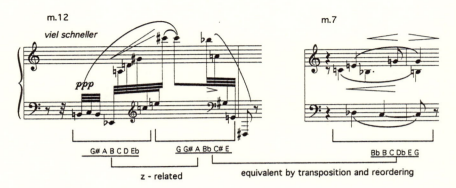

Example 11.6
Piano Piece, op. 11, no. 1, mm. 12–13 and 7.

according to the same types, suggesting an interpenetration of traditionally distinct textural components. Maegaard summarizes this viewpoint:

The structure of these chords is closely connected to the form of elements from the basic shape [the theme in mm. 1–3]. It seems that at this stage in the elucidation of a music whose shapes can be articulated by melody, arpeggiations, or pure chords, it becomes ever more irrelevant to speak of harmony per se.[38]

Technical writings on Schoenberg's twelve-tone works have a somewhat different history from those on his earlier atonal pieces, but they show the same diversity of outlook on basic issues. There were very few detailed analyses of twelve-tone pieces prior to the end of World War II. In part this reticence stems from Schoenberg's own silence on the nature of his method. The lecture-essay ''Composition with Twelve Tones,'' first published in 1950, is the composer's principal statement about the method, which had earlier come to be known through a few general descriptions by writers from the composer's circle, including Erwin Stein, Felix Greissle, and Theodor Adorno. There was also confusion in the literature about the relation between Schoenberg's method and the twelve-tone idea of Josef Matthias Hauer. Hermann Erpf, for example, in a discussion of twelve-tone music in his 1927 *Studien zur Harmonie- und Klangtechnik der neuen Musik*, mentions only the theories of Hauer.

These prewar statements on Schoenberg's twelve-tone music have in common the underscoring of traditional forms and compositional procedures. Schoenberg's own remarks about the method reinforce this viewpoint. In a 1923 talk to his students regarding the method, he concluded by saying: '' 'You use the row and compose as you had done it previously.' That means: 'Use the same kind of form or expression, the same themes, melodies, sounds, rhythms as you used before.' ''[39] Elsewhere in his writings on the method, he chose terminology and concepts associated with the classical repertory. A twelve-tone work, he said, rests on a *Grundgestalt* and its subsequent development. The first half of a row was its "antecedent," the latter half, its "consequent." While composing the Piano Suite, Op. 25 (1921–23), he even referred to row forms at their initial transposition level as "tonics" and those transposed to the tritone as "dominants."[40] The evidence from Schoenberg's writings and music suggests that he viewed twelve-tone composition as a mixed genre: it partook of certain new constructive elements derived from structural features of tone rows, but it also maintained formal features of traditional composition. This synthesis became highly controversial in the 1950s and has remained so in analytic studies even to the present.

Felix Greissle's "Die formalen Grundlagen des Bläserquintetts von Arnold Schönberg" (1925) is typical of early twelve-tone analyses.[41] The author first describes rudiments of the method. He points to the presence of a basic shape that contains the primary ordering of the twelve tones, shows how other forms of the row are derived, and illustrates their deployment in the work's themes. "Probably to maintain comprehensibility despite these [new] premises," he writes, "Schoenberg fell back upon classical formal types."

The first movement ("Schwungvoll") is in a pronounced sonata form, the second ("Anmutig und Heiter") is a large-scale scherzo with two trios, the third ("Etwas langsam") is in a two-part form with the interpolation of a quick, dancelike interlude, and the fourth is a rondo. And something else also recalls the classics: thematic work [and] differentiated extension of subsidiary ideas, which, despite their great diversity of character, always maintain the closest relation to the main idea and to one another. It is apparent that in many ways it is a matter of the continuation and further development of old methods. Formal unity is ensured by the new means, and music can again go forward from where it had to pause in its search for a replacement for tonality.[42]

In the decades following World War II, there was a remarkable increase in attention among theorists both to the twelve-tone method and to Schoenberg's works of this type. Interest in this repertory was no doubt stimulated by the international revival of serial composition during the same years. Some technical writings—such as book-length analyses of the Variations for Orchestra, Op. 31, by René Leibowitz (1949) and Carl Dahlhaus (1968)—continue the approach of their prewar counterparts, as they describe (now in considerably greater detail) traditional formal phenomena and rudimentary row manipulations.[43] But the postwar revival of serialism also produced a new analytic direction that was much less concerned with the ostensibly traditional features of twelve-tone music. The new direction reflects both a critical reassessment of Schoenberg's music by the younger generation of serial composers and a new independence of thought from the prevailing viewpoints set forth by earlier writers, including Schoenberg himself. Schoenberg's approach to twelve-tone music as a synthesis now came under attack. Its traditional texture was forcefully dismissed by Pierre Boulez in his widely read essay "Schoenberg Is Dead" (1952). Milton Babbitt expressed disappointment both in Schoenberg's analytic statements regarding his twelve-tone music and, by implication, in the music itself. "One is obliged to conclude,'' wrote Babbitt, ''that Schoenberg, like many other great innovators, was not . . . entirely aware of the implications of his own discovery.''[44]

In a letter to Rudolf Kolisch of 27 July 1932, Schoenberg had expressed skepticism about the value of tracing row manipulations and, by implication, other explorations of systematic features of the method. ''The only sort of analysis there can be any question of for me,'' he concluded, ''is one that throws the idea into relief and shows how it is presented and worked out.''[45]

But for many writers on twelve-tone music following World War II, the ''idea'' in such pieces had become synonymous with the method itself, which was then viewed in a far more systematic light than Schoenberg had apparently intended. The central figure in this revisionist analytic direction was the composer Milton Babbitt. His writings investigate the structural potential of the twelve-tone ''system'' (a term that Schoenberg rejected); they suggest a mode of analysis, based on mathematical models, that looks for an explanation of musical forms within the elements and operations of the system itself, rather than within traditional music.

Schoenberg's Wind Quintet is analyzed in this manner in Andrew Mead's article '' 'Tonal' Forms in Arnold Schoenberg's Twelve-tone Music'' (1987).[46] The author's approach to the Quintet makes an instructive comparison with that of Greissle, despite its much greater detail and use of highly specialized language. Greissle held that Schoenberg's application of traditional forms was a compensation for the presence of unfamiliar tone rows. Mead's viewpoint is the opposite. The tonal forms, he says, far from being imposed from outside on the musical material, grow from the very structure of the row and its transformations.

The surfaces of his music reveal compositional strategies animated by relations provided by the twelve-tone system. Despite surface similarities to tonal idioms, Schoenberg's twelve-tone music represents a distinctly different form of musical life. . . . The first movement of the Wind Quintet, op. 26, . . . appears to be a text-book sonata allegro. . . . But we shall see that each feature, even the transposition in the recapitulation, reflects relations within the piece's row class working in an overriding compositional strategy for the whole movement.[47]

In the sonata form of the first movement, Mead finds the various formal sections set apart by the choice of row forms. The first thematic area, for example, uses different row forms from the transition and from the second thematic area. Also, the lines and other pitch adjacencies are extracted from the operative row forms differently in each of these formal areas, reflecting a different ''strategy'' in each section.

Mead draws these and other conclusions from a different perspective from Greissle or, for that matter, from Schoenberg. The difference can be illustrated by a relatively minor observation that Mead makes regarding a parallel passage in mm. 1–3 and 42–45 (Example 11.7). The flute line beginning in m. 1 is the

Example 11.7
Woodwind Quintet, op. 26, first movement, mm. 1–3 (a); 42–45 (b).
Schoenberg Bläserquintett, op. 26, movement I
Copyright 1925 by Universal Edition / Copyright renewed / All Rights Reserved
Used in the territory of Canada by permission of European American Music Distributors Corporation, sole U.S. agent and Canadian agent for Universal Edition. Reprinted also by permission of Belmont Music Publishers, Pacific Palisades, CA 90272.

opening of the main theme of the first movement, which contains the notes of the basic series (Mead calls this row "P"). The oboe line in mm. 42–45 opens the second theme group, and it embodies the inversion of the basic series, transposed up four semitones ("It [P]") Mead interprets the large leaps—each a minor ninth—that occur in mm. 3 and 44–45 as marking off the first five notes of the two row forms. These five-note segments are identical in pitch-class content although different in order. He concludes: "The musical surface at the opening of the first and second sections emphasizes the relationship between P and It (P). . . . In both passages, the shared collection is projected in a narrow span, with the differing pitch class separated by a large skip."[48]

In other words, the primary meaning of the minor ninth does not come from its motivic role—an idea that demands development—but is instead a means of clarifying a structural similarity of two row forms. The musical surface, according to Mead's perspective, is essentially controlled by the system, which it serves to articulate. Its harmonic and motivic materials reify an abstract system of relationships which are themselves the essential musical idea.

The many different conclusions about Schoenberg's music reached by leading interpreters may seem baffling in their diversity and lack of consensus. These have arisen in part because the study of Schoenberg's music has involved many factors outside the music itself. They have been significantly informed, for example, by changing compositional styles having nothing to do with Schoenberg. The mathematically based analytic approaches of Babbitt and Forte, for example, would be unthinkable without the application of mathematical systems in works of numerous composers of the 1950s and 1960s. Critical attitudes toward Schoenberg's music have also been important shaping forces. The condemnation of Schoenberg's conservative style made by Boulez in the early 1950s is reflected in the search by theorists for alternatives to the composer's traditionalist theoretical viewpoint concerning posttonal music.

It is more difficult and controversial to assess the role of Schoenberg's own analytic conclusions on the interpretation of his music. Can they be considered factors "outside the music itself" or do they have a more basic and timeless significance? Technical writing on this music to date suggests that Schoenberg's interpretation of his music is not the only valid one. History has shown that any music rests on conceptions that change over time and imply new analytic directions. It can be expected that the future will hold even more disparate analytic conclusions than heretofore about a music that is so richly enigmatic.

NOTES

1. Paul A. Pisk, "Arnold Schoenberg as Teacher," American Society of University Composers, *Proceedings of the Second Annual Conference* (1976): 52–53.

2. See Bryan R. Simms, commentary upon Arnold Schoenberg's *Theory of Harmony*, in *Music Theory Spectrum* 4 (1982): 156–57.

3. Schoenberg, *Theory of Harmony*, trans. Roy E. Carter (Berkeley, Los Angeles: University of California Press, 1978), 16.

4. Schoenberg, "The Orchestral Variations, Op. 31: A Radio Talk," *Score* 27 (1960): 39.

5. Stein, "New Formal Principles," in *Orpheus in New Guises* (London: Rockliff, 1953), 62, 65.

6. Die Methode der Komposition mit zwölf Tönen substituiert die Ordnung, welche durch die beständige Rückbeziehung auf ein tonartliches Zentrum geleistet wird, durch eine andere Ordnung, derzufolge jedes in sich geschlossene Teilstück sich als ein Derivat der Tonbeziehungen in einer zwölftönigen "Grundgestalt" in faßlichem Zusammenhang mit allen anderen Teilstücken befindet, weil es sich ununterbrochen auf diese selbe Grundgestalt rückbezieht.

Published in *Stimmen* 2 (1948–49): 433–38. "Rückblick" is a German version of the essay "My Evolution" (*Style and Idea*, ed. Leonard Stein [Berkeley and Los Angeles: University of California Press, 1984], 79–91). In the English version, Schoenberg (perhaps erroneously) equates basic shape with basic set.

7. In *Style and Idea*, 290.

8. Stein, *Form and Performance* (New York: Limelight, 1989), 72.

9. Ibid., 83.

10. Eine Gestalt oder Phrase besteht aus der festen Zusammenfassung, festen Formung eines oder mehrerer Motive mit ihren (variierten) Wiederholungen. Sie umfaßt in der Regel 2 bis 3 Takte mit nur einem guten d.i. betonten Taktteil.

Rufer, "Begriff und Funktion von Schönbergs Grundgestalt," *Melos* 7 (1971): 282.

11. Schoenberg, *Coherence, Counterpoint, Instrumentation, Instruction in Form*, ed. Severine Neff, trans. Charlotte M. Cross and Severine Neff (Lincoln and London: University of Nebraska Press, 1994), 39.

12. Schoenberg, *Fundamentals of Musical Composition*, ed. Gerald Strang and Leonard Stein (New York: St. Martin's Press, 1967), 58.

13. *Style and Idea*, 288.

14. See Carl Dahlhaus, "Satz und Periode: Zur Theorie der musikalischen Syntax," *Zeitschrift für Musiktheorie* 9 (1978): 16–26.

15. *Fundamentals of Musical Composition*, 58.

16. Lissa, "Geschichtliche Vorform der Zwölftontechnik," *Acta musicologica* 7 (1935): 15–21.

17. Also see the English version: *Composition with Twelve Notes Related Only to One Another*, trans. Humphrey Searle (London: Rockliff, 1954).

18. David Epstein, *Beyond Orpheus: Studies in Musical Structure* (Cambridge, London: MIT Press, 1979), 19.

19. See, for example, Jack Boss, "Schoenberg's Op. 22 Radio Talk and Developing Variation in Atonal Music," *Music Theory Spectrum* 14 (1992): 125–49; Patricia Carpenter, "Grundgestalt as Tonal Function," *Music Theory Spectrum* 5 (1983): 15–38; Graham H. Phipps, "A Response to Schenker's Analysis of Chopin's Etude, Opus 10, No. 12, Using Schoenberg's Grundgestalt Concept," *Musical Quarterly* 69 (1983): 543–69; Walter Frisch, *Brahms and the Principle of Developing Variation* (Berkeley, Los Angeles: University of California Press, 1984); Janet Schmalfeldt, "Berg's Path to Atonality: The Piano Sonata, Op. 1," in *Alban Berg: Analytical and Historical*

Perspectives, ed. Robert P. Morgan, David Gable (Oxford: Clarendon Press, 1991), 79–109; and Ethan Haimo, "Atonality, Analysis, and the Intentional Fallacy [analyzing Schoenberg's Piano Piece, Op. 11, No. 1]," *Music Theory Spectrum* 18 (1996): 167–99.

20. Anton Webern, *The Path to the New Music*, ed. Willi Reich, trans. Leo Black (Bryn Mawr: Theodore Presser, 1963), 27.

21. Form (ist) die sinnliche Erscheinungsweise einer Idee. In der Form nimmt die Idee sichtbare oder hörbare Gestalt an. Damit tritt sie aus der Raum-und Zeitlosigkeit ihrer geistigen Realität in die materielle Welt von Raum und Zeit ein. . . . Solche kleinste Gruppen, die den Ausgangspunkt für den formalen Aufbau bilden, können einen oder auch mehrere Takte umfassen. In ihnen ist die besondere Eigenart des betreffenden Stückes oder auch eines bestimmten Formteiles bereits weitgehend festgelegt und damit das weitere Geschehen wie im Keime veranlagt.

Erwin Ratz, *Einführung in die musikalische Formenlehre: Über Formprinzipien in den Inventionen J. S. Bachs und ihre Bedeutung für die Kompositionstechnik Beethovens* (Vienna: Österreichischer Bundesverlag für Unterricht, Wissenschaft und Kunst, 1951), 7, 9.

22. Der achttaktige Satz, (2 × 2) + 4, besteht aus einem Zweitakter, seiner Wiederholung und einer viertaktigen Entwicklung, deren Wesen darin besteht, daß ein Teil der im Zweitakter exponierten Motive fallen gelassen und so eine Verdichtung und Beschleunigung der musikalischen Darstellung erzielt wird. In der Regel findet im Entwicklungsteil auch eine Beschleunigung in der harmonischen Disposition statt.

Ratz, *Einführung in die musikalische Formenlehre*, 22.

23. Caplin, "Funktionale Komponenten im achttaktigen Satz," *Musiktheorie* 1 (1986): 239–60.

24. English translations as "The Orchestral Variations, Op. 31: A Radio Talk," *Score* 27 (1960): 27–40, and "Analysis of the Four Orchestral Songs Opus 22," trans. Claudio Spies, *Perspectives of New Music* 3 (1965): 1–21. The original German texts are found in Schoenberg's *Gesammelte Schriften*, vol. 1, ed. Ivan Vojtech (Nördlingen and Reutlingen: S. Fischer, 1976) 255–72 and 286–300.

25. Schoenberg, *Theory of Harmony*, 323.

26. Schoenberg, "Composition with Twelve Tones," in *Style and Idea*, 217.

27. Schoenberg, *Theory of Harmony*, 421.

28. See the literature survey in Reinhold Brinkmann, *Arnold Schönberg: Drei Klavierstücke Op. 11* (Wiesbaden: Franz Steiner Verlag, 1969), 40–57.

29. Gleichgültig, welcher Meinung man beipflichtet, so viel steht fest, daß eine konstruktiv im großen wie im kleinen gebändigte Anlage das Resultat der Analyse ist. Klar erkennbare Tonalitätszusammenhänge in jedem Takt lassen es einfach unbegreiflich erscheinen, daß man unbeirrt mit dem nichtssagenden Schlagwort "atonal" den Gesetzen dieser Musik Genüge zu tun glaubte.

Nüll, *Moderne Harmonik* (Leipzig: Fr. Distner and C. F. W. Siegel, 1932), 104.

30. See Schoenberg's discussion of this term in his *Theory of Harmony*, 383–84, and *Structural Functions of Harmony*, rev. ed., ed. Leonard Stein (New York: W. W. Norton, 1969), 111.

31. Tonale und atonale Elemente werden gegeneinander ausgespielt, halten sich zumindest im Vertikalen in der Schwebe. Brinkmann, *Arnold Schönberg: Drei Klavierstücke*, 64.

32. Dieses Buch könnte ebensogut vor 25 Jahren geschrieben sein. Es ist die typische Symptom-Forschung, die zu einer Theorie der "Symptom-Erzeugung" führt. Nichts

könnte unwesentlicher sein, als der gezwungene Beweis, dass angeblich "Atonales" dennoch "tonal" ist. . . . Insbesondere erkennt er in keiner Weise den organischen Zusammenhang zwischen Melodie und Harmonie. Los Angeles, Arnold Schoenberg Institute.

33. Der 1. Akkord, der Fünfklang b-cis-f-ges-a, gleicht klanglich der 1. Umkehrung eines Nebenfünfklangs, der aus einem großen Dreiklang, großer Sept und überm. Non besteht. Der 2. Akkord, der Sechsklang g-as-b-c-des-f, gleicht einem Nebensechsklang, der aus einem Vierklang mit verm. Dreiklang und kleiner Sept sowie aus einem kleinen Dreiklang besteht, dessen Grundton Sept des Sechsklangs ist. Weigl, *Harmonielehre*, vol. 1 (Mainz: B. Schott's Söhne, 1925), 403.

34. Howard Hanson, *Harmonic Materials of Modern Music: Resources of the Tempered Scale* (New York: Appleton-Century-Crofts, 1960).

35. Forte, "The Magical Kaleidoscope: Schoenberg's First Atonal Masterwork, Opus 11, Number 1," *Journal of the Arnold Schoenberg Institute* 5 (1981): 127–68.

36. Ibid., 137.

37. Der primäre Sinn des Systems ist, die Akkorde durch wahrnehm-und vorstellbare Zusammenklangskriterien zu charakterisieren. Daher setzte ich auch getrost die vieltönigen Klänge unter das gleiche Symbol, M; denn eben an wahrnehm-und vorstellbarer Klangcharakteristik sind solche Akkorde meist wenig unterschiedlich. Zwar sind sie nach Dichte graduierbar; aber das hängt ebenso sehr von der Verteilung wie von der Anzahl der Töne ab. Eine neuntöniger Klang kann für das Gehör dichter erscheinen als ein elftöniger. Die Vorstellbarkeit nimmt mit Anwachsen der Anzahl von Tönen gewaltig ab.

Maegaard, *Studien zur Entwicklung des dodekaphonen Satzes bei Arnold Schönberg*, vol. 2 (Copenhagen: Wilhelm Hansen Musikforlag, 1972), 18.

38. Die Struktur dieser Akkorde (hängt) aufs engste mit der Form der Grundgestaltelemente zusammen. Es scheint also auf dieser Stufe der Entwicklung mit einer Musik, deren Gestalten entweder melodisch oder gebrochen oder rein akkordisch artikuliert werden können, allmählich belangloser zu werden, von Harmonik gesondert zu sprechen.

Ibid., vol. 2, 195.

39. Schoenberg, "Schoenberg's Tone Rows," in *Style and Idea*, 213.

40. See Rudolf Stephan, "Ein frühes Dokument zur Entstehung der Zwölftonkomposition," in *Festschrift Arno Forchert zum 60. Geburtstag*, ed. Gerhard Allroggen, Detlef Altenburg (Kassel: Bärenreiter, 1986): 296–302. Stephan reproduces an anonymous typescript, titled "Komposition mit zwölf Tönen," from the Berg Collection at the Österreichische Nationalbibliothek in Vienna. This is clearly a writing by Schoenberg (or possibly an incomplete transcription of a Schoenberg lecture) from about 1923.

41. Greissle, "Die formalen Grundlagen des Bläserquintetts von Arnold Schönberg," *Musikblätter des Anbruch* 7 (1925): 63–68.

42. Wohl um also trotz dieser Voraussetzungen verständlich zu bleiben, greift Schönberg auf klassische Formtypen zurück. Der erste Satz ("Schwungvoll") hat ausgesprochene Sonatenform, der zweite ("Anmutig und Heiter") ist ein groß angelegtes Scherzo mit zwei Trios, der dritte ("Etwas langsam") in zweiteiliger Form mit Einschaltung eines raschen, tanzartigen Zwischenteiles gehalten, der vierte ein Rondo. Und noch etwas anderes erinnert an die Klassiker. Die thematische Arbeit, der differenzierte Ausbau der Nebengedanken, die, trotz größter Mannigfaltigkeit der Charaktere, immer die engsten Beziehungen zueinander und zum Hauptgedanken haben. Man sieht, daß es sich hier vielfach um die Fortsetzung und Weiterentwicklung der alten Technik handelt. Die for-

male Geschlossenheit ist von neuem gesichert und die Musik kann wieder dort weiter-
gehen, wo sie haltmachen muβte, um einen Ersatz für die Tonalität zu suchen.

Ibid., 67–68.

43. Leibowitz, *Introduction à la musique de douze sons* (Paris: L'Arche, 1949), 111–
219; Dahlhaus, *Arnold Schönberg: Variationen für Orchester*, op. 31 (Munich: Wilhelm
Fink Verlag, 1968).

44. Babbitt, review of a French edition of Schoenberg's "Composition With Twelve
Tones," in *Journal of the American Musicological Society* 3 (1950): 266.

45. In Arnold Schoenberg, *Letters*, ed. Erwin Stein, trans. Eithne Wilkins and Ernst
Kaiser (Berkeley and Los Angeles: University of California Press, 1987), 165.

46. Mead, " 'Tonal' Forms in Arnold Schoenberg's Twelve-tone Music," *Music Theory Spectrum* 9 (1987): 67–92.

47. Ibid., 67, 73.

48. Ibid., 74–75.

12

Schoenberg as Teacher

Leonard Stein

THE PUPILS AND THEIR RESPONSE TO HIS TEACHING

In the preface to his *Theory of Harmony (Harmonielehre)*, which dates from 1911, Schoenberg writes: "This book I have learned from my pupils."[1] Lest one consider this only as an obligatory statement, in reality it acknowledges Schoenberg's respect for the many devoted pupils he had acquired in the few years preceding the publication of the book. In 1904 Alban Berg, one of these students, attracted by a newspaper announcement, came to study with Schoenberg.[2] Despite the lack of training shown by the young pupil, Schoenberg was impressed by the talent Berg exhibited in the many songs he had already written. Noting the technical deficiencies displayed in these compositions, Schoenberg proceeded to fill in his student's background with a systematic study of harmony and counterpoint. The resultant "Stunden," or exercises, preserved in notebooks by Berg, show the step-by-step procedure employed by Schoenberg in his teaching, a veritable "Gradus ad Parnassum" that lay as the basis of the teaching methods he employed throughout his long pedagogical career.[3] In addition, the numerous harmony exercises that came out of these Stunden were later incorporated into the *Theory of Harmony*, and Berg himself was enlisted by his mentor in the often onerous task of helping to put the book together.[4]

Within a year of the publication of the *Theory of Harmony*, the first book about Schoenberg appeared (*Arnold Schönberg* [Munich: R. Piper, 1912]). It consisted of a collection of articles by his pupils and friends, including a biography, discussion of his music, a description of the *Theory of Harmony*, information about Schoenberg's paintings, and statements about his teaching. This last section, called "Der Lehrer (sämtliche Beiträge von seinen Schülern)," includes testimonials by Alban Berg, Anton von Webern, Karl Linke, Egon

Wellesz, Robert Neumann, Erwin Stein, Heinrich Jalowetz, Karl Horwitz, and Paul Koniger to Schoenberg's pedagogical mastery. Typical of these statements is the one by Jalowetz, who writes: "Schoenberg has the admirable gift of adapting himself to the individuality of even the least of his students in such a way that no two of his students are led by him along similar paths. . . . The teacher does not have 'the method'—rather it rises from the interaction with the student."[5]

By the end of the First World War, the number of Schoenberg's pupils increased even more rapidly. A photograph album presented by some of these students to Schoenberg on his fiftieth birthday, in 1924, lists their names and gives information on their studies with Schoenberg or his assistants over a number of years.[6] His earliest student in this group, Vilma Webenau, studied privately with Schoenberg in Vienna in 1898. From 1903 to 1904 Schoenberg taught at the Schwarzwald school, where students from the Vienna Academy came to study with him on the recommendation of Dr. Guido Adler. Eight of the students in the album began their private studies with him in 1904, among them Berg, Webern, Horwitz, Jalowetz, and Wellesz. A total of twenty-one students studied with him between 1904 and 1912. Whereas only three names appear from 1912 to 1917, most likely as a consequence of the war, the bulk of the students in the album studied with Schoenberg both privately and at the Schwarzwald school in Vienna from 1917 to 1924.[7] Fifty-five of them were enrolled in classes in 1918–19 and twenty-two in 1919–20. Many of these later students also participated in the activities of the Society for Private Musical Performances (*Verein für musikalische Privataufführungen*) during those years.[8] Most of the students in the album mention their studies in harmony, counterpoint, and analysis, while others attended the seminar in composition. Prominent among these students of composition were Hanns Eisler, Hans Erich Apostel, Paul Pisk, Roberto Gerhard, Rudolf Kolisch, Josef Polnauer, Karl Rankl, Erwin Ratz, Josef Rufer, Erwin Stein, Fritz Zweig, and Viktor Ullmann, all of whom were to make distinguished careers for themselves as composers, conductors, solo performers, scholars, and teachers.

In 1926, after his appointment to the Prussian Academy of the Arts in Berlin, Schoenberg continued his teaching to a select group of gifted composers. His pedagogical methods proved to follow much the same course as those of the preceding period, as the musical examples preserved by Josef Rufer, his assistant at the Academy, testify.[9] Schoenberg's composition students at the Academy included Erwin Stein, Winfried Zillig, Karl Rankl, Nikos Skalkottas, Peter Schacht, and Erik Schmid, among others.

With the Nazi assumption of power in March 1933, Schoenberg was forced from his position at the Academy and soon left Germany. After a brief sojourn in France, Schoenberg, his wife, and young daughter decided to come to the United States in the fall of 1933. Traveling between Boston and New York— he had students in both cities—Schoenberg once again had to earn his living as a teacher of theory and composition, this time employed by the small Malkin

Conservatory in Boston. The many examples of harmony and counterpoint he provided his American students at the Conservatory again followed the methods laid down in his earlier instructions in these subjects.[10] Unwilling to face another cold winter on the East Coast of the United States, Schoenberg and his family headed west to the more salubrious climate of California in October 1934, shortly after his sixtieth birthday. As he wrote, rather optimistically, about prospects in the new land soon after his arrival: "I am sure that, once people know that I teach, those who can pay more will also come, and I shall be able to exist here quite well."[11] For the next seventeen years, until his death in 1951, Schoenberg earned his living principally by teaching both privately and at the two major universities in Los Angeles.[12]

Near the close of his life, Schoenberg summed up his career as a teacher in these terms:

In my fifty years of teaching I have taught certainly more than a thousand pupils. Though I had to do it in order to make a living, I must confess that I was a passionate teacher, and the satisfaction of giving to beginners as much as possible of my own knowledge was probably a greater reward than the actual fee I received. This was also the reason why I accepted so many pupils who could not pay, even if they had not the background to study with me. Thus I said in such a case once: "After all, if they cannot digest what I give them, it will damage them less to study with me than with a poorer teacher."[13]

His aim in teaching composition, he explains in the same article, is to achieve such matters as clear phrases, logical continuations, fluency, variety, and characteristic contrasts in the works of his pupils, as well as to influence their taste, "thereby excluding triviality, talkativeness, superficiality, bombast, complacency, and other poor habits" from their work. "A true teacher," he asserts, "must be a model to his pupils, possessing the ability to achieve several times what he demands of his pupil once." This is but one of many articles Schoenberg wrote about teaching, where he stated his aims and named some of his important pupils over the years.[14]

PROPOSALS FOR EDUCATING MUSICIANS

As previously mentioned, Schoenberg not only taught privately but in various schools, some public, some private. For his classes in the music schools he devised extensive curricula which included courses in harmony, counterpoint, composition, and analysis. At UCLA he also created classes in orchestration and a new course, which he called Structural Functions of Harmony. In addition, Schoenberg made several proposals for music schools, based on his experience in such institutions as the Schwarzwald school in Vienna and the Prussian Academy of the Arts in Berlin. One of these proposals was a plan for the foundation of an "International School for the Formation of Style" (*Internationale Stilbildungs-Schule*) which Schoenberg first conceived in 1920 and developed later in 1927.[15] In it he proposed to acquaint teachers and pupils from various nations with a knowledge of styles of composition and performance from the leading musical nations. "In general," he wrote, "less weight would have to be laid on theoretical teaching than on practical but, of course, the theorist should in no way be excluded." Another more extensive plan was promulgated by Schoenberg in August 1934 while he was spending the summer in Chautauqua, New York. This one is entitled "Proposal for the Foundation of a Musical Conservatory in Keeping with the Times" *(Vorschlag zur Errichtung einer Zeitgemaessen Musikunterrichts Institutes).*[16] The first of its seven proposals states that the pupils will have to develop "a superior command of all traditional techniques, as well as bringing them up to the latest contemporary art, so that with their powers well and widely trained they are able to collaborate in the work involved in further developing the resources of art." In the sixth proposal Schoenberg spells out in capital letters the dictum that "ALL PUPILS MUST MAKE IT A LIFE'S MAXIM THAT IN ARTISTIC QUESTIONS COMPROMISES ARE RULED OUT AND THAT INFLEXIBILITY IS A PART OF TALENT." Thus, to a great extent, Schoenberg stated in this tract his own philosophy of art and his aims in teaching. Several years later, while teaching at UCLA (1936–44), Schoenberg, influenced by discussions with his colleague, the acoustician Vern Knudsen, made a very detailed proposal for a "School for Soundmen" which, in contrast to the foregoing plans, is quite specific and practical in nature as to its goals.[17]

TEACHING RELATED TO COMPOSITION AND TRADITION

As we have clearly seen, Schoenberg's reasons for teaching went beyond making a living, though that was a very practical matter for a composer whose income for the most part was not greatly enhanced by the amounts he received for his music. Probably there have been very few distinguished composers who spent so much time in their career teaching, and with such "passionate" dedication to this task, as he did. One of the principal reasons for this strong passion lay in the belief that teaching constituted an indispensable means of passing along the tradition that he believed in so fervently and of which he considered himself to be a part. Schoenberg was never reluctant to pay homage to those composers who had influenced him, as he testified in his article "National Music," where he cited as his primary teachers, Bach and Mozart, and secondarily, Beethoven, Brahms, and Wagner.[18]

In his own compositions this adherence to traditional methods is most evident in certain works of a didactic character, such as the Suite in G Major for string orchestra, composed in 1934 for performance by American college orchestras. Describing this work, which consists of a fugal Overture, an Adagio, a Menuet, a Gavotte and a Gigue in G major and related tonalities, Schoenberg states its aim as a "piece [that] will become a veritable teaching example of the progress that can be made within tonality, if one is really a musician and knows one's craft."[19] In an unpublished "Sketch of a Foreword" to the work, Schoenberg described more fully its goals to "give genuine, real teachers and propagators of culture an opportunity to educate their students to have the deepest respect for artistic capacity, and to make it clear to them that culture can be maintained only through growth."[20]

PEDAGOGICAL TEXTS

The heritage of Schoenberg's teaching may be found in the texts on harmony, counterpoint, and composition which he authored and which, for the most part, were the outgrowth of his private and class instruction. Thus the examples in the *Theory of Harmony* came from Berg's private studies and those in the later books of counterpoint, harmony, and composition, all published in English, were the results of examples prepared for classes at UCLA by Schoenberg himself. The principal texts in these subjects are *Harmonielehre* (1911 and 1922), translated into English by Roy E. Carter as *Theory of Harmony* (Faber and Faber, 1978), *Models for Beginners in Composition* (G. Schirmer, 1942; revised edition, 1972, Belmont Music Publishers), *Structural Functions of Harmony* (W. W. Norton, 1954; revised edition, 1969), *Preliminary Exercises in Counterpoint* (Faber and Faber, 1963), and *Fundamentals of Musical Composition* (Faber and Faber, 1967). Other texts on these and related subjects were also planned by Schoenberg and were left in various unfinished states at his death. They include second and third volumes on counterpoint ("Contrapuntal Composition" and "Counterpoint in Homophonic Music"), a book on orchestration (with many citations from the literature), and a large volume with the general title of *Der musikalische Gedanke und die Logik, Technik und Kunst seiner Darstellung* (in English, *The Musical Idea and the Logic, Technique, and Art of Its Presentation*, published in both languages by Columbia University Press, 1995), a project on which Schoenberg worked from 1924 to 1936 and from which he extracted many ideas for his later books. All these books vary in degree from giving practical advice, including numerous examples in problem solving and analysis of masterworks, to presenting theoretical and philosophical discourses on musical terminology and concepts. Undoubtedly the most comprehensive book covering both aspects of study is the *Theory of Harmony*, which deals equally with practical matters as with the theory and philosophy of music.[21]

This dichotomy exists as well in numerous articles by Schoenberg, where he expounds, on the one hand, on philosophical concepts dealing with teaching and, on the other hand, affords explicit instructions for the solution of problems in composition. Thus in the article "Problems in Teaching Art" (1911), Schoenberg discusses his basic philosophy that "art is born of 'I must,' not of 'I can.' " In line with this dictum he states that for the student, "belief [only] in technique would have to be suppressed, and the urge to truthfulness encouraged." And, he continues, "the pupil would have to gather [from the methods of art] the *fact* that one must come to grips with all the problems—not *how* to. Technique could be demonstrated—but only as the grammar of a language might be. . . . But the ideas, the feelings—these are one's own contributions."[22] However, on the opposite side, Schoenberg is very explicit about the methods he uses in teaching the techniques of music. As he states in his counterpoint book, "advice will be given in more or less strict form which will be changed corresponding to a pedagogical point of view." The aim of the exercises therein, presented in a very systematic order, "will not be considered as theory, but as a method of training, and the foremost purpose of this method will be to teach the pupil so that he becomes able to use his knowledge later when he composes."[23] The methods for the practice (not theory) of, and the eventual goal in acquiring this technique is thus clearly presented in the writings of Schoenberg. The master teacher thus fortifies his pupils with both the ideals and the means to accomplish his task.

NOTES

1. Arnold Schoenberg, *Harmonielehre* (Vienna: Universal Edition, 3rd edition, 1922); English translation by Roy E. Carter, *Theory of Harmony* (Berkeley and Los Angeles: University of California Press, 1978). This statement appeared at first in the foreword of the first edition, 1911, and then was repeated in the third edition.

2. Actually it was Charley Berg, Alban's brother, who saw the advertisement and brought some of Alban's songs to Schoenberg (Willi Reich, *Alban Berg*, trans. Cornelius Cardew [New York: Harcourt, Brace, and World, 1965], 18).

3. The Berg exercises are listed in *Katalog der Musikhandschriften und Studien Alban Bergs*, collected and edited by Rosemary Hilmar (Vienna: Universal Edition, 1980). Hilmar also writes about their use in the *Theory of Harmony* in *Alban Berg: Leben und Wirken in Wien bis zu seinen ersten Erfolgen als Komponist* (Vienna: Böhlau, 1978).

4. Berg's work on the *Theory of Harmony* is described in several letters he wrote to Schoenberg in 1911. See *The Berg-Schoenberg Correspondence: Selected Letters*, edited by Juliane Brand, Christopher Hailey, and Donald Harris (New York: W. W. Norton, 1987), 5, 6, 10, 20.

5. From Jalowetz's statement in *Arnold Schönberg* (Munich: R. Piper, 1912), 83.

6. See "Dem Lehrer Arnold Schönberg" by Jerry McBride in the *Journal of the Arnold Schoenberg Institute* 8/1 (June 1984); 31–38. Photographs of some of the students in the Birthday Album are reproduced, along with the classes they took.

7. See "The Schwarzwald School," chapter 7 of *Schoenberg and His Circle* by Joan Allen Smith (New York: Schirmer Books, 1986), for information on Schoenberg's teaching there.

8. The *Verein* also served as a vehicle for teaching insofar as each work to be played was prepared by a *Vortrag Meister* (a "coach," typically one of Schoenberg's advanced students) and judged by Schoenberg himself before being performed. It is to be assumed that these works were also discussed and analyzed in class. Thus the *Verein* itself served as a sort of didactic forum.

9. The exercises in Rufer's handwriting are preserved in the archives of the Arnold Schoenberg Institute in Los Angeles.

10. See "Classes with Schoenberg, January through June 1934" by Lovina May

Knight in the *Journal of the Arnold Schoenberg Institute* 13/2 (November 1990); 137–63.

11. "Circular to My Friends on My Sixtieth Birthday," in *Style and Idea: Selected Writings of Arnold Schoenberg*, ed. Leonard Stein, trans. Leo Black (Berkeley and Los Angeles: University of California Press, 1984), 28.

12. After his retirement from UCLA in 1944 Schoenberg taught only privately, including a seminar in his home, although he did give one class for the Music Academy of the West, Carpenteria, CA, in 1948 and made plans for other courses elsewhere.

13. "The Task of the Teacher" (1950), in *Style and Idea*, 388.

14. Other articles on teaching include "Problems in Teaching Art" (1911), "On the Question of Modern Composition Teaching" (1929), "Teaching and Modern Trends in Music" (1938), "Eartraining Through Composing" (1939), "The Blessing of the Dressing" (1948), and "Against the Specialist" (c. 1940). See *Style and Idea*, Part VIII: Teaching. However, many other articles make frequent references to teaching methods and pedagogical advice regarding technical matters and analysis.

15. Two paged, single-spaced typed proposal, signed and dated "Marz 1927." Note at the end (in German): "Proposal for the Internationale Stilbildungs-Schule which I conceived about 1920 and put forward for the first time in connection with the Mahler Society founded in Holland." MS in the archives of the Arnold Schoenberg Institute, Los. Angeles.

16. Two paged, single-spaced typed proposal, in German, with the heading "Arnold Schoenberg, Chautauqua, New York, Box 346, August 1934." MS in the archives of the Arnold Schoenberg Institute, Los Angeles.

17. Handwritten nine-page proposal, in English, with one page of notes. At the head of the first page is written: "A.S. prof of Music at UCLA/ proposes the creation of a/ 'School for Soundmen.' " Before the description of the proposal there is written: "I herewith invite the Academy of M.P.A. & S. [Motion Pictures Arts & Sciences] to take into consideration of [*sic*] the following plan:". The note on the final page contains this statement: "Soundmen who know only music are as inefficient as soundmen who know only science. A true soundman need be trained in both music and science." MS in the archives of the Arnold Schoenberg Institute, Los Angeles.

18. "National Music (2)" (1931), in *Style and Idea*, 173.

19. "Circular to My Friends on My Sixtieth Birthday," in *Style and Idea*, 29.

20. Martin Bernstein, "On the Genesis of Schoenberg's Suite for School Orchestra," *Journal of the Arnold Schoenberg Institute* 11/2 (November 1988); 158–62; reprinted from the *Newsletter of the Institute for Studies in American Music* 14/1 (November 1984).

21. See Roy E. Carter, "Translator's Preface" to *Theory of Harmony*.

22. "Problems in Teaching Art" (1911), in *Style and Idea*, 365.

23. Preface I in Appendix A in *Preliminary Exercises in Counterpoint* (London: Faber and Faber, 1963), 221.

13

Schoenberg's Influence

Gunther Schuller

Arnold Schoenberg died nearly a half century ago, and he was during his entire lifetime one of the most controversial composers of the first half of the twentieth century, a period which had its fill of controversy, musical revolutions and *scandales*. During his stormy career, Schoenberg and his music provoked either the most abject scorn and rejection or the fiercest loyalty and commitment. It seemed impossible to remain passive vis-à-vis Schoenberg's music. In the great feuds of the 1930s and 1940s between the neoclassicists (Stravinsky, Copland, Hindemith) and the twelve-tone camp (Schoenberg and his followers), composers—especially young composers—were expected to take one side or the other. It was generally assumed that there was no common ground between the two warring factions and therefore no room for any negotiation or compromise. The larger public, not privy to or even particularly interested in the argumentations raging in academic and specialized music journals, was even less than passive: it remained completely ignorant, quite satisfied with its daily dosage of Brahms, Beethoven, and Tchaikovsky.

Things have not changed very much in the last fifty years. The various enclaves of rejection, passivity, and ignorance regarding Schoenberg's music—and by extension that of any music of "atonal" or "twelve-tone" persuasion—are, if anything, more deeply ensconced than ever before. This condition persists despite the fact that for a relatively brief period in the mid-1950s and 1960s, after Stravinsky had defected from the neoclassic to the twelve-tone camp and after the resultant sudden discovery of Webern's music, the aesthetic pendulum had swung dramatically to the dodecaphonic side, much to the consternation and horror of the neoclassic ranks. Another pendulum swing to the right followed in due course, precipitated and exacerbated by many of the musical and self-promotional excesses of the European serial avant-garde of the 1960s, with the inevitable backlash swing to the other extremes of minimalism, neoromanticism, and Cageian amateurism.[1]

It would seem then that through all the various aesthetic/stylistic twists and turns we have experienced in this century, Schoenberg's influence and reputation have been mercurial at best and remain variously so. Depending upon whom one is addressing they are characterized as "inconclusive," "ambiguous," "irrelevant," "nonexistent," or, on the other side, "profound," "revelatory," "life-changing," "inspiring."

While there is—and has been for sometime—a general and largely uncontested consensus that Stravinsky and Bartók, for example, are two of the "greatest," the "best," the "most important"—even the 'most popular'!—composers of our time, no such consensus exists regarding Schoenberg's reputation. In fact, if one asks the question, who are the two leading and most influential composers of the twentieth century, most people will offer the seemingly contradictory and confusing answer: Stravinsky and Schoenberg. What this seems to suggest is that there is a dichotomy between how a composer, Schoenberg in this case, is viewed by two basic constituents: the lay public on one hand, the serious professional on the other. That is to say, the one (first stated) consensus is based primarily on the extent to which a composer has become "popular" (in the broadest sense) and to what extent that composer's music has been assimilated into the general repertory, while the other consensus reflects a deeper understanding of that contribution, even if one does not necessarily share its aesthetic and philosophy. There is among many opponents of Schoenberg's aesthetic and the twelve-tone technique a dim recognition that something important was proposed therein, even if they cannot relate positively to the specific realization of that aesthetic in Schoenberg's own music. There is the further twist that many people, both lay and professional, have great difficulty in accepting Schoenberg's works, but find Berg's and Webern's twelve-tone music much more accessible. (More on that subject later.)

Before we can properly assess Schoenberg's legacy and its potential future influence, we must assess the reality of how his music has fared thus far, both in performance and in its impact on contemporary music in general. To say that Schoenberg had a difficult career with audiences and critics—and right from the start—is to understate things seriously. Even his early *Verklärte Nacht*—now a popular staple of the concert repertory—was immediately and roundly attacked, misunderstood, and sarcastically ridiculed by the critics. The Viennese public of the time did not know what to make of this young upstart's music, rejecting it summarily or, at best, enjoying the public *scandales* it always caused—this despite the fact that Vienna's leading musician and composer, Gustav Mahler, was very much interested in Schoenberg's music and often defended it with the public.

To fully appreciate that the criticism and rejection of Schoenberg's works never once let up, one need only to read the documentation of this sorry history in *Arnold Schönberg, 1874–1951: Lebensgeschichte in Begegnungen* (1992), assembled, edited, and produced by Nuria Schoenberg-Nono. Even Schoenberg's tonal *Gurrelieder*, premiered by Franz Schreker in 1913, a dozen years after it was composed, was not spared the critical venom of its early listeners and critics. This process continued more or less throughout Schoenberg's life, whether in Austria, later in Germany, or still later in the United States, despite the fact that by the second decade of the twentieth century, major figures such as Schreker, Busoni, Mengelberg, and Henry Wood began to support Schoenberg's music, take it seriously as an important new music, as something more than a chance for another public *scandale*, and began to perform it widely. In addition, Schoenberg's music began to attract students and followers, not only Berg and Webern and other composers such as Krenek and Skalkottas, but conductors (Mitropoulos, Stiedry), performers (Kolisch, Steuermann), and writers (Stuckenschmidt, Adorno, Rufer).

Nonetheless, it didn't seem to matter whether it was Schoenberg's earlier (1909–24), freely atonal music or the later twelve-tone works: they were all either summarily rejected or received with uncomprehending puzzlement, admired only by a small (but growing) minority of loyal followers. Schoenberg's emigration to the United States did nothing to alter this situation. Though by now world famous—more because of the sensation his music caused than any positive reception of it—Schoenberg found it difficult to find work in the States and to get his music performed, especially his orchestral works. Sporadic engagements as conductor (Boston, New York,[2] Los Angeles, San Francisco) and as teacher (Boston, New York—a more substantial one in Los Angeles) either led nowhere or were abruptly terminated. In the United States resistance to Schoenberg and his music grew despite some recognition of his stature (by, for example, Elizabeth Sprague Coolidge's commissioning his Fourth String Quartet through the Library of Congress), despite conductors such as Mitropoulos and Stokowski defending and performing his works,[3] and despite the occasional serious appraisal of his work(s) in journals like *Modern Music*. Schoenberg's music continued to be largely ignored or rejected, thus basically unperformed, as were the works of his pupils Webern and (less so) Berg, in an aesthetic and stylistic environment dominated entirely by the neo-classic school(s) of Stravinsky and Copland.

It wasn't until several crucial events occurred that the tide turned for Schoenberg: (a) Mitropoulos's appointment to the New York Philharmonic as music director, and his performances of many Second Viennese School works, in most cases never heard before in New York (or elsewhere in America for that matter); (b) Robert Craft's espousal as a fledgling conductor and proselytizing writer/ polemicist of the works of Schoenberg, Berg, and Webern, as well as his considerable influence on Stravinsky; and (c) Stravinsky's abandonment of neo-classicism in the early 1950s, when he adopted dodecaphony and serialism. Suddenly everyone was discovering (or rediscovering) Schoenberg and the twelve-tone concept, not only here in America (through Babbitt and Sessions) but in Europe (through Stockhausen, Boulez, Nono, Berio, Messiaen, and many others). Before long the complete (at least then-known) works of Webern were recorded (by Craft) and the post-Webern era had begun in full force. (Webern had died in 1945.)

While Schoenberg was not at first widely accepted and performed (or recorded), the lion's share of attention was given to Webern, while Berg's music with its more "romantic" outlook and frequent allusions to tonality began to be increasingly assimilated into the standard orchestral and chamber repertory.

Much of this happened after Schoenberg's death in 1951. I think he would have deplored the excesses of the new twelve-tone/serial avant-garde, especially in Europe, where the new young radicals (in Darmstadt, Donaueschingen, a little later in Warsaw) began, as mentioned, to boo Schoenberg's (and Berg's) music as "old-fashioned," "conventional," "conservative," and "reactionary." By the 1970s the serial avant-garde had reached such extremes of intellectualization and mathematecization—at the hands, to be sure, of many mediocre composers who had merely jumped onto the twelve-tone/serial bandwagon (Schoenberg by now long forgotten)—that a major cyclical swing to the "right" was virtually inevitable, a matter which I began to predict by the late 1960s and early 1970s in my work at Tanglewood, at the New England Conservatory, and in lectures.

The present fascination with minimalism, postminimalism, tonality, and neo-romanticism is the immediate (though I predict temporary) manifestation of that latest gigantic pendulum swing. Schoenberg and twelve-tone music again carry in most circles a negative connotation, and as readers of the *New York Times* were assured back in the 1970s and 1980s, that "awful," "dissonant," "ugly," twelve-tone music was a thing, thankfully, of the past, never to rise again. Thus spake the critic John Rockwell, for example.

Quite apart from the fact that the final tallies are not in—far from it—and that very quietly any number of fine, important composers have continued to feed on Schoenberg's legacy, the above-related developments would appear to be the history as seen and viewed in the broader public arena, from total rejection to virtually total acceptance back to near-total rejection—all in less than a century.

And if that history is true, how is one to understand it? How is one to fathom the difficulty Schoenberg's atonal works have encountered in being accepted into the mainstream? One wag many years ago had a very clever answer to those questions. He is reported to have suggested that Schoenberg, both as a person and in his music, was inherently complex, tinged with bitterness and strife, and that "even if Schoenberg had composed entirely in C-major, his music would still be impossibly complex and destined for rejection." There is some truth in this, although I believe—and what I think our wag meant—that it was neither Schoenberg's atonality and twelve-tonality nor the full chromaticism of his tone-center-less music, but rather his penchant for constant polyphony, the radical avoidance of repetition, and other complex factors that have made his music so hard to digest and accept for the broader public.[4] These are all basic characteristics which one does not find (anywhere to that extent) in

Stravinsky or Bartók—or if one does, they are always couched in a more tonally oriented context. Nor, for that matter, are they found in Berg or Webern. Ultrapolyphony in a *tonal* context is found to be more or less acceptable—if not fully comprehensible (see late Beethoven, mature Ives, and Reger)—while the same degree of counterpoint and sheer multithematic/rhythmic complexity in an atonal context remains indigestible for most people.

Given that inherent complexity of thought in Schoenberg's music, it will perhaps not come as a surprise that most of his music, especially his orchestral music, has not yet—or at least *very* rarely—been played well. That is, Schoenberg's music is not played with full understanding, especially of its harmonic content, nor is it played with the kind of understanding which orchestras have been able to achieve in the playing of Brahms symphonies only in this century.[5] By that I mean even the most average musician can now hear and *feel* Brahms's music more or less correctly. But this is not yet the case in respect to Schoenberg's complex orchestral music, such as some of his finest works—the Variations for Orchestra, op. 31, *Erwartung*, and even the earlier *Pelleas und Melisande*, Five Orchestra Pieces. and the Four Songs for voice and orchestra, op. 22. Orchestras such as the Chicago Symphony, and the Berlin and New York philharmonics can play the notes of these works correctly, at least technically, but do not yet play them with any stylistic sensitivity, harmonic understanding, thematic and textural awareness—in short with a comprehending *feeling* for the music. Playing all the notes technically correctly—hear the several Chicago Symphony recordings with Solti—does not by a long shot represent a deep, feeling understanding of the music, of Schoenberg's complex polyphonic writing, perpetual subtle variation of material, and even more subtle complicated "chamber" orchestration.[6] Thus a music which the best musicians cannot yet perform with full comprehension cannot reach or speak to an audience—especially when most of that audience will probably have no experience in listening to Schoenberg or atonal music anyway.

Since we tend to think of the main corpus of a composer's work as representing and defining his legacy, it seems rather premature to try to assess Schoenberg's legacy at this time—at least solely on the basis of his compositions and their performances.[7] But other aspects of his work—as teacher, theorist, writer, lecturer, and above all as creator of the twelve-tone method (or as he preferred to call it, "method of composing with twelve tones which are related only with one another")—can be evaluated more tellingly in terms of a legacy. That Schoenberg was a dedicated teacher, in Vienna as well as Berlin and Los Angeles, can hardly be disputed.[8] Many of his pupils and disciples rank as important composers and musical thinkers of the mid- to late twentieth century. In addition there are perhaps even more important composers (Milton Babbitt, Roger Sessions, Elliott Carter, George Perle, Mario Davidovsky, Donald Erb, Robert Lewis, Robert DiDomenica, Claudio Spiess, Bernard Rands, Alexander Goehr, Oliver Knussen, Pierre Boulez, Karlheinz Stockhausen, and Luigi Nono come to mind) who did not actually study with Schoenberg, but who nonetheless were tremendously influenced by his works and his theories. Beyond that there are many composers (like Andrew Imbrie, John Harbison) who do not now write in the Schoenbergian twelve-tone or serial concept, but who also were profoundly influenced by the compositions of the Second Viennese School. This legacy has manifested itself in a broadly varied and extensive repertory (chamber, orchestral, vocal and operatic) that survives, even to some extent flourishes, in our contemporary concert repertory.

Perhaps one of Schoenberg's greatest achievements is as a theorist and this may well be recognized someday (soon?) as one of the most important aspects of his legacy. For his *Theory of Harmony (Harmonielehre)* of 1911 is one of the most searching, all-embracing, exhaustive—even profoundly moving—expositions of the workings of "common practice" functional tonality that has ever been set forth, ranking easily with Rameau, Schenker, and Kirnberger. It is tragic that *Theory of Harmony* is not used in the majority of music schools and other training centers—teaching in harmony is altogether neglected nowadays, alas. I believe it ought to be required reading and study in all serious curricula.

Schoenberg's achievements as writer and lecturer are perhaps not as consistently brilliant as his work in classical theory. They are nevertheless important contributions to twentieth-century musical-intellectual literature, often stimulating and provocative in highly innovative ways.

Ultimately, however, the true legacy of Schoenberg, beyond even his compositions, will be his invention and conception of the twelve-tone technique. Obviously not everyone shares that view, but the fact remains that of all the concepts, techniques, systems, and theories that have been proposed in the twentieth century, none has (a) survived as well—against many odds and obstacles— and (b) proliferated in so many varied, constantly expanding/extending forms and expressions. What is often ignored (mostly out of ignorance or for polemical purposes) is that already the first generation of twelve-tone composers (Schoenberg, Berg, Webern) composed music of vastly differing styles. No one could ever confuse the music of these three masters among each other, proof that even in the somewhat restrictive assumptions of the orthodox twelve-tone technique of the 1920s, each of the three composers found a highly distinctive and original voice with which to express himself. What more can one ask of a (so-called) system, technique, or method?

Seventy years later the twelve-tone concept has been broadened and deepened in a myriad variety of ways, almost to the point that twelve-tone per se has become a meaningless term and one must inquire in what *kind* of twelve-tone or serial concept one is working. To put this another way, if there are several thousand "twelve-tone composers" in the world today, there are without question several thousand subtly varied but nonetheless basic twelve-tone systems at work, permitting—and this is the main point—a vast array of creative individuality and personality. Therefore to condemn "twelve-tone" as if it were some single, monolithic system that was created in the 1920s and never updated or broadened and refined is to completely ignore reality and historical process (let alone progress).

One need only to look at the music of say, Babbitt, Boulez, Sessions, Messiaen, and the serial music of Stravinsky, to realize how open and inspirational the twelve-tone system (in its broadest manifestations) can be. None of those composers' music sound even remotely alike, a clear sign that "twelve-tone" is anything but pedantically restrictive, denying of personality and originality, as many pundits would want us to believe. A system that is so broad-ranging and capable of such personal/stylistic diversity cannot be "all bad" and in fact seems to have about the same capacity for personal/stylistic/expressive exploration as did functional tonality in the nineteenth century.

Perhaps Elliott Carter put it best some years ago in an article in *Perspectives of New Music*, entitled "The American Composer Speaks: A Further Step," when he wrote: "the twelve-tone system has been particularly helpful, since it allows considerable latitude while limiting the composer's choices and giving these choices a kind of hierarchy of relationships. Once you have chosen the row, you have chosen a method of harmony and a collection of motives that are all interrelated. This is of enormous advantage, for it helps to put the composer in that situation of *focused freedom* that finds its counterpart in all species of musical training."[9] I would add: "of all musical endeavors."

There is one aspect of Schoenberg's work, especially his orchestral and chamber ensemble compositions, that is hardly ever discussed, let alone praised. That is his, in my view, extraordinary orchestration. It is extraordinary, not only because it is remarkably idiomatic—for any and whatever instrument—a sine qua non of orchestration, but also because it is at the same time totally original, using instruments in strikingly new and challenging ways. The early twentieth century produced many superior orchestrators (Ravel, Debussy, Stravinsky, Prokofiev, Respighi, Rachmaninov, and Delius—to name but a few), but Schoenberg's orchestration is even more original, more daring, more imaginative, more refined, as one can hear in any number of works such as *Erwartung, Gurrelieder*, "Herzgewächse," the Songs, op. 22, and the Variations for Orchestra. Somehow Schoenberg had an instinctive knack for writing instrumental parts of great difficulty and daring that are nonetheless totally idiomatic and, after some practice, eminently playable and logical.

To what extent all these achievements accumulate into an ongoing and living legacy of widespread influence remains to be seen. In these highly eclectic and fractious times it may very well be that no single composer can have the kind of impact a Beethoven or Wagner had in their era. But what must now be clear to many is that Schoenberg is hardly the negligible, even laughable, figure that many would-be taste makers would like the world to believe. Whether Schoenberg's legacy will reside in the short-term impact of his compositions, the long-term residual influence of his twelve-tone method and serialism, or the even broader, unpresumptuous influence left by Schoenberg's many students, disciples, and followers (from Kolisch and Steuermann to Babbitt and Carter, from

Richard Hoffman and George Wilson to Marcel Dick and Eugene Lehner, from Mitropoulos to Abbado)—or perhaps drawing upon all these legacies—the next decade or so will show. In the meantime, signs of the durability of Schoenberg's influence in a quiet, unostentatious way can be seen and heard in many places, if not necessarily in the *New York Times*. The early pronouncements of the death of Schoenberg's legacy seem to me, once again, somewhat premature.

NOTES

1. It is ironic that during the heyday of serialism in the 1950s and 1960s, a movement stimulated much more by Webern's particular twelve-tone and serial concepts than by Schoenberg's works and teachings, Schoenberg was more or less rejected by many serialist insiders, considered to be "hopelessly old-fashioned," "academic," "irrelevant," and the like. I vividly recall the works of Schoenberg and Berg being booed in Darmstadt, Donaueschingen, and other contemporary music festivals in the early 1960s, while Webern and advanced serialism were praised to the sky.

2. Although Schoenberg was never rated highly, even by his closest friends and followers, as a performer (cello and viola) and as a conductor, I must interject that, judging by his 1934 performance of the second movement of Mahler's Second Symphony with the Cadillac Symphony, a freelance orchestra heard weekly on NBC for a few years (sponsored by the Cadillac Motor Company), Schoenberg must have been—at least on that occasion—a first-rate conductor, equal to many of his more famous contemporary maestri. Not only is this a superb performance interpretationally—a wonderful synthesis of respect for Mahler's score (notation) and subtle interpretive freedom—but it is technically excellent; and an orchestra, especially a freelance orchestra, will not—cannot—give a clear performance of a work if the conductor's technique is faulty.

3. It is little known and appreciated that Stokowski, for example, waged a lengthy battle with his Philadelphia Orchestra board and management to give the premiere of Schoenberg's Violin Concerto with Louis Krasner as soloist. Despite continued and vehement opposition by the board, Stokowski persisted and the performance came to pass. But the frustrating, painful battle with his board was one of the crucial elements that led Stokowski to resign from the Philadelphia Orchestra.

4. Schoenberg himself sensed this problem and implied as much when he wrote, "I know the obstacles to comprehension lie even more on my musical thoughts than on their presentation and on my musical language. I know that little niceties repeated over and over without or with little variation or development are easier to grasp and provide better for temporary success than a language which insists on brevity and accordingly would not repeat without exhibiting the new form of an idea, the new form resulting from the *destiny of an idea*." (Again the profound influence of Brahms and Beethoven!)

5. But be it noted in passing that while harmonic/intervallic comprehension of Brahms's music has made great strides in the twentieth century, most of his most radical metric/rhythmic ideas (for example in his Fourth Symphony) have never to my knowledge been performed correctly. This is of some consequence for the performance of Schoenberg's works, since in respect to polyphony, rhythmic complexity and the concepts of "developing variation" and "nonrepetition," Schoenberg's major influence was Brahms (not Wagner).

6. If for example Schoenberg writes three- or four-part harmonies distributed among

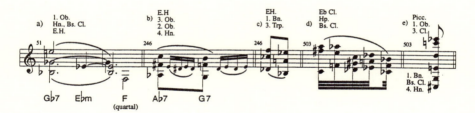

Example 13.1
Variations for Orchestra, op. 31.

several disparate instruments (e.g., in Example 13.1)—as he does hundreds of times in his Variations for Orchestra—and if, as is very common, the players involved are not even aware that they have a three- or four-part chord in consort, let alone understanding or feeling what that harmony is, how it is to sound, and how it is to be tuned, then of course that performance—multiply this by several hundred similar performance problems—cannot even begin to reveal the true essence and content of that music. These and similar other problems have to be solved before any meaningful assessment of Schoenberg's music can be made by critics and a lay public, problems that are not in the slightest addressed in any music training in schools, universities, and colleges. Since we have barely learned how to play Brahms and Wagner—and more recently Stravinsky and Bartók and other chromatic but still partly tonal composers—it will be a long time before Schoenberg's works will be fully understood, felt, and assimilated into the repertory.

7. In saying this I am putting the case forward on the most objective, pragmatic basis, i.e., on the basis of his compositions' reception and assimilation into the standard repertory. For all that I and several hundred composer colleagues and a few professionals feel that Schoenberg is the most important composer of our time, this is somewhat meaningless in terms of assessing his legacy when a majority of musicians of all disciplines (including conductors) disagree with such a view and/or find the whole subject irrelevant to their careers.

8. Be it noted that Schoenberg in his class teaching rarely, if ever, taught his twelve-tone method, adhering strictly to the traditional "common practice" functional tonality.

9. Another way of putting this is to say that working with a row as the basic, seminal pitch material provides an inner coherence and stylistic consistency which, while achievable in other non-twelve-tone ways, is of enormous help and inspiration to the composer.

IV

Sources

14

Selective Bibliography

Jerry McBride

INTRODUCTION

Research into the music of Schoenberg is still very much in the early stages of its development, especially when compared to the literature for major composers of the nineteenth century and earlier. This situation is not too surprising considering it is just slightly less than fifty years since his last composition was written. Nonetheless there is an increasingly large body of scholarly and critical work written about one of music's most controversial composers. In fact, controversy is one of the peculiar aspects of the literature on Schoenberg, and it has fueled the proliferation of writings and perhaps even hindered the objective evaluation of his music and his place in Western culture.

It is interesting to note that even today, nearly one hundred years after the composition of the first atonal pieces, there are still articles and entire books challenging the validity of atonal and twelve-tone music. Some of this literature is aimed at all art music of the twentieth century and seeks to confirm the tastes of the broad mass of the concertgoing public, who have generally disliked atonal and twelve-tone music. *The Agony of Modern Music* by Henry Pleasants (New York: Simon and Schuster; 1955) was a widely read and cited work at the middle of the century and is representative of this type of popular invective against twentieth-century music. However, there are also more recent attacks from the academy as well, such as *Schoenberg's Error*, by William Thomson, and *The Idea of Music: Schoenberg and Others*, by Peter Franklin. Of course, Schoenberg complained of the severe criticism of his music from as early as the first performances in Vienna at the beginning of the century, and he blamed it on critics who misrepresented his musical ideas or who did not even try to understand or listen to his music. It appears that there are still those who are more interested in political diatribe than in a more objective analytical discourse on the music itself.

On the other side of the spectrum are the supporters of Schoenberg's music and music by other composers of atonal and twelve-tone music. Just as Schoenberg's critics attacked him without mercy, his students and supporters (frequently referred to as ''disciples'') upheld and promoted his music and ideas with equal fervor. Added to this was the battle between the supporters of Stravinsky and those of Schoenberg—an aesthetic war not too different from that between the Brahmsians and Wagnerites of the previous century.

It is important for the reader to be aware of these biases in evaluating any literature about Schoenberg. Of course, not all of the literature on the music of Schoenberg can be invalidated as a result of these opposing viewpoints, and in general literature by individuals not directly or personally involved in the politics of Schoenberg's reception, which has only begun to appear within the last twenty to forty years, tends to be more objective and freer from these biases. The newer scholarship on Schoenberg will undoubtedly reassess his place in the history of music.

Biography

The principal biographers of Schoenberg are Egon Wellesz, Willi Reich, and H. H. Stuckenschmidt, all of whose works were originally published in German and subsequently translated into English. The biographies by Wellesz were written during Schoenberg's lifetime and with his cooperation and authorization. Reich's biography blends lengthy quotations from documents into the narrative text and presents the events of Schoenberg's life chronologically. The latest biography, by Stuckenschmidt, *Schönberg, Leben, Umwelt, Werk* (published in English as *Schoenberg: His Life, World, and Work*, 1978), is the most complete and authoritative biography to date. In fact, the author seems almost overwhelmed by the large body of source material to which he had access. A comprehensive study of Schoenberg, with well-organized and -documented biographical material and up-to-date commentary on the musical works, has still to be written.

The letters of Schoenberg pose another problem. The selected collection of letters prepared by Erwin Stein remains the primary publication of Schoenberg's correspondence. In recent years, full-length monographs have been published consisting of the letters between Schoenberg and one or two individuals. The collections of correspondence with Berg and Kandinsky are among the most important of these. Other less significant, although still important, collections of letters are scattered throughout the literature. Bringing the letters of Schoenberg currently published under bibliographic control would be a great service to Schoenberg scholarship until a complete edition of the letters is undertaken. Because of the size of the Schoenberg correspondence (some estimates place it at over 17,000 letters in the Library of Congress collection alone), the complete collection will probably not be published for some time.

Bibliography and Discography

The bibliographic literature on Schoenberg remains scattered and fragmentary. Josef Rufer's *Das Werk Arnold Schönbergs* (published in English as *The Works of Arnold Schoenberg: A Catalogue of His Compositions, Writings and Paintings*, 1962 and 1963) is the most complete published catalog of the Schoenberg manuscripts. Although a pioneering work, the treatment was not systematic or consistent throughout the volume. Volume 1 of Jan Maegaard's *Studien zur Entwicklung des dodekaphonen Satzes bei Arnold Schönberg*, while more detailed in its descriptions and consistent in its treatment, catalogs only the music manuscripts through 1933. The bibliography of Jean and Jesper Christensen, *From Arnold Schoenberg's Literary Legacy: A Catalog of Neglected Items*, supplements the Rufer catalog by describing the smaller text manuscripts in much greater detail. The critical commentary that accompanies the *Arnold Schönberg Sämtliche Werke* (in progress) is the most thorough and systematic bibliography of the manuscripts and published editions of the music of Schoenberg. A catalog of the archives of the Arnold Schoenberg Institute at the University of Southern California was a complete listing and description of the Schoenberg manuscripts and holdings of that repository. The catalog was accessible through the Research Libraries Information Network (RLIN) and was available in print upon demand from 1984 through 1997.

The only published bibliography of the literature and music of Schoenberg that approaches comprehensiveness is *A Bibliographic Catalog with Discography and a Comprehensive Bibliography of Arnold Schönberg*, by Tetsuo Satoh et al. However, the book is limited in that the citations are drawn primarily from the collection of the Kunitachi Music College Library in Japan and was completed in 1974. The *Journal of the Arnold Schoenberg Institute* has published an irregular series of current bibliography articles beginning with its first issue in October 1976 through November 1992 (vol. 15, no. 2). In contrast to the bibliographical control of Schoenberg literature, the recordings of Schoenberg's music have been thoroughly and carefully documented by R. Wayne Shoaf in *The Schoenberg Discography*, now in its second edition.

Music

This bibliography does not document the printed editions of Schoenberg's music, since all of his works will eventually be available in *Arnold Schönberg Sämtliche Werke* (Mainz: Schott; Wien: Universal Edition, 1966) and the edition is widely available. This collected works set is a meticulously prepared critical edition of all of the works of Schoenberg, including the unfinished works, sketches, and arrangements with complete descriptive bibliographic aparatus. The set can only be obtained in its entirety and is projected to consist of sixty-four volumes upon its completion. However, Belmont Music Publishers issues many of the works from the complete edition as individual publications without the critical notes. As with many major scholarly enterprises, it is not without controversy. One of the main criticisms of the edition by certain scholars is how deviations from the twelve-tone row are treated in the final text of the music and in the critical notes.[1] In response to these criticisms, the editorial principles of the edition are printed in every volume of critical notes published after 1984.

Most of Schoenberg's music has remained in print. The primary publishers of his music are Belmont Music Publishers, Universal Edition, Schott, Boelke Bomart, G. Schirmer, and Wilhelm Hansen. Belmont is the main publisher and distributor of Schoenberg's music. As more of Schoenberg's works enter the public domain, publishers including Dover, Kalmus, and Masters Music are reprinting earlier editions.

Writings

The major theoretical writings and textbooks of Schoenberg are essential for a complete understanding of his compositional methods and his role as a teacher. The *Harmonielehre* (3rd ed., 1922, translated into English by Roy Carter) goes far beyond a practical guide to tonal harmony. It is Schoenberg's main aesthetic and philosophical treatise on music theory. The other major theoretical treatise remained unfinished and has only recently been published in German-English parallel translation as *The Musical Idea and the Logic, Technique and Art of Its Presentation*, edited by Patricia Carpenter and Severine Neff. The textbooks, *Structural Functions of Harmony, Preliminary Exercises in Counterpoint*, and *Fundamentals of Musical Composition*, which were written for his students at UCLA toward the end of his life, although intended to satisfy the more practical needs of his students, still provide a wealth of information concerning his aesthetic and his compositional and pedagogical methods.

Schoenberg expressed his opinions on many topics in addition to music. The major collection of his essays first appeared in 1950, edited by Dika Newlin and entitled *Style and Idea*. It was later expanded by editor Leonard Stein in 1975 under the same title. Stein's compilation includes all of the essays from the earlier volume and a sample of some of the more significant essays. A comprehensive edition of all of Schoenberg's writings is appearing in German as *Gesammelte Schriften*, edited by Ivan Vojtech. Many of Schoenberg's writings have been published in full or in part in various books and journals. A comprehensive listing of these articles up to 1979 appeared in the *Journal of the Arnold Schoenberg Institute* in "Schoenberg's Published Articles: A List of Titles, Sources, and Translations," by Walter Bailey. Also the *Journal* continued to publish and translate into English essays and documents by Schoenberg until it ceased publication with the 1996 volume.

Analytical and Critical Studies

The music of Schoenberg is frequently divided into early, middle, and late works, which roughly correspond to the three stylistic periods: tonal, atonal, and twelve-tone. Schoenberg revealed a great deal about his theories of tonal composition through textbooks, essays, and teaching; however, he chose not to articulate his ideas with regard to atonal or twelve-tone writing to any great degree. Theorists are only now beginning to develop methods to explore the atonal and twelve-tone works.

The early tonal works have understandably received less critical attention as they can be approached using standard analytical techniques. Walter Frisch has explored these works extensively in *The Early Works of Arnold Schoenberg, 1893–1908* as well as in other articles. The most frequently performed work by Schoenberg is *Verklärte Nacht*, whose harmonic and structural features are described in "1/XII/99: Tonal Relations in Schoenberg's Verklärte Nacht," an article from *19th Century Music*, by Richard Swift.

In contrast, the atonal works dating from about 1907 through 1922 have received a great deal of scholarly attention. Theorists have approached atonal music with different methodologies ranging from traditional tonal analyses to mathematical set theory. Two notable attempts to place the round peg of atonality into the square hole of a tonal structure are "Chapter XXII. Arnold Schönberg: Opus 11 and Opus 19" from *Musical Form*, by Hugo Leichtentritt and *Aspects of Harmony in Schoenberg's Six Little Piano Pieces, Op. 19*, by Kenneth L. Hicken.

Many have noted that the atonal works were miniatures and that larger scale atonal works relied on verbal texts to extend the musical structure. One of the major books to explore this area is *Music and Text in the Works of Arnold Schoenberg: The Critical Years, 1908–1922*, by Alan Lessem.

One of the greatest influences on music theory relating to atonal music has been the work of Allen Forte, beginning with *Contemporary Tone-structures* (New York: Teachers College, Columbia University; 1955. xii, 194 p. Teachers College Studies in Education) and including *The Structure of Atonal Music*, 2nd ed. These two works combine mathematical set theory and Schenkerian analysis to provide a systematic theoretical explanation of atonal music. As a professor at Yale University and as an editor of the *Journal of Music Theory*, Forte has served as a mentor to a whole generation of younger scholars who have carried on this work. Because these studies are highly detailed examinations of the music and rely on sophisticated mathematical operations, they are recommended only for specialists.

The twelve-tone and late works of Schoenberg together with his immigration to the United States open many avenues for exploration. The first book to explain the basic principles of twelve-tone composition, and still one of the most complete, is *Die Komposition mit zwölf Tönen* (published in English as *Composition with Twelve Notes Related Only to One Another*), by Josef Rufer. As

Schoenberg's teaching assistant in the 1920s, Rufer was in an ideal position to absorb and communicate the principles of the twelve-tone technique. A number of other studies have focused on the evolution of the twelve-tone technique. The pioneering work of Jan Maegaard, *Studien zur Entwicklung des dodekaphonen Satzes bei Arnold Schönberg*, has been the basis for further research into how Schoenberg devised the principles of twelve-tone composition. More recent work on the development of the twelve-tone principle is *Schoenberg's Serial Odyssey: The Evolution of His Twelve-tone Method, 1914–1928*, by Ethan Haimo. Martha Hyde has pointed out the need to consider the importance of harmony and rhythm as it relates to twelve-tone composition, especially in *Schoenberg's Twelve-tone Harmony: The Suite Op. 29 and the Compositional Sketches* and related articles.

The influence of religion and spirituality on the life and works of Schoenberg has prompted a number of studies. Alexander Ringer has published extensively on Schoenberg's relationship to Judaism culminating in his book *Arnold Schoenberg: The Composer as Jew*. While it is not possible in the context of this essay to cite important writings on every work of Schoenberg, *Moses und Aron* contains the essence of so much of Schoenberg's personal and artistic philosophy that several studies should be mentioned. Karl Wörner's *Gotteswort und Magie: Die Oper "Moses und Aron" von Arnold Schönberg* (published in English as *Schoenberg's "Moses and Aaron"*) was the first extended study of the opera as a whole. The book by Pamela White, *Schoenberg and the God-Idea: The Opera Moses und Aron*, examines the philosophical, religious, and aesthetic aspects of the work, while *Schönbergs Oper Moses und Aron: Analyse der diastematischen, formalen und musikdramatischen Komposition* (Mainz; New York: Schott, 1988. 335 p. [Schott Musikwissenschaft]) by Christian Martin Schmidt is a thorough analysis based on source documentation. Hopefully it will be translated into English.

Criteria for Inclusion

The purpose of this bibliography was to select important writings that can serve to introduce the informed layman and musician to the life and works of Arnold Schoenberg. Consequently, the citations focus on works in English, although there are a few inclusions of studies of great importance in other languages and of sources that can be used with a moderate knowledge of that language. Highly technical musical analyses were generally avoided except to provide a few samples of this type of literature by significant theorists. The annotations attempt to be descriptive rather than evaluative and quote from the source in cases where there was a succinct statement to be found summarizing the work.

Although the selection of material emphasizes newer research, older materials are included for their significance to scholarship. For example, Richard Hill's article, ''Schoenberg's Tone-Rows and the Tonal System of the Future,'' has largely been supplanted by more recent studies, but it is included here because it was so influential when it first appeared. Only works through December 1995 could be included.

Producing a select bibliography always entails the use of subjective judgment. There are many interesting and valuable studies excluded from this list. However it is hoped that these items can serve as a beginning point to further the reader's interest in Schoenberg.

SELECTED BIBLIOGRAPHY

Writings

Berg, Alban, and Arnold Schoenberg. *The Berg-Schoenberg Correspondence: Selected Letters*. Juliane Brand, Christopher Hailey, and Donald Harris, eds. New York: W. W. Norton, 1987. xxviii, 497 p. The correspondence covers the twenty-five years from 1911 through Berg's death in 1935 with two letters to Berg's wife from 1936 appended. This work is indispensable to Schoenberg studies, since Berg was an important student, colleague, and friend of Schoenberg. The letters shed light not only on the personal and professional lives of the two composers but also chronicle the musical and cultural life of central Europe during the period, especially as it relates to the Second Viennese School and their associates.

Goehr, Alexander. "The Theoretical Writings of Arnold Schoenberg." *Proceedings of the Royal Musical Association*. 1973–74; 100: 85–96. This article is a cross between a survey of Schoenberg's published writings on music and a bibliographic essay. The majority of the essay discusses the *Harmonielehre*, and there are smaller sections devoted to *Structural Functions of Harmony, Preliminary Exercises in Counterpoint*, and *Fundamentals of Musical Composition*.

Schoenberg, Arnold. "Der biblische Weg = The Biblical Way." Moshe Lazar, ed. and trans. *Journal of the Arnold Schoenberg Institute*. June & November 1994, 17(1–2). 460 p. The stage play *Der biblische Weg* was the dramatic precursor to *Moses und Aron*. In this play, many of the philosophical ideas, which were to be expressed and developed in *Moses und Aron*, first appear. This volume contains the entire German text with an English translation, complete facsimiles and transcriptions of the first two drafts of the play, supporting documentation for the work, an extensive introductory essay by the editor, and a listing by R. Wayne Shoaf of the manuscript sources for the play.

―――. *Fundamentals of Musical Composition*. Gerald Strang and Leonard Stein, eds. New York: St. Martin's Press, 1967. xiv, 224 p. This book represents the culmination of Schoenberg's teaching of musical composition. It is intended as a textbook for the average music student and for the beginning composition student. In addition, it is a textbook in musical analysis focusing on works from the eighteenth and nineteenth centuries. Schoenberg believed that it was necessary for a composer to thoroughly understand and master the musical forms of this period in order to be able to attempt to compose in more modern idioms. Although the book contains many musical examples, a copy of the Beethoven Piano Sonatas is necessary to follow the discussion in the book.

―――. *Gesammelte Schriften*. Ivan Vojtech, ed. Gudrun Budde, trans. Nördlingen and Reutlingen: S. Fischer, 1976–. 2 v. This is a complete collection of the writings of Schoenberg. It includes all of the essays appearing in *Style and Idea* and all of the many other shorter essays. Schoenberg's writings originally in English have all been translated into German. As of this writing, only the first volume has been published.

———. *Letters.* Erwin Stein, ed. Eithne Wilkins and Ernst Kaiser, trans. New York: St. Martin's Press, 1965. Reprint. Berkeley and Los Angeles: University of California Press, 1987. 309 p. First published in German as *Arnold Schönberg: Ausgewählte Briefe.* Mainz: B. Schott's Söhne, 1958. This is a general selection from the massive correspondence of Schoenberg. The letters which were selected focus on musical and artistic matters, but there are also letters which give the reader a glimpse of Schoenberg's personality.

———. *The Musical Idea and the Logic, Technique, and Art of Its Presentation.* Patricia Carpenter and Severine Neff, ed., trans., and commentary. New York: Columbia University Press, 1995. xxiv, 462 p. This is a presentation in parallel translation of one of Schoenberg's most important, albeit unfinished, theoretical writings. "Four long essays in the manuscript provide a broad base for Schoenberg's theoretical concerns. Those on comprehensibility and coherence explicate his notions on perception and cognition. 'Principles of Construction' gives us his most precise ideas on organicism and the dynamic of the living artwork. 'The Constructive Function of Harmony' presents his understanding of cadence as a background of the tonal composition, his initial representation of monotonality, and his most detailed studies of Brahms's music. The definitions of the elements of form . . . and formal procedures . . . demonstrate his theory of form. The many short essays (on development, popular music, performance and gestalt, and introduction . . .) develop such topics in a manner not found elsewhere. . . . The aim of this volume is to present the main *Gedanke* manuscript in such a way as to project Schoenberg's writings on the musical idea and its presentation as a cogent body of thought about music."

———. *Preliminary Exercises in Counterpoint.* Leonard Stein, ed. New York: St. Martin's Press, 1970. xv, 231 p. (St. Martin's Music Paper Backs). This textbook by Schoenberg systematically and exhaustively examines species counterpoint for up to four voices and includes exercises in imitation and canon. Fugal writing was intended for another book which was never completed.

———. *Structural Functions of Harmony.* New York: W. W. Norton, 1954. xii, 200 p. Revised ed. New York: Norton, 1969. This textbook on harmony is designed to be used for self-study or in the classroom. It provides a brief review of the basic principles of harmony which are treated more comprehensively in the *Theory of Harmony.* This book emphasizes the role of chord progression in tonal composition.

———. *Style and Idea: Selected Writings of Arnold Schoenberg.* Leonard Stein, ed. Leo Black, trans. London: Faber & Faber, 1975. Reprint. New York: St. Martins, 1975. Paperback reprint. Berkeley and Los Angeles: University of California Press, 1984. 559 p. This book includes all of the essays published in the 1950 edition edited and translated by Dika Newlin and adds most of the other important essays by Schoenberg. Except for the last chapter, which deals with social and political ideas, all of the essays are about music. This is the main compendium of Schoenberg's writings in English.

———. *Theory of Harmony.* Roy E. Carter, trans. Berkeley and Los Angeles: University of California Press, 1978. xxi, 440 p. Schoenberg's text is one of the most thorough treatments of traditional harmony ever written and includes many statements of his aesthetic philosophy. Only the last three chapters, comprising a very small portion of the book, discuss chords outside tertian harmonies, including quartal chords, whole-tone harmonies, and chords containing five or more notes. This translation is based on the third edition of 1922.

————. "Unpublished Schoenberg Letters: Early, Middle and Late." Hans Keller, ed. *Music Survey.* June 1952, 4(3): 499–471. These fourteen letters form a miscellaneous collection. The most interesting are the letters to Schoenberg's longtime friend and astrologer Oscar Adler and one to Humphrey Searle discussing the possibility of a BBC program on twelve-tone composition.

Schoenberg, Arnold, and Hans Nachod. *The Arnold Schoenberg–Hans Nachod Collection.* John A. Kimmey, Jr., ed. Detroit: Information Coordinators, 1979. 119, 230 p. (Detroit Studies in Music Bibliography, no. 41). Schoenberg's cousin, Hans Nachod, sang the part of Waldemar in the premiere of the *Gurrelieder.* This book contains facsimiles of the entire Nachod collection at the University of North Texas. The collection contains letters from 1909 to 1949. About half of the letters, through the 1920s, concern performances of the *Gurrelieder.* The second half of the letters is primarily concerned with family matters and Nachod's frequent appeals to Schoenberg to help him immigrate to the United States pending the Austrian *Anschluss.* The vocal score containing performance annotations in Waldemar's part is reproduced in full, and there are also manuscripts of original compositions by Schoenberg dating from the 1880s and 1890s.

Schoenberg, Arnold, and Wassily Kandinsky. *Arnold Schoenberg, Wassily Kandinsky: Letters, Pictures, and Documents.* Jelena Hahl-Koch, ed. John C. Crawford, trans. London; Boston: Faber and Faber, 1984. 221 p. The primary section of the book is the correspondence between these two artists, which begins in 1911. Although working in different fields (music and art) Schoenberg and Kandinsky discovered that they shared a common artistic aesthetic, and they were both interested in creating a *Gesamtkunstwerk.* Many of the letters discuss Schoenberg's opera, *Die glückliche Hand,* and Kandinsky's play, *Der gelbe Klang.* The letters also touch on their theoretical writings, *Theory of Harmony* and *On the Spiritual in Art,* which were both published in 1911. Aside from being a composer, Schoenberg also painted throughout his life, but most of his paintings date from 1907 to 1912. His relationship with Kandinsky led to his being included in exhibitions in 1909 and 1912 of the group of painters organized by Kandinsky known as *Der blaue Reiter.* In addition to the letters, the book contains the writings of Schoenberg about *Die glückliche Hand* and Kandinsky's writings about *Der gelbe Klang.* The text concludes with essays about the relationship of Schoenberg and Kandinsky and about Schoenberg as an artist.

Bibliography

Bailey, Walter B. "Schoenberg's Published Articles: A List of Titles, Sources, and Translations." *Journal of the Arnold Schoenberg Institute.* November 1980, 4(2): [155]–191. This is a comprehensive bibliography of Schoenberg's essays published up to 1979.

Christensen, Jean, and Jesper Christensen. *From Arnold Schoenberg's Literary Legacy: A Catalog of Neglected Items*. Warren, MI: Harmonie Park Press, 1988. xii, 164 p. (Detroit Studies in Music Bibliography; no. 59). This book is a catalog of the manuscript writings of Schoenberg not listed in other published catalogs and complements the catalog by Josef Rufer, *The Works of Arnold Schoenberg*.

Rufer, Josef. *The Works of Arnold Schoenberg: A Catalogue of His Compositions, Writings and Paintings*. Dika Newlin, trans. London: Faber and Faber, 1962. 214 p. First published as *Das Werk Arnold Schönbergs*. Kassel: Bärenreiter, 1959. xii, 224 p. This is the only published catalog to date of the manuscripts of Schoenberg. Descriptions of the music manuscripts are very detailed while the descriptions of the manuscripts of the writings and other archival materials are inconsistent or mere listings. Since the book was first published in German in 1959, some of the locations or the arrangement of certain manuscripts has changed. Nonetheless, it is still a valuable resource as a one-volume catalog. More up-to-date and scholarly descriptions of the music manuscripts are found in the critical notes for the Schoenberg complete works.

Satoh, Tetsuo, et al. *A Bibliographic Catalog with Discography and a Comprehensive Bibliography of Arnold Schönberg=Shemberuku Shoshi*. Tokyo: Kunitachi Ongaku Daigaku Fuzoku Toshokan, 1978. 8, 156 p. (Kunitachi Music College Library Bibliography Series; 1). This is the first attempt at a comprehensive bibliography and discography on Schoenberg covering the literature through 1974. Most of the citations are in Western European languages.

Schoenberg, Arnold. *Sämtliche Werke*, Reihe B. Josef Rufer [and others], eds. Mainz: B. Schott's Söhne; Wien: Universal Edition; 1972–. 34 v. Series B of the *Collected Works* consists of the critical notes for all of Schoenberg's music. Each volume contains a section that lists and describes all of the manuscripts, sketches, and published editions for every musical work. When finished, this will be the most complete and detailed bibliography of the music of Schoenberg. The text is in German, but the bibliographic citations are accessible to English speakers.

Shoaf, R. Wayne. *The Schoenberg Discography*. 2nd ed., rev. and expanded. Berkeley, CA: Fallen Leaf Press, 1994. xv, 264 p. (Fallen Leaf Reference Books in Music; 18). This comprehensive discography lists every commercially produced recording of Schoenberg's music from the first piano rolls through the early 1990s. The exhaustive listing includes a list of the works of Schoenberg, a chronology of recordings and indexes to names, titles, recording labels, and reviews.

Biography

Armitage, Merle, ed. *Schoenberg*. Westport, CT: Greenwood Press, 1977. 319 p. Reprint of the ed., New York: G. Schirmer, 1937. The list of the contributors to this volume of essays reads like a who's who in the arts from the 1930s. In addition to reprinted and original essays, the book includes an interview with Schoenberg by the journalist José Rodriguez; a chronology by Nicholas Slonimsky; the essays "Tonality and Form" and "Problems of Harmony" by Schoenberg; reproductions of art works by Gershwin, Schoenberg, and Carlos Dyer; and photographs by Edward Weston and Otto Rothschild. The original edition of the book itself is an interesting example of art deco graphic design.

Arnold Schönberg, 1874–1951: Lebensgeschichte in Begegnungen. Nuria Schoenberg-
Nono, ed. Klagenfurt: Ritter Klagenfurt, 1992. 467 p. This monumental documentary biography covers Schoenberg's entire life. It includes facsimiles of music
and text manuscripts, letters, photographs, and illustrations presented in chronological order.

Bach, David Josef. "A Note on Arnold Schoenberg." *Musical Quarterly.* January 1936,
22(1): 8–13. As an early friend of Schoenberg, the author provides a glimpse into
Schoenberg's musical life in his early twenties. This is one of the very few
firsthand accounts of the events leading to Schoenberg's decision to become a
musician. Bach also emphasizes Schoenberg's predilection for the music of
Brahms and how his own compositions show this influence.

MacDonald, Malcolm. *Schoenberg.* London: J. M. Dent & Sons Ltd., 1976. xii, 289 p.
(The Master Musicians Series). The author's intention is "to explain and popu-
larize Schoenberg—to present some basic information about him, to survey his
music, to delineate the principal issues, and to ask some questions." The biographical section of the book presents the major events and influences of his life.
About two-thirds of the text is devoted to a discussion of the musical works. It
is one of the best introductions to the life and music of Arnold Schoenberg, being
neither too technical nor condescendingly simplified in presentation. The author
enjoys the music for its own sake and has no agenda to either promote or criticize
the music. The appendices include a chronology, list of works, biographical
sketches of people important in Schoenberg's life, and a selective bibliography
and discography.

Milhaud, Darius. "To Arnold Schoenberg on His Seventieth Birthday: Personal Recollections." *Musical Quarterly.* October 1944, 30(4): 379–384. Milhaud recounts
his interest in Schoenberg's music dating back to 1910 as a music student. Although he did not choose to write atonal or twelve-tone music, he admired
Schoenberg's work and promoted its performance in France. As a member of *Les
Six*, he performed *Pierrot lunaire* with the French singer, Marya Freund throughout Europe.

Neighbour, Oliver [W.]. "Schoenberg." In Neighbour, Oliver [W.], Paul Griffiths, and
George Perle, eds. *The New Grove Second Viennese School: Schoenberg, Webern,
Berg.* New York: W. W. Norton & Co., 1983: 1–85. (The Composer Biography
Series). This article is an updated version of that contained in *The New Grove
Dictionary of Music and Musicians.* Consisting of four parts—biography, the
works of Schoenberg, an exhaustive list of works, and a bibliography—it is an
excellent introductory essay on the life and music of Schoenberg.

Newlin, Dika. *Bruckner, Mahler, Schoenberg.* Rev. ed. New York: W. W. Norton, 1978.
First published in 1947. The author shows how the music of Schoenberg evolved
from the Viennese classical tradition and specifically how the music of Bruckner
and Mahler led to the most radical of his works. Very little is changed in the
revised edition except for a few corrections, a few additions to the bibliography,
and an additional chapter about the last seven years of Schoenberg's life.

———. *Schoenberg Remembered: Diaries and Recollections (1938–76).* New York: Pendragon Press, 1980. x, 369 p. The author began her studies with Schoenberg at
the age of 14 in 1939. During this time she kept a daily diary of all of her
activities. This book consists of extracts from those diaries of events concerning
Schoenberg and covers all of the years up to his death in 1951. Although the

tone of the book is what one might expect from a young girl, it is the only published account of Schoenberg that gives such a detailed picture of the composer's personality. The book is also rich in details about musical life in Los Angeles during this time, contains a wealth of information about Schoenberg's students and friends, and describes his teaching methods.

————. "Schöenberg in America, 1933–1948: Retrospect and Prospect." *Music Survey*. 1949, 1(5, 6): 128–131, 185–189. Schoenberg's career as a teacher and theorist is outlined including his classes at UCLA and the composition textbooks he wrote during this period. The second part of the article examines his compositions written after coming to America in 1933.

Reich, Willi. *Schoenberg: A Critical Biography*. Leo Black, trans. New York: Praeger Publishers, 1971. 268 p. (Books That Matter). First published in German as *Arnold Schönberg, oder, Der konservative Revolutionär*. Wien: Verlag Fritz Molden; 1968. 328 p., [16] p. of plates. (Glanz und Elend der Meister). This biography emphasizes the life of Schoenberg and is particularly useful for its chronological arrangement. A wealth of quotations from source material is also interspersed throughout the text. The appendix includes three essays by Schoenberg, Berg's dedication of *Lulu* to Schoenberg, and an essay by Oscar Adler, a lifelong friend of Schoenberg. The book concludes with a brief bibliography, chronological list of works, and an index.

Rubsamen, Walter H. "Schoenberg in America." *Musical Quarterly*. October 1951, 37(4): 469–489. The author gives a full account of Schoenberg's activities as a musician from his arrival in the United States in 1933 until his death in 1951. This includes his compositional activity, lecture engagements, teaching positions, work on various books and articles, and interactions with friends and colleagues.

Smith, Joan Allen. *Schoenberg and His Circle: A Viennese Portrait*. New York: Schirmer Books, 1986. xiv, 319 p. By means of oral history interviews, "this study is an attempt to place an event of major cultural importance, the development of the twelve-tone method, within a cultural-historical framework." The material from twenty-five interviews is arranged into five sections: "[Schoenberg's] cultural surroundings, his involvement with performance, his teaching activities, . . . the evolution of the twelve-tone method, . . . [and his] life after his disclosure of the method and before his immigration to the United States."

Steiner, Ena. "Schoenberg's Quest: Newly Discovered Works from His Early Years." *Musical Quarterly*. July 1974, 60(3): 401–420. This is one of the most complete accounts of Schoenberg's life up through his early twenties. The author discusses compositions from Schoenberg's childhood and his development as a musician and composer. Much of this information is based upon manuscripts that were in the possession of Schoenberg's cousin, Hans Nachod.

Steuermann, Edward. "A Conversation with Steuermann." Gunther Schuller, ed. *Perspectives of New Music*. Fall-Winter 1964, 3(1): 22–35. Steuermann was a student of Schoenberg and is considered by many to have been the foremost interpreter of Schoenberg's piano works. This interview is invaluable for firsthand information and covers Steuermann's early studies with Schoenberg, his participation in the premiere performance of *Pierrot lunaire*, the Society for Private Musical Performances, and his work in Vienna and Berlin with other composers and conductors during the 1920s.

Stuckenschmidt, H. H. *Schoenberg: His Life, World, and Work*. Humphrey Searle, trans.

New York: Schirmer Books, 1978. 581 p. First published in German as *Schön-berg: Leben, Umwelt, Werk*. Zurich: Atlantis Musikbuch-Verlag, 1974. This is the most comprehensive biography of Schoenberg written to date. The author's narrative weaves discussions of the music and writings of Schoenberg in with biographical information, giving a total picture of him as a man and a musician. It is clear that the author was working from a wealth of source material but also drew from his own experience as one who knew Schoenberg and was one of Germany's most prominent musical figures.

Wellesz, Egon. *Arnold Schönberg*. W. H. Kerridge, trans. London: J. M. Dent, 1925, New York: E. P. Dutton, 1925. (A. Eaglefield-Hull, ed. Dent's International Library of Books on Music). Several reprint ed. were published 1969–1971. This earliest biography by a pupil of Schoenberg was first published in German in Vienna in 1921. The translation was revised and updated for publication in 1925 with additional material by the editor. There are three chapters covering Schoenberg's life, his activity as a teacher and conductor, and his works through the early twelve-tone pieces. A brief chronology and index complete the book. It gives a unique contemporary account of the first half of Schoenberg's life by an admiring student.

General

Adorno, Theodor Wiesengrund. "Arnold Schoenberg, 1874–1951." In his *Prisms*. Samuel and Shierry Weber, eds. London: Neville Spearman, 1967: 147–172. 272 p. Originally published in German as *Prismen*. Berlin: Suhrkamp Verlag, 1955. The author explains and defends the music and aesthetic of Schoenberg. Individual works from the three main compositional periods of Schoenberg's life (tonal, atonal, and twelve-tone) are examined. The essay is a summary of Adorno's views of Schoenberg's music.

———. *Philosophy of Modern Music*. Anne G. Mitchel and Wesley V. Blomster, trans. New York: Seabury Press, 1973. xiv, 220 p. (A Continuum Book). Originally published in German as *Philosophie der neuen Musik*. Tubingen: Mohr, 1949. The book consists of two sections, "Schoenberg and Progress" and "Stravinsky and Restoration," written in 1941 and 1948, respectively. Adorno sees the music of Schoenberg and Stravinsky as dialectical opposites. By examining these two extreme positions, the essence of the music of other twentieth-century composers can be revealed. The philosophical underpinnings of both positions is examined by using Hegelian dialectics. Adorno views the Schoenbergians as the progressive elements in music—as the champions of authenticity, originality, and artistic integrity. Conversely the music of Stravinsky is dependent upon music of the past and to a certain extent is derivative. Adorno's language and argument, even in translation, can be difficult to follow for those with little background in aesthetic philosophy.

———. *Quasi una fantasia: Essays on Modern Music*. Rodney Livingstone, trans. London, New York: Verso, 1992. 336 p. Originally published in German as *Quasi una fantasia: Musikalische Schriften II*. Frankfurt am Main: Suhrkamp, 1963. The essays in this collection date primarily from the late 1950s and early 1960s. Adorno continues to expound the ideas he articulated in *Philosophy of Modern*

Music, but the style of the language and the expression of his ideas is clearer. The book is divided into three parts. In the first part, "Improvisations," he analyzes the role music plays in society as a "commodity" and how it is used by society for purposes other than artistic expression. In "Evocations," there are essays about the music of Mahler, Zemlinsky, Schreker, and Stravinsky. In part three, "Finale," he discusses the uniqueness of some of Berg's compositional techniques, the continued lack of recognition of the Second Viennese School in Viennese cultural circles, Schoenberg's *Moses und Aron*, and the meaning of the term "New Music" in the 1960s.

Boretz, Benjamin, and Edward T. Cone, eds. *Perspectives on Schoenberg and Stravinsky*. Rev. ed. New York: W. W. Norton, 1972. x, 284 p. (The Norton Library, N618). Nine essays from *Perspectives of New Music* dating from 1965 to 1968 are contained in this book. They include Robert Craft's article on the Five Orchestra Pieces, op. 16; an English translation of Schoenberg's 1932 "Analysis of the Four Orchestral Songs, Opus 22"; three essays by Milton Babbitt; two articles by David Lewin on the first act of *Moses und Aron* and the *Phantasy for Violin with Piano Accompaniment*, op. 47; a contribution by Glenn Watkins on Schoenberg's organ works; and an article by Boris Schwarz on Schoenberg's trip to the Soviet Union. A discography appears only in the first edition, published in 1968 (pp. 253–267).

Boulez, Pierre. "Schoenberg Is Dead." In Pierre Boulez, *Stocktakings from an Apprenticeship*. Paule Thévenin, ed. Stephen Walsh, trans. Oxford: Clarendon Press, 1991. 209–214. Also in *Notes of an Apprenticeship*. Herbert Weinstock, trans. New York: Alfred A. Knopf, 1968. 268–278; and a shorter version in *Score*. February 1952, 6: 18–22. This essay is a manifesto for the post–World War II serial movement. Boulez credits Schoenberg for the creation of the twelve-tone technique but criticizes him for remaining tied to nineteenth-century German romanticism through the use of classical forms. Boulez thinks that twelve-tone composition, as a new means of organizing pitch, requires a new means of organizing and employing all parameters of musical composition. The use of the twelve-tone technique with classical forms is seen as illogical and contradictory.

Brown, Julie. "Schoenberg's Early Wagnerisms: Atonality and the Redemption of Ahasuerus." *Cambridge Opera Journal*. 1994, 6(1): 51–80. Wagner's influence on music, and on Schoenberg and other central European composers at the turn of the century in particular, extends beyond technical matters to aesthetics, philosophy, religion, and race. In a 1935 lecture Schoenberg acknowledges the influence that Wagner's ideas, including anti-Semitism, had on him. Schoenberg's reaction to this prevailing Wagnerian *Weltanschauung* had a profound effect in the formation of the Second Viennese School and the transition from tonal to atonal writing. The complex interrelationship between religious, philosophical, and musical ideas is explored in this article.

Christensen, Jean. "The Spiritual and the Material in Schoenberg's Thinking." *Music & Letters*. October 1984, 65(4): 337–344. Drawing upon the many small and largely unpublished essays and fragmentary writings which Schoenberg first organized in 1932 and added to thereafter, the author examines Schoenberg's philosophy concerning artistic creation. Throughout these writings Schoenberg sees the role of the artist to be the expression of a central idea of spiritual truth and not necessarily to be concerned with a search for beauty or to please the audience.

Examples of this philosophy are frequently seen in *Die Jakobsleiter* and *Moses und Aron*.

Cross, Charlotte M. "Three Levels of 'Idea' in Schoenberg's Thought and Writings." *Current Musicology*. 1980, no. 30: 24–36. The author outlines three concepts of idea depicted throughout the writings of Schoenberg. The first of these is the musical idea or *Gedanke*, which the composer receives all at once by inspiration and then articulates through working out the details of a composition. The second concept is the necessity for self-expression, which leads to the third aspect, humanity's desire to reach toward and become one with God.

Dahlhaus, Carl. *Schoenberg and the New Music: Essays*. Derrick Puffett and Alfred Clayton, trans. Cambridge and New York: Cambridge University Press, 1987. viii, 305 p. These essays, written between 1964 and 1984, are mainly selected from Dahlhaus's 1978 publication, *Schönberg und andere*. The author explores the concept of the New Music, which arose in the 1920s, and relates that idea to Schoenberg's music and theories.

————. "Schoenberg and Schenker." *Proceedings of the Royal Musical Association*. 1973–74, 100: 209–215. Also published in *Schoenberg and the New Music: Essays by Carl Dahlhaus*. Derrick Puffett and Alfred Clayton, trans. Cambridge and New York: Cambridge University Press, 1987. 134–140. Schoenberg's and Schenker's theories of consonance and dissonance are diametrically opposed. Schenker's theory searches for the unchanging fundamental basis of a musical work which is concealed by middle and foreground elements. That is, the essence of a work is its background level to which foreground elements and, therefore, dissonant notes are subordinate. Schoenberg views a musical work as the product of a musical idea. In this conception, no note is incidental or subordinate to true musical understanding. Dissonances are of equal importance to consonances in the expression of the musical idea.

Forte, Allen. "Schoenberg's Creative Evolution: The Path to Atonality." *Musical Quarterly*. April 1978, 59(2): 133–176. The author shows how Schoenberg gradually developed the compositional means to compose atonal music using unordered pitch sets during the years 1905–1909. The first instance of the use of a pitch set begins in the song, "Am Wegrand," op. 6, no. 6, with the use of a "signature set" composed of the pitch equivalents of the letters in Schoenberg's name (E-flat, C, B, B-flat, E, and G). The use of this set (or a derivative of it) can be found in all of the works from this period of transition from tonal to atonal composition. With the composition of the song "Am Strande" of 1909, Schoenberg has fully developed atonal composition. The article is highly technical and may require the reader to refer to Forte's seminal work *The Structure of Atonal Music* (2nd ed. New Haven: Yale University Press, 1977. ix, 224 p.).

Franklin, Peter. *The Idea of Music: Schoenberg and Others*. Basingstoke: Macmillan, 1985. xv, 188 p. The author provides a critical reassessment of the music of the first half of the twentieth century. He believes that progressive movements such as the Second Viennese School have produced propaganda to promote their own music at the expense of more conservative elements. His purpose is "to establish a case for Mahler as a landmark rather than a bridge, and for Strauss as a 'survivor' from whom much may yet be learned." The music of Schreker and Pfitzner are reevaluated and accorded a much more historically important role in music history than is generally recognized. The writings of Schopenhauer, Adorno, and

Thomas Mann are used to support his viewpoint. The book is intended to be provocative and highly critical of the music of Schoenberg.

Goehr, Alexander. "Schoenberg and Karl Kraus: The Idea Behind the Music." *Music Analysis*. March–July 1985, 4(1/2): 59–71. Throughout his life, Schoenberg was concerned with the concept of the "Idea." This concept is expressed through music most fully in the opera *Moses und Aron*. Schoenberg's writings and essays explore the concept of the musical "Idea," especially in a series of unfinished manuscripts known as the *Gedanke* manuscripts. The Viennese writer and critic, Karl Kraus, had an enormous influence on Viennese cultural and intellectual life prior to his death in 1936. Schoenberg was also influenced by Kraus's theories and philosophy which Goehr relates to Schoenberg's concept of the "Idea."

Gould, Glenn. *Arnold Schoenberg: A Perspective*. Cincinnati: University of Cincinnati; 1964. viii, 22 p. (University of Cincinnati Occasional Papers; no. 3). This is the text of a lecture delivered at the University of Cincinnati. Gould views Schoenberg's music as being a transition between late nineteenth-century romanticism and the modern era in much the same way that Monteverdi's work was the link between the late Renaissance and the early baroque. In Monteverdi's time music was moving from polyphony toward a greater reliance on tonal harmony based on the major and minor systems. Schoenberg was to reverse this trend three hundred years later. Tonal harmony had become so complex that he developed the twelve-tone technique, which emphasizes linear polyphony over harmony. Gould explores this idea through a brief chronological overview of Schoenberg's music.

Gradenwitz, Peter. "The Religious Works of Arnold Schönberg." *Music Review*. February 1960, 21(1): 19–29. The music of Schoenberg having religious content, beginning with *Die Jakobsleiter* and ending with his last work, the "Modern Psalms," is examined from both a philosophical and musical standpoint. Schoenberg's interest in spiritual and religious subjects occupied most of his life and grew more important at the end of his life. Religious ideas were closely intertwined with musical ideas and were expressed symbolically as in *Moses und Aron*. Schoenberg uses Jewish cantillation in several of his later works, especially the *Kol nidre*.

Gray, Cecil. "Arnold Schönberg—A Critical Study." *Music and Letters*. January 1922, 3(1): 73–89. Published with minor editorial changes as "Arnold Schönberg," in Gray, Cecil. *A Survey of Contemporary Music*. 2nd ed. London: Oxford University Press; Humphrey Milford, 1927, 162–183. This is a critical survey of Schoenberg's published works from opp. 1–22. The author attempts to provide an impartial assessment of the music. He admires Schoenberg's daring new musical language but clearly does not care for the compositions. Gray represents a viewpoint that was widely shared by knowledgeable musicians of the time. He sees Schoenberg as the culmination of the romantic movement taken to its ultimate extreme and also sees him as the end of a musical era rather than the beginning of a new one. He concludes that there are no new musical discoveries to be made and that Schoenberg and future composers need not consider further advances into unknown territory. The article is of interest as it comes just before Schoenberg's first twelve-tone compositions.

Harvey, Jonathan. "Schönberg: Man or Woman?" *Music & Letters*. July-October 1975, 56(3–4): 371–385. The author seeks to answer the question as to why Schoen-

berg's compositions were able to develop from late romanticism, to expressionism, to neoclassicism when other composers of the same and later generations
were unable to release tonality as the primary organizing aspect of their work.
The question is answered in two parts: spiritual and musical. Spiritually Schoenberg synthesized cultural traditions with his own highly individualistic personal
artistic expression. This spirituality was most fully explored philosophically in
Moses und Aron. The remainder of the article explores how Schoenberg expresses
this spirituality in musical terms.

Jalowetz, Heinrich. "On the Spontaneity of Schoenberg's Music." *Musical Quarterly.*
October 1944, 30(4): 385–408. The author argues that Schoenberg's music emphasizes melody over harmony and tonality. It is this emphasis on melody that
gradually led to the twelve-tone technique as a coherent substitution for tonality.
Through an analysis of the Piano Concerto, it is shown how the twelve-tone
technique allows for freedom of expression while preserving a multitude of musical interrelationships.

Journal of the Arnold Schoenberg Institute. Los Angeles: Arnold Schoenberg Institute;
1976–1996. 19 v. The *Journal of the Arnold Schoenberg Institute* at the University of Southern California published articles about Schoenberg and related subjects. It was issued three times annually for the first two volumes and twice
annually thereafter. The director of the Institute served as the editor of the *Journal.* Leonard Stein, a pupil of Schoenberg, was the editor of volumes 1–14. With
volume 15, the next director, Paul Zukofsky, changed the *Journal*'s emphasis
from scholarly articles to the publication of Schoenberg's archival documents.
The last issue of the *Journal,* volumes 18–19 (1995–1996), was published as one
physical volume in late 1997.

Leibowitz, René. *Schoenberg and His School: The Contemporary Stage of the Language
of Music.* Dika Newlin, trans. New York: Philosophical Library, 1949. This work
explores the music of the Second Viennese School and how Schoenberg's ideas
transformed twentieth-century music. The book concludes with an index, bibliography, discography, and lists of works for the three composers.

Lessen, Alan [Philip]. "Schönberg and the Crisis of Expressionism." *Music & Letters.*
October 1974, 55(4): 429–443. The social, political, cultural, and artistic forces
in central Europe between 1908 and 1925 are explored as they relate to Schoenberg's music of that period. The work of Karl Kraus, Adolf Loos, Wassily Kandinsky and others shared many of the same influences. A pivotal year for
Schoenberg and his students was 1908, when the first atonal pieces appeared.
There was also a move away from nineteenth-century romantic representation of
emotion and feeling in the arts toward a direct depiction of feelings, psychological
states, and dreams.

———. "Schoenberg, Stravinsky, and Neo-Classicism: The Issues Reexamined." *Musical Quarterly.* October 1982, 68(4): 527–542. During their lifetimes, the aesthetic principles of Schoenberg and Stravinsky were generally viewed as polar
opposites. Revisionists in the last quarter of the century proposed that the differences were not as great as earlier thought since both composers wrote works of
a neoclassical nature. The author proposes: "A reexamination of the issues may
show that the differences between the two composers remain significant and that
Neo-Classicism, far from serving as an agent of mediation, is useful only as a
key to the understanding of such differences."

Mitchell, Donald. *The Language of Modern Music*. Rev. ed. Philadelphia: University of Pennsylvania Press, 1994. This extended essay examines the major currents in the first half of the twentieth century by focusing primarily on the contributions of Schoenberg and Stravinsky. The author discusses how the development of the twelve-tone technique was one of the major impediments to the acceptance and performance of Schoenberg's music. The unifying aspect of early twentieth-century music for both Schoenberg and Stravinsky was melody. The dissolution of tonality paved the way for a new treatment of melody in the form of the twelve-tone technique. While it is possible to create abstract, "nonthematic" works, both Schoenberg and Stravinsky retain melody and themes as a primary aspect of their music—Schoenberg's themes being developmental and Stravinsky's being static.

Neighbour, O[liver] W. "In Defence of Schönberg."*Music & Letters*. January 1952, 33(1): 10–27. Following Schoenberg's death, an article was published in *Music & Letters* consisting of contributions from eminent British musicians who presented their assessments of the music of Schoenberg. This article is a reply to those comments. The author first examines the twelve-tone method and focuses on the use of harmony. He notes that Schoenberg left no "rules" for twelve-tone harmony, and this is where the inventiveness and flexibility of the technique challenges the composer and links twelve-tone music to older musical tradition. The second half of the article is a survey and evaluation of Schoenberg's musical works.

Newlin, Dika. "Arnold Schoenberg's Debt to Mahler." *Chord and Dischord*. 1948; 2(5): 21–26. The author recounts the meeting and personal relationship that developed between Mahler and Schoenberg. In addition, several types of musical influences that Mahler had on Schoenberg are described and are most clearly seen in Schoenberg's String Quartet no. 2 in F-sharp Minor, op. 10. These influences are beginning and ending a multimovement composition in different keys, the use of quotation, the use of very large orchestral forces, and innovative orchestration. The blending of orchestral and chamber music forms, such as the programmatic sextet, *Verklärte Nacht*, and the use of soprano voice in the String Quartet no. 2, are cited as other influential characteristics.

Peyser, Joan. "Schoenberg, Webern, and the Austro-German Tradition." In Joan Peyser, *The New Music: The Sense Behind the Sound*. New York: Delacorte Press, 1971. 1–79. The music of Schoenberg and the development of twelve-tone music is viewed as being a defining influence in twentieth-century music. This extended essay on the life and music of Schoenberg is written in a very accessible style for one approaching this music for the first time. It also clearly reflects the author's interpretations and opinions of musical history and aesthetics.

Ringer, Alexander L. *Arnold Schoenberg: The Composer As Jew*. Oxford: Clarendon Press, 1990. xii, 260 p. This compilation of essays discusses the influence of Judaism on the music and life of Arnold Schoenberg. A common theme throughout the essays is Schoenberg's unswerving belief and dedication to his musical and aesthetic ideals, even and especially in the face of almost overwhelming opposition. He was a leader of a musical minority and also a member of a social, racial, and religious minority. When Schoenberg formally recognized his heritage in 1933 by his return to the Jewish community, he maintained his belief in Judaism with the same fervor that characterizes his artistic philosophy.

———. "Schoenberg, Weill and Epic Theater." *Journal of the Arnold Schoenberg In-*

stitute. November 1980, 4(1): 77–98. Schoenberg's views on the aesthetic theories of Kurt Weill and the dramatic music of Germany in the 1920s are examined. His extensive annotations to a newspaper article by Weill entitled "Der Musiker Weill" and an essay commenting on another article by Stuckenschmidt about Brecht's idea of "Epic Theater" entitled "Stuckenschmidt-Brecht Operngesetzte" provide insight into the philosophical and aesthetic differences between Schoenberg's ideas about opera, which stem from the operatic tradition, and Epic Theater, in which Brecht and Weill reacted against that tradition.

Rognoni, Luigi. *The Second Vienna School: Expressionism and Dodecaphony*. Robert W. Mann, trans. London: John Calder, 1977. xxix, 417 p. Published in Italian as *La scuola musicale di Vienna: espressionismo e dodecafonia*. Torino: G. Einaudi, 1966. x, 539 p. The author blends commentary and analyses of the music of Schoenberg, Berg, and Webern with observations on the social and cultural context in which those works were written, enhancing the reader's understanding of this music. The introduction provides the historical background leading up to Schoenberg's early works. There are chapters exploring the relation of expressionism, *Gebrauchsmusik*, and neoclassicism to the music of the Second Viennese School. The author combines a chronological and a stylistic approach to the discussion by focusing on selected genres, such as vocal music or dramatic music, and following those genres through the life of the composer.

Rosen, Charles. *Arnold Schoenberg*. Chicago: University of Chicago Press, 1996. xiv, 113 p. Originally published by: New York: Viking Press, 1975 (Modern Masters). Rosen notes that Schoenberg's music has elicited intense criticism and dislike from many audiences and from many parts of the musical establishment. He explores the reasons behind this controversy by discussing the move from late nineteenth-century chromatic harmony to atonality. The author believes that the works from the years 1908–13 transformed music of the twentieth century and are central to the understanding of the music of the Second Viennese School. There is a brief chapter about the Society for Private Musical Performances, and the book concludes with a discussion of twelve-tone music and Schoenberg's neoclassicism.

Rufer, Josef. "Schoenberg—Yesterday, Today, and Tomorrow." William Drabkin, trans. *Perspectives of New Music*. Fall-Winter 1977, 16(1): 125–138. The author briefly describes the three main periods of Schoenberg's composition: tonal, atonal, and twelve-tone. He argues that Schoenberg's music grew out of the German musical tradition and that new ideas in no way contradict that tradition but are a continuation of it.

Stadlen, Peter. "Schoenberg's Speech-Song." *Music & Letters*. January 1981, 62(1): 1–11. Questions about how Schoenberg intended Sprechstimme to be performed have existed because the instructions for its performance seem to contradict the exact notation of pitch in *Pierrot lunaire*. Schoenberg's own statements about how Sprechstimme is to be performed are not consistent. In addition, in his later works he no longer notated the speaking voice on a full five-line staff. The author concludes that the difficulty in speaking on pitch but not singing, lies in being able to shorten the length of the notes and/or lingering on consonants such as l, m, and n.

Stein, Erwin. *Orpheus in New Guises*. Hyperion reprint ed. Westport, CT: Hyperion Press, 1979. vii, 167 p. (Encore Music Editions). First published: London: Rockliff, 1953. This is a collection of essays primarily about the music of Mahler, Schoenberg, and Britten dating from 1924 to 1953 by one of Schoenberg's most devoted students. The articles on Schoenberg include "Mahler, Reger, Strauss and Schoenberg"; "Schoenberg"; "The *Gurrelieder*"; "New Formal Principles"; "Some Observations on Schoenberg's Twelve Note Rows"; "Performing Schoenberg's Music"; "The Treatment of the Speaking Voice in *Pierrot Lunaire*"; and "Musical Thought: Beethoven and Schoenberg."

Stein, Leonard. "The Privataufführungen Revisited." In *Paul A. Pisk: Essays in His Honor.* John Glowacki, ed. Austin: College of Fine Arts, University of Texas, 1966. 203–207. The formation and activities of the *Verein für musikalische Privataufführungen* (Society for Private Musical Performances) are outlined briefly. The names of the principle performers and selective lists of compositions performed by the Society are included.

Weiss, Adolph. "The Lyceum of Schönberg." *Modern Music.* March–April 1932, 10(3): 99–107. This is an outline of Schoenberg's basic compositional principles as perceived by the author, who was a student of Schoenberg's in Berlin in the 1920s. After setting out five fundamental principles of an art work, the essential aspects of the twelve-tone series (melody, rhythm, harmony, counterpoint, and instrumentation) are discussed.

Analysis and Criticism: General

Ashforth, Alden. "Linear and Textural Aspects of Schoenberg's Cadences." *Perspectives of New Music.* Spring-Summer 1978, 16(2): 195–224. "The intent of this study is to assess some of Schoenberg's means of phrase articulation, in non-tonal works after 1907, through a classification of the cadential devices he typically employs in two important dimensions: the linear and the textural."

Bailey, Walter B. *Programmatic Elements in the Works of Schoenberg.* Ann Arbor, MI: UMI Research Press, 1984. x, 188 p. (Studies in Musicology, no. 74). This study examines the role of extramusical elements in the compositions of Schoenberg. *Verklärte Nacht* and *Pelleas und Melisande* are generally considered to be Schoenberg's only programmatic works. It is revealed that many of Schoenberg's works throughout his life were inspired by programs or extramusical ideas although not explicitly stated. These include the String Quartets nos. 1–3; the Five Orchestra Pieces, op. 16; the Suite, op. 29; the Piano Concerto, op. 42; and the String Trio, op. 45. In addition to these pieces, a number of unfinished works having programs survive among Schoenberg's sketches.

Berg, Alban. "The Berg Guides." Mark DeVoto, ed. and trans. *Journal of the Arnold Schoenberg Institute.* June & November 1993, 16(1–2): 331 p., 1 leaf insert. This volume of the *Journal* is devoted almost entirely to the analytical guides prepared by Berg for the *Gurrelieder*; the Chamber Symphony no. 1 in E Major, op. 9; and *Pelleas und Melisande.* Each one of the guides is reprinted in the original German with an accompanying parallel English translation by Mark DeVoto, who also contributed an introductory essay. R. Wayne Shoaf concludes the volume with an article comparing the various printings of the published guides. The volume also includes the text and translation of an analysis of the String Quartet no. 2 in F-sharp Minor, op. 10, written in 1909 by a member of Schoenberg's circle.

————. "Why Is Schönberg's Music So Difficult to Understand?" In Willi Reich. *Alban Berg*. Cornelius Cardew, trans. New York: Harcourt, Brace & World, Inc., 1965. [189]–204. First published as "Warum ist Schönbergs Musik so schwer verständlich?" *Musikblätter des Anbruch*. August/September 1924, 6(7/8): 329–341. Berg answers this question with the phrase: "by its immeasurable richness." He illustrates this by analyzing the opening bars of the String Quartet no. 1 in D Minor, op. 7. Within these few measures he shows how all of the parts are motivically related to the principal theme; how the themes are constructed freely and asymmetrically; how themes, rhythms, and harmonies are continually subjected to variation; and how the harmony reflects the richness of the melodic invention. All of this occurs within a compressed period of time compared to music of the past. In Schoenberg's atonal works, it is these factors and not the unfamiliar harmonic language that makes the music more difficult for the listener to grasp.

Friedheim, Philip. "Rhythmic Structure in Schoenberg's Atonal Compositions." *Journal of the American Musicological Society*. Spring 1966, 19(1): 59–72. The rhythmic complexities of Schoenberg's published works from 1908 to 1913 are surveyed in this article. The works all contain frequent tempo changes, ambiguous metrical designations, and a rich variety of rhythmic values. In several of the works an ostinato is used as a referential rhythmic device. These characteristics contrast with rhythmic treatment in the early twelve-tone works, where the composer returns to more regular rhythms.

Frisch, Walter. *The Early Works of Arnold Schoenberg, 1893–1908*. Berkeley: University of California Press, 1993. xix, 328 p. "This book is fundamentally about Schoenberg the composer: about the compositional decisions he made and the compositional strategies he adopted or abandoned both in individual works and across or between works." In this chronological survey, the author analyzes the most significant works of Schoenberg's tonal period. There are individual chapters on the early songs, *Verklärte Nacht, Gurrelieder, Pelleas und Melisande*, the String Quartets nos. 1 and 2, and the Chamber Symphonies nos. 1 and 2.

Goehr, Walter, and Alexander Goehr. "Arnold Schönberg's Development Towards the Twelve-note System." In *European Music in the Twentieth Century*. Howard Hartog, ed. London: Routledge & Kegan Paul, 1957. 76–93. The essay attempts "to trace the continuity of musical thought employed in Schoenberg's compositions from the *Gurrelieder* (1901) to the Serenade, Op. 24 (1923), [and deals] separately with the different aspects of construction: first, with his treatment and subsequent dissolution of the functions of tonal harmony; then with the significance of his return to the use of counterpoint; and finally, with the character of his rhythm and with other elements which contribute to his conception of form and the novelty of his expression."

Keller, Hans. "Whose Fault Is the Speaking Voice?" *Tempo*. Winter 1965–1966, no. 75: 12–17. There have been numerous critics of combining the speaking voice with music including Willi Apel, Edmund Tracey, Hugo Riemann, and Alfred Einstein, while composers such as Mozart and Schoenberg have composed works in this genre. The reaction against the speaking voice in Schoenberg's works is due largely to its use in *Pierrot lunaire*, which was also one of his first atonal works.

Lessem, Alan Philip. *Music and Text in the Works of Arnold Schoenberg: The Critical Years, 1908–1922*. Ann Arbor, MI: UMI Research Press, 1979. vii, 247 p. (Studies in Musicology; no. 8). The period under examination is Schoenberg's atonal period—the works following his early tonal compositions and preceding the twelve-tone compositions. The majority of works in this period have texts which provide their structure. Schoenberg was not interested in depicting or reflecting the surface details of the text in musical terms, but rather the underlying ideas, feelings, and emotions conveyed in a text served as the inspiration for musical ideas. Several pieces are discussed in detail including the String Quartet no. 2 in F-sharp Minor, op. 10; *Fifteen Poems from the Book of the Hanging Gardens*, op. 15; *Erwartung; Die glückliche Hand; Pierrot lunaire*; "Herzgewächse"; Four Songs for voice and orchestra, op. 22; and *Die Jakobsleiter.*

Lewin, David. "Inversional Balance as an Organizing Force in Schoenberg's Music and Thought." *Perspectives of New Music.* Spring-Summer 1968, 6(2): 1–21. Just as the dominant and subdominant chords define and balance the tonic in tonal harmony, the author describes how Schoenberg uses the principle of inversion in a similar fashion in twelve-tone composition. The use of this inversion principle occurs both within the set itself and by the choice of sets and their transpositions. Examples of this practice are taken from "Die Kreuze" of *Pierrot lunaire*; the first movement of the Serenade, op. 24; the String Quartet no. 3, op. 30; act 1, scene 3 of *Moses und Aron*; and several of the later works based on sets constructed from hexachords.

Lewis, Christopher. "Mirrors and Metaphors: Reflections on Schoenberg and Nineteenth-century Tonality." *19th-Century Music.* Summer 1987, 11(1): 26–42. Post-romantic music employs different harmonic, melodic, and structural means, yet analysts frequently discuss these works using the language and analytical techniques developed for music of the common practice period. One of the primary characteristics of this music is progressive tonality (starting in one key and ending in another) and the use of two tonic keys within the same piece. This creates dissonance and key relationships which appear aberrant if analyzed from the viewpoint of a single tonality. Three early works of Schoenberg ("Traumleben," op. 6, no. 1; "Lockung," op. 6, no. 7; and "Voll jener Süsse," op. 8, no. 5) are examined to illustrate this point.

Maegaard, Jan. *Studien zur Entwicklung des dodekaphonen Satzes bei Arnold Schönberg.* København: Wilhelm Hansen Musikforlag, 1972. 3 v. Publisher's no.: Wilhelm Hansen 29024. This is the first major study of the development of twelve-tone composition, and it examines the music of Schoenberg from 1907 to 1933. The main part of the work (v. 2) comprises analyses of pieces from this period which the author believes were important landmarks in Schoenberg's gradual movement from tonal harmony through "atonal" music to the mature twelve-tone technique of composition. Volume 1 is an extensive listing of Schoenberg's library, music manuscripts, and sketches pertaining to the study. It generally provides more detail than Rufer's, *The Works of Arnold Schoenberg*, for the music under consideration. The third volume consists of the musical examples for Volume 2.

Nelson, Robert U. "Schoenberg's Variation Seminar." *Musical Quarterly.* April 1964, 50(2): 141–164. The article draws on a series of lectures on variation form in Schoenberg's works given by Schoenberg himself during 1948 and 1949. Seven compositions in variation form are analyzed: "Litanei" from the String Quartet no. 2 in F-sharp Minor, op. 10; "Nacht" from *Pierrot lunaire*; Variations from the Serenade, op. 24; Theme and Variations from the Suite, op. 29; Variations for

Orchestra, op. 31; *Variations on a Recitative*, op. 40; and Theme and Variations in G Minor for band, op. 43a. From these analyses it is shown that Schoenberg generally does not follow the practice of free variation from short motives; rather his variation forms are derived from an identifiable melodic theme.

Odegard, Peter S. "Schönberg's Variations: An Addendum." *Music Review*. May 1966, 27(2): 102–121. Robert Nelson asserts in his article "Schoenberg's Variation Seminar" that the Adagio of the String Quartet no. 3, op. 30, is not a variation form and that Schoenberg did not consider it a theme and variations either. Odegard outlines six characteristics of Schoenberg's variation forms. Erwin Stein, whose analysis was included with the published score, analyzed the movement as a theme and variations, while Schoenberg claimed that it was closer to a rondo. Stein's analysis is found to be plausible and the music does follow the six characteristics of Schoenberg's variation forms.

Payne, Anthony. *Schoenberg*. London; New York: Oxford University Press, 1968. 61 p. (Oxford Studies of Composers; 5). In this short monograph the author concerns himself exclusively with musical analysis. In the preface he states his purpose: "An examination of one aspect of the composer's work was obviously called for, and it seemed that style and form as these grew out of his psychological and expressive needs gave the best opportunities for probing beneath the music's surface." The book is an introduction to the many facets of Schoenberg's musical creativity, although the early tonal works are not discussed at all. The primary concern is to discuss the essential compositional elements of the atonal and twelve-tone works.

Phipps, Graham H. "The Tritone as an Equivalency: A Conceptual Perspective for Approaching Schoenberg's Music." *Journal of Musicology*. Winter 1985–86, 4(1): 51–69. "The purpose of this article is to present the view that the tritone represents tonal equivalency; that is to say, pitches which are a tritone apart serve the *same* tonal function. . . . this writer asserts that the concept of tritone equivalency exists as a latent phenomenon in the mainstream of eighteenth- and nineteenth-century music, both as seen in music literature and as explained by music theorists of the time; that it becomes one of the significant features of late nineteenth- and early twentieth-century music; and that it is adopted as a basic constituent of Schoenberg's musical language. Included in the discussion will be: 1) a short history of this point of view from the eighteenth century up to and including Schoenberg's concept; 2) some observations regarding the misinterpretation and omission of this opinion in writings of various theorists past and present; and 3) musical illustrations to amplify this point of view."

Pillin, Boris William. *Some Aspects of Counterpoint in Selected Works of Arnold Schoenberg*. Los Angeles: Western International Music, 1971. ii, 200 p. The book examines "Arnold Schoenberg's contrapuntal methods, and . . . assess[es] the effects, if any, of the abnegation of tonality and the use of the twelve-tone technique upon his contrapuntal writing." Schoenberg applied the contrapuntal techniques of the eighteenth century with Bach's music as the model. The differences between the use of counterpoint in the three main periods of Schoenberg's writing (tonal, atonal, and twelve-tone) are examined. With the abandonment of tonality, counterpoint becomes the unifying device of a piece of music.

Samson, James. "Schoenberg's 'Atonal' Music." *Tempo*. June 1974, no. 109: 16–25. The author calls for a more balanced approach to the analysis of atonal works.

In particular, he sees the use of set theory as proposed by Allen Forte as too narrow a methodology for understanding atonal music because it emphasizes the role of pitch organization to the almost total exclusion of other factors in composition such as rhythm, dynamics, structure, counterpoint, and residual tonal implications.

Simms, Bryan R. "New Documents in the Schoenberg-Schenker Polemic." *Perspectives of New Music*. Fall-Winter 1977, 16(1): 110–124. Previously unpublished writings of Schoenberg about Schenker are published and translated here for the first time. Many of these writings appeared in little-known journals or as marginalia in publications by Schenker. The role of repetition in music was one of the fundamental differences between their theories. Schoenberg's idea of developing variation stands in stark contrast to Schenker's theory of an *Urlinie* which is repeated at various levels of a composition.

Spratt, John F. "The Speculative Content of Schoenberg's *Harmonielehre*." *Current Musicology*. 1971, no. 11: 83–88. The *Harmonielehre* by Schoenberg contains practical instructional material and also philosophical commentary related to the underpinnings of musical harmony. This article examines the speculative and philosophical parts of the book.

Thomson, William. *Schoenberg's Error*. Philadelphia: University of Pennsylvania Press, 1991. x, 217 p. (Leonard B. Meyer, ed., Studies in the Criticism and Theory of Music). The author believes that Schoenberg saw the development of atonal and twelve-tone composition as the next logical and inevitable step in the evolution of Western music. Thomson argues that there is no analogy between biological evolution and an evolutionary process in the arts. Instead, he believes that Schoenberg's theories and the music upon which they are based are faulty in their logic and cannot be substantiated by the history of Western music. He sees many inconsistencies in Schoenberg's theoretical writings.

"Towards the Schoenberg Centenary, I–VI." *Perspectives of New Music*. Fall-Winter 1972—Fall-Winter 1975, 11–14. Each issue contains three to four articles about Schoenberg primarily by American music theorists and composers. The articles are similar in subject matter to the earlier compilation *Perspectives on Schoenberg and Stravinsky*.

Van den Linden, R. Cort. "Arnold Schönberg—I." Scott Goddard, trans. *Music & Letters*. October 1926, 7(4): 322–331. This devoted pupil of Schoenberg extols the genius of a master composer. The article examines the principles found in the *Harmonielehre*.

———. "Arnold Schönberg—II." Scott Goddard, trans. *Music & Letters*. January 1927, 8(1): 38–45. In the second half of this article, the author looks at aspects of Schoenberg's compositions beyond the *Harmonielehre*. He discusses the use of more daring harmonies, counterpoint, thematic structure, etc., by including examples of the String Quartets nos. 1 and 2 and an early song. He believes that Schoenberg's music will gain wider acceptance in the future.

Webern, Anton. *The Path to the New Music*. Willi Reich, ed. Leo Black, trans. Bryn Mawr, PA: Theodore Presser; London: Universal Edition; 1963. 67 p. First published in German as *Die Wege zur Neuen Musik*. Wien: Universal Edition, 1960. This is a series of sixteen lectures delivered in 1932–33 as recorded by Willi Reich. In the first eight lectures, Webern shows how all of Western musical history naturally leads to the dissolution of tonality. The remaining lectures are about the early atonal works and the development of the twelve-tone technique as a new means of creating unity within a composition. In an appendix, the editor includes excerpts from letters Webern wrote to him from 1938 to 1944.

Whittall, Arnold. *Schoenberg Chamber Music*. Seattle: University of Washington Press, 1972. 64 p. (BBC Music Guides; 21). This is a series of extended analytical essays on the chamber works which include *Verklärte Nacht*; the String Quartet in D Major; the String Quartets nos. 1–4; the Chamber Symphony no. 1 in D Major, op. 9; "Herzgewächse;" *Pierrot lunaire*; the Serenade, op. 24; the Woodwind Quintet, op. 26; the Suite, op. 29; the *Ode to Napoleon Buonaparte*, op. 41; the String Trio, op. 45; and the *Phantasy for Violin with Piano Accompaniment*, op. 47.

Wörner, Karl H. "Arnold Schoenberg and the Theater." Willis Wager, trans. *Musical Quarterly*. October 1962, 48(4): 444–460, [1] leaf of plates. This article discusses Schoenberg's four operas from a dramatic viewpoint. Schoenberg's early operas, *Erwartung* and *Die glückliche Hand*, broke new ground musically and dramaturgically. The operas of Berg contain many of the elements first presented in these operas. The most successful of Schoenberg's operas are those where the libretti are rich in material that can be developed musically. This is true of *Erwartung* and *Moses und Aron*, which are both complex psychological dramas, but in *Die glückliche Hand* and *Von heute auf morgen*, the characters and the plots are so abstract that dramatic portrayal is difficult.

Analysis and Criticism: Twelve-tone Music

Brindle, Reginald Smith. *Serial Composition*. London, New York: Oxford University Press, 1966. 210 p. This text focuses on the mechanics of twelve-tone and serial composition. It covers the basics of constructing a tone row, writing melodies, two and multivoice counterpoint, harmony, form and structure, and orchestration in twelve-tone compositions. In many ways it is a basic text for the beginning twelve-tone composer but may also be used by others to understand how twelve-tone works are constructed.

Gerhard, Roberto. "Tonality in Twelve-tone Music." *Score*. May 1952, no. 6: 23–35. The author sees similarities between twelve-tone composition and counterpoint before the seventeenth century when harmony was determined more as a result of independent melodic lines. Following this reasoning, the basic set of a twelve-tone composition plays the same function as tonality in a tonal work. The formulation of the basic set is essential to establishing coherence and unity of the composition in that it is "a fixed series of intervals (independent of metre and rhythm) as an abstract form of musical thought implying its own complete system of accompaniment." It is shown how hexachords can be used in their original order or permuted to allow for enough flexibility to be used as harmonies. The author concludes that "the twelve-tone technique is in fact a new formulation of the principle of tonality."

Haimo, Ethan. *Schoenberg's Serial Odyssey: The Evolution of His Twelve-tone Method, 1914–1928*. Oxford: Clarendon Press; 1990. ix, 192 p. The author shows how Schoenberg gradually developed and perfected the twelve-tone technique of composition through the years 1914–28 focusing on the oratorio, *Die Jakobsleiter*, and the published works, opp. 23–32. This penetrating study describes the evolution of Schoenberg's idea of a new method of composition from an abstraction to a fully integrated musical idea.

———. "Schoenberg's Unknown Twelve-tone Fragments." *Journal of the Arnold Schoenberg Institute.* June 1988, 11(1): 52–69. Jan Maegaard listed all of the twelve-tone sets used by Schoenberg in an earlier article ("Schönbergs Zwölf-tonreihen." *Die Musikforschung.* October/December 1976, 29(4): 385–425). Ten additional sets were discovered and added to the list, which now numbers 125.

Hill, Richard S. "Schoenberg's Tone-Rows and the Tonal System of the Future." *Musical Quarterly.* January 1936, 22(1): 14–37. This is one of the earliest articles to survey Schoenberg's use of the twelve-tone technique in his compositions. Although some parts of the article have been superseded by later research, Hill makes some interesting observations about the types of sets that can be used in twelve-tone composition. The twelve-tone technique is seen as a natural extension and evolution of Western music's harmonic resources which started with pentatonicism, moved to diatonic tonality, and evolved through atonality to result in twelve-tone compositions. The author finds Schoenberg's free use of the sets within some of the compositions to be too complicated and confusing. Maintaining a stricter use of the sets would aid in greater comprehensibility.

Hyde, Martha M[acLean]. "The Format and Function of Schoenberg's Twelve-tone Sketches." *Journal of the American Musicological Society.* Fall 1983, 36(3): 453–480. Through a survey of Schoenberg's sketches for the twelve-tone works, four categories are determined: row tables, row sketches, compositional sketches, and form tables and charts. It is discovered that the amount of sketches for longer and shorter works is about the same, because Schoenberg worked out the compositional principles of a composition through the basic set. Thus, "[Schoenberg] would regularly structure the basic set to maximize certain properties, work out the fundamental succession of row forms and the overall form of the movement, compose the melodic line, and only then fill in the secondary voices. Once established, this 'conscious control' over his new means and form allowed Schoenberg to compose without needing to sketch the details of individual passages."

———. "Musical Form and the Development of Schoenberg's Twelve-tone Method." *Journal of Music Theory.* Spring 1985, 29(1): 85–143. The pieces from Schoenberg's "atonal" period tend to be shorter works. Composing works in more extended forms without tonality as a structural principal resulted in the formulation of the twelve-tone technique. Some musicologists have attempted to show that Schoenberg's development of the twelve-tone technique unfolded continuously through the composition of the pieces opp. 23–25 and that by studying these works in chronological order it is possible to see this progression. The author shows that the development of the twelve-tone technique was a response to the compositional problem of creating large-scale forms in works without a central tonality. Through an analysis of the Suite for Piano, op. 25, the author describes how Schoenberg created harmonic and motivic unity in a composition derived from a single set.

———. "The Roots of Form in Schoenberg's Sketches." *Journal of Music Theory.* Spring 1980, 24(1): 1–36. Schoenberg's sketches reveal how the basic set of a twelve-tone composition is used to generate harmonies and the formal structure of a work. Contrary to what is commonly believed, that a twelve-tone composition

is based on a single twelve-tone set, several works are examined in which Schoenberg has extended the technique by using a basic set comprised of three related
hexachords or by using three different sets whose first five pitches are the same.
The sketches show that Schoenberg used harmonies derived from the basic set to
articulate major structural points in his pieces.

Maegaard, Jan. "A Study in the Chronology of Op. 23–26 by Arnold Schoenberg."
Dansk Årborg for Musikforskning. 1962, 2: 93–115. The author first examines
the manuscripts and sketches for these four works to establish the chronology of
their inception and completion. The works were started as early as July 1920 and
finished by 1924 with most of the compositional activity concentrated during the
year of 1923. Through these works it is possible to see several stages through
which the twelve tone technique developed until it took its final form in the
Woodwind Quintet, op. 26.

Milstein, Silvina. *Arnold Schoenberg: Notes, Sets, Forms.* Cambridge, New York: Cambridge University Press, 1992. xix, 210 p. (Arnold Whittall, ed. Music in the
Twentieth Century). This unique study looks at Schoenberg's twelve-tone writing
from several viewpoints. Schoenberg's own theoretical writings lend information
concerning the melodic, harmonic, and structural aspects of composition. His
compositional sketches yield insight into the construction and application of the
set to a composition. His writings and place in music history provide the setting
and the link to musical traditions and procedures of the past. The author shows
how these elements influence one another in his compositions and how the later
twelve-tone works are frequently infused with tonality by examining the Suite,
op. 29; the String Quartet no. 4, op. 37; the *Ode to Napoleon Buonaparte*; and
the String Trio, op. 45.

Perle, George. "Schönberg's Late Style." *Music Review.* November 1952, 13(4): 274–
282. This article is a critique of Schoenberg's essay "Composition with Twelve
Tones." While Perle admires Schoenberg's genius and the importance of the
twelve-tone technique, he also finds what he considers many inconsistencies in
Schoenberg's late compositions and in the technique itself. The practice of la-
beling the principle and secondary themes and the strict avoidance of octaves in
twelve-tone composition are two such criticisms of Perle's.

———. *Serial Composition and Atonality: An Introduction to the Music of Schoenberg,
Berg, and Webern.* 6th rev. ed. Berkeley and Los Angeles: University of California Press, 1991. xv, 164 p. In this analytical survey of the music of the Second
Viennese School, the author shows various ways in which pitches are combined
in atonal and serial compositions. The discussion includes an examination of
atonal works (those which are not tonal and yet are not based on a twelve-tone
set) and works which are based on pitch sets not consisting of all twelve tones
of the chromatic scale. The three main chapters of the book examine twelve-tone
melodic, harmonic, and formal structure.

Rufer, Josef. *Composition with Twelve Notes Related Only to One Another.* 2nd impression rev. Humphrey Searle, trans. London: Barrie and Rockliff, 1961. xiv, 218,
xxiv p. First published as *Die Komposition mit zwölf Tönen.* Berlin: Max Hesses
Verlag, 1952. This is the first book to explain the historical basis and the technique of composing twelve-tone music. Rufer was Schoenberg's teaching assistant
when Schoenberg was formulating the principles of twelve-tone composition. The
book discusses not only pitch material for composition but also the function of

rhythm and form. There is an appendix which consists of statements by various composers about their use of twelve-tone technique. Other supplementary material includes an index, a list of works and writings by Schoenberg, and an outline of a composition curriculum by Schoenberg.

Simms, Bryan R. "Who First Composed Twelve-tone Music, Schoenberg or Hauer?" *Journal of the Arnold Schoenberg Institute.* November 1987, 10(2): 108–133. The author looks at correspondence between Hauer and Schoenberg and examines the theoretical writings and compositions of the two composers to establish a chronology of the appearance of the twelve-tone idea. In the end he concludes: "The question defies a simple answer not only because the dodecaphonic idea was embodied in different ways in the works of Hauer and Schoenberg, but also because it was the outcome of a gradual historical evolution."

Walker, Alan. "Back to Schönberg." *Music Review.* May 1960, 21(2): 140–147. Two of the principles of twelve-tone composition are the transformation of the basic set from its original form to the inversion and retrograde versions and the principle of octave equivalence. Some critics of twelve-tone composition assert that it is not possible for listeners to discern that a melody played in inversion or retrograde is related to the original. Some proponents assert that row manipulations are strictly a method for the composer and are not intended to be perceptible. Through a series of tests given to fifteen music students, four of whom had absolute pitch, the author tests the hypothesis that it is possible to identify related sets. The experiment shows that it is possible to hear related sets and that the more a listener is acquainted with twelve-tone compositions, the greater success there is in hearing the relationships. The students with absolute pitch achieved a 90 percent success rate.

Wellesz, Egon. *The Origins of Schönberg's Twelve-Tone-System.* Washington, DC: Library of Congress, 1958. 14 p. Reprinted in *Lectures on the History and Art of Music: The Louis Charles Elson Memorial Lectures at the Library of Congress, 1946–1963.* Irving Lowens, ed. New York: Da Capo Press, 1968. [167]–186. (Da Capo Press Music Reprint Series). The author relates the development of Schoenberg's music beginning in 1904 through the first twelve-tone works. He credits Josef Matthias Hauer with giving Schoenberg the idea of using twelve-tone rows but leaves to Schoenberg the idea of creating a unified method of composition using the rows. He concludes that the twelve-tone method is successful only in the hands of a gifted composer.

Analysis and Criticism: Selected Works

Erwartung, op. 17.

Buchanan, Herbert H. "A Key to Schoenberg's *Erwartung* (Op. 17)." *Journal of the American Musicological Society.* Fall 1967, 20(3): 434–449. The opera *Erwartung* is considered by many to be a prime example of an "atonal" and "athematic" composition. However, there are recurrent intervallic and rhythmic motives which provide the work its essential unifying structure. The author shows how Schoenberg has used material from one of his earlier songs, "Am Wegrand," op. 6, no. 6, for the motives of *Erwartung,* even to the extent of quoting portions of the song's text and melody in the opera.

Fifteen Poems from the Book of the Hanging Gardens, op. 15.

Stroh, Wolfgang Martin. "Schoenberg's Use of the Text: The Text as a Musical Control in the 14th *Georgelied,* Op. 15." Barbara Westergaard, trans. *Perspectives of New Music.* Spring-Summer 1968, 6(2): 35–44. This analysis of op. 15, no. 4, shows how the text of the poem contributed to the structure and composition of the piece. The analysis attempts to show that the key words of the text and the form of the text provide the basis upon which motives and the overall structure of the music are composed.

Five Orchestra Pieces, op. 16.

Dahlhaus, Carl. " 'The Obbligato Recitative.' " In Carl Dahlhaus. *Schoenberg and the New Music: Essays by Carl Dahlhaus.* Derrick Puffett and Alfred Clayton, trans. Cambridge, New York: Cambridge University Press, 1987. 144–148. First published as " 'Das obligate Rezitativ.' " *Melos/NZ.* 1975, 1(3): 193–195. The title which Schoenberg gave to the Orchestra Piece, op. 16, no. 5 *(Das obligate Rezitativ),* appears to be an oxymoron. Yet, what Schoenberg means by obligato in this sense is an endless and nonrepeating melody. This manifests itself in the composition as a series of continuously new yet related musical ideas and melodies. The title expresses the presence of opposites just as the piece itself is constructed of highly organized yet apparently free melodies.

Lambourn, David. "Henry Wood and Schoenberg." *Musical Times.* August 1987, 128(1734): 422–27. The article recounts the history of the premiere (3 September, 1912) and second performance (17 January, 1914) of the Five Orchestra Pieces, op. 16, in England conducted by Henry Wood and Schoenberg. The audience and critical reactions to the work are described together with comments on the reception of Schoenberg's music in England in general.

Die glückliche Hand, op. 18.

Auner, Joseph. "Schoenberg's Aesthetic Transformations and the Evolution of Form in *Die glückliche Hand.*" *Journal of the Arnold Schoenberg Institute.* November 1989, 12(2): 103–128. Schoenberg frequently refers to the need for inspiration to compose a musical work. This was especially apparent in 1909, when Schoenberg wrote an amazing number of his most important works in a very short time. The author sees *Die glückliche Hand* as a pivotal work in which Schoenberg's basic musical aesthetic begins to shift and in which Schoenberg begins to rely less on a purely inspirational or intuitive process of musical composition in favor of compositional processes.

Crawford, John [C]. "*Die glückliche Hand*: Further Notes." *Journal of the Arnold Schoenberg Institute.* June 1980, 4(1): 68–76. Through an examination of the manuscripts and other source materials, the date when Schoenberg began the composition of the opera is determined to be the end of June 1910 rather than the previously determined 1908. This places it after the composition of *Erwartung.*

———. "*Die glückliche Hand*: Schoenberg's *Gesamtkunstwerk.*" *Musical Quarterly.* October 1974, 60(4): 583–601. "This study . . . investigate[s] the artistic influences present in the multifold dimensions of *Die glückliche Hand,* the opera's aesthetic aims, and the degree to which these are successfully realized."

Steiner, Ena. "The 'Happy' Hand: Genesis and Interpretation of Schoenberg's *Monumentalkunstwerk.*" *Music Review*. August 1980, 41(3): 207–222, [2] p. of plates. The composition of *Die glückliche Hand* occupied nearly five years of Schoenberg's life (1908 to 1913) from its initial inception to its completion. The autobiographical nature of the opera, which deals with Schoenberg's marital crisis and the suicide of Richard Gerstl (the man with whom Schoenberg's wife had an affair) less than a month after the first musical sketches of the opera, accounts for this long period of creation. The author also explores some of the musical and dramatic aspects of the opera which had to be worked out, as *Die glückliche Hand* integrates music, lighting, plot, and staging in a novel way.

Gurrelieder.

Nachod, Hans. "Schoenberg: The Very First Performance of Schoenberg's 'Gurrelieder.' " *Music Survey*. Summer 1950, 3(3): 38–40. This is a firsthand account of the premiere performance of the *Gurrelieder* with piano accompaniment by Schoenberg's cousin Hans Nachod, who sang the part of Waldemar.

"Herzgewächse," op. 20.

Hough, Bonny. "Schoenberg's *Herzgewächse* and the *Blaue Reiter Almanac.*" *Journal of the Arnold Schoenberg Institute*. November 1983, 7(2): 197–221. The *Blaue Reiter Almanac* is composed of contributions of various Central European artists who were associated with Kandinsky and were active around 1910. The *Almanac* is a sort of artistic and spiritual manifesto of the modern arts. Schoenberg was clearly sympathetic to the general aesthetic ideas of the *Blaue Reiter* group and contributed two items to the *Almanac*: the composition, "Herzgewächse," and an essay, "Das Verhältnis zum Text." This article examines the relationship between the philosophy of the *Blaue Reiter* and "Herzgewächse" and includes an analysis of the piece.

"Modern Psalms."

Ringer, Alexander L. "Faith and Symbol—On Arnold Schoenberg's Last Musical Utterance." *Journal of the Arnold Schoenberg Institute*. June 1982, 6(1): 80–95. Schoenberg's last composition, "Modern Psalm no. 1," op. 50c, remains unfinished, as do many of his major religious works. The work ends on the words, "trotzdem bete ich" (and yet I pray), which the author finds to be significant in relation to Jewish religious thinking and other philosophies with which Schoenberg was familiar. Schoenberg was also greatly influenced by numerology, and there appears to be a connection between the number six and various aspects of the piece.

Moses und Aron.

Goldstein, Bluma. "Word, Image, Idea: Schoenberg and Moses—A Tragic Coexistence?" In Bluma Goldstein, *Reinscribing Moses: Heine, Kafka, Freud, and Schoenberg in a European Wilderness*. Cambridge, MA: Harvard University Press, 1992. [137]–167. Schoenberg's conception of Moses was influenced by the social, cultural, and political events through which he lived in Europe and America. His ideas and views of Moses and Judaism are expressed in the unpublished drama *Der biblische Weg* and the unfinished opera *Moses und Aron*. In both works, the protagonists, Max Aruns and Moses, bear a certain resemblance to Schoenberg himself through their idealism and uncompromising adherence to noble aims—Aruns to the establishment of a utopian Jewish nation, Moses to an abstract and indescribable God, and Schoenberg himself to the highest artistic ideals and standards.

Keller, Hans. "Moses, Freud and Schönberg." *Monthly Musical Record*. January–February, March–April 1958, 88: 12–16, 63–67. The author explores the preoccupation of Freud and Schoenberg with Moses as revealed in the former's book, *Moses and Monotheism*, and the latter's opera, *Moses und Aron*. While some have asserted that Freud's psychoanalytical techniques paralleled and influenced expressionist composers, the link that Keller sees between Freud and Schoenberg is their personal identification with Moses.

Lewin, David. "*Moses und Aron*: Some General Remarks, and Analytical Notes for Act 1, Scene 1." *Perspectives of New Music*. Fall-Winter 1967, 6(1): 1–17. The author finds a correlation between "the multiple proportion—God: Moses: Aron: Volk equals 'the idea' (row): composer (Schoenberg): performer: audience." God uses his intermediaries, Moses and Aron, to communicate with his people just as the pure musical idea is communicated through Schoenberg and the performers to the audience. The analysis of the dramatic structure is followed by a detailed musical analysis of the pitch and formal structure of the first scene of the opera.

Weaver, Robert. "The Conflict of Religion and Aesthetics in Schoenberg's *Moses and Aaron*." In Robert Weaver, ed. *Essays on the Music of J. S. Bach and Other Divers Subjects: A Tribute to Gerhard Herz*. Louisville, KY: University of Louisville; New York: Pendragon Press, 1981. 291–303. (Festschrift Series; 4). The author sees a similarity between Schoenberg's nineteenth-century romantic concept of the artist as misunderstood genius, and the main characters of his opera, *Moses und Aron*. In the opera, Moses is the misunderstood spiritual leader who must rely on Aron to communicate his idea to the masses. A synopsis of the plot is compared to the corresponding events as mentioned in the Bible to show how Schoenberg altered the basic story to emphasize this idea. The fact that the third act remains unfinished indicates Schoenberg's internal struggle between this romantic ideal and a world that no longer accepts that ideal.

White, Pamela C. "The Genesis of *Moses und Aron*." *Journal of the Arnold Schoenberg Institute*. June 1982, 6(1): 8–55. "The purpose of this article is to establish a chronology for the known extant sources of both text and music of the opera, and then, by examining these sources, to gain new insight into Schoenberg's compositional procedure."

———. *Schoenberg and the God-Idea: The Opera Moses und Aron*. Ann Arbor, MI: UMI Research Press, 1985. xii, 339 p. (Studies in Musicology, no. 83). The author states that "*Moses und Aron* . . . is the product of [Schoenberg's] knowingly futile effort to express 'the holy fire,' or . . . to give Representation to the Idea of the holy." The book is one of the first comprehensive studies of the source material for the opera, including the manuscript scores and sketches, and all of the drafts and final versions of the libretto. A study of Schoenberg's library reveals that Schopenhauer's and Karl Kraus's writings greatly influenced Schoenberg's religious and philosophical views. There is also an analysis of the music and its relation to the libretto. Through this holistic analysis of *Moses und Aron*, the author shows that this work is central to Schoenberg's creative output.

Wörner, Karl H. *Schoenberg's "Moses and Aaron."* Paul Hamburger, trans. New York: St. Martin's Press, 1963. 208 p. Note: First published in German as: *Gotteswort und Magie: Die Oper "Moses und Aron" von Arnold Schönberg.* Heidelberg: Lambert Schneider, 1959. 93 p. The author sees in Schoenberg's epic opera the expression of three symbols (God as an idea, God the infinite, and God's promise) in musical and dramatic terms. There is an analysis of the formal structure and the twelve-tone sets of the work. The complete libretto with an English translation by Allen Forte is included as an appendix.

Passacaglia.

Haimo, Ethan. "Redating Schoenberg's Passacaglia for Orchestra." *Journal of the American Musicological Society.* Fall 1987, 40(3): [471]–494. The sketch page of the unfinished work, *Passacaglia* for orchestra, is dated 5 March 1920. However, accompanying musical sketches comprised primarily of row charts show twelve-tone compositional procedures far more advanced than any other piece Schoenberg had written up to that time. The author concludes that the final digit of the date is a badly written six. Accepting the 1926 date places the *Passacaglia* between the completion of the Suite, op. 29, and the Variations for Orchestra, op. 31. The *Passacaglia*'s use of a combinatorial set is consistent with the op. 29 and op. 31 works. The *Passacaglia* and the Variations for Orchestra also share similarities in their opening themes, which leads to the conclusion that the *Passacaglia* is an early version or sketch for the Variations for Orchestra.

Phantasy for Violin with Piano Accompaniment, op. 47.

Lewin, David. "A Study of Hexachord Levels in Schoenberg's Violin Fantasy." *Perspectives of New Music.* Fall-Winter 1967, 6(1): 18–32. The article is not a full analysis of the *Phantasy for Violin with Piano Accompaniment* but focuses on the use of hexachords in the piece. Different transpositions of the hexachords occupy sections or areas of the piece. The transpositions follow a pattern of intervals analogous to the minor thirds of a diminished triad, which is similar to the modulatory patterns in many of Liszt's compositions. The author considers the ideas put forth in the article to be a starting point for further analyses of the piece and as an attempt at a greater understanding of Schoenberg's methods.

Piano Concerto, op. 42.

Bailey, Walter B. "Oscar Levant and the Program for Schoenberg's Piano Concerto." *Journal of the Arnold Schoenberg Institute.* June 1982, 6(1): 56–79. A short program connected with the basic themes of the Piano Concerto, op. 42, is written on one of the leaves of sketches: "1. Life was so easy; 2. Suddenly hatred broke out; 3. A grave situation was created; 4. But life goes on." These general moods were the basic inspiration for the work. The author examines the genesis of this piece as revealed through the manuscripts and sketches. There is also an account of Oscar Levant's role as the commissioner of the work and how, when he renounced the obligation, the work was dedicated to another Schoenberg student, Henry Clay Shriver.

Piano Pieces, opp. 11, 19, 23, 25, and 33.

Bailey, Kathryn. "Row Anomalies in Opus 33: An Insight into Schoenberg's Understanding of the Serial Procedure." *Current Musicology*. 1976, no. 22: 42. One of the basic principles of twelve-tone composition is the avoidance of repeating a pitch until all the tones of the set have sounded. The author discusses this principle and the conditions under which pitch repetition is allowed by Schoenberg. Using op. 33 as an example, she shows that through the use of set segmentation, pitch repetition is not avoided as regularly as stated by Schoenberg in theory. Set segmentation and the reordering of pitches within set segments causes the pitches of the set to be presented in a different order than the actual set originally presented them. That is, actual compositional practice uses unordered set segments (hexachords, tetrachords, trichords, etc.). The author concludes that Schoenberg's unwillingness to strictly follow the set's pitch order in actual composition casts doubt on his assertion to be the originator of the twelve-tone technique.

Brower, Candace. "Dramatic Structure in Schoenberg's Opus 11, Number 1." *Music Research Forum*. 1989, 4(1): 25–52. A motivic and structural analysis of the Piano Piece, op. 11, no. 1, follows a survey of the analytical literature on the piece. Descriptions of general subjective emotional states are applied to various motives and themes to explain how they are developed. These descriptions of dramatic elements ("character, events, actions, and the expression of thoughts and emotions") are combined with a more traditional musical analysis of the pitch content and form to enhance understanding of the piece.

Forte, Allen. "Context and Continuity in an Atonal Work: A Set-Theoretic Approach." *Perspectives of New Music*. Spring 1963, 1(2): 72–82. Through the use of mathematical set theory, the author explains the structural basis of the Six Little Piano Pieces, op. 19 as it relates to a single interval, G–B. After defining ten sets of pitches related to this interval, he shows how these pitch sets interact to produce a coherent and continuous composition. This short article is a succinct introduction to the use of set theory as applied to atonal compositions.

Friedberg, Ruth. "The Solo Keyboard Works of Arnold Schönberg." *Music Review*. February 1962, 23(1): 39–50. This is a motivic analysis of each of the five piano works.

Glofcheskie, John. " 'Wrong' Notes in Schoenberg's Op. 33a." *Studies in Music* [Canada]. 1976, 1: 88–104. The author argues that two pitches in this piece deviate from the normal ordering of the set. Many have assumed that these notes are "mistakes" or "wrong" notes. However, it is shown that Schoenberg intentionally exchanged these pitches at critical points in the piece so as to emphasize important structural aspects of the work.

Hicken, Kenneth L. *Aspects of Harmony in Schoenberg's Six Little Piano Pieces, Op. 19*. Winnipeg: Frye Publishing, 1984. x, 79 p. This analysis shows how an atonal composition (op. 19) is indebted to traditional tonal compositional techniques. The author believes that the piece contains a succession of tonal centers rather than just one, that modulation occurs generally through the means of common chords, and that the harmonies consist of extensions of triads and quartal chords.

Harmonic analyses of all six pieces using standard tonal harmonic chord symbols and a modified Schenkerian analysis of several of the pieces is included in the book. The author states "that the harmonic organization of almost all of this composition [op. 19] could be viably explained in an aurally defensible fashion, in terms of outgrowth from the traditional [tonal] language."

Leichtentritt, Hugo. "Chapter XXII. Arnold Schönberg: Opus 11 and Opus 19." In *Musical Form*. Cambridge, MA: Harvard University Press, 1951. 425–450. These analyses show that Schoenberg's atonal piano pieces can be understood in terms of traditional tonal practices. The melodies sound quite traditional when transposed into the space of a single octave. Also many of the melodies have tonal implications when played without the accompaniment. The author does not think that the pieces are atonal. Rather his analyses reveal a polytonal harmonic structure with rapidly changing key areas. There are also simultaneously sounding chord structures whose implied resolution is never sounded. Phrase and formal structures generally follow traditional forms.

Travis, Roy. "Directed Motion in Schoenberg and Webern." *Perspectives of New Music*. Spring-Summer 1966, 4(2): 85–89 (preceded by 7 p. of musical examples). This is an analysis of Six Little Piano Pieces, op. 19, no. 2, using Schenkerian methodology.

Tuttle, T. Temple. "Schönberg's Compositions for Piano Solo." *Music Review*. November 1957, 18(4): 300–318. The author analyzes all six piano pieces.

Pierrot lunaire, op. 21.

Bailey, Kathryn. "Formal Organization and Structural Imagery in Schoenberg's *Pierrot Lunaire*." *Studies in Music from the University of Western Ontario*. 1977, 2: 93–107. The textual imagery of three of the settings in *Pierrot lunaire* ("Der Mondfleck," "Parodie," and "Nacht") is particularly rich, and it is in these pieces where there is the most structural organization, including fugues, canons, and a passacaglia. The author analyses these forms and their relationship to the text.

Brinkmann, Reinhold. "What the Sources Tell Us . . . : A Chapter of *Pierrot* Philology." Evan Bonds, trans. *Journal of the Arnold Schoenberg Institute*. June 1987, 10(1): 11–27. Through careful study of the primary manuscripts, published scores, and early secondary sources for *Pierrot lunaire*, the author provides a history of the composition of the work. The sources reveal much about the compositional process.

Dossier de presse = *Press-Book de Pierrot lunaire d'Arnold Schönberg*. François Lesure, Emily Good [et al.], eds. Genève: Editions Minkoff, 1985. 259 p. (François Lesure, ed. Dossiers de presse: anthologie de la critique musicale = Press-books: anthology of musical criticism; t. 2). This is a compilation of reviews from performances of *Pierrot lunaire* in newspapers and magazines dating from the premiere in 1912 through 1924. The articles are reproduced in facsimile and are arranged in chronological order. The most significant reviews have been selected and are written in English, French, German, Italian, and Spanish. There are brief biographical notes about the individual reviewers concluding the volume.

Dunsby, Jonathan. *Schoenberg: Pierrot lunaire*. Cambridge: Cambridge University Press, 1992. x, 84 p. (Julian Rushton, ed. Cambridge Music Handbooks). Following background information on the commedia dell'arte and Schoenberg's early career, the author discusses how *Pierrot lunaire* came to be. The central part of the book is an examination of each of the twenty-one settings of Giraud's poems, including musical analyses.

Fleury, Louis. "About 'Pierrot Lunaire': The Impressions Made on Various Audiences by a Novel Work." A. H. Fox Strangways, trans. *Music & Letters*. October 1924, 5(4): 347–356. This is a firsthand account by the flutist of the Pierrot ensemble of performances of *Pierrot lunaire* during its European tour of 1923 and 1924, including Paris, London, and Italy.

Lessem, Alan [Philip]. "Text and Music in Schoenberg's 'Pierrot Lunaire.' " *Current Musicology*. 1975, no. 19: 103–112. The relation between the text and music in *Pierrot lunaire* is brought about through the use of subtle rhythmic and intervallic motives. A motive consisting of seven notes of equal length with a jagged melodic contour appears throughout the work in connection with *Pierrot*. Similarly, generalized three-note intervallic cells are used to underscore meaning in the text in ways reminiscent of Wagner.

Serenade, op. 24.

Lester, Joel. "Pitch Structure Articulation in the Variations of Schoenberg's Serenade." *Perspectives of New Music*. Spring-Summer 1968, 6(2): 22–34. The author applies the analytical methods used by Milton Babbitt in his article "Set Structure as a Compositional Determinant" (*Journal of Music Theory*. 5: 72–94) to the variation movement of the Serenade, op. 24. In this way he is able to examine the properties of the Serenade's fourteen-pitch set and the compositional processes that operate throughout the movement.

String Quartets, opp. 7, 10, 30, and 37.

Dale, Catherine. *Tonality and Structure in Schoenberg's Second String Quartet, Op. 10.* New York: Garland Publishing, 1993. xix, 380 p. (John Caldwell, ed. Outstanding Dissertations in Music from British Universities). In this study "Schenkerian and Salzerian techniques of hierarchical, voice-leading analysis combine with Schoenbergian concepts of motivic shape and Fortean pitch-class-set theory in an attempt to mirror the stylistic diversity of Schoenberg's score." Part 1 of the book explores Schoenberg's and Schenker's theories of harmony and voice leading so as to justify the analytical methodology employed in the study. Part 2 is a verbal analysis of the entire work based on the methodologies discussed in Part 1, followed by a complete graphic, Schenkerian analysis in Part 3.

Frisch, Walter. "Thematic Form and the Genesis of Schoenberg's D-Minor Quartet, Opus 7." *Journal of the American Musicological Society*. Summer 1988, 41(2): 289–314. The sketches for the String Quartet no. 1 in D Minor, op. 7, are examined to see how Schoenberg was able to achieve thematic unity throughout the piece and to determine his compositional working method.

Gradenwitz, Peter. "The Idiom and Development in Schoenberg's Quartets." *Music & Letters*. July 1945, 26(3): 123–142. The author proposes four main periods of compositional development for Schoenberg: 1898–1906, 1907–14, 1923–27, and 1936–44. The four string quartets are viewed as the culmination of Schoenberg's stylistic development in each period. Schoenberg's development as a composer is explored through analyses of each of the quartets.

————. "A Talk on Schoenberg for Composers' Concourse." *Score and I.M.A. Mag-*

azine. June 1956, no. 16: 19–28. The article consists of two sections: an analysis of the first movement of the String Quartet no. 4, op. 37, followed by general comments on Schoenberg's use of twelve-tone composition and its relation to tonal music.

String Trio, op. 45.

Hyamson, William. "Schönberg's String Trio (1946)." *Music Review.* August 1950, 11(3): 184–194. The article begins with an analytical overview of the Trio's structure and unique instrumental techniques. Most of the discussion focuses on the properties of the combinatorial set. The author concludes that the hexachords of the set are used as "modes." That is, Schoenberg does not always observe the order of the notes within the hexachords, but treats the hexachords as a set of pitches which may be used in any order.

Neighbour, O[liver] W. "Dodecaphony in Schoenberg's String Trio." *Music Survey.* June 1952, 4(3): 489–490. The author describes the rows and how they are used in the String Trio, op. 45.

Whittall, Arnold. "Schoenberg and the 'True Tradition': Theme and Form in the String Trio." *Musical Times.* September 1974, 115(1579): 739–743. This brief analysis of the String Trio, op. 45, points out the important ways in which themes and motives are generated from the basic set. The thematic process employed by Schoenberg is distributed throughout the entire work so that unity is achieved not only through the use of a single twelve-tone set but also by the presence of recurring motives.

Suite, op. 29.

Hyde, Martha M[acLean]. *Schoenberg's Twelve-Tone Harmony: The Suite Op. 29 and the Compositional Sketches.* Ann Arbor, MI: UMI Research Press, 1982. x, 160 p. (George Buelow, ed. Studies in Musicology; no. 49). Many have asserted that only themes and melodies are created from the pitches of the basic set. The author reevaluates this view in light of veiled evidence from Schoenberg's essay "Composition with Twelve Tones," which indicates that harmonies are determined from orderings and groupings of the pitches of the basic set. This hypothesis is validated through a study of the sketches of the Suite, op. 29. The study is extended to propose a theory of twelve-tone meter which is related to twelve-tone harmony.

———. "The Telltale Sketches: Harmonic Structure in Schoenberg's Twelve-Tone Method." *Musical Quarterly.* October 1980, 66(4): 560–580. "This essay undertakes to justify Schoenberg's claim [that harmonies are also regulated by the order of the pitches of the basic set] and to resolve the 'harmonic problem,' first by reinterpreting some key passages in 'Composition with Twelve Tones' and then by analyzing portions of the *Suite,* Opus 29, with the help of Schoenberg's manuscript sketches."

A Survivor from Warsaw, op. 46.

Strasser, Michael. " 'A Survivor from Warsaw' as Personal Parable." *Music & Letters.* February 1995, 76(1): 52–63. The history of how *A Survivor from Warsaw* came to be written and premiered is explained through Schoenberg's correspondence.

The origin and meaning of the text is also examined. From this study the author concludes "that Schoenberg saw in this story of a small group of condemned Jewish prisoners both a striking crystallization of his own inner struggle with his Jewishness and a modern parable confirming the message of *Moses und Aron*: God has a special role for His Chosen People, and that only by acknowledging and accepting the uniqueness of their status can the Jews endure and triumph over the adversities that confront them."

Variations for Orchestra, op. 31.

Hicken, Kenneth [L]. "Schoenberg's 'Atonality': Fused Bitonality?" *Tempo*. June 1974, no. 109: 27–36. The author hypothesizes that the harmonic structures of Schoenberg's twelve-tone music can be explained in terms of "fused bitonality." Fused bitonality is the simultaneous and integrated use of two tonalities. A series of harmonic analyses of the Variations, op. 31, shows how the keys of F and B major are used to harmonize the principal themes. The principle of fused bitonality is also extended to the formal structure of the piece as can be supported through a Schenkerian analysis.

Variations on a Recitative for organ, op. 40.

Watkins, Glenn E. "Schoenberg and the Organ." *Perspectives of New Music*. Fall-Winter 1965, 4(1): 119–135. Schoenberg's views about the organ can be found in an early essay, *"Die Zukunft der Orgel,"* and a letter from 1949 to a Dr. David. The letter explains Schoenberg's ideas about registration and about how the organ could be improved as a musical instrument. There is a motivic analysis of the *Variations on a Recitative*, op. 40, and a discussion of the keyboard figurations of the unfinished Sonata for Organ. The author concludes that Schoenberg was aiming for clarity of the individual lines in these organ works and that the revival of baroque organs will be able to produce a sound much closer to Schoenberg's ideal than larger organs using heavy registrations.

Verklärte Nacht, op. 4.

Swift, Richard. "1/XII/99: Tonal Relations in Schoenberg's *Verklärte Nacht.*" *19th Century Music*. July 1977, 1(1): 3–14. This analytical essay describes the formal structure and harmonic relationships in *Verklärte Nacht*. The author believes that the work consists of two sonata forms (the first in the minor key, the second in the major key) linked together by a transition section. The primary tonal areas move in a stepwise motion (tonic, supertonic, mediant, tonic). The Neapolitan and its dominant permeate the work.

Von heute auf morgen, op. 32.

Davison, Stephen. "Of Its Time, or Out of Step?: Schoenberg's *Zeitoper, Von heute auf morgen.*" *Journal of the Arnold Schoenberg Institute*. November 1991, 14(2): 271–298. The opera, *Von heute auf morgen*, was written at the time when the genre of the *Zeitoper*, as exemplified by works such as *Jonny spielt auf*, by Ernst Krenek, and *Die Dreigroschenoper*, by Kurt Weill, enjoyed immense popular success. It was Schoenberg's belief that the twelve-tone technique could be applied to this genre and be equally successful. While the libretto of *Von heute auf morgen* exhibits all of the traits of a *Zeitoper*, the music does not. Instead, it remains true to all of Schoenberg's aesthetic ideals. No doubt this explains why the opera never received popular acceptance or became part of the opera repertory. Nonetheless, it is an expertly crafted work, and this article also includes an analysis of the main features of the opera.

Woodwind Quintet, op. 26.

Corson, Langdon. *Arnold Schoenberg's Woodwind Quintet, Op. 26: Background and Analysis*. Roy Christensen, ed. Nashville, TN: Gasparo, 1984. 84 p. This extended essay consists of historical background on the composition of the Woodwind Quintet, op. 26, followed by thorough analyses of the pitch content of the basic set of the piece and the form of the work. While musical examples are provided, access to a score of the work would be very useful for following the argument. The book was published to accompany a recording by the Oberlin Woodwind Quintet (Gasparo GS-204).

Analysis and Criticism: Arrangements

Jacob, Gordon. "Schoenberg and Brahms's Op. 25." *Music & Letters*. July 1951, 32(3): 252–255. This is a critique of Schoenberg's orchestration of Brahms's Piano Quartet no. 1 in G Minor, op. 25.

Spies, Claudio. "The Organ Supplanted: A Case for Differentiations." *Perspectives of New Music*. Spring-Summer 1973, 11(2): 24–55. Schoenberg transcribed three organ pieces by Bach for orchestra: *Komm, Gott, Schöpfer, heiliger Geist, BWV 631; Schmücke dich, O liebe Seele, BWV 654*; and the Prelude and Fugue in E-flat major, BWV 552. After a short discussion of Schoenberg's transcription of the Piano Quartet no. 1 in G Minor, op. 25 by Brahms, the orchestrational techniques employed in each of the Bach transcriptions is examined. The author shows how Schoenberg used orchestral colors and transferred important lines into higher and lower registers to enhance the music beyond what the organ can do.

Straus, Joseph N. "Recompositions by Schoenberg, Stravinsky, and Webern." *Musical Quarterly*. July 1986, 72(3): 301–328. Motivic development is one of the strongest elements in Schoenberg's music. Schoenberg "recomposed" pieces by Bach, Handel, Brahms, and Monn and emphasized the richness of the motivic content of these pieces by changing their orchestration and texture. The article examines portions of the Concerto Grosso op. 6, no. 7, of Handel and the chorale prelude, *Schmücke dich, O liebe Seele, BWV 654*, by Bach as altered by Schoenberg.

NOTE

1. This issue is treated at length in Ethan Haimo, "Editing Schoenberg's Twelve-tone Music," *Journal of the Arnold Schoenberg Institute* (November 1984), 8(2): [141]–57.

15

Selective Discography

Jerry McBride

It is safe to say that Schoenberg is one of the most underrepresented of the major composers of Western music in the catalogs of recording companies. During his lifetime, only twenty-seven of his works appeared on thirty-nine different commercial recordings.[1] It is no wonder that it has taken so long for his music to gain general acceptance.

Fortunately in the last fifty years the situation has improved considerably; and while the number of recordings available at any one time still remains relatively small, it is possible to obtain recordings of most of Schoenberg's music, and certainly all of the major works. Just as in Schoenberg's time, there are a few dedicated performers who have recorded his music; and although this has not lead to a wealth of varying interpretations, it has generally insured recordings of authoritative and high-quality performances.

Some of Schoenberg's students were also world-class performers. Rudolf Kolisch, also Schoenberg's brother-in-law, was the first violinist of the Kolisch String Quartet and, later in the United States, the Pro Arte Quartet. Kolisch performed a number of major new works for string quartet and was known for uncompromisingly high standards of performance, to the point where the Quartet was able to play many works in its repertory from memory. The recordings made of the four Schoenberg quartets during the winter of 1936–37 are legendary. Unfortunately, the masters of these recordings have been lost. Although the sound quality of even the best transfers leaves something to be desired, the intensity of these performances still comes through.

Along with Kolisch, few did more to advance the cause of Schoenberg's compositions than pianist, Edward Steuermann. Steuermann played in the premiere of *Pierrot lunaire, Ode to Napoleon Buonaparte*, the Five Piano Pieces, op. 23, and the Piano Concerto, op. 42, and was active in the Society for Private

Musical Performances in Vienna. His recording of the piano music of Schoenberg has long stood as the most important interpretation of these pieces.

Interest in the performances of conductor Hans Rosbaud has recently been renewed. Rosbaud was also a champion of new compositions, and as the conductor of the Southwest German Radio Symphony Orchestra, he presented many performances of the Second Viennese School. Rosbaud will probably best be remembered for conducting the premiere concert and stage performances and the first recording of *Moses und Aron*. Given the special affinity that he had for this music, his other recordings are also highly recommended.

Pierrot lunaire is the only work to be recorded with Schoenberg himself conducting. Although there are a number of excellent performances of *Pierrot*, this recording will always serve as a reference for other interpretations.

The fact that so few of Schoenberg's works had been recorded at the time of his death led to attempts to record all of his works. In the 1960s, Robert Craft supervised the recording of an eight-volume set of LPs. This monumental undertaking contained numerous recorded premieres and was the first time that all of Schoenberg's music was widely available. Although very important for its time, the quality of the interpretations is rather uneven and many of these recordings are now out of print. In a similar project, the London Sinfonietta under David Atherton recorded all of the chamber music to coincide with the Schoenberg centenary in 1974. But it is Pierre Boulez whose name dominates the current listing of the Schoenberg recorded repertory and whose work has supplanted the earlier Craft recordings. While Boulez's interpretations may not always be the last word on every work of Schoenberg, listeners may be assured that the performances are accurate, well executed, and highly spirited, in most cases.

This listing of recorded performances will provide the reader with a sample of some of the best interpretations of Schoenberg's music. The titles of the compositions are listed alphabetically under each classification and are followed by the names of the performers and the date of the recording session. Label names and numbers have been omitted from this list, because recordings go out of print rapidly, may be reissued under various label names and numbers, and/ or may be reissued in different combinations.

The emphasis here is on recordings through December 1995 that are currently available. However, recordings of historical significance and other noteworthy performances are included even if they are currently out of print. Hopefully, this list will serve as a guide to significant performances that will remain available for many years. For complete discographic information consult *The Schoenberg Discography* by R. Wayne Shoaf and catalogs of recordings such as *Schwann Opus*[2] for current availability.

I. VOCAL MUSIC

A. Stage Works

Erwartung, op. 17 (monodrama).

Dorothy Dow, soprano; New York Philharmonic; Dimitri Mitropoulos, conductor. (18 November, 1951).

Janis Martin, soprano; BBC Symphony Orchestra; Pierre Boulez, conductor. (14–15 April, 1977).

Jessye Norman, soprano; Metropolitan Opera Orchestra; James Levine, conductor. (April 1989).

Die glückliche Hand, op. 18 ("drama with music").

Siegmund Nimsgern, bass-baritone; BBC Symphony Orchestra; BBC Singers; Pierre Boulez, conductor. (12 March, 1981).

Moses und Aron (opera).

Hans Herbert Fiedler, speaker; Helmut Krebs, tenor; Ilona Steingruber-Wildgans, soprano; Ursula Zollenkops, alto; Helmut Kretschmar, tenor; Chorus of the Hamburg Academy of Music; Chorus of the North German Radio; Orchestra of the North German Radio; Hans Rosbaud, conductor. (12 March, 1954).

Richard Cassilly, tenor; Günter Reich, speaker; Richard Angas, bass; Felicity Palmer, soprano; Gillian Knight, mezzo-soprano; John Winfield, tenor; Roland Hermann, baritone; John Noble, bass; BBC Symphony Orchestra; BBC Singers; Orpheus Boys' Choir; Pierre Boulez, conductor. (November-December 1974).

Franz Mazura, speaker; Philip Langridge, tenor; Barbara Bonney, soprano; Aage Haugland bass; Mira Zakai, alto; Daniel Harper, tenor; Thomas Dymit, tenor; Herbert Wittges, baritone; Chicago Symphony Orchestra and Chorus; Glen Ellyn Children's Chorus; Georg Solti, conductor. (April-May 1984).

Von heute auf morgen, op. 32 (opera in one act).

Erika Schmidt, soprano; Magda László, soprano; Herbert Schachtschneider, tenor; Derrik Olsen, baritone; Holland Festival Orchestra; Hans Rosbaud, conductor. (12 July, 1958).

B. Works with Chorus

1. Chorus and Orchestra

Gurrelieder (for soloists, choirs, and orchestra).

Jeanette Vreeland, soprano; Rose Bampton, mezzo-soprano; Paul Althouse, tenor; Robert Betts, tenor; Abrasha Robovsky, bass; Benjamin de Loache, speaker; Philadelphia Orchestra; Princeton Glee Club; Fortnightly Club; Mendelssohn Club; Leopold Stokowski, conductor. (11 April, 1932).

Inge Borkh, soprano; Hertha Töpper, mezzo-soprano; Herbert Schachtschneider, tenor; Lorenz Fehenberger, tenor; Keith Engen, bass; Hans Herbert Fiedler, speaker; Bavarian

Radio Chorus and Symphony Orchestra; Rafael Kubelík, conductor. (9–12 March, 1965).

Marita Napier, soprano; Yvonne Minton, mezzo-soprano; Jess Thomas, tenor; Kenneth Bowen, tenor; Siegmund Nimsgern, bass-baritone; Günter Reich, speaker; BBC Symphony Orchestra; BBC Singers and Choral Society; Goldsmith's Choral Union; Men's voices of the London Philharmonic Orchestra Chorus; Pierre Boulez, conductor. (October-December 1974).

Susan Dunn, soprano; Brigitte Fassbänder, mezzo-soprano; Siegfried Jerusalem, tenor; Peter Haage, tenor; Hermann Becht, bass; Hans Hotter, speaker; Berlin Radio Symphony Orchestra; St. Hedwig's Cathedral Choir; Düsseldorf Municipal Choral Society; Riccardo Chailly, conductor. (May-June 1985).

Die Jakobsleiter (oratorio).

Mady Mesplé, soprano; Ortrun Wenkel, alto; Kenneth Bowen, tenor; Ian Partridge, tenor; Anthony Rolfe-Johnson, tenor; John Shirley-Quirk, baritone; Siegmund Nimsgern, bass-baritone; Paul Hudson, bass; BBC Symphony Orchestra; BBC Singers; Pierre Boulez, conductor. (1 April, 1980).

Kol nidre, op. 39 (for speaker, mixed choir, and orchestra).

John Shirley-Quirk, speaker; BBC Chorus; Pierre Boulez, conductor. (19 (February, 1984).

"Modern Psalm no. 1," op. 50c (for speaker, mixed choir, and orchestra).

John Shirley-Quirk, speaker; BBC Chorus; Pierre Boulez, conductor. (19 February, 1984).

Prelude to the *Genesis* Suite, op. 44 (for mixed choir and orchestra).

Festival Singers of Toronto; CBC Symphony Orchestra; Robert Craft, conductor. (1963)

A Survivor from Warsaw, op. 46 (for speaker, men's choir, and orchestra).

Günter Reich, speaker; BBC Symphony Orchestra; BBC Chorus; Pierre Boulez, conductor. (23 September, 1976).

Gottfried Hornik, speaker; Vienna Philharmonic Orchestra; Vienna State Opera Concert Chorus Male Choir; Claudio Abbado, conductor. (May 1989).

2. Chorus (accompanied and a cappella)

Canons

Gregg Smith Singers; Robert Craft, conductor. (1968).

"De profundis" (Psalm 130), op. 50b (for mixed choir).

BBC Singers; Pierre Boulez, conductor. (8 September, 1982).

"Dreimal tausend Jahre," op. 50a (for mixed choir).

BBC Singers; Pierre Boulez, conductor. (8 September, 1982).

Four Pieces for Mixed Choir, op. 27.

BBC Chorus; London Sinfonietta; Pierre Boulez, conductor. (8, September, 1982).

"Friede auf Erden," op. 13 (for mixed choir).

BBC Chorus; Pierre Boulez, conductor. (8 September, 1982).

Six Pieces for Men's Choir, op. 35.

BBC Chorus; Pierre Boulez, conductor. (19 February, 1984).

Three Folk Song Movements arr. for mixed choir.

BBC Singers; Pierre Boulez, conductor. (26 October, 1986).

Three Folk Songs arr. for mixed choir, op. 49.

BBC Singers; Pierre Boulez, conductor. (26 October, 1986).

Three Satires for mixed choir, op. 28.

BBC Singers; London Sinfonietta; Pierre Boulez, conductor. (8 September, 1982).

C. Solo Vocal Music

1. Voice and Orchestra

Four Songs, op. 22.

Yvonne Minton, soprano; BBC Symphony Orchestra; Pierre Boulez, conductor. (12 March, 1981).

Ode to Napoleon Buonaparte, op. 41 (arr. for speaker, piano, and string orchestra).

Mack Harrell, speaker; New York Philharmonic; Edward Steuermann, piano; Artur Rodzinsky, conductor. (23 November, 1944).

Kevin McMillan, speaker; I Musici de Montréal; Marc-André Hamelin, piano; Yuli Turovsky, conductor. (28–29 May, 1992).

Six Songs, op. 8.

Anja Silja, soprano; Vienna Philharmonic Orchestra; Christoph von Dohnányi, conductor. (September 1979).

"Song of the Wood Dove" from *Die Gurrelieder* arr. for mezzo-soprano and chamber orchestra.

Lili Chookasian, mezzo-soprano; Boston Symphony Orchestra; Erich Leinsdorf, conductor. (18–24 October, 1964).

Jessye Norman, soprano; Ensemble InterContemporain; Pierre Boulez, conductor. (15 September, 1979).

Jard van Nes, mezzo-soprano; Schönberg Ensemble; Reinbert de Leeuw, conductor. (1986).

String Quartet no. 2 in F-sharp Minor, op. 10 (arr. for orchestra): see section II.A.3 (String Orchestra).

2. Voice and Ensemble

"Herzgewächse," op. 20 (for voice and small ensemble).

Lucy Shelton, soprano; Da Capo Chamber Players; Oliver Knussen, conductor. (July 1991).

"Nachtwandler" from *Brettl-Lieder*: see section I.C.3 (Voice and Piano)

Ode to Napoleon Buonaparte, op. 41 (for speaker, piano, and string quartet).

Derrik Olsen, speaker; Southwest German Radio Symphony Orchestra; Hans Rosbaud, conductor. (20 December, 1953).

Kenneth Griffiths, speaker; LaSalle Quartet; Stefan Litwin, piano. (August 1985).

David Wilson-Johnson, speaker; Ensemble InterContemporain; Pierre Boulez, conductor. (31 March, 1980).

Thomas Allen, speaker; Nash Ensemble; Lionel Friend, conductor. (May 1990).

Pierrot lunaire, op. 21 (for speaker and small ensemble).

Erika Stiedry-Wagner, speaker; Leonard Posella, flute/piccolo; Kalman Bloch, clarinet/bass clarinet; Rudolf Kolisch, violin/viola; Stefan Auber, cello; Edward Steuermann, piano; Arnold Schoenberg, conductor. (24 September, 1940).

Jeanne Héricard, speaker; Southwest German Radio Symphony Orchestra; Hans Rosbaud, conductor. (4–5 April, 1957).

Jan DeGaetani, speaker; Contemporary Chamber Ensemble; Arthur Weisberg, conductor. (May 1970).

Mary Thomas, speaker; Fires of London; Peter Maxwell Davies, conductor. (July 1973).

Yvonne Minton, speaker; Michel Debost, flute/piccolo; Antony Pay, clarinet/bass clarinet; Pinchas Zukerman, violin/viola; Lynn Harrell, cello; Daniel Barenboim, piano; Pierre Boulez, conductor. (20–21 June, 1977).

Jane Manning, speaker; Nash Ensemble; Simon Rattle, conductor. (1977).

Lucy Shelton, speaker; Da Capo Chamber Players, Oliver Knussen, conductor. (17–18, 20–21 December, 1990). Performed once in German and once in an English translation by Andrew Porter.

Phyllis Bryn-Julson, speaker; New York New Music Ensemble; Robert Black, conductor. (20–21, 23, September, 1992).

Serenade, op. 24 (for baritone, clarinet, bass clarinet, mandolin, guitar, and string trio): see section II.B (Chamber Music).

String Quartet no. 2 in F-sharp Minor, op. 10: see section II.B (Chamber Music)

3. Voice and Piano

"Am Strande."

Dietrich Fischer-Dieskau, baritone; Aribert Reimann, piano. (22–24 January 1983).

"Die Beiden."

Marni Nixon, soprano; Leonard Stein, piano. (1975).

Brettl-Lieder.

Phyllis Bryn-Julson, soprano; Ursula Oppens, piano. (songs 1–7, 1990).

Jessye Norman, soprano; James Levine, piano; Mary Ann Archer, piccolo; Mark Gould, trumpet; Gregory Zuber, snare drum. (songs 1–8, April 1990).

Jody Karin Applebaum, soprano; Marc-Andre Hamelin, piano. (songs 1–7; 2 November 1990).

"Ecloge."

 Donella Del Monaco, voice; Maurizio Carnelli, piano. (1979).

Fifteen Poems from the Book of the Hanging Gardens, op. 15.

 Jan DeGaetani, mezzo-soprano; Gilbert Kalish, piano. (November 1974).

 Phyllis Bryn-Julson, soprano; Ursula Oppens, piano. (1990).

Four Songs, op. 2.

 Dietrich Fischer-Dieskau, baritone; Aribert Reimann, piano. (22–24 January 1983).

 Phyllis Bryn-Julson, soprano; Ursula Oppens, piano. (1990).

 Lucia Popp, soprano; Irwin Gage, piano. (3–6 May 1991).

"Ein Schilflied."

 Marni Nixon, soprano; Leonard Stein, piano. (1975).

Songs [complete].

 Lars Thodberg Bertelsen, baritone; Susanne Lange, mezzo-soprano; Tove Lønskov, piano. (1988–1989).

Two Songs, op. 1.

 Dietrich Fischer-Dieskau, baritone; Aribert Reimann, piano. (22–24 January 1983).

II. INSTRUMENTAL MUSIC

A. Large Ensemble Music

1. Orchestra

a. Full Orchestra

Accompaniment to a Film Scene, op. 34

 Southwest German Radio Symphony Orchestra; Hans Rosbaud, conductor. (15 July 1966).

 BBC Symphony Orchestra; Pierre Boulez, conductor. (9 February 1976).

 Chamber Orchestra of Europe; Heinz Holliger, conductor. (September 1992).

Chamber Symphony no. 1 in E major, op. 9b (arr. for orchestra).

 BBC Northern Symphony Orchestra; Jascha Horenstein, conductor. (1970).

Five Orchestra Pieces, op. 16.

 Chicago Symphony Orchestra; Rafael Kubelík, conductor. (1953).

 Southwest German Radio Symphony Orchestra; Hans Rosbaud, conductor. (22 September 1958).

 BBC Symphony Orchestra; Pierre Boulez, conductor. (23 September 1976).

 Berlin Philharmonic Orchestra; James Levine, conductor. (June 1986).

 City of Birmingham Symphony Orchestra; Simon Rattle, conductor. (1988).

 Royal Concertgebouw Orchestra; Riccardo Chailly, conductor. (1990).

Cleveland Orchestra; Christoph von Dohnányi, conductor. (21 January 1991).

Five Orchestra Pieces, op. 16 (rev. 1949).

London Symphony Orchestra; Antal Dorati, conductor. (14–22 July 1962).

Pelleas und Melisande, op. 5.

New Philharmonic Orchestra; John Barbirolli, conductor. (1968).

Berlin Philharmonic Orchestra; Herbert von Karajan, conductor. (January 1974).

Chicago Symphony Orchestra; Pierre Boulez, conductor. (6–10 December 1991).

Houston Symphony Orchestra; Christoph Eschenbach, conductor. (1995).

Theme and Variations in G Minor, op. 43b (arr. for orchestra).

Philadelphia Orchestra; Eugene Ormandy, conductor. (1967).

Variations for Orchestra, op. 31.

Southwest German Radio Orchestra; Hans Rosbaud, conductor. (1961).

Berlin Philharmonic Orchestra; Herbert von Karajan, conductor. (January-February 1974).

Chicago Symphony Orchestra; Georg Solti, conductor. (May 1974).

BBC Symphony Orchestra; Pierre Boulez, conductor. (23 September 1976).

Chicago Symphony Orchestra; Pierre Boulez, conductor. (6–10 December 1991).

City of Birmingham Symphony Orchestra; Simon Rattle, conductor. (April 1993).

b. Solo Instrument(s) and Full Orchestra

Cello Concerto after a keyboard concerto by Georg Matthias Monn.

Yo-Yo Ma, cello; Boston Symphony Orchestra; Seiji Osawa, conductor. (1985).

Piano Concerto, op. 42.

Edward Steuermann, piano; Hessian Radio Symphony Orchestra; Hermann Scherchen, conductor. (1954).

Glenn Gould, piano; New York Philharmonic; Dimitri Mitropoulos, conductor. (16, March 1958).

Alfred Brendel, piano; Bavarian Radio Symphony Orchestra; Rafael Kubelík, conductor. (December 1971).

Peter Serkin, piano; London Symphony Orchestra; Pierre Boulez, conductor. (October 1985).

Maurizio Pollini, piano; Berlin Philharmonic Orchestra; Claudio Abbado, conductor. (September 1988).

Emmanuel Ax, piano; Philharmonia Orchestra; Esa-Pekka Salonen, conductor. (20–21 December 1992).

String Quartet Concerto after Handel.

Kolisch String Quartet; Los Angeles Philharmonic Orchestra; Otto Klemperer, conductor. (January 1938).

American String Quartet; New York Chamber Orchestra; Gerard Schwarz, conductor. (March 1987).

Violin Concerto, op. 36.

Louis Krasner, violin; West German Radio Orchestra; Dimitri Mitropoulos, conductor. (16 July 1954).

Zvi Zeitlin, violin; Bavarian Radio Symphony Orchestra; Rafael Kubelík, conductor. (September 1971).

2. Chamber Orchestra

Chamber Symphony no. 1 in E major, op. 9.

Ensemble InterContemporain; Pierre Boulez, conductor. (16 September 1979).

Berlin Philharmonic Orchestra; Giuseppe Sinopoli, conductor. (June 1981).

Marlboro Music Festival. (1982).

Schönberg Ensemble; Reinbert de Leeuw, conductor. (1986).

Orpheus Chamber Orchestra. (April 1989).

Chamber Orchestra of Europe; Heinz Holliger, conductor. (June 1989).

Concertgebouw Orchestra; Riccardo Chailly, conductor. (January 1992).

Chamber Symphony no. 2, op. 38.

Ensemble InterContemporain; Pierre Boulez, conductor. (5 April 1980).

Orpheus Chamber Orchestra. (April 1989).

Chamber Orchestra of Europe; Heinz Holliger, conductor. (September 1992).

Three Pieces for Chamber Orchestra.

Ensemble InterContemporain; Pierre Boulez, conductor. (15 September 1979).

Schönberg Ensemble; Reinbert de Leeuw, conductor. (1986).

3. String Orchestra

String Quartet no. 2 in F-sharp Minor, op. 10 (arr. for string orchestra).

I Musici de Montréal; Nadia Pelle, soprano; Yuli Turovsky, conductor. (28–29 May 1992).

Suite in G major.

Deutsche Kammerphilharmonie; Mario Venzago, conductor. (October 1987).

Verklärte Nacht, op. 4 (arr. for string orchestra).

Concertgebouw Orchestra; Otto Klemperer, conductor. (7 July 1955).

Symphony of the Air; Leopold Stokowski, conductor. (17 November 1960).

Los Angeles Philharmonic Orchestra; Zubin Mehta, conductor. (1967). 1943 version.

English Chamber Orchestra; Daniel Barenboim, conductor. (1968).

New York Philharmonic; Pierre Boulez, conductor. (24 September 1973).

Berlin Philharmonic Orchestra; Herbert von Karajan, conductor. (December 1973).

Academy of Saint Martin-in-the-Fields; Neville Marriner, conductor. (1974).

Berlin Radio Symphony Orchestra; Riccardo Chailly, conductor. (April 1987).

Orpheus Chamber Orchestra. (April 1989).

Sinfonia Varsovia; Emmanuel Krivine, conductor. (12–17 August 1990).

Chamber Orchestra of Europe; Heinz Holliger, conductor. (September 1992).

4. Band

Fanfare on Motifs of Die Gurrelieder (for brass and percussion).

Hollywood Bowl Orchestra; John Mauceri, conductor. (February 1991).

Theme and Variations in G Minor, op. 43a.

Eastman Symphonic Wind Ensemble; Frederick Fennell, conductor. (1957).

Cincinnati College Conservatory of Music Wind Symphony; Eugene Corporon, conductor. (29–31 May 1993).

B. Chamber Music

"Der eiserne Brigade" (for piano quintet).

London Sinfonietta. (October-December 1973).

Schönberg Ensemble. (1981).

Phantasy for Violin with Piano Accompaniment, op. 47

Adolf Koldofsky, violin; Edward Steuermann, piano. (1951).

Yehudi Menuhin, violin; Glenn Gould, piano. (25–26 October 1965).

Boston Symphony Chamber Players (Joseph Silverstein, violin; Gilbert Kalish, piano). (1977).

Schönberg Ensemble (Janneke van der Meer, violin; Marja Bon, piano). (January 1983).

Scherzo in F Major (for string quartet).

Schönberg Quartet. (1981).

Ensemble Avantgarde. (1995).

Serenade, op. 24 (for baritone, clarinet, bass clarinet, mandolin, guitar, and string trio).

Warren Galjour, baritone; ISCM Concert Group; Dimitri Mitropoulos, conductor. (1949). Sung in English.

Thomas Paul, baritone; Marlboro Festival Ensemble; Leon Kirchner, conductor. (30 July 1966).

John Shirley-Quirk, baritone; Ensemble InterContemporain; Pierre Boulez, conductor. (10 April 1979).

"Ein Stelldichein" (for oboe, clarinet, piano, violin, and cello).

Ex Novo Ensemble. (January 1989).

String Quartet in D major.

    LaSalle Quartet. (March 1970).

    Juilliard Quartet. (May-June 1975).

String Quartets nos. 1–4.

    Kolisch Quartet; Clemence Gifford, alto (in no. 2). (1936–1937).

    LaSalle Quartet; Margaret Price, soprano (in no. 2). (1968–1970).

    Juilliard Quartet; Benita Valente, soprano (in no. 2). (May–June 1975).

    Arditti String Quartet; Dawn Upshaw, soprano (in no. 2). (1994).

String Trio, op. 45.

    Koldofsky Trio. (1950).

    Santa Fe Chamber Music Festival. (4–6 September 1981).

    LaSalle Quartet. (December 1982).

    Schönberg Ensemble. (March 1983).

    Juilliard String Quartet. (21 May 1985).

Suite, op. 29 (for E-flat clarinet, clarinet, bass clarinet, and piano quartet).

    Marlboro Music Festival. (1969).

    London Sinfonietta; David Atherton, conductor. (1973–1974).

    Boston Symphony Chamber Players. (1977).

    Ensemble InterContemporain; Pierre Boulez, conductor. (14 June 1982).

    Schönberg Ensemble; Reinbert De Leeuw, conductor. (30 June–1 July 1988).

Verklärte Nacht, op. 4 (for string sextet).

    Hollywood String Quartet; Alvin Dinkin, viola; Kurt Reher; cello. (21–22 August 1950).

    Santa Fe Chamber Music Festival. (4–6 September 1981).

    LaSalle Quartet; Donald McInnes, viola; J. Pegis, cello. (November 1982).

    Schönberg Ensemble. (March 1983).

    Ensemble InterContemporain. (6 November 1983).

    Raphael Ensemble. (12–14 April 1990).

    Nash Ensemble. (May 1990).

    Juilliard String Quartet; Walter Trampler, viola; Yo-Yo Ma, cello. (3–5 April 1991).

"Weihnachtsmusik" (for 2 violins, cello, harmonium, and piano).

    Arditti String Quartet; Hakon Austbö, harmonium; Louise Bessette, piano; Michel Béroff, conductor. (13–22 November 1989).

Woodwind Quintet, op. 26.

    London Sinfonietta; David Atherton, conductor. (1973–1974).

    Danzi Quintet. (1975).

Vienna Wind Soloists. (1977).

Aulos Wind Quintet. (1992).

C. Keyboard

1. Piano

Chamber Symphony no. 1 in E major, op. 9 (arr. for piano 4 hands).

Zoltán Kocis and Adrienne Hauser, piano. (August–October 1988).

Chamber Symphony no. 2, op. 38 (arr. for two pianos).

John Ogden and Brenda Lucas. (1974).

Piano Music (opp. 11, 19, 23, 25, and 33).

Edward Steuermann. (1957).

Glenn Gould. (1958–1965).

Maurizio Pollini. (May 1974).

Paul Jacobs. (1975).

Three Piano Pieces (1894).

Yuji Takahashi. (15–16 December 1977).

Six Piano Pieces (1896) (for piano 4 hands).

Victoria Postnikova and Gennadi Rozhdestvenski. (1980).

Dana Muller and Gary Steigerwalt. (August–September 1991).

2. Organ

Sonata for Organ (unfinished).

Michael-Christfried Winkler. (July 1992).

Variations on a Recitative, op. 40.

Marilyn Mason. (1968).

Livia Mazzanti. (November 1991).

Michael-Christfried Winkler. (July 1992).

III. ARRANGEMENTS

A. Orchestra

Bach, Johann Sebastian. Two Chorale-Preludes. *Komm, Gott, Schöpfer, heiliger Geist, BWV 631; Schmücke dich, O liebe Seele*, BWV 654 (for orchestra).

Berlin Philharmonic Orchestra; Jascha Horenstein, conductor. (1929).

Bavarian Radio Symphony Orchestra; Michael Tilson Thomas, conductor. (1986).

————. Prelude and Fugue in E-flat Major, BWV 552 (for orchestra).

Boston Symphony Orchestra; Seiji Osawa, conductor. (October 1989).

Brahms, Johannes. Piano Quartet no. 1 in G Minor, op. 25 (for orchestra).

Los Angeles Philharmonic Orchestra; Otto Klemperer, conductor. (7 May 1938).

City of Birmingham Symphony Orchestra; Simon Rattle, conductor. (19 June 1984).

London Symphony Orchestra; Neeme Järvi, conductor. (1988–1989).

London Philharmonic Orchestra; Gennadi Rozhdestvensky, conductor. (March 1990).

B. Chamber Ensemble

Denza, Luigi. *Funiculi, funiculá* (for voice, clarinet, mandolin, guitar, violin, viola, cello).

Schönberg Ensemble; Reinbert de Leeuw, conductor. (1981).

Mahler, Gustav. *The Song of the Earth* (arr. by Schoenberg and Webern, and completed by Rainer Riehn, for voice, flute, clarinet, harmonium, piano, string quartet, double bass, and percussion).

Ingrid Schmithüsen, soprano; Aldo Baldin, tenor; Ensemble Köln; Robert Platz, conductor. (1992).

————. *Songs of a Wayfarer* (for baritone, flute, clarinet, harmonium, piano, string quartet, double bass, and percussion).

Jean-Luc Chaignaud, baritone; Michel Moraguès, flute; Paul Meyer, clarinet; Hakno Ausbö, harmonium; Louise Bessette, piano; Arditti String Quartet; Marc Marder, double bass; Michel Béroff, conductor. (13–22 November 1989).

Reger, Max. A Romantic Suite, op. 125 (arr. by Schoenberg and Kolisch for flute, clarinet, harmonium 4 hands, piano 4 hands, and string quartet).

Schönberg Ensemble; Reinbert de Leeuw, conductor. (1981).

Schubert, Franz. *Serenade*, D. 889 (for voice, clarinet, bassoon, mandolin, guitar, and string quartet).

Schönberg Ensemble. (1981).

Sioly, Johann. *Weil i a alter Drahrer bin* (for clarinet, mandolin, guitar, and string trio).

Schönberg Ensemble. (1981).

Strauss, Johann. *Emperor Waltz* (for flute, clarinet, and piano quintet).

Schönberg Ensemble. (1981).

Michel Moraguès, flute; Paul Meyer, clarinet; Arditti String Quartet; Louise Bessette, piano; Michel Béroff, conductor. (13–22 November 1989).

Strauss, Johann. *Roses from the South* (for harmonium, piano, and string quartet).

Schönberg Ensemble. (1981).

Arditti String Quartet; Louise Bessette, piano; Hakno Ausbö, harmonium; Michel Béroff, conductor. (13–22 November 1989).

NOTES

1. R. Wayne Shoaf, *The Schoenberg Discography*, 2nd ed., rev. and expanded (Berkeley, CA: Fallen Leaf Press, 1994), [143]–144. These statistics were obtained from the chronological listing given on these pages.

2. *Schwann Opus* (Santa Fe: Schwann Publications, 1990–).

Index of Musical Works

General Index

Abbado, Claudio, 266
Adler, Guido, 18, 252
Adler, Oscar, 14, 282
Adorno, Theodor Wiesengrund, 36, 237, 242, 261, 283–84
aggregate, 123, 135, 164, 226
all interval tetrachord, 240
American Academy of Arts and Letters, 38
Amsterdam, 23, 24, 25
Ansorge Verein, 20
anti-Semitism, 12, 28, 31–32, 34, 205
Apostel, Hans Erich, 252
Arachon, 31, 32
Armitage, Merle, 36
Arnold, Robert Franz, 60
Arnold Schönberg (Berg and Webern), 23, 251
atonality, 5, 52, 83–99, 160, 236, 237, 259, 293–95
Austrian Society of Authors, Composers, and Publishers, 34, 39

Babbitt, Milton, 243–44, 246, 261, 263, 265
Bach, J. S., 5, 11, 23, 53, 159, 178, 200, 223, 224, 225, 229, 234, 254
Bagar, Robert, 8

Balzac, Honoré de, 25
Barcelona, 29, 31, 35
Bartók, Béla, 36, 177, 236, 260, 263, 267 n.6
basic shape (''Grundgestalt''), 54, 201, 223, 225, 226, 228, 230, 231, 232, 233, 235, 242, 243
Bauhaus, 28
Beethoven, 6, 11, 14, 26, 39, 51, 53, 54, 55, 70, 72, 178, 188, 197, 224, 230, 231, 232, 234, 254, 259, 263, 265, 266 n.4; Symphony No. 3 in E-flat, *Eroica*, 70, 197
Berg, Alban, 19, 20, 23, 24, 25, 33, 34, 35, 65, 66, 70, 177, 251, 252, 260, 261, 262, 263, 264, 266 n.1
Berio, Luciano, 261
Berlin, 12, 15-16, 17, 18, 19, 22, 26, 30, 32, 33, 181, 190, 263; Berlin Philharmonic Orchestra, 17, 263
Bernstein, Martin, 182
Bierbaum, Otto Julius, 16
Boston, 4, 32, 33, 204, 252, 253, 261; Boston Symphony Orchestra, 33, 37
Boulez, Pierre, 7, 12, 261, 263, 265; ''Schoenberg Is Dead,'' 243, 284, 310
Brahms, Johannes, 4, 11, 14, 51, 52, 53, 54, 55, 56, 57, 59, 72, 195–96, 200,

Contributors

WALTER B. BAILEY is Associate Professor of Musicology and Director of Graduate Studies at Rice University's Shepherd School of Music. He received his Ph.D. from the University of Southern California, and his dissertation was the first from that institution to take advantage of the archives of the Arnold Schoenberg Institute. He is the author of several articles on Schoenberg and the book *Programmatic Elements in the Works of Schoenberg*.

PATRICIA CARPENTER, Professor Emerita at Barnard College, Columbia University, served as chair of the Barnard Department of Music and Director of the Graduate Theory Program, Columbia School of Arts and Sciences, and as vice-president of the Society for Music Theory. A student of Arnold Schoenberg both at UCLA and privately, she later earned her Ph.D. in musicology from Columbia University. She is the author of a number of articles on Schoenberg and co-editor of Schoenberg's *The Musical Idea and the Logic, Technique, and Art of its Presentation*.

ETHAN HAIMO, Professor in the Department of Music at the University of Notre Dame, received his Ph.D. in music composition and theory from Princeton University. His published work includes articles on Schoenberg's twelve-tone music and the book *Schoenberg's Serial Odyssey*. He is currently writing a book on Schoenberg and the birth of atonality. Haimo has also written on other topics, including Haydn and Stravinsky. Active as a composer, his catalog includes more than thirty compositions.

JAN MAEGAARD, musicologist and composer, is Professor Emeritus at the University of Copenhagen and has been a visiting professor at the State University of New York at Stony Brook and the University of California, Los

Angeles. He is the author of the groundbreaking *Studien zur Entwicklung des dodekaphonen Satzes bei Arnold Schönberg*, several other books, and many articles on music. As a composer, he has created works ranging from small choral pieces to large-scale concertos, and many of his compositions are printed and/or recorded. A recent recording of his Concerto for Cello and Orchestra, op. 98, and *Triptykon* for violin and orchestra, op. 72, includes Maegaard's orchestration of Schoenberg's *Variations on a Recitative*, op. 40 (Da Capo/Marco Polo DACOCD415).

JERRY McBRIDE is Music Librarian at Middlebury College, Middlebury, Vermont. He was archivist of the Arnold Schoenberg Institute from 1979–86, where he was project director for an NEH Research Resources grant to catalog the Institute's collection. He has published numerous articles and bibliographies on Schoenberg in the *Journal of the Arnold Schoenberg Institute*. He is active in the Music Library Association, where he has served on the board of directors, as a member and chair of various committees, and as chair of the Southern California and New England chapters.

GUNTHER SCHULLER has developed a musical career that ranges from composer and conductor to educator, administrator, music publisher, and record producer. At the age of seventeen he was principal French hornist with the Cincinnati Symphony and two years later was appointed to a similar position with the Metropolitan Opera Orchestra. In 1959 he gave up performing to devote his time primarily to composition. He has received commissions from major orchestras throughout the world and, since 1980, has been a member of the American Academy of Arts and Letters. Over 75 percent of his over 150 works have been commissioned, and most of them have been recorded. Among other awards, he has received two Guggenheim fellowships, the Darius Milhaud Award, the Rodgers and Hammerstein Award, the William Schuman Award, a MacArthur Award, a Pulitzer Prize, and numerous honorary degrees. As a conductor, Schuller travels throughout the world, leading major ensembles. As an educator, he has taught at the Manhattan School of Music and Yale University, and he served as head of the composition department at the Berkshire Center at Tanglewood from 1963 to 1984. From 1967 to 1977 he was president of the New England Conservatory of Music. He is currently artistic director of the Festival at Sandpoint, Idaho, the Connoisseur Society, and co-artistic director of the Smithsonian Jazz Masterworks Orchestra. Schuller has written dozens of essays and four books, the most recent of which are *The Swing Era: The Development of Jazz, 1930–1945* (1989) and *The Compleat Conductor* (forthcoming).

BRYAN R. SIMMS is Professor and Director of Graduate Studies in the School of Music at the University of Southern California. He is formerly editor of *Music Theory Spectrum* and the *Journal of Music Theory*, and he specializes in music and musical theory of the twentieth century. He is the author of *Music of the*

Twentieth Century: Style and Structure, The Art of Music: An Introduction, Alban Berg: A Guide to Research, and general editor of *Schoenberg, Berg, and Webern: A Companion to the Second Viennese School*, the last of which will shortly appear from the Greenwood Publishing Group.

LEONARD STEIN, Director Emeritus of the Arnold Schoenberg Institute, was director of the Institute and editor of the *Journal of the Arnold Schoenberg Institute* from 1976 to 1991. His association with Schoenberg began in 1935, when he studied theory and composition with the composer at the University of Southern California and the University of California, Los Angeles; later he served as Schoenberg's teaching assistant and editor of his books on theory and composition, including *Style and Idea: Selected Writings of Arnold Schoenberg* and *Fundamentals of Musical Composition*. A pianist, Mr. Stein has lectured and concertized throughout the United States and Europe.

ISBN 0-313-28779-1

90000>

EAN

9 780313 287794

HARDCOVER BAR CODE